WOMEN WAGING W

THE AMERICAN REVOLUTION

Women Waging War
in the American Revolution

Edited by Holly A. Mayer

University of Virginia Press
CHARLOTTESVILLE & LONDON

This book was published with the assistance of the National Society of the Sons of the American Revolution and Joseph W. Dooley.

University of Virginia Press
Printed in the United States of America on acid-free paper

First published 2022
First paperback edition published 2024
ISBN 978-0-8139-5226-0 (paper)

9 8 7 6 5 4 3 2 1

The Library of Congress has cataloged the hardcover edition as follows:

Names: Women Waging War in the American Revolution (Conference)
(2019 : Philadelphia, Pa.) | Mayer, Holly A., editor.
Title: Women waging war in the American Revolution /
edited by Holly A. Mayer.
Description: Charlottesville : University of Virginia Press, 2022. |
Includes bibliographical references and index.
Identifiers: LCCN 2022011411 (print) | LCCN 2022011412 (ebook) |
ISBN 9780813948270 (hardcover) | ISBN 9780813948287 (ebook)
Subjects: LCSH: United States—History—Revolution, 1775–1783—Women. |
United States—History—Revolution, 1775–1783—Participation, Female.
Classification: LCC E276 .W668 2022 (print) | LCC E276 (ebook) |
DDC 973.3082—dc23/eng/20220308
LC record available at https://lccn.loc.gov/2022011411
LC ebook record available at https://lccn.loc.gov/2022011412

Cover art: *Moving On*, Bryant White. (whitehistoricart.com)

To Carol Berkin,
educator, scholar, and advocate
of the history of women in early America

CONTENTS

PREFACE

WOMEN AND the American Revolution—their effects on it, and its effects on them—has become an essential topic in the study of the emergence of the early republic over the past forty-plus years. The contributions, conundrums, and changes of, by, and for women, as well as the offenses against them, were legion, and thus there are still many threads to spin, yarns to weave, and materials to cut and sew in new ensembles. Among them are those of women's agency for and in the War for American Independence specifically. How did women wage the Revolution's war, and within it their own? What did their battles look like if they were not so much about aiming muskets but words, if they sometimes entailed shouldering knapsacks but more often other burdens, and when they included enduring bodily, material, and emotional wounds? How did their choices in war reflect and affect personal and public losses or achievements?

These and other questions are addressed in this volume's chapters. The essays began as presentations at the tenth annual conference sponsored by the National Society of the Sons of the American Revolution (SAR), which was held in Philadelphia in June 2019. Each SAR conference addresses a different theme, and in this case the call for papers asked for participants to examine the significance of women warriors, followers, and activists in the American Revolution's War for Independence. The essays were to reflect on why women's wartime and martial, not necessarily military, actions mattered then and why they have mattered since then in interpreting the Revolution. The call invited public history practitioners as well as academic scholars so that the conference could encourage not only discussion about women and the Revolution's warfare but also a conversation about how we "do" history—how various researchers discover subjects in the shadows and then present their methods and results to different audiences. We all want to engage people with interest in the Revolution whether in the classroom, at public venues, or laid out on a couch, but we also recognize the difficulties in bridging an author's and audience's inclinations in integrating narratives and analyses. This work represents a bridge always under construction.

This book, like the conference, is dedicated to Carol Berkin, Presidential Professor of History, Emerita, at Baruch College and the Graduate Center, City University of New York (CUNY). Professor Berkin has adeptly constructed and tread bridges between academic and public history as an educator, author, editor, and advisor. Among the dozen books she has written or edited, the ones most related to this volume are *First Generations: Women in Colonial America* (1996) and *Revolutionary Mothers: Women in the Struggle for America's Independence* (2005). She also authored *Civil War Wives* (2009) and other works about the creation of the American nation.

The conference and this book benefited from generous sponsorships and gracious collaborations. First and foremost, enduring thanks go to the Sons of the American Revolution for creating and maintaining the conference series as part of its search for knowledge and understanding. Particular and deep appreciation goes to Joseph W. Dooley, a past president general of the SAR and its continuing annual conference director, who models the principles as well as initiative, energy, and courtesy so representative of the society. Such recognition also goes to the conference committee members who worked with Mr. Dooley, including David N. Appleby, Edward F. Butler Sr., Howard F. Horne Jr., John O. Thornhill, and Larry D. McClanahan.

We also applaud other benefactors. They include the George Washington Endowment Fund of the National Society of the SAR and the George Knight–Kenneth C. Patty Memorial Trust Fund of the Virginia Society of the SAR; the National Society SAR Ladies Auxiliary, as well as the California Society SAR Ladies Auxiliary and Missouri Society SAR Ladies Auxiliary; Powell Enterprises and the WinSet Group LLC; the George Mason Chapter of the Virginia Society SAR; and the George Washington Chapter of the Virginia Society SAR. Generous individuals included Thomas Cayle and Anee-Dörte Epstude Adams; Warren and Nancy Alter; Ronald J. and Constance H. Barker; Mark S. Brennan Sr. (in memory of Mark S. Brennan Jr.); Derek and Janet Brown; the Rt. Rev. and Mrs. Louis V. Carlson Jr.; Ernest B. Coggins Jr.; Peter M. Davenport, COL, USA (Ret.); Joseph R. Godfrey, Ph.D.; Mr. and Mrs. John H. Franklin Jr.; William M. Marrs; Lanny and Ann Patten; Samuel C. Powell, Ph.D.; Mrs. Diane Stephens; Edward W. Ward; and Timothy E. Ward.

Sincere thanks also go to the Museum of the American Revolution, which opened in 2017 after many dedicated people waged a long and successful campaign to "bring to life the diverse array of people who created a new nation" that we celebrate as the United States. Bows especially go to the museum's president, Dr. R. Scott Stephenson; Dr. Philip Mead, its chief historian and director of curatorial affairs; and the staff members who provided such fine hospitality to our participants.

We also thank the Mount Vernon Ladies' Association for its contributions to this conference and its continued support of academic and public histories of the American Revolution in general. And we deeply appreciate the contributions of all of the participants who energized discussions and whose comments spurred reconsiderations.

All of the contributors to this volume are profoundly grateful to the University of Virginia Press, especially Nadine Zimmerli, editor of history and social sciences; Helen Chandler, acquisitions assistant; Margaret A. Hogan, for her keen copyediting; and the other editorial and publishing staff members whose labors set our words to paper and on screen. We also thank the anonymous reviewers whose comments helped better the essays individually and collectively.

Furthermore, all of the authors give heartfelt thanks to family members and friends who have been so supportive of our historical enterprises (you know who you are), but some contributors wish to add specific professional acknowledgments. Jackie Beatty thanks Rosemarie Zagarri, whose dissertation comments helped shape her thinking on women's political power, as well as Kristen Beales, Lauren Duval, and Shira Lurie for helping clarify her argument. Carin Bloom thanks Middleton Place Foundation, specifically Barbara Doyle, Mary Edna Sullivan, and Tracey Todd for their earlier work upon which Carin could build her analysis. Ben Carp is grateful to Cassandra A. Good, Nancy Isenberg, Cynthia A. Kerner, Miriam Liebman, the Washington Early American Seminar at the University of Maryland, and others for comments on drafts. His research was supported by a Jacob M. Price Visiting Research Fellowship from the William L. Clements Library and an award by the Professional Staff Congress and the City University of New York. Lauren Duval is grateful to Kate Haulman, Kristen Beales, Jacqueline Beatty, and Shira Lurie for their generous, insightful feedback on her essay, as well as for research support from the David Library of the American Revolution and American University, including the Office of the Provost and the Dorothy and Victor Gondos Jr. Research Fellowship. Lorri Glover, who drew some material from her book *Eliza Lucas Pinckney: An Independent Woman in the Age of Revolution* (2020) to deliver a refocused aspect here, is grateful to Ami Plugrad-Jackisch, Craig Thompson Friend, and the Fred W. Smith National Library for the Study of

George Washington. Martha King also gratefully recognizes Mount Vernon's Fred W. Smith National Library for its fellowship support. The contributors all conclude with thanks to the organizations and institutions that have supported their work including academic homes, research establishments, and historical societies.

WOMEN WAGING WAR IN
THE AMERICAN REVOLUTION

INTRODUCTION

Women's Wars of the Revolution

—~~~~~~—

CHARACTERIZATIONS OF "Molly Pitcher" at the Battle of Monmouth and Margaret Corbin at Fort Washington conjure images of a woman, tattered skirt hiked up with a bucket at her feet, ready to fire a cannon. The stories of Deborah Sampson herald a woman who donned a uniform, shouldered a musket, and served in the Continental Army as Robert Shurtliffe. Along with accounts of Martha Washington and other officers' wives and daughters, including Angelica and Elizabeth Schuyler, these tend to be the primary popular tales of women waging war during the American Revolution. Countless other women, however, battled against or maneuvered among the Revolution's challenges as they sought security and opportunities while trying to reconcile public and personal aims and needs. The Revolution's war was not a woman's war but comprised many women's wars. The essays here illuminate women's tremendously diverse and complex lived experiences from the onset through the immediate aftermath of the War for American Independence, revealing distinctions and intersections of place, rank or class, and ethnicity on those experiences, and suggest some of their effects on both the nature and recounting of that war.

"War," Carl von Clausewitz wrote, is "an act of force to compel our enemy to do our will." He reminded readers of its inherent brutality even though social conditions and political relations might "circumscribe and moderate" it.[1] War may thus be defined as armed conflict between hostile parties that, when legally declared and conducted, operates according to political, cultural, and social constructs. Historically, war has often resulted in unsanctioned as well as sanctioned violence depending on who did what to whom and how and why. That was the case in the War for American Independence, during which women advocated, participated in, and were victimized by such acts of force.

Waging war is not just about combat, although active, armed fighting between enemy forces is rightfully a predominant definition. Warfare may be the essence of war, but war also happens to societies as it encompasses actions and peoples outside armed and uniformed ranks. Some women were directly engaged in the Revolution's warfare but all of them had to navigate a world at war. Their engagement or navigation has affected where they appear, or not, in histories. Traditional military history tends to focus on doctrine, organization, strategy, and tactics, while "war and society," or better yet "war, culture, and society" history encompasses social and cultural causation and effects. Modern military history incorporates both, but individual works still generally lean one way or the other.[2]

Developing and deciding on strategies and tactics requires an understanding of ends—objectives—and the ways and means—people and resources—to accomplish them. That is relevant on a personal level, seen in women's actions during the Revolution, as well as in the public military theater. Strategies and tactics in war are myriad although often lumped or categorized for interpretation. The War for American Independence has been described as a war of attrition between the main British and Continental Armies. The strategies of the major forces, reflecting the policies of their political leaders, focused on wearing down the enemy's will and ability to fight until that enemy either conceded to British authority or accepted American independence. Each side planned to reincorporate the other (such as Americans accepting loyalists). The Revolution also, however, included battles of annihilation in the borderlands where militias, irregular forces, and Native Americans fought to defend or destroy property and push out persons or eradicate peoples. The type and extent of coercion—how militants managed violence in word and deed to achieve their ends—is revealing of the persons, societies, and cultures involved.[3] Why combatants tried to win in the ways they did affected their treatment of civilians, which affected women's interests and security and how and why they acted as they did.

Combatant and civilian actions on all sides also provoke consideration of a question posed by Alfred F. Young and Gregory H. Nobles: "Whose American Revolution was it?" That expands to whose war for or of independence was it? Histories of the American Revolution have always included the stories of elite leaders, with the narratives—and their particular subjects—rising and falling in popularity and including hagiographic or iconoclastic interpretations. Generations have praised and criticized the men made famous by the Revolution and its war. Fame—and infamy—accorded with definitions of character and demonstrations of courage and heroism.[4] But what about women? Decorous women were not supposed to be public actors or courting fame: They were to be good "but aim not to be great / A Woman's noblest Station is retreat." Society ranked what constituted courage, heroism, and honor in gendered terms.[5]

Seeking answers to "whose revolution" or "whose war" has also been complicated by how sources by and about women were created and maintained. There are generally more primary sources, and subsequently secondary literature, available on elite, literate women. Yet how much did their stories sync with those of other, more marginalized women? While women lived within a broad, gendered categorization, there were nuances contingent to class, ethnicity, region, and loyalties. There had always been social ranks in early America, but inequality was increasing by the late eighteenth century. Revolutionary rhetoric espoused political equality and power, but often as gendered patriarchally in terms of fathers, brothers, and sons, and reinforced by wartime hierarchical associations and militaries trying to secure old or new orders. If the type of political or military service was related to social rank or class, what about the "classes" of wives, mothers, sisters, and daughters?

The war created military wives. Some of them lived and worked, and in a few cases fought, with the contending forces. Others were like mariners' wives, who took on "deputy husband" roles and "masculine" responsibilities for the periods of their spouses' service. The assumption of such powers was not revolutionary, for they were socially acceptable as financial necessities spurred them, and they were trimmed, if not taken away, upon the husband's return.[6] Such an arrangement rested on a traditional understanding of marriage as an economic partnership, which was changing to a "companionate" model through the revolutionary era. Sara T. Damiano teases out the nature and timing of the shift when arguing that "the war increased marriages' importance as economic alliances," with wives taking on more responsibilities. But she also remarks, given her examination of literate elite and middling couples, that they adopted the responsibilities while in correspondence with their husbands, which in turn "reshaped power relations within marriage, increasing spouses' interdependence on one another." Such correspondence, with its mixture of business, affective, and gendered language, tended to keep the husbands in command and the wives as their agents.[7]

As Damiano acknowledges, looking at upper-ranked, literate, married White women leaves out the economic challenges that beset others. Illiterate wives also had to deal with family finances but, especially if their husbands were similarly illiterate, possibly without spousal communication. Did that provide more room for their own agency rather than as their husbands' agents? Furthermore, war made widows and made it likelier for other women to remain single who had to assume such roles permanently, which in turn challenged the domestication of the household into a separate, private, feminized home.

Sources and synthesis are even more of a challenge in developing the histories of African American and Native American women. African Americans as active contributors to the American Revolution and participants within military ranks were both seen and unseen then and later. The "seeing"—a group's visibility to the wider contemporary society and later generations—related to how they complicated the story of the Revolution with their "struggle within a struggle."[8] There were layers to the fight for freedom: there was the ideological big "L" Liberty of the Declaration of Independence, and the smaller "l" liberties related to personal liberation and the autonomy of collectives.

The Black struggle, by those free and enslaved, to break restrictions and confinement both connected and contrasted to Native American struggles against increasing constraints and containment. The Revolution included "Indian independence movements" and brutal borderland fights between Native and colonial inhabitants, as each tried to erect boundaries against the other, which fed into increasing racist sentiments.[9] Social and cultural constructions of race did not begin with the Revolution, but it added political layers. Its war, like other wars, also revealed a gendered component to race and, vice versa, a racial component to gender. Combatants derided male opponents deemed weak or dishonorable as womanlike, while they othered the enemy's women by pronouncing them not womanly enough in virtue and propriety. That was particularly the case with Native American women deemed "insolent" who exercised a master's authority with captives or assumed a warrior's role in the field.[10]

The War for American Independence included female warriors of various sorts although not all, like Deborah Sampson, were recognized as women when they bore arms. As Gina M. Martino has noted, Indigenous and European beliefs about gender conceived "space for women to act as leaders and combatants" in the conflicts of the seventeenth- through mid-eighteenth-century northeastern borderlands. Women could and did make war, and were lauded for it, as long as they did so within acceptable boundaries. Over time, the praise shifted more to their functionary and economic roles in support of wars until, finally, martial women were reconfigured in memory as resolute mothers, wives, and daughters.[11] Women's martial participation during the Revolution challenged evolving perceptions and precepts about women's roles in war and society. War women were still respected in Indigenous cultures, but transatlantic European, including Anglo-American, cultures of the revolutionary era both dramatized and derided women who warred as their societies sought to celebrate female heroism but also to confirm gender roles in war as in peace.[12] The Revolution tested women's places and power in America as its war imposed extra obligations on most women, offered freedom or liberties to some, but did not immediately ensure independence for all.

The Revolution did not emancipate America's women or ensure them equality under the law, whether White, Black, Native American, or other ethnicities: that required generations of struggles. It did, however, lay the foundations—in words and actions—for those struggles into the modern era. Aside from the universal principles expressed in declarations and constitutions, women's actions in the War for Independence and its aftermath, as evidenced in these essays, showed that most were not and could not be protected within a private social sphere, nor were they so delicate or unfit, mentally and physically, that they needed to be. The Revolution provided proof, but because of powerful social and cultural norms affirmed in the early republic's laws and literature, confirming its tenets was only beginning.

HISTORIANS HAVE long looked at the Revolution as a social as well as political movement, within which the War for Independence was a military and cultural event that affected the speed and nature of broader changes. The participants defined their societies through their actions within their respective cultures of war, which included hierarchical rank structures, gendered roles, and ethnic distinctions. The essays featured here present a war of many layers and spaces, including domestic ones, beyond the commonly recognized battlefields. In examining the war's invasion of domestic places and women's actions within military spaces, the essay authors consider how a situation, time, place, and person may explain how and why women during the Revolution's conflicts acted similarly and differently, individually and as groups. In doing so, they reveal the war as diverse women's wars. Women's situations and the choices they made in them, as investigated through varying methodologies over time, have affected how historians have lumped and split them in their analyses.[13] Historical events, memory, and interpretations run along intersecting, parallel, and skew lines, all of which appear in these essays and in the literature from which they draw and to which they contribute.

Modern academic studies on women in the American Revolution date to the last quarter of the twentieth century. There were earlier investigations, but most reflected popular tastes rather than scholarly methodology. There is a vast difference between one of the first accounts of a woman in the Revolution, Herman Mann's memoir of Deborah Sampson, *The Female Review*, published in 1797, and Alfred Young's "life and times" biography of Deborah Sampson, *Masquerade*, in 2004.[14] In between, in a period marked by struggles for "woman's" rights against an increased focus on female domesticity, Elizabeth F. Ellet collected accounts for her multivolume *The Women of the American Revolution*, published between 1848 and 1850. Ellet engaged in scholarly research, setting an agenda for women historians and historians of women in America, but interpretively she celebrated women, primarily among the elite, who showed feminine heroism within domestic bounds.[15]

By the 1890s, female writers of popular colonial history shifted their attention from the founding leaders and soldiers to include ordinary women as role models. Their histories were "civic primers" as they presented "an idealized view of feminine character to young female readers." But ambiguity creeped into that ideal, as in Alice Morse Earle's *Colonial Dames and Good Wives*, where she "championed the Victorian ideals of maternal piety and feminine deference at the same time she introduced embryonic versions of the twentieth-century 'new woman'— self-sufficient, independent, politically invested, and even sexual—as a heroic model of femininity."[16]

Such interpretations—and ambiguity—continued into the twentieth century as history professionalized and most of its practitioners dismissed women's history. A few women scholars, however, such as Mary Ritter Beard and Julia Cherry Spruill in the 1930s, dug deeper into women's agency through history, including in the colonial and revolutionary eras, marking trails for later trackers. Then Elizabeth Cometti, writing as Americans were recovering from World War II, detailed how "war was very real to the women of the Revolutionary period" as they took on more work, dealt with shortages, and demonstrated their patriotism.[17] By the 1970s, as part of the new social history that was coincident with the era's social movements and bicentennial celebration of the American Revolution, more scholars were publishing innovative works that asked readers to consider race, class, and gender as they analyzed the choices revolutionaries and loyalists made. They also questioned the nature and permanency of the Revolution's changes for women.[18]

Reflecting the earlier pattern, it was still generally women writing about women, but more had breached graduate program walls and could offer greater challenges to academic myopia. Linda K. Kerber's *Women of the Republic* and Mary Beth Norton's *Liberty's Daughters*, both published in 1980, heralded the changes and the continuing challenges "to earn for the field of women's history an enduring place in the historiography of early America."[19] Although Kerber and Norton addressed how the war affected women's roles and self-conceptions, they and many of the other authors that constructed that "enduring place" through the 1990s—including Joan R. Gundersen, who provided a survey of women in revolutionary America, and Cynthia A. Kierner, whose analysis of women's public and domestic roles or places in the South offers a fine comparison to Spruill's earlier work—tended to concentrate on the cultural and social effects of the political revolution. That has continued in the twenty-first century as authors such as Kate Haulman examine the "culture wars" about gendered as well as political identities in the Revolution.[20]

Some historians then and since have more fully included women's actions in the war and the effects of that war on their roles. A few look specifically at women with the military forces and the gendered issues intrinsic to war, with which the authors here also engage. A major bridge builder has been Carol Berkin. Her *Revolutionary Mothers* presents the actions and effects of women in a range of social ranks, ethnicities, and loyalties primarily through the war years. Among the earliest scholars focusing on women within armed forces, Linda Grant De Pauw surveyed women in war through the ages, including the "Age of Revolution."[21] Over the past few decades, besides Alfred Young with *Masquerade*, others who have addressed the Revolution's war and women have included Nancy K. Loane writing about "camp followers" at Valley Forge, Ruma Chopra and Judith Van Buskirk on those who were loyalist or "disaffected," and, on a somewhat different track, Sarah J. Purcell, whose book *Sealed with Blood* is about women as well as White and Black men remembering their participation in the war to advance their interests afterward. Overall, along with continuing emphasis on the Revolution's "ladies," recent scholarship has included more work on the women that the revolutionaries themselves and later generations of Americans preferred not to "see."[22]

Popular histories of women in the Revolution and its war continue, of which some hark back to the role-model themes in earlier works from Ellet to Cometti, while others more carefully incorporate the advancing scholarship. The historians' labors have added biographies of disparate individuals, monographs offering comparative analyses, and anthologies collecting examples of such works, which integrate women and gender issues within histories of early America and expand our knowledge of the diverse experiences of different participants.[23] This collection builds on those but concentrates on the War for Independence to advance the study of women within military histories and support war studies within gendered histories.

Integrating women, and the history of women, into the narrative of the War for American Independence illuminates how gender—a cultural concept—as well as ethnicity and social rank, or class, affected lived experiences in and contributions to it. Legal status too—with classifications for citizen or non-, free or enslaved, as well as gender—affected women's experiences and identities in the war and its history. An adult single woman, whether never or once married, had the legal identity of *feme sole*: she was independent (within social and financial constraints) and could own property, make contracts, and institute legal actions under her own name, in her own person. A married woman was a *feme covert*; under the laws of coverture, her identity was subsumed within and her rights abridged by those of her husband. Such subordination limited and hid women's actions in the Revolution and interpretations of them since. The war also both challenged and confirmed dependency for women as it made them evaluate, navigate, and often alter their relationships with their families, communities, and local, national, and imperial authorities. They had to consider what they wanted—their objectives—and how—with or by what and whom—they were to achieve them. Women's options and the choices they made among them, their challenges and how they met them, and the costs they bore because of the war contributed to the bifurcated—conservative and radical—nature of the American Revolution both at the time and in its histories since then.

THE ESSAYS in *Women Waging War* reveal the great variety of women's experiences in the war, the effects of some of their actions on it, and the significance of those to interpretations of that war. The authors' choices and treatment of their subjects also reflect their venues—academic or public history—as well as the type and availability of resources. Women's wartime agency is sometimes as covert in documents as their persons were then in law. Region, rank, race, and religion shaped not only their experiences but also the records.

Whether interrogating those records for one woman's story or many women's common experiences, the authors share a goal of identifying—when possible, naming—women as actors. "Molly Pitcher" is a nickname attached to the camp follower Mary Ludwig Hays but may have been

meant as a catchall tag for other such active female contributors to the
Continental Army's efforts. Furthermore, using the diminutive Molly
(for Mary or Margaret) both familiarized and hid the real person or persons. Public use of intimate nicknames detracted from the status of an
individual. The flip side, reflecting a married woman's *feme covert* status,
was to identify a woman through her husband's name. That buried her
separate identity then and has made it tougher for historians to disinter
it since. At least, however, there were those names.

A major challenge in history is that of recovering the histories of the
misnamed, as often occurred with Native Americans, and the nameless.
One way is to record and interpret them by numbers and another by connections to known persons and places, but even that is difficult if the reference is not specific or obscured by spelling issues in the records. Persons
and places disappear, and thus names and no names are part of the story.
Yet what does it mean when a society does not think it necessary to record
a person's name? What are the circumstances that lead people to disappear in history? To paraphrase Caroline Cox, the treatment of people's
names, identities, and actions reveals something about the involved persons' status, where they fit within the context of power dynamics, and
how others then and since have seen their value to history and public re-
membrance.[24] The authors here probe such treatments as they develop
their own arguments about women's agency in the War for Independence.

In some form or another all of the essays analyze the challenges that
women faced, the choices that they made, the costs they bore, and their
contributions, both direct and indirect, to the character of the Revolution's war. The articles both differ and connect as the authors consider
such factors as various women's social ranks and ethnicity, at what period and where they acted in the conflict that engulfed all of America's
peoples, how women responded to threats and opportunities, and the
results of acting or not acting. Another consequence not often considered but presented in some of the chapters is that of how women's actions affected military operations. In effect, the essays reveal a spectrum
of women's options and agency as tied to position, privilege, power, or
lack thereof, and how the consequences reflected the same.

Another connection among the essays are relationships: war experiences were generally relational to families and communities as women
acted as wives, widows, mothers, sisters, daughters, and neighbors.[25]
Those connections, in turn, also serve as a reminder that men in the
war likewise made choices related to personal connections as well as
economic or political matters, faced the challenges of maintaining or

securing their families, and bore the costs of those choices. Acknowledging affiliations in analyses of decision-making helps explain the spectrum and limits of loyalties in the conflict. Yet although the relational elements may sometimes be given short shrift in accounts of men's actions, so too are women's independent choices.

The essays incorporate all of the volume's themes—war and (in)dependency, options and choices, challenges and actions, short-term costs and longer-term consequences—to some degree, but the emphasis in each informed organization. The opening chapters focus on women passionately engaged in actions that helped establish the nature, or natures, of the war. Those that follow examine how women's bodies, livelihoods, and reputations were targets, and how they proactively and reactively tried to secure them. The concluding essays survey the war's consequences for women personally and its impact on social order, gender roles, and government responsibilities. The book opens with a woman igniting war's destruction and another urging bloodshed in support of liberty. It closes with women battling the altered social and economic states that resulted from the warfare.

A WOMAN set fire to New York City and paid for it with her life. Her act of rebellion had far-reaching as well as personal consequences, yet laws, attitudes, and histories that assigned women domestic and supportive roles, says Benjamin L. Carp, explain why this firebrand remains an unnamed activist. Her mode of action was disreputable. Carp contends that the revolutionaries "publicized victims of their enemies' violence and the heroism of domesticated women on their side, but they almost never publicized female allies who behaved badly." In an amendment to Laurel Thatcher Ulrich's assertion that "well-behaved women seldom make history," it depends on who was writing the history and for what purpose.[26] In this case, the woman who chose to "misbehave" was not remembered individually but within revolutionary archetypes, both positive and negative.

Mercy Otis Warren stoked fires with words, but as a model of "republican motherhood" or, as presented here, sisterhood, her mode of action and elite status engendered more renown than rebuke. J. Patrick Mullins, like many of the authors, credits the importance of family connections in evaluating wartime choices. Women undertaking a male relative's work were not revolutionary. Eighteenth-century women, like those before and since, in America and elsewhere, managed farms and businesses on the absences of their fathers and husbands. Mercy Otis Warren, however, took up her brother James Otis Jr.'s campaign promoting radical action and, in so doing, assumed the power of public persuasion. As the words of a woman, however, were often dismissed, and because there could be prosecution for libel and sedition, Warren anonymously published political commentaries as dramatic compositions. Her forays before the war were about personal and local matters, but during and after she published under her own name plays and histories that continued to support radical government and individual rights. She waged war by writing war.[27]

Revolutionaries amplified colonial archetypes about Native American women during the war, especially those who, acting on their own allegiances to families, tribes, and nations, supported actions with the British. Whether they chose to engage as allies on one side or the other, all Native Americans conducted their own anticolonial wars of independence.[28] Barbara Alice Mann explains how Native American social and cultural principles affected the ways Indian women of the Eastern Woodlands waged war, and how "Western" social and cultural preconceptions, along with material interests, affected their interpretations of those actions. Mann's observation that Degonwandonti (Molly Brant) walked in two worlds, British and Mohawk, extends to other Native American women. Navigating both worlds became more perilous in the wars of the Revolution, as Indian women, especially women warriors, combated physical and cultural assaults on their places, peoples, and identities.

Agitators rhetoricized rape and rapine to defame opponents and make them enemies. American revolutionaries politicized rape in discourse and images as they accused the British Empire of trying to despoil the colonies along with depriving colonists of their rights. Britain and its loyalists, in turn, accused rebel activists of seducing (an act committed by "immoral" men and women) Americans from their proper allegiance.[29] Such political rhetoric, however, became personally real for women when they suffered attacks on their bodies, property, and reputations.

Domestic or private spaces were not privileged as warfare invaded homesteads and disorderly soldiers assaulted women sexually. As Lauren Duval reveals, women tried to combat the threats through tactics of diversion, dissemblance, avoidance, and obstruction. When those did not work, some challenged victimization by bearing witness against the attackers. The nature of the crime meant it was underreported, but when the women or their adherents officially complained and demanded justice, the sufferers had to endure another trauma, that of recounting the attacks to strangers in the masculine and military space of courts martial.

Warfare, as Duval proves, was not an abstraction to women on the home front waging personal battles during the American Revolution.

Steven Elliott provides another perspective on the challenges to women living amid armed forces garrisoned in their communities and quartered in their homes. He confirms that armies of occupation and on the march menaced women with assault, abuse, plunder, and displacement, but he focuses on how New Jersey women managed disruptions caused by the Continental Army and found opportunities to advance and sustain themselves and their families. He emphasizes the pragmatism, which sometimes also served patriotic ends, of women negotiating personal and economic arrangements in the civil-military communities created by war.

Such communities included refugees, and Sean M. Heuvel interrogates wartime propaganda and subsequent lore to clarify the challenges of one refugee wife and postwar widow. Some contemporary tales credited, and others maligned, the loyalist Elizabeth "Betsey" Loring for keeping General Sir William Howe in her arms instead of with the army, thereby helping American forces. Evidence shows that she was Howe's social companion, but Heuvel argues there is no proof that the "infamous Betsey" was his mistress, a designation meant to sully her and disparage Howe. Given her family ties and postwar actions, he directs readers to other conclusions about her actions in politically and economically perilous times, and in so doing shows how the personal became political and vice versa.

During the Revolutionary War, armies invaded domestic spaces and women entered military ones. Wives—and daughters, sisters, and mothers—who followed the war's forces shared similar trials in trying to remain alive and with family members, but there were distinctions related to their origins, social ranks, and theaters of operations. The stories of soldiers' wives, like their deaths, were usually unremarked or overlooked within diverse records. Followers, therefore, in more ways than one, were buried without the "honors of war," but Don N. Hagist exhumes accounts, if not always names, that reveal both honorable and dishonorable actions.[30] Followers labored to sustain their families and maintain the forces, and took risks to deliver information or supplies. But some also plundered, and thus women were at times the perpetrators, not just victims, of the crimes that accompanied military movements.

On the other end of the social spectrum from soldiers' wives were the general officers' ladies. Their choices included visiting rather than following their spouses, which could lead to challenges in travel, security and supplies, and deputizing, whether acting as deputies for their husbands at home or finding deputies for themselves when they headed for camp. Yet many of the younger wives, such as Lucy Flucker Knox and Catharine Littlefield Greene, focused on opportunities rather than challenges. Martha J. King recounts aspects of one elite woman's war that stand against the standard conditions faced by other military wives. Catharine "Caty" Greene experienced the war as a period of liberation, of sociability, leisure, and even peace, whereas postwar challenges had her, like other women but to a different degree, battling to contain the costs of her husband's service. The spirited bride of the Revolution became an entrepreneurial postwar widow.

Eliza Lucas Pinckney had long been an entrepreneurial widow. She was so successful that Lorri Glover categorizes her as a planter-patriarch rather than family matriarch. As a patriarch, like a matriarch, her focus was family, but with more emphasis on securing its prosperity, power, cohesion, and continuance. The war threatened all of that but especially bled the family's wealth and undermined its stability. After the British occupied Charleston in 1780, the battle to extend royal authority beyond the city became, Glover asserts, a woman's war. Women, including Eliza, her daughter, and daughters-in-law, who refused to evacuate and instead maintained family farms and businesses, faced enemy assaults, plundering, and, if they had them, the loss of enslaved workers. Pinckney started the war with extensive resources and ended it with them much depleted. Yet she still had far more resources and political connections than her sister sufferers, which meant she could more easily rebuild and ensure her independence, though it came at the expense of the further enslavement of others.

While the Pinckney and Middleton families (Sally Middleton Pinckney was one of Eliza Pinckney's daughters-in-law) fought to preserve their properties and power, some of the enslaved people on their estates accepted the war's invitations to freedom. And while Catharine Greene escaped domestic duties by visiting with American officers in South Carolina, Lucy Banbury escaped slavery on a Middleton estate and pursued freedom by fleeing northward to British forces. As Carin Bloom presents Banbury's story, she reveals some of the challenges and opportunities of the enslaved and of researchers incorporating both persons and travails within interpretations of historic sites.[31] A major issue is tracing names so as to account for individuals that were representative or exceptional of other enslaved peoples and their options for liberty through the war. African American women shared the experiences of other women at home and in camps but also, in choosing to stay or not in those places, embarked on other campaigns for independence that bore different costs. Lucy Banbury's war did not end with the treaty of peace in 1783: for her, the challenges and costs of independence continued with passages to Nova Scotia and then, as a widow, to Sierra Leone.

Todd W. Braisted addresses the tribulations of other loyalist women, including those of color, in the refugee crises that were part of the war. The crises included personal loss and desperate searches for security and sustenance by and for the women, and spiraling expenses for the British Army that affected logistics support for the troops and operations. As this war to assert or reassert authority was also a war for hearts and minds, the British could not ignore the refugees.[32] By evicting loyalists, including women who could have been deemed apolitical, the revolutionaries not only secured areas and gained resources; they also denied the same to their enemies and put more financial pressure on those opponents. In effect, the victims became weapons as the women who had been dependent on their own and their families' labors and lands drew on military resources and, in some cases, sailed to England to petition directly for government recompense and assistance. On the other side, the revolutionaries' state and local governments had to assist their own refugees, for such economic intervention supported their political authority.[33] The war's costs for women, and by extension the British and American governments, continued for decades.

As Jacqueline Beatty shows, many women who were themselves loyalists or of loyalist families petitioned American governments, in this case that of South Carolina, for recognition and assistance as they sought to remain in their homes and preserve family property after the British Army evacuated Charleston. In the political act of petitioning, in which they named themselves as both actors and victims, most expressed deference and dependence as they exercised the socially sanctioned prerogatives of wives, widows, and mothers to sustain their households. Political allegiances had cost them, but commonly held beliefs in familial allegiance and duties provided a way to exercise a gendered jiu-jitsu to persuade legislatures to accede to their requests. Some women made even more forthright declarations of their own allegiances and rights to property, but assertions of independence rather than dependence generally rebounded on those petitioners.

Personal independence cost many women dearly as the war wounded, sometimes fatally, family dynamics and economic security. Alisa Wade presents the other side of husbands' service and sacrifice as she examines the challenges and costs of provisional and permanent widowhood. In effect, showing how war affected the gendered distinction between patriarch and matriarch, many women had to assume both roles. Some women abhorred the extra responsibilities of the "widow's state," whether permanent or temporary, but others embraced head-of-household duties. How they chose to act, within the legally relaxed constraints (compared to *feme covert*) of a provisional or real *feme sole* status, affected the financial security of their families and by extension the broader market economy. Wade's examination of wartime widowhood shows the criticality of household production to the revolutionary era's political and economic culture, and how women's empowerment and autonomy came through sacrifice.

SOCIAL AND cultural interpretations have tended to argue that the Revolution was not all that revolutionary, but, as Alan Taylor has countered, "the revolution appears more traumatic and transformative if we pay closer attention to military conflict and its civilian consequences. The long, hard, wrenching war compelled people to change in ways unanticipated in 1775." The war displaced and injured people, destroyed property, and wrecked trade.[34] It engaged not only soldiers but also military dependents, associates, and targets. It made widows. Whether, as Wade categorizes them, provisional or permanent, widows were transformed from *feme covert* to *feme sole* and, in effect, as Glover notes with Pinckney, from matriarchs to patriarchs, from managers to proprietors, as the command of households required that they negotiate economic and political challenges outside the home. As intermediaries, administrators, entrepreneurs, and claimants, they exercised power.[35]

As men made war, women had to make money. They also had to tend to their homes, which they sometimes made in military camps, challenging a cultural turn to separate the public from private, in this case military from domestic, in both places and persons. That continued for widows after the war if they had to labor for others in or out of their houses in order to maintain their homes. To separate work and home, there had to be a familial or other pecuniary partner, such as government (with pensions or other assistance), to finance such separation.[36] If "the revolution was a struggle for economic independence that became a colonial independence movement," then the war escalated struggles for economic independence by and for widows, and by extension all women, that ultimately contributed to another kind of independence movement in succeeding generations.[37]

Women, whether widowed, married, or neither, were essential agents, willing and unwilling, in the dynamic theaters—military and political, social and economic—of the War for American Independence. Accounting for their challenges and choices, sacrifices and support, on varied fronts confirms the broader and deeper ramifications of the American Revolution. As this volume could not possibly include all women's experiences, there continues to be room and need for more on diverse women's actions in and contributions to the war and Revolution and, in turn, the war's revolutionary effects on their lives and power in America. The authors here, who deeply appreciate the work of their predecessors and colleagues who have explored women of the revolutionary era in academic and public history venues, eagerly anticipate the research of others to come.

Notes

1. Carl von Clausewitz, *On War*, ed. and trans. Michael Howard and Peter Paret (1832; Princeton, NJ: Princeton University Press, 1976), 75–76. Clausewitz's wife assisted, edited, and ensured the 1832 publication of that seminal work; see Vanya Eftimova Bellinger, *Marie von Clausewitz: The Woman behind the Making of* On War (New York: Oxford University Press, 2015).

2. Wayne E. Lee, "Early American Ways of War: A New Reconaissance, 1600–1815," *Historical Journal* 44, no. 1 (2001): 269–89; Lee, "Mind and Matter—Cultural Analysis in American Military History: A Look at the State of the Field," *Journal of American History* 93, no. 4 (March 2007): 1116–42. For a general definition and summary of types and interpretations of warfare, see Matthew S. Muehlbauer and David J. Ulbrich, *Ways of War: American Military History from the Colonial Era to the Twenty-First Century* (New York: Routledge, 2014), 1–5. Revolutionary War and society (with women) histories include David Hackett Fischer, *Washington's Crossing* (New York: Oxford University Press, 2004); John Resch and Walter Sargent, eds., *War and Society in the American Revolution: Mobilization and Home Fronts* (DeKalb: Northern Illinois University Press, 2007); and Harry M. Ward, *The War for Independence and the Transformation of American Society* (London: UCL Press, 1999).

3. For the question of "why did they try to win that way?" and a summary of Russell Weigley's duality of attrition and annihilation, see Lee, "Mind and Matter," 1120–21, with culture and violence introduced on 1128–29. See also Fred Anderson and Andrew Cayton, *The Dominion of War: Empire and Liberty in North America, 1500–2000* (New York: Penguin, 2005), 167–76.

4. Alfred F. Young and Gregory H. Nobles, *Whose American Revolution Was It? Historians Interpret the Founding* (New York: New York University Press, 2011), with Nobles reviewing "Founders Chic" in "Refocusing on the Founders," 137–41, esp. 138–39.

5. "Advice to the Ladies," *Virginia Gazette* (Williamsburg; ed. Alexander Purdie and John Dixon), 16 May 1771. See also Ruth H. Bloch, "The Gendered Meanings of Virtue in Revolutionary America," *Signs: Journal of Women in Culture and Society* 13, no. 1 (1987): 37–58.

6. Laurel Thatcher Ulrich, *Good Wives: Image and Reality in the Lives of Women in Northern New England, 1650–1750* (New York: Oxford University Press, 1983), 38–50; Lisa Norling, "'How Frought with Sorrow and Heartpangs': Mariners' Wives and the Ideology of Domesticity in New England, 1790–1880," *New England Quarterly* 65, no. 3 (September 1992): 422–46.

7. Sara T. Damiano, "Writing Women's History through the Revolution: Family Finances, Letter Writing, and Conceptions of Marriage," *William and Mary Quarterly*, 3rd series, 74, no. 4 (October 2017): 697–728, 701, 716 (quotations).

8. Borrowing from Anne Firor Scott's reflection on women's voluntary associations in "On Seeing and Not Seeing: A Case of Historical Invisibility," *Journal of American History* 71, no. 1 (June 1984): 7–21. Gregory H. Nobles notes the layered struggle in summarizing the work of Benjamin Quarles and other historians who have explored Black wartime endeavors, in "Redefining Freedom in the Revolution," in Young and Nobles, *Whose American Revolution*, 148. For more on African American struggles in the armies of the Revolution and afterward, see Sylvia R. Frey, *Water from the Rock: Black Resistance in a Revolutionary Age* (Princeton, NJ: Princeton University Press, 1991), and Judith Van Buskirk, *Standing in Their Own Light: African American Patriots in the American Revolution* (Norman: University of Oklahoma Press, 2017). In addition, see Jacqueline Jones, "Race, Sex, and Self-Evident Truths: The Status of Slave Women during the Era of the American Revolution," in *Slavery and Freedom in the Age of the American Revolution*, ed. Ira Berlin and Ronald Hoffman (Charlottesville: University Press of Virginia, 1983), 293–337.

9. Gregory H. Nobles, "Facing the Revolution from Indian Country," in Young and Nobles, *Whose American Revolution*, 175, 186–88.

10. For applicable material, although about earlier warfare, see Ann M. Little, *Abraham in Arms: War and Gender in Colonial New England* (Philadelphia: University of Pennsylvania Press, 2007): wartime duty as the "measure" of a man (169), whereas weakness was a "womanlike state" (220); quoting Cotton Mather's "insolent" for Indian women and the power they wielded in peace and war within their communities, 98–102. Race, manliness, and Native women (in passing) in frontier warfare are also noted in Gregory T. Knouff, *The Soldiers' Revolution: Pennsylvanians in Arms and*

the Forging of Early American Identity (University Park: Pennsylvania State University Press, 2004), 163–64, 168–70.

11. Gina M. Martino, *Women at War in the Borderlands of the Early American Northeast* (Chapel Hill: University of North Carolina Press, 2018), 3, 106, 136–37.

12. Holly A. Mayer, "Bearing Arms, Bearing Burdens: Women Warriors, Camp Followers and Home-Front Heroines of the American Revolution," in *Gender, War and Politics: Transatlantic Perspectives, 1775–1830*, ed. Karen Hagemann, Gisela Mettele, and Jane Rendall (Basingstoke, UK: Palgrave Macmillan, 2010), 170–76.

13. Acknowledging Sarah Knott's "situational narratives" in "Narrating the Age of Revolution," *William and Mary Quarterly*, 3rd series, 73, no. 1 (January 2016): 3–36, esp. 5, 24–25 (definitions), 34 (about the "imagined reader").

14. [Herman Mann], *The Female Review: Memoirs of an American Young Lady* (Dedham, MA: Nathaniel and Benjamin Heaton, 1797); Alfred F. Young, *Masquerade: The Life and Times of Deborah Sampson, Continental Soldier* (New York: Knopf, 2004).

15. Elizabeth F. Ellet, *The Women of the American Revolution* (c. 1848–50; reprint, Williamstown, MA: Corner House, 1980); Scott E. Casper, "An Uneasy Marriage of Sentiment and Scholarship: Elizabeth F. Ellet and the Domestic Origins of American Women's History," *Journal of Women's History* 4, no. 2 (Fall 1992): 10–35. See, for example, the Declaration of Sentiments, Seneca Falls, New York, 1848, and Catharine Beecher's *A Treatise on Domestic Economy* (Boston: T. H. Webb, 1842) and *The Duty of American Women to Their Country* (New York: Harper and Brothers, 1845).

16. Julie Des Jardins, *Women and the Historical Enterprise in America: Gender, Race, and the Politics of Memory, 1880–1945* (Chapel Hill: University of North Carolina Press, 2003), 1–4, 15–17, 19; Alice Morse Earle, *Colonial Dames and Good Wives* (Boston: Houghton Mifflin, 1895).

17. Julia Cherry Spruill, *Women's Life and Work in the Southern Colonies* (Chapel Hill: University of North Carolina Press, 1938); "Making the Revolution," in *America through Women's Eyes*, ed. Mary Ritter Beard (New York: Macmillan, 1933), 54–87; Elizabeth Cometti, "Women in the American Revolution," *New England Quarterly* 20, no. 3 (September 1947): 329–46.

18. Elizabeth Evans, *Weathering the Storm: Women of the American Revolution* (New York: Charles Scribner's Sons, 1975); Sally Booth Smith, *Women of '76* (New York: Hastings House, 1973); Debra L. Newman, "Black Women in the Era of the American Revolution in Pennsylvania," *Journal of Negro History* 61, no. 3 (July 1976): 276–89; Mary Beth Norton, "Eighteenth-Century American Women in Peace and War: The Case of the Loyalists," *William and Mary Quarterly*, 3rd series, 33, no. 3 (July 1976): 386–409; Joan Hoff Wilson, "The Illusion of Change: Women and the American Revolution," in *The American Revolution: Explorations in the History of*

American Radicalism, ed. Alfred F. Young (DeKalb: Northern Illinois University Press, 1976), 383–431.

19. Mary Beth Norton, *Liberty's Daughters: The Revolutionary Experience of American Women, 1750–1800* (Boston: Little, Brown, 1980); Linda K. Kerber, *Women of the Republic: Intellect and Ideology in Revolutionary America* (Chapel Hill: University of North Carolina Press, 1980). Richard R. Beeman revealed the challenge of acceptance in "A New Era in Female History," *Reviews in American History* 9, no. 3 (September 1983): 341. In "Women and Revolution: 1750–1800, 1980–2005," a session dedicated to Norton's and Kerber's work at the annual meeting of the Society for Historians of the Early American Republic (SHEAR), on 23 July 2005, participants considered these seminal works still "fresh" but that they also highlighted how women's history had developed since their publication. For the state of the field at the end of the 1980s, see Ronald Hoffman and Peter J. Albert, eds., *Women in the Age of the American Revolution* (Charlottesville: University Press of Virginia, 1989).

20. Joan R. Gundersen, *To Be Useful to the World: Women in Revolutionary America, 1740–1790* (New York: Twayne, 1996); Gundersen, "'We Bear the Yoke with a Reluctant Impatience': The War for Independence and Virginia's Displaced Women," in Resch and Sargent, eds., *War and Society in the American Revolution*, 263–88; Cynthia A. Kierner, *Beyond the Household: Women's Place in the Early South, 1700–1835* (Ithaca, NY: Cornell University Press, 1998); Kate Haulman, "Fashion and the Culture Wars of Revolutionary Philadelphia," *William and Mary Quarterly*, 3rd series, 62, no. 4 (October 2005): 625–62. Some other works, besides those noted elsewhere in this essay, include Barbara E. Lacey, "Women in the Era of the American Revolution: The Case of Norwich, Connecticut," *New England Quarterly* 53, no. 4 (December 1980): 527–43, and Betsy Erkkila, "Revolutionary Women," *Tulsa Studies in Women's Literature* 6, no. 2 (Autumn 1987): 189–223.

21. Carol Berkin, *Revolutionary Mothers: Women in the Struggle for America's Independence* (New York: Knopf, 2005); Linda Grant De Pauw, *Battle Cries and Lullabies: Women in War from Prehistory to the Present* (Norman: University of Oklahoma Press, 1998); De Pauw, "Women in Combat: The Revolutionary War Experience," *Armed Forces and Society* 7 (Winter 1981): 209–26, with Janice E. McKenney's rebuttal in "'Women in Combat': Comment," *Armed Forces and Society* 8 (Summer 1982): 686–92. For an early incorporation of women's activities into military history, see also Paul E. Kopperman, "Medical Services in the British Army, 1742–1783," *Journal of the History of Medicine* 34 (October 1979): 428–55, and "The British High Command and Soldiers' Wives in America, 1755–1783," *Journal of the Society for Army Historical Research* 60 (1982): 14–34.

22. Young, *Masquerade*; Nancy K. Loane, *Following the Drum: Women at the Valley Forge Encampment* (Washington, DC: Potomac Books, 2009). See

also Holly A. Mayer, *Belonging to the Army: Camp Followers and Community during the American Revolution* (Columbia: University of South Carolina Press, 1996); Mayer, "Wives, Concubines, and Community," in Resch and Sargent, eds., *War and Society in the American Revolution*, 235–62; Mayer, "Bearing Arms, Bearing Burdens"; Ruma Chopra, "Loyalist Women in British New York City, 1776–1783," in *Women in Early America*, ed. Thomas A. Foster (New York: New York University Press, 2015), 210–24; Judith Van Buskirk, "They Didn't Join the Band: Disaffected Women in Revolutionary Philadelphia," *Pennsylvania History* 62, no. 3 (Summer 1995): 306–29; and Sarah J. Purcell, *Sealed with Blood: War, Sacrifice, and Memory in Revolutionary America* (Philadelphia: University of Pennsylvania Press, 2002).

23. Recent anthologies about early American women with some essays related to the Revolution's war include Barbara B. Oberg, ed., *Women in the American Revolution: Gender, Politics, and the Domestic World* (Charlottesville: University of Virginia Press, 2019), and Foster, ed., *Women in Early America*. Integration as a major goal of women's and gender history is noted in Cornelia H. Dayton and Lisa Levenstein's "The Big Tent of U.S. Women's and Gender History: A State of the Field," *Journal of American History* 99, no. 3 (December 2012): 793–817, 794–95 (quotation). They also point out the growing interdisciplinarity and innovations in studies of race, class, gender, sexual orientation, relational differences among women, and the construction of norms and their destabilization. Other "tent" essays on women and the Revolution that present recent interpretive directions and literature include the following: Gregory H. Nobles, "Writing Women into the Revolution," in Young and Nobles, *Whose American Revolution*, 224–55; Terri L. Snyder, "Refiguring Women in Early American History," *William and Mary Quarterly*, 3rd series, 69, no. 3 (July 2012): 421–50; the forum of essays on "Politics in and of Women's History in the Early Republic," *Journal of the Early Republic* 36, no. 2 (Summer 2016): 313–57; and Kate Haulman, "Women, War, and Revolution," in *The Oxford Handbook of American Women's and Gender History*, ed. Ellen Hartigan-O'Connor and Lisa G. Materson (New York: Oxford University Press, 2018), 551–69.

24. Caroline Cox examined the treatment of men's bodies and status in *A Proper Sense of Honor: Service and Sacrifice in George Washington's Army* (Chapel Hill: University of North Carolina Press, 2004), xi.

25. Relationships connect to the broader interpretive category of affiliations, which has been used to track and understand women's activism. See Dayton and Levenstein, "Big Tent," 797.

26. Laurel Thatcher Ulrich, *Well-Behaved Women Seldom Make History* (New York: Vintage, 2007).

27. See Eileen Hunt Botting, "Women Writing War: Mercy Otis Warren and Hannah Mather Crocker on the American Revolution," *Massachusetts Historical Review* 18 (2016): 88–118, esp. 91, 109–11.

28. Colin G. Calloway, *The American Revolution in Indian Country: Crisis and Diversity in Native American Communities* (New York: Cambridge University Press, 1995), xiii.

29. Sharon Block, "Rape without Women: Print Culture and the Politicization of Rape, 1765–1815," *Journal of American History* 89, no. 3 (December 2002): 849–68. For "seduction," see Charles Inglis, *The Deceiver Unmasked; or, Loyalty and Interest United* (New York: Samuel Loudon, 1776), preface.

30. Cox, *Proper Sense of Honor*, 163–65.

31. The War for Independence and individual freedom flights offer additional "Transition to Freedom" accounts to those of place-based "slavery to freedom" interpretations. Based on the latter, Brian Graves provides a thoughtful review of how southern historic plantation sites are grappling with how to interpret slavery—through themes of reconciliation, reparations, or, apropos to this volume, generating shared historical memory—in "'Return and Get It': Developing McLeod Plantation as a Shared Space of Historical Memory," *Southern Cultures* 23, no. 2 (Summer 2017): 75–96.

32. This inserts women into the "triangularity" of the conflict as analyzed by John Shy in "The American Revolution: The Military Conflict Considered as a Revolutionary War," in *Essays on the American Revolution*, ed. Stephen G. Kurtz and James H. Hutson (Chapel Hill: University of North Carolina Press, 1973), 121–56.

33. Matthew P. Dziennik looks at the dispossessed in general, not women particularly, in connecting refugee relief to establishing institutional authority in "New York's Refugees and Political Authority in Revolutionary America," *William and Mary Quarterly*, 3rd series, 77, no. 1 (January 2020): 65–96.

34. Alan Taylor, "Expand or Die: The Revolution's New Empire," *William and Mary Quarterly*, 3rd series, 74, no. 4 (October 2017): 625.

35. See Michael A. McDonnell and David Waldstreicher, "Revolution in the Quarterly? A Historiographical Analysis," *William and Mary Quarterly*, 3rd series, 74, no. 4 (October 2017): 652–53; Carole Shammas, "Anglo-American Household Government in Comparative Perspective," *William and Mary Quarterly*, 3rd series, 52, no. 1 (January 1995): 104–44; and Ellen Hartigan-O'Connor, "The Personal Is Political Economy," *Journal of the Early Republic* 36 (Summer 2016): 335–41.

36. Connections between government aid and dependent domesticity appear in Kristin A. Collins, "'Petitions without Number': Widows' Petitions and the Early Nineteenth-Century Origins of Public Marriage-Based Entitlements," *Law and History Review* 31, no. 1 (February 2013): 1–60, esp. 5–7, 13, 36, 39, 42, 48–49, 56–57.

37. McDonnell and Waldstreicher, about a Staughton Lynd and Waldstreicher interpretation, in "Revolution in the *Quarterly?*" 654.

"The First Incendiary"

A Female Firebrand and the New York City Fire of 1776

BENJAMIN L. CARP

—◦◦◦◦◦◦—

THE BRITISH Army captured New York City on 15 September 1776. Six days later, a group of rebels spoiled the king's prize: they set fires that laid waste to hundreds of buildings. Soldiers on the scene caught and summarily executed several unnamed incendiaries. The *St. James's Chronicle* of London, printing a "private Letter" from New York, reported "that the first Incendiary who fell into the Hands of the Troops was a *Woman*, provided with Matches and Combustibles." The news was meant to shock readers who were conditioned to believe that women belonged at home, tending the hearth fires, not in the center of a warzone, starting house fires. To a British newspaper audience, this female incendiary became vivid proof that the American rebellion was a crime against the natural order.[1]

The laws of war were clear about what ought to happen next. Normally it was "a maxim of justice and humanity" not to mistreat women and other noncombatants, but according to Emer de Vattel, "If the women wish to be spared altogether, they must confine themselves to the occupations peculiar to their own sex, and not meddle with those of men by taking up arms." Furthermore, "incendiaries . . . may be exterminated wherever they are seized."[2] And so in the case of the "first Incendiary," the *Chronicle* continued, "her Sex availed her little, for without Ceremony, she was tossed into the Flames" by the soldiers. It was the ancient punishment for witches, traitors, heretics, and arsonists—a way to destroy the deep evil that lingered in the bodies of serious criminals. Indeed, British authorities still punished some women for petty treason (usually murdering their husbands) by burning them at the stake as "home-rebels" and "house-traitors."[3] Histories, too, try to suppress women who defy the strictures of marriage and domesticity.

Because of that suppression, we do not expect to encounter women committing acts of irregular warfare; most people regard such an image as a nightmare or ignore the idea entirely. This essay considers the story of the "first Incendiary" and argues for an honest reckoning with her frightful identity.[4]

PEOPLE OF the eighteenth-century British Empire relied on a small handful of stereotypes to fasten restrictive gender roles on women. The first type was the proper (usually White) woman, tender and subservient, except for when she ran a household in the absence of a father or husband. The second type was the "disorderly woman," apt to be mercurial, deceptive, oversexed, and unruly. More rarely, literature and history made room for a third role: that of a righteous warrior who defended the community and kept her family fed and intact at all costs. This type of woman—like Jeanne d'Arc (who also met a fiery death)—might be strong, politicized, and out on the frontlines of civil and military conflict. British society also tolerated—even grudgingly admired—the occasional hardy plebeian woman who dressed as a man and fought for her country, who displayed her own kind of masculinity and heroism. But for the most part, such women were not celebrated until they were neutralized or deceased.[5]

Prior to the outbreak of the Revolution, American women had become politically active, signing on to boycotts of British goods and producing homespun cloth. Then they supported the war effort with their money and labor. Female soldiers like Deborah Sampson Gannett, the Massachusetts woman who surreptitiously served in uniform, were rare. Women more often acted in informal or auxiliary military capacities. They encouraged beaux and relatives to fight, joined army communities, and entertained troops in garrison. Most of these activities were uncontroversial (at least among their own partisans), since they accorded with traditional notions of women's labor, nurturing, and subordination. In such cases, their male allies welcomed their presence.[6]

In a culture that tried to domesticate women and denigrate those outside a privileged sphere, politically and militarily active women might also transgress too far. Their enemies described them as being under an "epidemical kind of phrenzy." They became "little mischief-making devils," throwing aside modesty and delicacy. At that point, their bodies were at risk; Joan DeJean has pointed out that the emergence of violent women has often coincided with (or indeed precipitated) violence against women. Women became victims of war, as refugees, property owners, and vulnerable bodies. More specifically, the 1776 campaign around New York created new roles for local women as saboteurs and spies but also revealed shocking incidents of physical and sexual assault. Patriots twice punished Lorenda Holmes, a loyalist, for conveying messages and refugees across enemy lines: first, local patriot authorities stripped her of her clothes and exposed her before a crowd of people, then a few months later rebel soldiers burned her on the foot with coals. In August 1776, Captain Francis, Lord Rawdon, gave a heinous (if possibly fictive) account of rapes committed by British soldiers on Staten Island. Other women would later meet violent deaths, such as Jane McCrea (a loyalist's fiancée killed by Indians near Fort Edward, New York, in 1777) or Hannah Caldwell (a minister's wife who died from a stray bullet during a British raid on Connecticut Farms, New Jersey). In spite of the risks, women challenged social conventions by joining the political and military mobilization of the revolutionary era. Patriots publicized victims of their enemies' violence and the heroism of domesticated women on their side, but they almost never publicized female allies who behaved badly.[7]

Instead, in the case of the "first Incendiary," what "her Sex availed her" was an anonymous death at the hands of the king's men. While this punishment was permissible under the laws of war, it also occurred at a moment when the bonds of authority were especially loose: civic institutions were largely inoperable, and the American army (and most civilians) had fled. The British Army had just begun its occupation, and loyalists had barely begun to return. This unstable scenario had two effects: first, it gave license for British soldiers to punish women in ways they might not otherwise have done; second, it allowed Americans to disavow responsibility for the fire, and so the deeds of the "first Incendiary" would go unmentioned in the patriot press.

THE LONDON newspaper story of the "first Incendiary" is partly corroborated by two unprinted accounts. The first comes from Henry Strachey, a member of Parliament who served as secretary to Admiral Richard, Lord Howe, in his capacity as peace commissioner. Strachey wrote to his wife in England that he had seen the fire from aboard the *Eagle* flagship (about two miles from the city) and called it "the most shocking Scene" and "the most melancholly Catastrophe that ever came within my View." At Lord Howe's side, Strachey was well-positioned to receive the best intelligence from Manhattan. Strachey wrote that British soldiers and sailors had killed five or six "Incendiaries" and seized other "Contrivers." He added, "One Woman was caught with a Match, and her hands all over Gunpowder which she had been kneading into balls." But he said nothing further about her fate.[8]

The second account was the 1783 testimony of Private George Kerr of the 43rd Regiment of Foot. Kerr recalled entering a house behind St. Paul's Chapel, where he found "five men & a woman." The room had a cupboard with "a Kegg holding about 5 Gall[on]s with the [rest] out full of open powder & a bundle of matches near it." Kerr "seized the men, when the woman cried & offered me money to let them go." She hoped that Private Kerr would be swayed by sympathy—or, failing that, greed—and look the other way, but as the newspapers said, "her Sex availed her little." Instead, Kerr recalled, "I took the money & carried the 5 Men the Powder & Matches to the Provost." The soldiers took the men to jail and probably saved St. Paul's from destruction.[9]

Her tears may well have been genuine—she had just been cornered by armed men ("fell into the Hands of the Troops"). But Kerr apparently decided that her cries were a feminine ruse or an unfeminine outburst, especially since they preceded a bribe. The woman, having crossed the boundaries of gendered propriety, may well have tried to cross back by using her presumed weakness and irresponsibility as leverage to escape punishment.[10] Kerr said nothing more about the woman's fate in his recorded testimony. If this was the "first Incendiary" from the newspaper, then either he or Ward Chipman (the scribe) omitted what happened next: the Redcoats responded to this fallen woman's crime by immolating her "without Ceremony." Kerr pocketed the cash.

Who was she, and why had she done it? Given the nature of the evidence, we can only speculate. Perhaps the woman had taken an active part in the rebellious city's political culture or was connected to a patriot soldier. If so, then perhaps she and her companions were enacting their animus against wealthy local loyalists, the Church of England, the British Army. If she owned no property in the city, then she may have cared little for its fate. If she was a New Yorker, then she would have known many women who acted alongside men in commerce, sociability, and other endeavors, even in transgressive activities like keeping disorderly houses, theft, and criminal violence.

During the city's famous 1741 conspiracy trials, women had participated in the thefts and multiracial cabals that made up the city's counterculture. Because the "first Incendiary" was discovered in the "holy ground" neighborhood notorious for prostitution, she might have been a sex worker. If she had been part of the city's informal, marginal economy, then she may have felt that much more comfortable defying gender norms by confronting a soldier. Again, if she was a resident New Yorker, perhaps she perceived herself as defending her hometown; for centuries, women had defended besieged cities, protected their homes from pillage, and withheld their property from conquest. Possibly she made the affirmative choice to burn houses rather than let them fall into enemy hands.[11]

Still, her participation *as* a woman was distinctive and indicates something broader about the radical elements of the revolutionary movement. Although Continental Army officers wanted an orderly army, they also confronted soldiers who sowed chaos, disobeyed orders, and used non-traditional methods of war. As radical actors, patriots were willing to consider radical methods, including the deployment of women as spies and saboteurs. Such women could manipulate prevailing gender assumptions; as Judith L. Van Buskirk writes, "Considered weak and childlike, females could go where few males dared because they were considered no threat." The "first Incendiary" had a particular ability to act behind enemy lines. Her ability to exploit her presumed incapacity was exactly what made her dangerous.[12]

AT WESTMINSTER in London, the female firebrand's story drew the attention of Edmund Burke, an opposition member of Parliament. Burke used her story for a different political purpose. Omitting any male incendiaries from his version of events, he singled out an incendiary woman not to demonstrate the wrongness of the American rebellion but to denounce the wrongness of Great Britain's approach to fighting it. Burke had previously served as London agent for the colony of New York, and from the 1760s onward he had argued on behalf of the colonies and their grievances. On 6 November 1776, from the floor of the House of Commons, he bitterly criticized the ministry. They had hatched a two-faced strategy by sending the Howe brothers as peace commissioners to America, and furthermore Parliament's sluggish delays had given Congress time to declare independence. Now they had run out of ideas. The British commanders could only unleash "the healing, soothing, merciful measures of foreign [i.e., Hessian] swords, at the breasts of those unhappy people."[13]

What was worse, this strategy was bound to fail. Even if "the wreath of victory adorned your brow, still is not that continent conquered." As proof, he evoked the "one miserable woman" who was caught with the clear intention to burn New York. Burke's account noted her plans to use gunpowder ("Her train was laid and fired"). Unlike Kerr's weeping wheedler, however, Burke portrayed the woman as defiant upon capture: "She was brought forth, and knowing that she would be condemned to die, upon being asked her purpose, said, 'to fire the city!' and was determined" to seize the opportunity to do "what her country called for." By burning New York City, she had, "with her single arm . . . arrested your progress in the moment of your success," which not even George Washington's army had been able to do. "Providence was pleased to make use of those humble means to serve the *American* cause, when open force was used in vain." Britain's failure had motivated a "humble" woman to burn a British garrison. She died the day before Nathan Hale, who was hanged after declaring his own famously defiant valediction on behalf of his country.[14]

Dror Wahrman notes the "internal tension and disharmony" in Burke's rendering of this woman, which was shot through with an "unnatural confusion of fundamental identity categories."[15] As Burke described her, "This miserable being was found in a cellar, with her visage besmeared and smutted over, with every mark of rage, despair, resolution, and the most exalted heroism, buried in combustibles, in order to fire *New-York*, and perish in its ashes."[16] Her blackened face might have been a prepared disguise or the byproduct of a smoky night's work; either way, it had the effect of obscuring her. Burke called her "miserable" but praised her "exalted heroism." Had she, as Kerr testified, been crying or trying to bribe her way out of jeopardy? Or was she clear-eyed in her patriotic purpose? Was she weak and pitiable, as ladies were expected to be, or abominably masculine, by taking part in a war where women ostensibly had no place? Why was she kneading balls of gunpowder instead of bread dough? Burke hoped his listeners would conclude that the "unnatural rebellion" had gone so far beyond the norms of war that women were now stepping forward to perform the rebels' most horrid deeds. But perhaps we should not be so surprised to find a radical female incendiary at work.[17]

Burke accused the ministry of creating "this unhappy situation . . . by a succession of acts of tyranny." He listed a few of the Americans' grievances and concluded, "This it is that has burnt the noble city of *New-York*; that has planted the bayonet . . . in the bosom of the city; where alone your wretched Government once boasted the only friends she could number in *America*." In other words, British policy had so alienated the populace that the ministry had no one but themselves to blame for the destruction of New York City. Burke asked the men of Parliament to draw their eyes to the "bosom" at the business end of a Hessian bayonet. The British Army would regret its ham-fisted disregard for a sanctuary that should have nurtured them (the loyal city, the female chest). In its place, the soldiers now faced a torch-bearing arm, a "visage besmeared," and a cry of righteous rage and self-destruction. Burke imagined New York as a "bosom" of sociability, friendship, domesticity, and maternal embrace; the incompetent British ministry had provoked a very different kind of woman, who in turn destroyed hundreds of homes.[18] His friend Joshua Reynolds may have evoked her in his portrait of *Thaïs* (1781), depicting the courtesan who helped Alexander the Great to burn Persepolis in 330 BCE.[19]

In Burke's view, the king and his ministers had conjured the "miserable being" who dwelled in the New York cellar. Her soot-stained "visage" reflected Britain's early failures. Kerr's fellow redcoats had set aside her womanhood and thrown her into the inferno. The country's shame, Burke was saying, foretold its eventual defeat.

IN THE years that followed, the "first Incendiary" passed into the realm of the symbolic, crossed the English Channel, multiplied, echoed throughout later historical events, and then passed back into myth. The radical French writer Michel René Hilliard d'Auberteuil published his *Essais historiques et politiques sur les Anglo-Américains* in 1781–82. The *Essais* celebrated Americans' innate courage and republicanism, supported the justice of their rebellion, and criticized the conduct of the British Army.[20] In the author's account of the Great Fire of New York, both men and women deliberately set fire to the city and tried to stop the British from extinguishing the flames. Some of the men were captured and executed. Meanwhile, "The women in particular seemed to be animated by the wrath of the Furies." The author depicted them as seized with horror and despair at a moment of chaos, "running astray, with their hair scattered and bristling," while Jean-Jacques-François Le Barbier's illustration shows a child clinging to a mother who has collapsed in anguish.[21]

Yet Hilliard d'Auberteuil also crowed that New York women's audacity in setting the fire exceeded that of the women in Virgil's *Aeneid* who burned the Trojan ships in Sicily. He mentioned three women in particular. One woman loudly accused American men of cowardice for abandoning the city. Fearing rape at the hands of British soldiers, she was about to stab herself when an English officer disarmed her. A second woman fled north to Washington's camp and confessed to burning her own house so that the British tyrants would not have it. British soldiers arrested a third woman with a torch in her hand. While many of the suspects who were caught in 1776 with incendiary materials shrewdly claimed that they were carrying them to safety, in Hilliard d'Auberteuil's telling, this woman firmly and defiantly informed the soldiers that she was setting fire to the city. Le Barbier's image shows no male incendiaries but at least two women carrying torches—one has her hair pulled by a British soldier, while the other holds three torches aloft. The knife-wielding woman clutches her bosom. These women appear virtuous—a far cry from the Maenads that populated conservative nightmares. They are forthright about their aims, they prefer death to dishonor, and they sacrifice their private interest for the public good.[22]

Hilliard d'Auberteuil based his account in part on the speech by Burke (whom he admired) and British newspaper reports of the fire, but he also exercised quite a bit of poetic license.[23] In 1784, he retold the story in *Miss McCrea*. This novel offers a few different archetypes of womanhood, from tearful victims to cunning servants. Its main character is young, doomed Jane McCrea, a blushing, innocent girl who is astonished to find that the fictional Captain Belton (part of the British expedition landing in New York) would "respect my sex and the weakness of my age," unlike his comrades who had raped, slaughtered, and plundered their way across Long Island and Manhattan. The female "*incendiaires*" had multiplied since the *Essais*. Hilliard d'Auberteuil wrote that they "chose to burn their homes rather than let them become booty for the enemy." When a British officer asks one, "What are you doing, mad woman?" she replies defiantly (as in Burke's account): "I am setting the city afire!" Even as the soldiers arrest her, they "could not shake her firmness." Instead, the women cry, "Ground where we were born! We leave you forever rather than surrender our liberty." With that, "Several women stabbed themselves at the very instant of capture." In the novel, these women are stoic suicides rather than teary-eyed victims of British wrath. Hilliard d'Auberteuil twice translated the defiant (yet still ambiguous) woman of Burke's account into French: in his imagination, a number of New York women killed themselves and incinerated their city rather than live under tyranny.[24]

THE "FIRST Incendiary" of British newspaper accounts had become a potent revolutionary archetype, suspended halfway between truth and fiction. But then, strangely, the allegory of the "destructive woman" gained solid form during the tumultuous events of the next decades. Her spiritual descendants emerged as the *tricoteuses,* protestors, and *boutefeux* of the French Revolution and the *pétroleuses* of the Paris Commune in 1871; perhaps they were inspired in part by the literary examples that Hilliard d'Auberteuil had published in Paris. As Dominique Godineau writes, "They consciously assumed the role of detonator, of 'firebrands.'" She adds, "During certain periods of crisis, collective *mentalités* expected women to be the ones . . . to start the movement." Militant women had agency, but they were rapidly inspiring a backlash: during the Parisian riots of 1795, French authorities referred to female protestors as the "furies of the guillotine," making "incendiary remarks" and calling men "cowards."[25]

Back in England, Burke's own perspective on radical politics and disorderly women had changed, and he was no longer celebrating the "exalted heroism" of female firebrands. Burke was the target of crowd action during the Gordon Riots in London (2–8 June 1780), when suspected female incendiaries were also killed on the spot. In Parliament, he mocked female anti-Catholic protesters as illiterate "monsters," and subsequent English riots would offer more examples of burning houses, female firestarters, and summary executions. Yet an increasingly conservative British public refused to celebrate such women. In 1790, Burke described the French women who marched on Versailles in October 1789 as "the furies of hell, in the abused shape of the vilest of women."[26]

Mary Wollstonecraft, Burke's adversary, became as disillusioned as anyone else with the bloody turn that the French Revolution had taken in 1793. She too then wrung her hands over the "mob" that stormed Versailles in 1789: the "market women, and the lowest refuse of the streets, women who had thrown off the virtues of one sex without having power to assume more than the vices of the other." Still, in the scapegoating of revolutionary women, she smelled a rat: "It has . . . been the scheme of designing men very often since the revolution, to lurk behind them as a kind of safeguard, working them up to some desperate act, and then terming it a folly, because merely the rage of women." She had previously written that women's revolutionary violence was a byproduct of their oppression; now she predicted that men would denigrate such violence and dismiss its underlying causes, to the detriment of women's rights.[27]

AMERICANS EVENTUALLY celebrated some of women's contributions to the American Revolution. Yet they had no reason to commemorate or celebrate a female incendiary, even apart from their desire to conceal the perpetrators who burned New York City.[28] Peter Force included Burke's

1776 speech in his *American Archives*, but few historians made use of it. William Henry Shelton (a Civil War artillerist who became an author and illustrator) called Burke's "fancied description . . . more dramatic than historic" and labeled it the product of Burke's "fervid imagination." Otherwise, Americans largely forgot the "first Incendiary" until gender-conscious historians like Linda K. Kerber rediscovered her in the 1980s.[29] As a result, it will probably never be possible to recover her name, much less retrieve her thoughts or center her voice.

Yet the "first Incendiary" deserves to be remembered. Since she died less than three months after the Declaration of Independence, she may well have been the first woman of the United States to be killed in action by the British Army. She hardly typified those who challenged gender boundaries during the Revolution; by engaging in irregular, collective violence alongside male incendiaries, she stood at the revolutionary movement's most radical vanguard. Because violent women caused fear and discomfort, they fit awkwardly in history. These "furies" loomed large in the "fervid imagination" of conservative European thinkers (especially after the French Revolution), tempting us to dismiss them as fictional stories—as titillating fantasies or cautionary tales for well-behaved girls. The wider world scapegoated them as monstrous caricatures or suppressed them. They became "smutted over"—obscured—but beneath the ash and gunpowder, we can pinpoint 1776 as a moment when women were waging war in unexpected ways. Some contemporaries even briefly held up these female warriors as examples of "exalted heroism" and republican virtue.

NOTES

1. *St. James's Chronicle* (London), 9–12 November 1776; Benjamin L. Carp, "The Night the Yankees Burned Broadway: The New York City Fire of 1776," *Early American Studies* 4, no. 2 (Fall 2006): 487–91.

2. Emer de Vattel, *The Law of Nations; or, Principles of the Law of Nature*, ed. Béla Kapossy and Richard Whitmore (1758; 1797; Indianapolis: Liberty Fund, 2008), book 1, chap. 19, §233:228 ("incendiaries"); book 3, chap. 8, §145:549 ("maxim," "women"); book 3, chap. 15, §226:613. For a similar dynamic in 1871 Paris, see Gay L. Gullickson, *The Unruly Women of Paris: Images of the Commune* (Ithaca, NY: Cornell University Press, 1996), 189–90.

3. *St. James's Chronicle*, 9–12 November 1776; Romedio Schmitz-Esser, "The Cursed and the Holy Body: Burning Corpses in the Middle Ages," *Journal of Medieval and Early Modern Studies* 45, no. 1 (January 2015): 131–57;

Frank McLynn, *Crime and Punishment in Eighteenth-Century England* (London: Routledge, 1989), 121–24; Frances E. Dolan, "Home-Rebels and House-Traitors: Murderous Wives in Early Modern England," *Yale Journal of Law and the Humanities* 4, no. 1 (1992): 1–31.

4. On women and irregular warfare, see Stephanie McCurry, *Women's War: Fighting and Surviving the American Civil War* (Cambridge, MA: Harvard University Press, 2019), esp. chap. 1; LeeAnn Whites and Alecia P. Long, "Introduction," in *Occupied Women: Gender, Military Occupation, and the American Civil War*, ed. LeeAnn Whites and Alecia P. Long (Baton Rouge: Louisiana State University Press, 2009), 1–14; and Linda K. Kerber, "'History Can Do It No Justice': Women and the Reinterpretation of the American Revolution," in *Toward an Intellectual History of Women* (Chapel Hill: University of North Carolina Press, 1997), 63–99, esp. 70.

5. Natalie Zemon Davis, "Women on Top," in *Society and Culture in Early Modern France: Eight Essays* (Stanford, CA: Stanford University Press, 1975), 124–51; Teresa Ann Murphy, *Citizenship and the Origins of Women's History in the United States* (Philadelphia: University of Pennsylvania Press, 2013); Mary Beth Norton, *Liberty's Daughters: The Revolutionary Experience of American Women, 1750–1800*, paperback ed. (1980; Ithaca, NY: Cornell University Press, 1996); Elaine Forman Crane, *Ebb Tide in New England: Women, Seaports, and Social Change, 1630–1800* (Boston: Northeastern University Press, 1998), esp. 8, 76, 82–83, 96, 141, 178, 189, 208–9, 226–41; Ruth H. Bloch, "The Gendered Meanings of Virtue in Revolutionary America," in *Gender and Morality in Anglo-American Culture, 1650–1800* (Berkeley: University of California Press, 2003), 136–53; Kerber, "'History Can Do It No Justice,'" 72, 79–88, 96–98; Linda K. Kerber, *Women of the Republic: Intellect and Ideology in Revolutionary America* (Chapel Hill: University of North Carolina Press, 1980), 32, 85, 104–5, 112; Joan R. Gundersen, *To Be Useful to the World: Women in Revolutionary America, 1740–1790*, rev. ed. (1996; Chapel Hill: University of North Carolina Press., 2006), esp. 192–99; Fraser Easton, "Gender's Two Bodies: Women Warriors, Female Husbands and Plebeian Life," *Past and Present* 180 (August 2003): 131–74; Scarlet Bowen, "'The Real Soul of a Man in Her Breast': Popular Opposition and British Nationalism in Memoirs of Female Soldiers, 1740–1750," *Eighteenth-Century Life* 28, no. 3 (Fall 2004): 20–45; Robert B. Shoemaker, *Gender in English Society, 1650–1850: The Emergence of Separate Spheres?* (London: Routledge, 1998), 23–28, 37–38, 233–38; Ann Hughes, *Gender and the English Revolution* (London: Routledge, 2012), 10–29, 35–42, 54–61; Don Herzog, *Household Politics: Conflict in Early Modern England* (New Haven, CT: Yale University Press, 2013).

6. Norton, *Liberty's Daughters*, chap. 7; Kerber, *Women of the Republic*, chap. 2; Crane, *Ebb Tide*, 235–36; Linda Grant De Pauw, "Women in Combat: The Revolutionary War Experience," *Armed Forces and Society*

7, no. 2 (Winter 1981): 219–21; Holly A. Mayer, *Belonging to the Army: Camp Followers and Community during the American Revolution* (Columbia: University of South Carolina Press, 1996); Gundersen, *To Be Useful to the World*, chap. 9; Holly A. Mayer, "Bearing Arms, Bearing Burdens: Women Warriors, Camp Followers and Home-Front Heroines of the American Revolution," in *Gender, War and Politics: Transatlantic Perspectives, 1775–1830*, ed. Karen Hagemann, Gisela Mettele, and Jane Rendall (New York: Palgrave Macmillan, 2010), 169–87.

7. "Extract of a Letter from Boston Dated Oct. 25," *Middlesex Journal* (London), 22–24 November 1774 ("phrenzy," "devils"); Alfred F. Young, "'Persons of Consequence': The Women of Boston and the Making of the American Revolution, 1765–1776," in *Liberty Tree: Ordinary People and the American Revolution* (New York: New York University Press, 2006), 123, 126; Joan DeJean, "Violent Women and Violence against Women: Representing the 'Strong' Woman in Early Modern France," *Signs* 29, no. 1 (Autumn 2003): 117–47; Robert G. Parkinson, *The Common Cause: Creating Race and Nation in the American Revolution* (Chapel Hill: University of North Carolina Press, 2016), 339–49, 492–94; Norton, *Liberty's Daughters*, 175–76, 202–4; Sharon Block, *Rape and Sexual Power in Early America* (Chapel Hill: University of North Carolina Press, 2006), 41, 81–82, 210, 230–37; Holger Hoock, *Scars of Independence: America's Violent Birth* (New York: Crown, 2017), 98, 115, 120–21, 164–74. See also Don N. Hagist, "Rawdon's Ruse," *Journal of the American Revolution* (23 July 2014), https://allthingsliberty.com/2014/07/rawdons-ruse/; also compare Gullickson, *Unruly Women*, 180–81.

8. Henry Strachey to Jane Strachey, 25 September 1776, Henry Strachey Papers, box 2, William L. Clements Library, University of Michigan, Ann Arbor. Charles Stedman, who served with General William Howe's army, discussed the deliberate burning of New York and subsequent imprisonment of "between one and two hundred men and old women"; see Stedman, *The History of the Origin, Progress, and Termination of the American War* (London, 1794), 2:209.

9. Minutes of a Commission to Investigate the Causes of the Fire in New York City, 84–85, New York City Misc. MSS, New-York Historical Society.

10. On British soldiers' attitudes toward women, see Jennine Hurl-Eamon, *Marriage and the British Army in the Long Eighteenth Century: "The Girl I Left Behind Me"* (Oxford: Oxford University Press, 2014), 101–11, 122–31. On tears and other female bids for leniency, see Davis, "Women on Top," 146; Arlette Farge and Jacques Revel, *The Vanishing Children of Paris: Rumor and Politics before the French Revolution*, trans. Claudia Miéville (1988; Cambridge, MA: Harvard University Press, 1991), 97–100; Cynthia A. Bouton, "Gendered Behavior in Subsistence Riots: The French Flour War of 1775," *Journal of Social History* 23, no. 4 (Summer 1990): 742–43;

Dominique Godineau, *The Women of Paris and Their French Revolution*, trans. Katherine Streip (1988; Berkeley: University of California Press, 1998), 119–20, 143–44, 156, 176–79, 233, 318, 354–56, 358–62; Thomas J. Humphrey, *Land and Liberty: Hudson Valley Riots in the Age of Revolution* (DeKalb: Northern Illinois University Press, 2004), 70–71; Thomas Dixon, *Weeping Britannia: Portrait of a Nation in Tears* (Oxford: Oxford University Press, 2015), esp. part 2; Julie Ellison, *Cato's Tears and the Making of Anglo-American Emotion* (Chicago: University of Chicago Press, 1999), 4, 9–10, 16–20; and Nicole Eustace, *Passion Is the Gale: Emotion, Power, and the Coming of the American Revolution* (Chapel Hill: University of North Carolina Press, 2008).

11. On women (including prostitutes) in colonial New York, see Serena R. Zabin, *Dangerous Economies: Status and Commerce in Imperial New York* (Philadelphia: University of Pennsylvania Press, 2009), esp. chaps. 2–3, 6; Timothy J. Gilfoyle, *City of Eros: New York City, Prostitution, and the Commercialization of Sex, 1790–1920* (New York: Norton, 1992), 23–25; and Joyce D. Goodfriend, *Who Should Rule at Home: Confronting the Elite in British New York City* (Ithaca, NY: Cornell University Press, 2017), 228–32. For representations of prostitutes, see Madelyn Gutwirth, *The Twilight of the Goddesses: Women and Representation in the French Revolutionary Era* (New Brunswick, NJ: Rutgers University Press, 1992), 311, and Gullickson, *Unruly Women*. On the arsonists' motivations, see Carp, "The Night the Yankees Burned Broadway." On the Continental Army community, see Mayer, *Belonging*. See also John A. Lynn II, *Women, Armies, and Warfare in Early Modern Europe* (Cambridge: Cambridge University Press, 2008), chap. 4, esp. 202–8, and Gullickson, *Unruly Women*, 162.

12. Judith L. Van Buskirk, *Generous Enemies: Patriots and Loyalists in Revolutionary New York* (Philadelphia: University of Pennsylvania Press, 2002), 51; Charles Patrick Neimeyer, *America Goes to War: A Social History of the Continental Army* (New York: New York University Press, 1996), chap. 7.

13. "House of Commons, Wednesday, November 6, 1776," in *American Archives: Fifth Series*, ed. Peter Force (Washington, DC, 1851), 3:1012.

14. Ibid., 3:1012–13. Compare sabotage and arson in James C. Scott, *Weapons of the Weak: Everyday Forms of Peasant Resistance* (New Haven, CT: Yale University Press, 1985). While the literature on Hale is extensive, see the most recent work, Virginia DeJohn Anderson, *The Martyr and the Traitor: Nathan Hale, Moses Dunbar, and the American Revolution* (New York: Oxford University Press, 2017).

15. Dror Wahrman, *The Making of the Modern Self: Identity and Culture in Eighteenth-Century England* (New Haven, CT: Yale University Press, 2004), 223. See also Gullickson, *Unruly Women*, 174, 183.

16. "House of Commons, Wednesday, November 6, 1776," in Force, ed., *American Archives*, 3:1012. Compare dirty faces and "caves" as signifiers of lower-class status in Nancy Isenberg, *White Trash: The 400-Year Untold*

History of Class in America (New York: Penguin, 2016), 22, 112, 114, 120. On dirty faces' connections to bonfires, sexual perversion, and fertility rituals, see Peter Shaw, *American Patriots and the Rituals of Revolution* (Cambridge, MA: Harvard University Press, 1981), 214–16, and Susan E. Klepp, "Rough Music on Independence Day: Philadelphia, 1778," in *Riot and Revelry in Early America*, ed. William Pencak, Matthew Dennis, and Simon P. Newman (University Park: Pennsylvania State University Press, 2002), 164–66.

17. For "unnatural rebellion," see Kathleen Wilson, *The Sense of the People: Politics, Culture and Imperialism in England, 1715–1785* (Cambridge: Cambridge University Press, 1998), 281, and Ruma Chopra, *Unnatural Rebellion: Loyalists in New York City during the Revolution* (Charlottesville: University of Virginia Press, 2011), 3–4, 228n13.

18. "House of Commons, Wednesday, November 6, 1776," in Force, ed., *American Archives*, 3:1013; Lorrayne Carroll, *Rhetorical Drag: Gender Impersonation, Captivity, and the Writing of History* (Kent, Ohio: Kent State University Press, 2007), 109, 117–18; Linda Colley, *Captives: The Story of Britain's Pursuit of Empire and How Its Soldiers and Civilians Were Held Captive by the Dream of Global Supremacy* (New York: Pantheon, 2002), chap. 7.

19. Martin Postle, *Sir Joshua Reynolds: The Subject Pictures* (Cambridge: Cambridge University Press, 1995), 44–48; Charles Robert Leslie and Tom Taylor, *Life and Times of Sir Joshua Reynolds* (London, 1865), esp. 321–22, 325, 328.

20. Carine Lounissi, "French Writers on the American Revolution in the Early 1780s: A Republican Moment?" in *Beyond 1776: Globalizing the Cultures of the American Revolution*, ed. Maria O'Malley and Denys Van Renen (Charlottesville: University of Virginia Press, 2018), 74–104.

21. Michel René Hilliard d'Auberteuil, *Essais historiques et politiques sur les Anglo-Américains* (Brussels and Paris, 1782), book 2, part 1, 30 (and facing page). For unkempt hair, see also Linda Colley, *Britons: Forging the Nation, 1707–1837* (New Haven, CT: Yale University Press, 1992), 246, and Gullickson, *Unruly Women*, 171, 174–83, 196–97.

22. Hilliard d'Auberteuil, *Essais historiques*, 30–31; Minutes of a Commission, 50; Gutwirth, *Twilight*, esp. 257–59, chap. 8. The story of the officer who stopped a woman from stabbing herself derived from the *Gazetteer and New Daily Advertiser* (London), 11 November 1776, an anecdote about a pregnant woman named Packnell.

23. Thomas Jefferson dismissed the *Essais* as erroneous due to reliance on "impure" English newspaper accounts; his complaint may have been partisan rather than purely empirical. Jefferson to Jean Chas, 7 December 1786, in *The Papers of Thomas Jefferson*, ed. Julian P. Boyd et al. (Princeton, NJ: Princeton University Press, 1954–), 10:580; see also Jefferson to the Editor of the *Journal de Paris*, 29 August 1787, in ibid., 12:61–65.

24. Michel René Hilliard d'Auberteuil, *Miss McCrea: A Novel of the American Revolution*, trans. Eric LaGuardia (1784; Gainesville, FL: Scholars Facsimiles and Reprints, 1958), 8–9, 26 ("respect"), 28, 30, 34 ("chose to burn," "mad woman," "shake her firmness," "leave you forever," "stabbed themselves"), 35 ("instantly killed"), 40 ("*incendiaires*"). On "firmness," compare David Ramsay, *History of the Revolution in South Carolina from a British Province to an Independence State* (Trenton, NJ, 1785), 2:124; Ellison, *Cato's Tears*, 64–65; and Gullickson, *Unruly Women*, 174–83, 196–97.

25. Godineau, *Women of Paris*, esp. chaps. 12, 14, pp. 273 ("destructive woman"), 325 ("furies of the guillotine"), 327 ("incendiary remarks," "cowards"), 328 ("firebrands"), 329 ("start the movement"), 130; Gullickson, *Unruly Women*.

26. *Parliamentary Register* (London, 1782), 17:370 [8 June 1780] ("monsters"); Edmund Burke, *Reflections on the Revolution in France* (1790), in *Revolutionary Writings*, ed. Iain Hampsher-Monk (Cambridge: Cambridge University Press, 2014), 73 ("furies of hell"); Ian Haywood, *Bloody Romanticism: Spectacular Violence and the Politics of Representation, 1776–1832* (New York: Palgrave Macmillan, 2006), chap. 5; Ian Haywood and John Seed, eds., *The Gordon Riots: Politics, Culture and Insurrection in Late Eighteenth-Century Britain* (Cambridge: Cambridge University Press, 2012), esp. chaps. 5, 7, 10.

27. Mary Wollstonecraft, *An Historical and Moral View of the Origin and Progress of the French Revolution . . .* (London, 1795), 426; Mary Wollstonecraft, *A Vindication of the Rights of Woman with Strictures on Political and Moral Subjects* (London, 1792), 163; Claudia L. Johnson, *Equivocal Beings: Politics, Gender, and Sentimentality in the 1790s: Wollstonecraft, Radcliffe, Burney, Austen* (Chicago: University of Chicago Press, 1995), 39.

28. Kerber, "'History Can Do It No Justice,'" 75, 84; Peter C. Messer, "Writing Women into History: Defining Gender and Citizenship in Post-Revolutionary America," *Studies in Eighteenth-Century Culture* 28 (1999): 350; Murphy, *Citizenship*.

29. William Henry Shelton, *The Jumel Mansion* (Boston: Houghton Mifflin, 1916), 53–54.

"I Bare My Bosom, and Pour My Choicest Blood"

Republican Sisterhood and Political Violence in Mercy Otis Warren's *Adulateur*

J. Patrick Mullins

—∿∿∿∿∿—

IN THE spring of 1772, a Boston newspaper published one of the first public statements by a colonist offering moral justification for armed resistance against the Crown government of an American province. Three years before Patrick Henry made his celebrated appeal to arms and the God of Hosts, this vindication of revolutionary action came not from a statesman, nor indeed a man at all. Although not nearly as prominent in popular memory as Abigail Adams among America's "founding mothers," Mercy Otis Warren is notable as one of the first historians of the American Revolution and a contributor to the pamphlet debates on ratification of the U.S. Constitution. Long before Warren was a historian of the Revolution, however, she contributed to its intellectual origins through political drama. Historian Carol Berkin counted Warren "among the most famous and effective propagandists of the prewar period."[1] The first of Warren's political dramas—indeed, her first published writing—was *The Adulateur* of 1772. Appearing as "Dramatic sketches" in two editions of the *Massachusetts Spy*, *The Adulateur* has been largely forgotten as a contribution to prewar Whig opposition literature. Literary scholars have noted Warren's first work as a contribution to early American drama, but full illumination of its political content and meaning require close textual analysis within the historic context of political events in Massachusetts in the late 1760s and early 1770s. This approach highlights the signal radicalism of *The Adulateur* as a political document and Warren's distinctive role as a female contributor to the intellectual origins of the American Revolution.[2]

Warren's status as a published polemicist distinguished her from other civic-minded and politically engaged Yankee women like her friends Abigail Adams and Hannah Winthrop. Historian Linda K. Kerber called such women "republican mothers." A practitioner of and advocate for "republican motherhood," Warren took seriously her civic duty to educate her sons for the responsible exercise of power.[3] But the moral imperatives of republican motherhood do not explain why she—alone among other American republican mothers—emerged before the Revolutionary War as a literary political activist waging political war. Rosemarie Zagarri has observed that Warren's distinctive course may be partly attributed to the influence of her older brother, James Otis, alongside whom she received a liberal education, whose political fortunes she considered her own, and whose cause she embraced after his collapse into mental illness. By considering *The Adulateur* as Warren's continuation of James Otis's power struggle with the royal governor of Massachusetts, one can begin to understand how Mercy Otis Warren emerged as a literary political activist, as well as one of the most violently radical of Boston's notoriously radical Whigs. Barred from taking her brother's place on the dueling ground, battlefield, or assembly floor, she continued his crusade against the Thomas Hutchinson faction in a way legally open to her sex: literature. Drama, poetry, and novels were considered acceptable literary forms for female readers and writers, but Warren bent drama to political ends with violent implications. Unable to defend her brother's honor or her country's liberty by taking up arms herself, she took up her pen and with it issued a call to arms. To understand why Warren emerged as a public political thinker in the 1770s, beginning with *The Adulateur* of 1772, it is helpful to think of her less as a republican mother and more as a republican sister.[4]

The contest of political parties that defined Massachusetts politics in the 1760s and 1770s began as a struggle for office between two families. Before she married James Warren of Plymouth in 1754, Mercy Otis Warren's father, James Otis Sr., had secured his family's place in the Massachusetts elite. Otis served as a county court judge, legislator, attorney general, and member of the governor's council, and he anticipated appointment to the Massachusetts Superior Court upon the death of Chief Justice Stephen Sewall. He ran afoul, however, of the new royal governor,

Francis Bernard. In the fall of 1760, Bernard was prosecuting violators of the Trade and Navigation Acts aggressively, using general search warrants called writs of assistance. Otis and his son, James Otis Jr., the acting advocate general, opposed such writs as incompatible with colonial rights. Bernard chose Lieutenant Governor Thomas Hutchinson, a merchant with no legal training, to be chief justice, perhaps because Hutchinson was a friend to Crown prerogative who could be relied on to uphold the constitutionality of the warrants. The Otises were outraged.[5]

James Otis Jr. resigned his royal commission in protest and used the newspapers to accuse Hutchinson of "engrossing places of power & profit for himself, his family, and dependents." Hutchinson was now simultaneously lieutenant governor, chief justice, county probate judge, and member of the governor's council, and his brother-in-law Andrew Oliver served as provincial secretary. Hutchinson combined into his hands not just the salaries of multiple offices but the powers of the government's legislative, executive, and judicial branches. The separation of powers, Otis maintained, was a critical protection for the people's liberty from oppression by their own government. By contrast, Chief Justice Hutchinson would be adjudicating laws he helped to draft as a councilor and enforced as lieutenant governor. Otis believed that Hutchinson and Bernard had formed a "junto," a faction seeking public power to abuse it for private advantage. Indeed, the governor reaped one-third of the proceeds when customs officers used writs of assistance to seize merchant vessels for smuggling. The officers themselves gained another third, and the last third went to the Crown, from which customs agents drew payoffs for informants. It seemed to Otis that Bernard put Hutchinson on the court expressly to ensure that he could continue enriching himself through prosecutions for smuggling. In February 1761, Otis represented Boston merchants before Chief Justice Hutchinson in a suit to stop further issue of writs of assistance and misappropriation of Crown funds by the customs service. It came as little shock to anyone when Hutchinson ultimately ruled against the merchants.[6]

In March 1761, Otis was elected to the Massachusetts House of Representatives, emerging as leader of an organized political opposition who styled themselves Whigs or the "friends of liberty." Their legislative battles with the Bernard-Hutchinson faction and the "friends of government" framed Massachusetts politics throughout the 1760s. Otis fashioned the factional fight in exalted moral terms as a defense of liberty against tyranny. In his 1764 pamphlet opposing Parliament's taxation of the colonists under the Sugar Act, Otis further universalized the political stakes. He affirmed the natural right of all "individuals" to be bound only by governments to which they have consented. Casting the current taxation controversy in the abstract terms of individual natural rights, Otis followed the logical implication to apply the principle of natural rights equally to all humans, regardless of race or sex. "The Colonists are by the law of nature free born, as indeed all men are, white or black," he wrote, denouncing slavery and the slave trade as incompatible with natural rights. "Are not women born as free as men?" Otis added, "Would it not be infamous to assert that the ladies are all slaves by nature?" He asked whether, in the pre-political state of nature, women had "as good a right to give their respectable suffrages for a new king as the philosopher, courtier, petit maître and politician?"[7]

While colonial Whigs embraced natural rights political philosophy in the 1760s as the foundation of their opposition to parliamentary taxation, Otis was one of the few who acknowledged explicitly its radical implications for women as well as enslaved African Americans. Initially educated at home alongside his sister Mercy, Otis recognized what a difference educational opportunity could make for women. "His sister's brilliance," argued historian Rosemarie Zagarri, "led him to an unfashionable belief in the equality of the sexes." Otis had deep respect as well as heartfelt affection for his sister, and he and Mercy Warren saw their personal fortunes as inseparable. "No man ever loved a sister better," Otis wrote Warren in 1766, "and among all my conflicts I never forget that I am endeavoring to serve you and yours." If Mercy Otis Warren's example influenced James Otis to argue for women's rights, so Warren in turn followed Otis's example as a literary champion of "the rights of individuals." It was, however, Mercy Warren's response to her brother's downfall— a tragedy for the family taking place on the stage of public affairs—that set her on the course to becoming one of the most radical of Boston's radical Whigs before the outbreak of war with Britain.[8]

Under Parliament's Townshend Acts of 1767–68, the British Crown not only imposed new customs duties but also created an American Board of Customs Commissioners for the more effective collection of the duties. Commissioners were authorized to root out smuggling with writs of assistance, while the accused were prosecuted in vice-admiralty courts under royally appointed judges without juries. The increased Crown revenue would then be used to pay the salaries of the customs collectors, judges, and executive officers tasked with enforcing its collection. No longer dependent on payment of their salaries out of provincial taxes appropriated by the elected House of Representatives, these appointed officials would then be freed from any accountability to the people. They could enforce the new tax regime without regard to popular opposition to the parliamentary taxes. Boston merchants vowed not to import the taxed goods until Parliament lifted the new duties, and the Sons of Liberty harassed importers, purchasers of imports, and customs commissioners to prevent payment and collection of the duties. In the wake of the *Liberty* riot in June 1768, when the Sons of Liberty interfered with a royal warship and assaulted customs commissioners to prevent confiscation of a merchant ship, Governor Bernard appealed to the Crown for military support, and the first regiment of British regulars arrived in Boston on 1 October. Radical Whigs like Otis and Samuel Adams were fiercely opposed to the military occupation of the city. It was not lost on them that, only five months earlier in St. George's Fields, the king's troops had fired on Londoners protesting the incarceration of the English Whig hero John Wilkes, killing seven.[9]

By the end of 1768, James Otis Jr. was drinking heavily, suffering from bouts of mental illness, and displaying erratic behavior in public. When he heard that one of the royal customs commissioners, John Robinson, had called him an enemy of the Crown, a furious Otis demanded satisfaction. He called out Robinson in the *Boston Gazette* on 4 September 1769, writing, "I have a natural right if I can get no other satisfaction to break his head." The next day, he came looking for Robinson in the British Coffee House, known to be a haven for officers of the British Army and Navy, customs officers, and other "friends of government." Their exchange of angry words turned into a duel with canes, which degenerated into a general brawl. An army officer and naval officer restrained Otis while Robinson struck him in the head, leaving a cut down to the skull that bled profusely. Suffering from lacerations, bruises, and a concussion, Otis weathered a fever overnight but was out of danger the next day.[10]

Around 10 September, Mercy Otis Warren poured out her terror in a letter to her brother. "You know not what I have suffered for you within the last twenty four hours," she wrote, having imagined him "slain by the hands of merciless men." Interpreting this affair of honor in the context of the current political crisis, Warren asked rhetorically if "we have men among us under the guise of officers of the Crown, who have become open assassins?" She expressed horror that a customs commissioner "attacked a gentleman alone and unarmed with a design to take away his life." Although the Crown had sent the army and navy to Boston as "the *conservators* of the peace," royal officers in the coffee house had not stopped the fight but instead joined in, behaving like "a band of ruffians."

The well-known "errand" of the king's troops sent to Boston was "to uphold villainy, and protect villains," that is, to protect the customs commissioners from the Sons of Liberty. But Warren never imagined that they would "stand by" and allow a "miscreant" like Robinson "to spill the blood of citizens, who criminate the designs, and their measures." She urged Otis "with a sisterly affection" not to retaliate. Describing herself as "one who has your welfare more at heart, after very few exceptions, than that of any other person in the world," Warren acknowledged Otis's mental illness as a factor in the fiasco. Indeed, his deterioration accelerated in the months to come, requiring his withdrawal from public life. But she continued to see the assault on her brother as an attempted assassination by Crown officers, and it was the beginning of her emergence as a "republican sister" who took up the cause of liberty where her brother left it.[11]

Just before the coffee house row, Governor Bernard departed for England, and Hutchinson became acting governor of Massachusetts Bay as tensions continued to build between protesters and enforcers of the Townshend Acts. On 22 February 1770, a crowd of men and boys picketed the shop of Scotsman Theophilus Lillie because he continued to import and sell taxed goods. Ebenezer Richardson, a notorious customs informer, challenged the picketers and attracted the taunts of boys when he retreated to his home. Richardson and the angry crowd outside his house exchanged insults and brickbats until he pointed a musket out of an open window and fired randomly into the crowd. The spray of birdshot pierced the lung of a schoolboy, Christopher Seider. He died that night, and the coroner ruled the eleven-year-old's death an intentional homicide. A funeral procession of about two thousand participants, "the largest perhaps ever known in America" in Hutchinson's estimation, honored Seider, the child of poor German immigrants. Pronouncing Seider "this little hero and first martyr to the noble cause," the *Boston Gazette* compared his death to that of William Allen, the innocent boy whose killing by Scottish troops in London precipitated the 1768 Massacre of St. George's Fields. Just eleven days after Seider's death, on 5 March 1770, the American Whig cause had additional martyrs when British regulars fired into a crowd on King Street, killing four men and one seventeen-year-old.[12]

Boston's radical Whigs pressed for prosecution of the arrested British soldiers and their commanding officer for murder. Acting Governor Hutchinson postponed those trials, so Richardson was tried first on 20 April before a jury drawn from outside of Boston. At the conclusion of the trial, three of the four judges concluded that Richardson had committed manslaughter. Justice Peter Oliver, brother to Andrew Oliver and brother-in-law to Hutchinson, contended that Richardson acted justifiably in self-defense and that the Whigs who inflamed the mob and the magistrates who failed to suppress the mob were actually to blame for the boy's death. The jury deliberated all night and the next morning pronounced Richardson guilty of murder, in defiance of the judges' majority decision that the charge was manslaughter. The judges reluctantly recorded the verdict but declined to pass sentence. If the Whigs were frustrated enough by justice delayed for Richardson, they did not take the news well of justice denied when juries in October and November 1770 acquitted the British soldiers and their commanding officer of the charge of murder.[13]

Despite removal of the regiments from Boston and repeal of all Townshend duties except the tea tax, the Whig cause appeared in retreat. Then, on 14 March 1771, Thomas Hutchinson's royal commission took effect and he became governor of Massachusetts in his own right. His brother-in-law Peter Oliver replaced him as chief justice of the Superior Court, and his younger brother Foster Hutchinson also sat on the court. His other brother-in-law, Andrew Oliver, was promoted from provincial secretary to lieutenant governor. Hutchinson chose his nephew the importer Nathaniel Rogers as Andrew Oliver's replacement. When Rogers died before he could assume the office, the place of provincial secretary went instead to Thomas Flucker, one of the few nonrelatives in the new administration. These appointments confirmed for Mercy Otis Warren her brother's earlier warnings that Hutchinson was determined to engross all power and public wealth into his and his family's hands. If they accepted royal salaries out of the tea revenue, she feared, the Hutchinson junto could commit abuses with no check from the people's representatives. As if to confirm her worst anxieties, Hutchinson secured a pardon for Ebenezer Richardson from the Crown. In March 1772, Richardson paid his bail and fled town with the mob at his heels. For Warren, the cause of liberty had reached its lowest ebb in Massachusetts, and Richardson's pardon was the final spur she needed to leap into the fray of literary political activism.[14]

Her first attempt at a published political commentary was *The Adulateur,* which appeared in 1772 as two "Dramatic sketches" in the 26 March and 23 April issues of the *Massachusetts Spy.* Its target was the Hutchinson junto. Warren began writing the first sketch immediately after news broke of Richardson's release from confinement that March. While outrage against Hutchinson was general among Bostonians of Whiggish sentiments, there was a gendered character to Warren's decision to respond in the public prints at that moment. The intensity of her indignation over Hutchinson's pardon of a child murderer was distinctive among colonial Whigs and may have been maternal in its protectiveness. Historian Linda Kerber has noted that the centrality Warren gave to the boy's death in *The Adulateur* "helped solidify Seider's martyred status" in Whig political memory. But it was less as a republican mother than as a republican sister that Warren took up her pen against Hutchinson and his cronies, whom she blamed both for the current threat to New England liberty and for the assault and downfall of her brother. With James Otis Jr. incapacitated by mental illness and James Otis Sr. advanced in age, Warren assumed responsibility for continuing the Otis family's campaign against the Hutchinson junto at the moment when her brother's leadership was most needed by the public.[15]

Unable to stand for office or address politics in her own name due to the social and legal limits on her sex, Warren joined the public battle by writing a dramatic piece (rather than a political essay, as her brother had) and submitting it for newspaper publication anonymously. In early eighteenth-century England, Richard Steele and Joseph Addison contended in their essays on taste and manners that politics was not a suitable subject of discussion by refined women. Historian Mary Beth Norton has argued that the popularity of their essays in the colonies helped conventionalize this gender barrier. American readers might have dismissed Warren's efforts out of hand had they known the sex of *The Adulateur*'s author. Its anonymous publication, as Berkin has remarked, enabled Warren to offer the public a stinging critique of Massachusetts politics without compromising her class and gender status as a genteel, married woman. Warren's use of anonymity also likely had a political motive. As Zagarri has suggested, she may have "feared direct retribution by British officials or Tory sympathizers, and she did not want to expose her home or family to danger." In criticizing the most powerful men in the province, the author exposed herself to prosecution as a purveyor of sedition.[16]

For the same self-protective reason, Warren framed her anonymous critique of the Hutchinson junto as a fictionalized theater piece set in a fictionalized foreign land during an unspecified era, in which the targets of her fury were disguised, albeit thinly. Coupled with anonymous authorship, this method enabled her to publish a searing criticism of Crown government and a justification of revolutionary violence with sufficient deniability to immunize herself from government action

or extralegal retaliation. With delicious irony, Warren's strategy to by-
pass legal dangers and gender barriers by offering political commentary
in the format of a dramatic piece was inspired by Joseph Addison, the
Englishman who had so eloquently argued against female participation
in politics. Warren's model for her play was Addison's 1716 drama *Cato:
A Tragedy*, which used the historic last stand of Roman republicans
against Julius Caesar to comment on court politics in early eighteenth-
century England. Addison adopted an ancient Roman setting "to expose
the false arts of life, to pull off the disguises of cunning, vanity, and af-
fectations." Paraphrasing Addison, Warren observed that *The Adulateur*
and its two prewar sequels, *The Defeat* (1773) and *The Group* (1775), were
"offered [to] the public only as occasions arose, and the exigencies of the
times required the vizard should be stripped from the face of intrigue,
where flattery and illusion were hackneyed, as usual, by the minions of
a Court." Just as Addison aimed to "pull off the disguises of cunning," so
Warren crafted her political drama to strip the "vizard" from "the face of
intrigue." Paradoxically, her method for unmasking the intriguers of her
own time and place required creating new masks for them.[17]

Warren's literary method to expose the corruption of Massachusetts
government in 1772 required fashioning in words a stage set for a play
that was never written in full nor intended to be performed. When the
first dramatic sketch appeared in newsprint on 26 March, Warren gave
it the disguise of an "advertisement" submitted to the *Massachusetts Spy*.
The advertisement offered "a specimen" of a "Dramatic performance, consisting of three Acts," which was to be "exhibited for the entertainment
of the public, at the grand parade in Upper Servia." "Upper Servia" is a
subregion of Serbia and the seat of a late medieval Christian uprising
against Ottoman Turkish rule. Not only was the make-believe play to be
performed there but its story was set in the country's past. Warren described her archvillain Rapatio as "the Bashaw of Servia" and his minion
Gripeall as the "Captain Bashaw," and she called the courtroom in which
Judge Hazelrod presides a "Divan" (a judicial chamber in the Ottoman
Empire). Warren wanted her readers to be in on the joke; she did not
expect them to think that the sketch was really part of a play scheduled
for performance in Europe. Warren gave her characters names that were
neither Turkish nor Slavic but either Roman (in the tradition of Addison's *Cato*) or comically English (in eighteenth-century England's tradition of moralizing satire). Turkish-era Serbia was meant to connote
for Boston readers any formerly independent country suffering under
the yoke of foreign despotism, and this oblique comparison of Britain to
Turkey was itself revolutionary in its implications.[18]

Despite the exotic setting and disguised characters, Warren's intended meanings for *The Adulateur* become unmistakable as an attack on the Hutchinson junto when considered in the context of political events unfolding in Massachusetts from 1760 to 1772. Taking up her brother's accusation that Thomas Hutchinson was driven by ambition and avarice to seek total power, Warren satirized him as Rapatio, the collaborator appointed to power by the conquering Turks who serves the foreign oppressor in exchange for wealth. The first sketch opens with a soliloquy in which Rapatio ponders how "from my youth ambition's path I trod, / . . . and lust of power is still my darling lust, / Despotic rule by first, my sovereign wish." He schemes to

> quench the gen'rous flame, the ardent love
> Of liberty in Servia's freeborn sons,
> Destroy their boasted rights, and mark them slaves,
> To ride triumphant o'er my native land,
> And revel on its spoils!

Rapatio's brother Meagre represents Hutchinson's younger brother Justice Foster Hutchinson. His lackey Limpet is Lieutenant Governor Andrew Oliver, while Dupe, the "Secretary of State" for Servia, is Provincial Secretary Thomas Flucker. Rapatio's "minion of oppressive power," the Bashaw Captain Gripeall, represents Admiral John Montagu, commander-in-chief of the British Navy in North America in the early 1770s. Rapatio calls them "my myrmidons," part of "the venal herd" who serve and flatter him because he has corrupted them with office.[19]

In *The Adulateur*, all that stands between the rapacious bashaw and the realization of his "deep laid schemes" are virtuous citizens resolved to defend their liberty. At the conclusion of the third act, readers receive the soliloquy of "the virtuous Senator" Cassius, a classical hero in the style of Addison's protagonist Cato. He weeps for his "poor country," crying out that he "would have fought for thee, / And emptied ev'ry vein" to prevent its ruin. But

> now too late I fear
> The cruel manacles prepar'd by Brundo's hand,
> Cruel Rapatio, with more fatal arts,
> Has fix'd, has rivetted beyond redress.

Absent from the play except as a name, Brundo is the stand-in for the departed Governor Francis Bernard. With Rapatio's centralization of power complete and the "manacles" of slavery "rivetted beyond redress," no legal or political avenue remains to stop him. Like his ancient Roman namesake, the assassin of Julius Caesar, Cassius proposes revolutionary violence as the only remaining option. "My indignation rous'd" by "the shameless tyrant," Cassius says that "Servia's virtuous sons" will "execrate a wretch, who dare[s] enslave / A gen'rous, free and independent people." For Cassius, outrage is not enough. Such righteous anger demands action. But what action, and who should be the actor? He addresses "ye pow'rs divine," which "mark the movements of this nether world" to "bring them to account." Cassius appeals to divine providence to

> crush, crush these vipers,
> Who singled out by a community
> To guard their rights—shall for a grasp of oar [ore]
> Or paltry office, sell them to the foe.

Rapatio and his officers betrayed the people's trust in return for money and power. As traitors and usurpers, they are therefore "vipers" who should be crushed. Cassius conveys the desperation of the moment in the storyline that Warren and her fellow radical Whigs felt so keenly in March 1772.[20]

By providing in public a moral justification for the killing of Governor Hutchinson and his political allies, Warren staked out ground on the radical fringe of Boston's radical Whigs. She did, however, end the second act of *The Adulateur* with her republican hero calling on divine providence to intervene and give the villains the terrible justice they have earned. If there were any doubt in her readers that the villains of *The Adulateur* (and by extension the Hutchinson junto) warranted destruction, Warren resolved it in the second dramatic sketch, published in the *Massachusetts Spy* on 23 April. "Ebenezer, a friend to Government," makes his first appearance, offering a soliloquy as he sits in prison. Rapatio promised Ebenezer "honors, places, pensions," as well as a pardon, if only he would be Rapatio's tool in killing his opponents. Satirizing Chief Justice Peter Oliver's defense of Richardson at trial, Chief Justice Hazelrod extended to Ebenezer the hope of a pardon, but he now despairs that nothing can prevent his execution. Rapatio and Hazelrod "*seduc'd* my soul to laugh at virtue, / To give up all my right to future bliss," and "*encourag'd* me with hopes of pardon, / To glut *your* vengeance, for the cause was *yours*, / On weeping innocence." If any figure in Massachusetts politics lent himself to caricature as a conventional stage villain, it was Ebenezer

Richardson. Warren instead downplayed his personal culpability for the death of Christopher Seider, seeking to implicate the junto in the boy's death by treating Richardson in *The Adulateur* as Hutchinson's tool in the governor's larger plan to enslave Massachusetts. Richardson's name is the only one that Warren declined to disguise, perhaps because he had fled New England and no one would rise in his defense.[21]

In Warren's hands, the determination of the Superior Court not to sentence Richardson to death as the jury's verdict required was further evidence of the corruption of the judiciary. In the jail cell scene, Hazelrod chides Ebenezer for despairing over the jury's decision: "Can the verdict of some half-formed peasants, / Unmeaning dull machines, thus damp your courage?" The Superior Court justices are

> Steady and vigilant in *one sole* plan,
> To crush the friends of Freedom, extirpate
> The dear remains of Virtue, and like Nero,
> At one dread blow to massacre his millions.

Fully committed to Rapatio's conspiracy against Servia's liberty, the judges vow to protect Ebenezer. Warren retaliated against Peter Oliver for his conduct during the Richardson trial by portraying Hazelrod as a moral monster: "When Seider bled / We snuff'd the rich perfume.—The groans of youth / Gods! they were music in our ears." Hazelrod promises that Ebenezer will soon leave jail and provide the judges with "pleasing scenes of blood and carnage, / To glut *our* vengeance." The completion of Rapatio's conspiracy requires the slaughter of the patriots who oppose him, and Ebenezer will be needed again as his weapon of choice. Christopher Seider's death came eleven days before the Boston Massacre, and radical Whigs initially raised the alarm of an imminent general massacre of the town by the British Army. Warren attributed such a plan to her fictional Hutchinson.[22]

Warren had left the question open from her first dramatic sketch as to what action the patriots should take against their oppressor. In a scene change of the second sketch, Cassius is horrified by news of the impending release of Ebenezer from jail. "To see the Patriot / Reeking in Gore excites the keenest pleasure" for Rapatio, Hazelrod, and their conspirators. In a private conversation with "Marcus, a young patriot," Cassius concludes that the time is fast approaching when Servia's freedom-loving citizens can no longer wait for divine providence and must take justice into their own hands. Addressing again his "poor country," he asks rhetorically,

> When will it be,
> When high-soul'd honour beats within our bosoms,
> And calls to action; when thy sons, like heroes,
> Shall dare assert thy rights, and with their swords,
> Like men, like freemen, pave a way to conquest,
> Or on thy ruins gloriously expire.

Warren offered in Cassius's speech one of the first public defenses of armed resistance to Crown authority during the imperial crisis. She hedged only in having Cassius ask "when will it be" that patriots would answer the call to action, take up the sword, and fight to the death.[23]

Warren's second dramatic sketch concludes on a quieter, solemn note, with Cassius offering avuncular advice to his young companion regarding how to remain a good man in a corrupt world. In response to Cassius's defense of the use of arms, Marcus displays his public spirit by responding, "In such a cause pleas'd could I bare my bosom, and pour my choicest blood." He is moved to righteous violence by having witnessed Hazelrod's release of Ebenezer from justice. "I have seen, / Tho' young I've seen, such crimes by ermined wretches," like the chief justice, "as would have shocked a century." But he questions whether "deeds so foul should find abettors." An embittered Cassius explains to his friend, who "know[s] so little of the world," that vices and crimes are actually rewarded with "preferment" by those in power, looking for men without character prepared to serve their ends unquestioningly. The "man of honest mind" who "grasps alone at virtue" is "neglected" for political office. To gain "wealth and honors," one must "be a rascal, / Stoop low and cringe, stick not at oaths," and even be prepared to commit "MURDER!" Marcus recoils at the thought of selling his soul for worldly advancement and resolves to "live a poor man, / And die so too, while virtue and my conscience / Speak peace within." Cassius commends this decision, as "poverty must be thy fate, / If you're your country's friend." He tells Marcus, "When I am gone, as soon perhaps I may be," remember that the time may "soon arrive, when murders, blood and carnage / Shall crimson all these streets . . . forbid it Heaven!" But in this bloody warfare, the ruling regime will not triumph, Cassius predicts: "May these monsters find their glory fade, / Crush'd in the ruins they themselves have made." This concluding line of the second sketch may be an allusion to the story of Samson collapsing the temple, in which both the hero and his tormentors are destroyed together.[24]

Warren offered *The Adulateur* in the spring of 1772 to lift the morale of her fellow Whigs at a moment when it was at a low ebb. In the wake of the failure of nonimportation, Hutchinson's consolidation of power, the pardon of Ebenezer Richardson, and James Otis's accelerating mental decline, she felt compelled by civic virtue to carry on her brother's cause as a good republican sister. She could not duel with canes or take up the musket, but she could use her mastery over words to issue an emotionally charged call to arms. Her dramatic sketches were not explicit incitements to violence, but they did remind the radical Whigs that Hutchinson, the Olivers, and their allies were "monsters" and "vipers" who needed to be "crush'd." Armed violence against them and the overthrow of their corrupt regime was morally justified, and the time was fast approaching, she predicted, when patriotic New Englanders would indeed have to take up arms to prevent the loss of their liberty. Three years later, they did.

Warren spoke the words in her *Adulateur* that she thought her brother would say, if he still had control of his senses. If there were ever any doubts as to whom the public-spirited Cassius was meant to represent, she indicated her intentions in the manuscript notes to her plays, listing "James Otis Junior" as the heroic senator. She said of Otis in a note meant for her sons that "his time, his fortune, his happiness, and his life were sacrificed at the shrine of freedom." Making him the hero of her first play was "a tribute of gratitude" to an adored brother for his sacrifice to the public. If *The Adulateur* concluded with Cassius informing his young friend that his death might soon be at hand, presumably on the field of battle or in an attempt on the life of the tyrant, Warren thought of her brother's life having been destroyed by his severe beating at the hands of Robinson and Crown officers.[25]

There is, however, one lingering mystery as to the real-life referents of the characters in *The Adulateur*. Who was Marcus? He is the only character with a speaking role not listed in the "Dramatis personae." Indeed, characters are listed there who have no speaking role at all. He is only identified in the midst of the text as "Marcus, a young patriot." In her manuscript notes from the 1780s, Warren identified all of the major characters in *The Adulateur* and her two subsequent prewar plays, with the strange exception of Marcus. In the spring of 1775, with war finally at hand, Warren adopted the pseudonym Marcia in her private correspondence with Abigail Adams and other friends. If limits on her sex prevented Warren from entering public life in her own name, she could do so anonymously in the newspapers while playing the role of a virtuous Roman matron in letters with friends. Like young Marcus, Warren was committed to the cause of liberty, and "in such a cause pleas'd could I bare my bosom, and pour my choicest blood." But Cassius warns Marcus against chasing after office or taking up arms. The poignant conversation between Cassius and Marcus in *The Adulateur,* in which the older man advises the younger man to leave revolutionary violence to him, stay clear of politics, and keep his virtue intact and life secure, might have been Warren's stand-in for an imagined, much-wished-for conversation between James Otis Jr. and his younger sister. Just as she used the literary device of disguise to attack the Hutchinson junto in the press, did Mercy Otis Warren disguise herself as a male character in her own play? Did she thereby escape the limits set on her sex by writing herself into the public political struggle between James Otis Jr. and Thomas Hutchinson, between liberty and tyranny? Was Marcus actually Marcia?[26]

NOTES

1. Carol Berkin, *First Generations: Women in Colonial America* (New York: Hill and Wang, 1996), 171; Joan R. Gunderson, *To Be Useful to the World: Women in Revolutionary America, 1740–1790* (Chapel Hill: University of North Carolina Press, 2006), 176–78; Rosemarie Zagarri, *A Woman's Dilemma: Mercy Otis Warren and the American Revolution* (1995; Chichester, UK: Wiley, 2015), chap. 3, esp. 57–60 for Warren's *Adulateur.* For an understanding in popular memory of Mercy Warren, Abigail Adams, and other revolutionary-era women as "founding mothers," see Cokie Roberts, *Founding Mothers: The Women Who Raised Our Nation* (New York: William Morrow, 2004). For an introduction to Warren's historical thought, see Eileen Hunt Botting, "Women Writing War: Mercy Otis Warren and Hannah Mather Crocker on the American Revolution," *Massachusetts Historical Review* 18 (2016): 88–118.

2. For Warren's description of the short pieces as "Dramatic sketches," see Mercy Otis Warren, "Plays and Poetry" manuscript, n.d. [17—], 1, Houghton Library, Harvard University Libraries, Cambridge, MA (hereafter "Houghton Manuscript"). Note that the Houghton manuscript is written in the hand of Warren's son James Warren Jr. in his capacity as amanuensis, but it is a verbatim copy of the original manuscript, located in the Mercy Otis Warren Papers, Massachusetts Historical Society, Boston.

3. For the interpretive concept of "republican motherhood," see Linda K. Kerber, "The Republican Mother: Women and the Enlightenment—An American Perspective," *American Quarterly* 28, no. 2 (Summer 1976): 187–205, esp. 201–5; see also Linda K. Kerber, *Women of the Republic: Intellect and Ideology in Revolutionary America* (Chapel Hill: University of North Carolina Press, 1980). For Mercy Otis Warren and "republican motherhood," see Zagarri, *A Woman's Dilemma,* 28–29; Lester H. Cohen, "Mercy Otis Warren: The Politics of Language and the Aesthetics of

Self," *American Quarterly* 35, no. 5 (Winter 1983): 495–96; and Kate Davies, *Catharine Macaulay and Mercy Otis Warren: The Revolutionary Atlantic and the Politics of Gender* (Oxford: Oxford University Press, 2006), 268–70.

4. For the thesis that Warren began writing her political plays as a way of carrying on the political agenda of her father and brother, see Zagarri, *A Woman's Dilemma*, 50, 56.

5. Zagarri, *A Woman's Dilemma*, 11–12; J. Patrick Mullins, *Father of Liberty: Jonathan Mayhew and the Principles of the American Revolution* (Lawrence: University Press of Kansas, 2017), 99–100.

6. *Boston Gazette*, 11 April 1763; Zagarri, *A Woman's Dilemma*, 32–33; Mullins, *Father of Liberty*, 100–101.

7. Charles F. Mullett, ed., "Some Political Writings of James Otis," *University of Missouri Studies: A Quarterly of Research* 4, no. 3 (July 1929): 322, 303, 307; Zagarri, *A Woman's Dilemma*, 33–35, 15.

8. Kerber, "The Republican Mother," 187–88; Zagarri, *A Woman's Dilemma*, 15–16.

9. Benjamin L. Carp, *Rebels Rising: Cities and the American Revolution* (New York: Oxford University Press, 2007), 43–50; Hiller B. Zobel, *The Boston Massacre* (New York: Norton, 1970), 62–63, 69–76, 80–81, 94, 99.

10. Zagarri, *A Woman's Dilemma*, 52–53; Zobel, *Boston Massacre*, 147–50; Richard Archer, *As If an Enemy's Country: The British Occupation of Boston and the Origins of Revolution* (New York: Oxford University Press, 2010), 155–57.

11. Mercy Otis Warren to James Otis Jr., [c. 10 September 1769], in *Mercy Otis Warren: Selected Letters*, ed. Jeffrey H. Richards and Sharon M. Harris (Athens: University of Georgia Press, 2009), xiv, 3, 4; Zagarri, *A Woman's Dilemma*, 55; Craig Bruce Smith, *American Honor: The Creation of the Nation's Ideals during the Revolutionary Era* (Chapel Hill: University of North Carolina Press, 2018), 82–83; Nancy Rubin Stuart, *The Muse of the Revolution: The Secret Pen of Mercy Otis Warren and the Founding of a Nation* (Boston: Beacon Press, 2008), 41–42. For testimony of Otis's accelerating mental deterioration, see John Adams, *Works of John Adams*, ed. Charles Francis Adams (Boston: Charles C. Little and James Brown, 1850), 2:219–20, 226–28.

12. Archer, *As If an Enemy's Country*, 149, 178–81; Zobel, *Boston Massacre*, 172–79; Carp, *Rebels Rising*, 52.

13. Zobel, *Boston Massacre*, 222–26.

14. Ibid., 228, 240; Gerald Weales, "*The Adulateur* and How It Grew," *Library Chronicle* 43, no. 2 (1979): 105–6. For the debate on royal salaries for Massachusetts officials, see Richard L. Bushman, *King and People in Provincial Massachusetts* (1985; Chapel Hill: University of North Carolina Press, 1992), 172–75, and *Boston Gazette*, 16 March 1772.

15. Linda K. Kerber, "'History Can Do It No Justice': Women and the Re-interpretation of the American Revolution," in *Women in the Age of the American Revolution,* ed. Ronald Hoffman and Peter J. Albert (Charlottesville: University Press of Virginia, 1989), 23.

16. Carol Berkin, *Revolutionary Mothers: Women in the Struggle for America's Independence* (New York: Vintage, 2005), 106; Zagarri, *A Woman's Dilemma,* 69; Angela Vietto, *Women and Authorship in Revolutionary America* (Burlington, VT: Ashgate, 2005), 106. For Joseph Addison's influential argument against female discussion of political subjects, see Mary Beth Norton, *Separated by Their Sex: Women in Public and Private in the Colonial Atlantic World* (Ithaca, NY: Cornell University Press, 2011), 114–16, 118, 121, 149. For examples of Thomas Hutchinson's (unsuccessful) legal attempts to punish radical Whigs who criticized him or the Crown in Massachusetts newspapers in 1771, see Neil L. York, "Tag-Team Polemics: The 'Centinel' and His Allies in the 'Massachusetts Spy,'" *Proceedings of the Massachusetts Historical Society* 107 (1995): 102–3.

17. Fredric M. Litto, "Addison's Cato in the Colonies," *William and Mary Quarterly,* 3rd series, 43, no. 3 (July 1966): 433; Warren, Houghton Manuscript, 6.

18. Zagarri, *A Woman's Dilemma,* 57; Martha C. Nussbaum, "Friends, Romans, and Lovers: Political Love and the Rule of Law in *Julius Caesar,*" in *Shakespeare and the Law: A Conversation among Disciplines and Professions,* ed. Bradin Cormack, Martha C. Nussbaum, and Richard Strier (Chicago: University of Chicago Press, 2013), 267; Eran Shalev, *Rome Reborn on Western Shores: Historical Imagination and the Creation of the American Republic* (Charlottesville: University of Virginia Press, 2009), 66; Shalev, "Mercy Otis Warren, the American Revolution and the Classical Imagination," *Transatlantica,* no. 2 (2015): 7; Mercy Otis Warren to James Otis Jr., [c. 10 September 1769], in Richards and Harris, eds., *Selected Letters,* xiv, 3. For the fullest explanation that Warren set her play in Turkish-ruled Serbia, see Weales, "*The Adulateur* and How It Grew," 109–10. For the location and history of "Upper Servia," see Edward King, *Descriptive Portraiture of Europe in Storm and Calm* (Springfield, MA: C. A. Nichols, 1885), 671.

19. *Massachusetts Spy,* 26 March 1772; Warren, Houghton Manuscript, 1.

20. *Massachusetts Spy,* 26 March 1772; Warren, Houghton Manuscript, 1, 5. In her manuscript note, Warren mistakenly gives the name of "the virtuous Senator" as Brutus rather than Cassius, presumably conflating in memory her 1772 dramatic sketches with the plagiarized 1773 pamphlet version, in which Cassius's speeches are put in the mouth of a character named Brutus and Cassius's role in the plot is substantially reduced. For the (almost entirely) plagiarized 1773 pamphlet version of *The Adulateur* by an unknown writer, see *The Adulateur: A Tragedy, as It Is Now Acted in Upper Servia* (Boston: New Printing-Office, 1773).

21. *Massachusetts Spy*, 23 April 1772.

22. Ibid.

23. Ibid.

24. Ibid.

25. Warren, Houghton Manuscript, 5.

26. For the scholarly understanding that Warren's political writing was inspired by her brother's campaign against Hutchinson and fueled by anger at his beating and downfall, see particularly Zagarri, *A Woman's Dilemma*, 55, 58–59; see also Richards and Harris, eds., *Selected Letters*, xiv. For Warren's identification with classical republican virtue through her use of a classical pseudonym, see Philip Hicks, "Portia and Marcia: Female Political Identity and the Historical Imagination, 1770–1800," *William and Mary Quarterly*, 3rd series, 62, no. 2 (April 2005): 277; Davies, *Catharine Macaulay and Mercy Otis Warren*, 199–200; and Caroline Winterer, *The Mirror of Antiquity: American Women and the Classical Tradition, 1750–1900* (Ithaca, NY: Cornell University Press, 2007), 44–54, esp. 50.

War Women of the Eastern Woodlands

BARBARA ALICE MANN

—〰〰〰〰—

WOMEN AND men did battle on multiple fronts during the American Revolution, not only along the Atlantic coast where most colonial settlements lay but also to the west, especially in modern-day upstate New York, western Pennsylvania, and the Ohio Country. The coastal war was the full-on fight against Great Britain with which most people are familiar, whereas the western, total war against Native America is often neglected.[1] Yet the ravaging of Indian civilians compared to that of Napoleon's forces against civilians in his European campaigns. Although some scholars may credit Napoleon with conducting the first total war in modern times—a war waged completely against other Europeans—combat and casualties during the western Indian campaigns in the American Revolution reveal an earlier total war.[2] The Sullivan-Clinton campaign through Iroquoia in 1779 was but one example of the devastating warfare conducted by provincial, Continental, and state forces against the Indigenous inhabitants of North America.[3]

The nations of the Haudenosaunee, or Iroquois League, did not wish to fight either the British or the Americans—or to stand as proxy fighters for either side, which they made clear first to the British at Oswego and Montreal and second to the Americans at Albany when hostilities erupted in 1775. They reiterated their position in 1777, only to be forced into the war, especially by dirty tricks of the British.[4] If that is overlooked in Western histories, then the fact that the joint refusal to go to war had to have been a decision handed down by the women's councils is more so, as is evidence that in their culture a number of the Indigenous soldiers were always female.[5] This obscuring occurred despite researchers who had documented female cultural authority in the Wood-lands, with a dismayed Lucien Carr crying in 1884 that Lenape women's power was "but little short of despotic."[6] Carr hardly discovered this fact; Woodland women's power had been recorded by Europeans as a sort of freak of nature since at least 1656 by Jesuit missionaries, soon followed by Joseph François Lafitau in 1724 and Pierre de Charlevoix in 1761, just to name a few of the earliest sources.[7] Indian women's power made them not only actors but also targets in the total war of the western campaigns.

In regard to matriarchal and patriarchal authority, a culture's found-ing stories are revealing. If the European Christian story forefronts a First Father and his Only Son, then the Woodland stories forefront First Mothers and their Daughters. From Atensic (Ataensic, Yagendgi) of the Iroquois and Selu of the Cherokee, to Kokomthena of the Shawnee and Kahesana Xaskwim of the Lenape, First Women abound.[8] First Daugh-ters likewise were foundational, like the Iroquoian Katsitsianiionde, the Fat-Faced Lynx, daughter of Atensic.[9] Originally, such spirits (not "goddesses") were deliberately expelled from Western chronicles, like the female twins of north and south; falsified into an evil presence, like Atensic; or stunningly, like Kokomthena, sex-changed by later schol-ars from female to male.[10]

The importance of women in creation tradition forecast their cen-trality in social, economic, and political life. The women ran their own councils, had their own officials, managed all the farming, and held what Lafitau called "le tréfor public" ("the public treasury").[11] Only the women could "nominate" candidates, that is, put them in office, and they held the power of impeachment of errant officials. The women called—or called off—wars, and women named the "Young Men" who went for sol-diers.[12] (Although Western texts style them as "warriors," the Iroquois term huskë'ëthe, "he carries beechnuts on his back," is best understood as "Young Man."[13]) Rather than the men speaking for all, they were mere mouthpieces of the women's councils. This is why Lafitau called the women "l'ame des confeils" ("the soul of the councils").[14] Moreover, the older the woman, the more she was honored as "Grandmother."

Thus, despite intensive studies that seek to include the formerly ex-cluded of American history, the European belief that declaring war was a universal male prerogative still guides discussion. Because of the ma-triarchal nature of Woodlands societies, however, the Grandmothers de-clared war, and then, only for one action at a time—and the Young Men did not have to go if they did not agree on the necessity of war.[15] This was why Grandfathers were constantly telling Europeans that they "could not control the young men," that the chiefs were not their "masters."[16] The Grandfathers could and did, however, throw what cold water they could on hostile fervor, as when the Miami war chiefs of 1825 told the Young Men to stay home and "take care of the women and children" and not "trouble themselves" about things that would distract them from these, their primary duties.[17]

More horrifying yet to colonial Europeans was the sight of men at major Indian-European councils, proudly walking about in skirts and carrying women's corn pounders. Lafitau recounted that these cross-dressed men greatly surprised the earliest Europeans, and not in a good way. "Hermaphrodites!" they shuddered.[18] By the time Lafitau wrote in 1724, it was grudgingly understood that these men had been sent to an all-male council as the speakers of the women, dressing and acting as if they were women, but European men still disdained the practice. Indeed, the thought of female chiefs was still too much to bear, so Lafitau downgraded the *Femmes Chefs* he saw to just the mothers of (male) chiefs.[19] Still more astounding to Europeans were the women warriors they saw on the battlefields and in charge of the disposition of prisoners for adoption or execution.[20]

It is important to know that in Woodlands cultures, it is the job that is gendered, not the human being. Women could be "made" men, and men could be "made" women for the duration of a task, such as peace-making (woman) or war-making (man). In fact, whole nations had jobs, so that the Iroquois League anointed the entire Lenape nation "women." Instead of understanding that it was a high honor for the Lenape to become *Gantowisas* ("woman acting in her official capacity"), Westerners set about trying to take the dress off the Lenape. They celebrated British Indian agent Sir William Johnson for pushing the Lenape to go to war in 1755 (a violation of their position), so that by 1794 at the Greenville Treaty, they "formally declared" that they "were no longer women, but MEN."[21]

This last development might have felt "right" to Westerners, but they had it all wrong. Skirts on Indigenous men had nothing at all to do with sexuality but everything to do with social and governmental functioning in a matriarchy. The Lenape were "made women" to quell Lenape-Iroquois fighting. The Iroquois proposed, and the Lenape agreed, that "one nation shall be the *woman*," sitting at the center and giving up war entirely. The "male" nations would "live around" her, ensuring that none could "touch or hurt the woman." Should any warmonger attack her, the Iroquois (men) would "immediately say to him, 'Why do you beat the woman?' Then, all men shall fall upon him, who has beaten her."[22] In fact, the entire Lenape nation had thus been made judges, a female-gendered job, and, as Cayuga chief Deskaheh noted, "it was a compliment" to be called *Gantowisas*.[23]

By the same token, biological women could be "made men" to take on a male-gendered job such as Young Man. Traditions of such female leaders stretch far back in memory, to the time of the overthrow of the Mound Builder priesthood and the establishment of the Iroquois League in 1142, when the Mohawk people traveled under their female chief, Gaihonariosk, from Ohio, putting up briefly in Ontario, Canada, before moving south into upstate New York.[24] Although female chiefs abounded, if only incidentally, in European-inscribed texts, European colonists began denigrating as much as they reported, distorting proportions to favor men.[25] Indigenous women somehow managed not quite to disappear from settler texts, but they were heavily submerged by the contempt of chroniclers like James Adair, who in 1775 denigrated the supposed interference of Muskogee women with presumably male business as "petticoat-government."[26]

As a result of this bias, when European men saw women of influence in their own right, they immediately expected, and proceeded to record, the women not by name but as an appendage of some notable male, being his "daughter" or his "dusky queen."[27] For instance, one British report noted that five "Sinneke" (Seneca) women had "engaged" in battle along with 450 Young Men in 1687. The report's author simply assumed that these were wives who had "resolved not to leave their husbands," whereas they had been made men and were combat soldiers in their own right, alongside their lineage brothers.[28]

Female Grandmothers, chiefs, and soldiers were recorded very haphazardly, so that ferreting them out in the primary sources takes some searching and contextual knowledge. For instance, in 1745 a French militia's sneak attack on the Meskwaki killed an unenumerated "many" Indians and tracked down the survivors as they ran for their lives across two hundred miles. Finally catching up to their prey, the militia slew an undefined more, while capturing a "large number" of women and children, whom the militia began marching back to its town, presumably as slaves. Along the march, however, the militia was foiled. When the group paused to rest, one of the women saw her chance as the lone scout guarding the prisoners leaned into the river for a drink of water. Springing on him, she latched hold of his penis with both of her bound hands, twisting and squeezing for all she was worth while kneeing his head fully into the water until he drowned. She then hastily released herself and the rest of the captives, leading them all home. The chronicler claimed that she was made a chief for her bold and brave actions at the river, but she was most probably already a war chief.[29] It is not easy for a woman to kill a man with her bare, bound hands. That takes training.

By 1775, the settlers already knew of all these customs—and resented them mightily. It was bad enough that the Indians demanded to know by what right the colonists were on their land, but for Indian women to assume command of councils, economics, society, and war was too much. Colonists particularly resented the fact that the women were in charge of all prisoners taken in war, deciding their fate of adoption or execution. Umbrage over this was expressed on 27 May 1763 by Pierre-François-Xavier de Charlevoix, who recounted with ire that any prisoners not yet dead were "abandoned to the fury of the women." Any woman who had suffered a loss in war was empowered to attack the "first who falls under her hand, and one can scarcely imagine how far she is transported with Rage. She has no regard either to Humanity or Decency, and every Wound she gives him, one would expect him to fall dead at her Feet, if we did not know how ingenious these Barbarians are in Prolonging the most unheard of Punishment."[30] Presenting Indigenous women as the furies of hell was a way that the culture of Europe allowed the settlers to explain female warriors, for short of Celtic queen Boudica and French peasant Joan of Arc (both of whom died for their presumption), there were no such models in European history.

The reasons for the America Revolution were manifold, although most traditional histories focus narrowly on the genuinely glorious aspect of the Revolution, the war of liberation from British oppression. There were, however, other reasons for the Revolution beyond taxation without representation. One less acknowledged was the Royal Proclamation of 1763, which prohibited settler encroachment on Indian land, with British officers required to remove the offending squatters by force.[31] Freed from this order by the Revolution, former rebels rushed west, especially if they had been soldiers paid in warrants for land there. The greater their violation of Indigenous space, the greater their venom against the alleged savagery of Native resisters, especially the Iroquois, with particular hatred spewed at the *Gantowisas*. These rebels launched all-out attacks against the Indians in pursuit of Indian lands.[32]

An Indigenous woman whom Western scholars tend to mention in discussions of the Revolution is Grandmother ("Madame") Sacho, for she is recorded in multiple soldiers' journals of General John Sullivan's 1779 New York campaign. She is typically presented merely as speaking with Sullivan at Sheoquaga ("Catherine's Town") and being left with food when Sullivan departed, but her story is grimmer than that. First, there were two women involved, Grandmother Sacho and a never-named young woman who was murdered by Sullivan's soldiers. Although some stories say the second woman was found dead when the soldiers encountered Grandmother Sacho, the journals of the expedition tell another tale.[33]

Finding the sixty towns, which he burned, already evacuated, Sullivan took very few prisoners.[34] One was Grandmother Sacho, found at Sheoquaga on 1 September 1779, which was so unusual that twenty diarists noted her presence.[35] Many of the journals used racist, belittling terms to describe offensively the "very aged squaw" with Major Jeremiah Fogg dubbing her a "full blooded antideluvian hag."[36] Major John Burrowes recorded that Grandmother Sacho was deliberately hidden in a "bunch of bushes ... to be safe" as she could not be evacuated, at least not in time. Upon seeing the soldiers, she was "just ready to die with fear, thinking she was to be killed," said Burrowes, with Dr. Jabez Campfield and Major Fogg sharing in that last impression.[37]

The fear was not without merit. Fogg recorded that the soldiers "would readily have killed this helpless wretch" had Sullivan not "spared her," laying Sullivan's decision to the "dictates of humanity."[38] Based on Fogg's uncorroborated remark, Sullivan has since been lauded for his supposed mercy in allowing Grandmother Sacho to live.[39] This highlights the danger of consulting just one source. In fact, Sullivan kept her alive to pump her for information, which he "threatened her with punishment" to obtain. At first, probably leaning on the fact that she was a Tuscarora whose lineage had been adopted in by the Cayuga, she acted as though she did not understand what was being asked by one of Sullivan's Oneida scouts. The Oneida shifted through the various Iroquoian dialects, however, making it clear that she was being evasive.[40] Private Nathan Davis claimed that the interpreter then "drew his knife and told her he would take her scalp" if she did not talk, at which point she gave intelligence to save her life.[41] It was only after being informed that the army was not going to kill her that Grandmother Sacho "manifested the greatest degree of gratitude" to Sullivan "as her good angel," at least in the text usually cited. What Lieutenant Samuel M. Shute recorded as gratitude looks more like simple relief. When he left town, Sullivan built her a "bark hut," but on his return trip through Sheoquaga, finding her in tears and starving, he left her with one hundred pounds of flour and fifty pounds of beef.[42]

The second woman was not mentioned by most of the diarists, but Captain Daniel Livermore was quite clear that "two squaws" were taken alive at Sheoquaga, as was Reverend John Gano, who described the second woman as "a young one to take care of" Grandmother Sacho. Lieutenant Erkuries Beatty assumed that the second woman just "pretended to be lame" when discovered because, when the soldiers left to "get some others to help fetch her in," she seized the opportunity to hide so well that they could not locate her immediately. Twenty days later, when Sullivan's army passed back through Sheoquaga on its way home, the young woman with the limp was found dead, "forty rods distant" from the hut that Sullivan had had built for Grandmother Sacho. Sullivan ordered her buried.[43] According to Fogg, the young woman had been shot by nameless army "expresses," that is, couriers.[44] Knowing of the gang rape by Colonel Goose Van Schaick's 558 men of 126 Onondaga female and child prisoners, male and female, in late April 1779—an event still riling the Iroquois in 1816—the young woman's initial disappearing act is understandable, and her death most probably consequent of rape.[45]

Both Grandmother Sacho and her young aide fall into the victim category, with the elder surviving only because she provided intelligence. The soldiers' desire to kill the elder and the actual murder of the younger were not anomalies; women were regular targets of what Fogg termed the "enmity" of soldiers against the "savages."[46] Two Seneca chiefs, Egnohowin ("Esther Montour") and her sister, Catherine Montour, became particular targets of militia ire. Despite their European-sounding names and confusion in the Western record about who was the grandmother, the mother, the sisters, or the daughters, both Catherine and Esther necessarily derived from a Seneca mother to have held the offices that they did. All inheritance (male as well as female) runs through the female progenitrix, including position titles. Adoptees would have had no access to positions' titles, but the Montour women did, demonstrating their lineage.[47]

The original Catherine Montour ("Madame Montour") was the Seneca-adopted Wyandot grandmother—or perhaps great-aunt—of the revolutionary-era Esther and Catherine, with the French governor Louis Buade, Comte de Frontenac, rumored to have fathered her.[48] However she came to be, the first Catherine Montour spoke multiple Algonkin and Iroquoian dialects and acted as a diplomat.[49] Because she was highly regarded, her name ("Catherine") was perpetuated as a position title after her death, for the names of notable ancestors traditionally transmute into titles of office in later generations. This was how all

French governors became known by the name Onontio ("Big Mountain"), a translation into Mohawk of the surname of the first French governor, Montmagny ("Big Mountain").[50]

Egnohowin, or Esther, was originally married to a Munsee (Wolf Clan) Lenape man from Pennsylvania.[51] Shortened from the original Lenape Sheshequanink, the town of Sheshequin was in what is now Ulster Township, Bradford County, Pennsylvania, near the border of modern upstate New York. Egnohowin is portrayed in Western texts as taking control of Sheshequin when her husband died in 1772, but it is more likely that she was already a civil chief and he a war chief, for the non-League-aligned Munsee were intense resisters against European encroachment. After 1772, Egnohowin moved Sheshequin just opposite Tioga Point. Although when they moved, Woodlanders took their clan town names with them, the revolutionary militias dubbed its Tioga Point incarnation "Queen Esther's Town."[52]

Both Egnohowin and Catherine took on war duties, and Egnohowin prosecuted hers with extreme prejudice. Revolutionaries held her particularly to blame for the attack at the Battle of Wyoming in July 1778, at which she led a party of War Women. Settler accounts seemed to vie with one another for the most gruesome possible depiction of their actions, placing Egnohowin in the thick of battle, supposedly singing a war song (more probably her death song), and afterward leading the women in scalping the vanquished. Some reports had her personally scalping anywhere from eight to sixteen men, while others had her forming those to be executed into a circle, which she rounded, tomahawking and scalping each man in turn. Both of these execution reports were most likely true, as this was how executions were traditionally handled.[53] Other, specious reports had her viciously slitting her victims' throats, maniacally declaring that she would never grow tired of killing settlers.[54] Given the lurid, longstanding propaganda against women warriors as inhuman fiends from hell, that depiction of Egnohowin should be taken with a large dose of salt. Was she in charge of executions? Most probably. Did she rave inchoately about killing settlers? Most probably not. The insane were not allowed to act as chiefs.

The official excuse for hitting "Esther's Town" was revenge for the Wyoming Valley attack, but Colonel Thomas Hartley, who was mounting the offensive, noted the fertility of the land, calling the area "a valuable Country" while fearing, post-Wyoming, that it might be "depopulated" of settlers who would be "ruined" were the land not secured through attack.[55] Clearly, possession of the land was at issue. Ordered to establish some interior forts on the cheap in August 1778, Hartley had set off to raid Iroquoian lands, and perhaps saw Sheshequin as a soft target for being woman-led.[56] His "Expedition" against this and other "small Indian Towns on the North Branch of Susquehanna" was foiled when the towns along his intended route were warned by the only Indians with whom he engaged during his expedition. Upon discovery, following his sack of Sheshequin, upwards of seven hundred Indians and Rangers (European Tories) massed to meet his invasion. Hartley then decided that it was instead "most Expedient" simply to skedaddle for home, taking the Iroquois cattle and horses that his militia stole after destroying "Tioga & Shesiken."[57]

Sheshequin might have been evacuated, looted, and burned, but Egnohowin was not down for the count, for she reemerged during Sullivan's campaign in upstate New York in 1779. Although settler histories portray the campaign as war, it was not defined by battles. The primary action of the Iroquoian soldiers, male and female, was to evacuate all the townspeople ahead of the onslaught, as they had before Hartley.[58] This was standard practice, for war is not a value in matriarchies; saving the "Innocents"—a legal category including all noncombatants—is.[59] Clearly, Egnohowin was not an Innocent, however, for not only had she been at Wyoming but she was also at Newtown along the Chemung River in the one European-style engagement that General John Sullivan forced on the starving Iroquois during the 1779 campaign. Official reports of the battle mention specific men, but there was no word of Egnohowin except in the expedition journal of Sergeant Nathaniel Webb on 30 August 1779, the day after the engagement. Given settler animus against a woman who fought back, it is hardly surprising that the Continental soldiers treated her body with contempt after Newtown. At 8:00 a.m., four hundred men were ordered to "destroy corn, &tc." In the process of leveling the cornfield, they came across the bodies of "several Indians and Tories . . . some of which they had hove into the river—also the body of Queen Esther, who murdered many of the inhabitants of Wyoming last summer."[60]

Even as Iroquoia was under siege, in early June 1779 a Kentucky militia 296 strong engaged in a sneak attack against the Shawnee at "Little Chillicothe" (modern-day Xenia, Ohio). Roused from early morning sleep by the attack, the surprised forty men of the town lay down covering fire for the 260 civilians, as the women, perforce made "men" by the special circumstance of the emergency, shouted, "Kentuck! Kentuck," rousing and racing the children and old folks to the Council House. They next began hacking firing holes in the walls as the forty Shawnee men, engaged in a running fire-fight with the militia, retreated into the Council House.[61]

On the pretext of defecting to a Kentucky militia that most probably included slaveholders, an unnamed Black woman among the Shawnee rushed out of the Council House to the militia, warning them ominously (and quite falsely) that Katepakomen ("Simon Girty"), a much-feared Wyandot war chief, was on his way with a hundred reinforcements. This news panicked the militiamen. In the mayhem that followed, the Black woman mysteriously disappeared from the militia ranks, never to be seen again by them.[62] Indians traditionally had no color line, so the Black woman was probably a War Woman harboring no intention of eschewing Shawnee freedom for Kentucky slavery but every intention of spreading disinformation to flummox the militia. (The Shawnee won the engagement.)[63]

During the Revolution, the two hundred or so Lenape and Mahican converts to Moravian Christianity lived at Welhik Tuppeek ("Schonbrunn"), Goshchochking ("Gnadenhutten"), and Salem, the missionaries' "praying towns" in Ohio. The converts were perforce allies of the revolutionaries through the loyalties of the missionaries, particularly John Heckewelder, a friend of and informant for Colonel Daniel Brodhead, commander at Fort Pitt. This put the converts at odds with the primary body of Lenape and Mahican traditionals of Ohio, who successfully resisted rebel invasion of Ohio throughout the war. The traditionals realized that the Moravian missionaries were spying for the Americans, dispatching reports to Brodhead on a regular ten-day schedule, but hesitated to injure their relatives among the converts.[64] Thus, the revolutionaries were using the converts as a fifth column and a shield.

In the fall of 1781, however, the traditionals caught Heckewelder redhanded by intercepting a spy report to Brodhead. Spiriting the entire body of Moravian converts to Upper Sandusky, the Wyandot capital in Ohio, the traditionals eventually separated out the missionaries for delivery to the British commandant at Detroit as spies. Throughout the missionaries' 1781 captivity, the Lenape allowed civil Peace Women (who handled civic negotiations during peacetime and housed prisoners during wartime) to care for the missionaries with food and clothing because the missionaries were categorized as Innocents, being "Messengers of Peace," that is, officials enjoying safe conduct through enemy lands.[65] There was a Lenape War Woman, however, who decided to aid the Americans. Given in the texts only as Chief Glickhican's "niece," as

soon as Heckewelder was arrested she stole the best war horse of the
chief leading the traditionals and risked speeding off to Fort Pitt with
the news. Albeit not a convert herself, her family members were, and
she intended to protect them.[66] Alas, the protection was short-lived. In
return for their war-long accommodation of the rebels, the converts were
massacred by Pennsylvania militia in March 1782.[67]

Meanwhile, among the British was Degonwandonti ("Molly Brant,"
c. 1736–1796), often mispresented as a War Woman. Fluently bilingual
as well as English literate, Degonwandonti walked in two worlds, the
upscale portion of the British colonial world and the Mohawk world of
her birth. She was used more than appreciated by the British during the
Revolution, whereas the Mohawk regarded her as both their Speaker to
the Crown and as the female civil chief in whatever town she resided. She
reinforced her Indigenous identity by always appearing in traditional
buckskin dress, whether in a formal drawing room or in the "box of a
house" arranged for her use by the British.[68]

Western sources rumored that she was an "Indian princess," but
"princess" is an entirely Western station.[69] Iroquoian Clan Mothers
held lineage "titles," that is, authorization to hold public office, the rough
equivalent of the title U.S. senator or representative. Degonwandonti
was not from a titled lineage. Had she been, she would have hobnobbed
with other title-holding women, so that her little brother Thayendanegea
("Joseph Brant," 1743–1807) would not have had to depend on the British
command to make him important.[70] It was the British, not traditional
culture, that elevated both the brother and sister.

Degonwandonti maintained her British-engineered status during
the Revolution primarily by supporting the British insistence that the
Iroquois take part in the war. Despite her influence and the engagement of her brother and others like him in combat, the Iroquois did not
wish to take part in the war and heavily resisted the blandishments of
both the British and the Americans, preferring to remain "in a State
of Neutrality."[71] The actions of these few who favored war obscured that
Iroquoian sentiment largely favored noninvolvement. It is false, however,
to say that the eventual participation of Iroquoian nations with either
British or American armies meant that the Iroquois League "split." Whenever the League as a whole could not come to a consensus, the council
fire was put out, signaling that each nation was free to act according to its
own lights. The fire had been doused many times before; it did not signal
the end of the Iroquois League, which still exists.[72]

The British desperately wanted—needed—the participation of the
Iroquois, especially of the Seneca, the Guardians of the Western Door,

where the revolutionaries' western front lay. When the Seneca war chief Sayenqueraghta noised about his desire to withdraw from the war to stand neutral, his decision could easily have influenced many other Iroquois to chuck the British alliance. At this point, Degonwandonti served the British agenda by openly drubbing Sayenqueraghta's decision.[73] A Clan Mother publicly calling out a male official on his performance in office was the first step in a formal impeachment proceeding. As Sayenqueraghta certainly knew, Iroquoian women did not hesitate to impeach errant male officials, including the women's Speaker to the men, Sagoyewatha (c. 1750–1830)—"Red Jacket" himself—when he obviated their intentions.[74] Sayenqueraghta got the message and changed his tune.[75]

In 1782, as revolutionaries on the Pennsylvania-Ohio frontier engaged in bloody campaigns to expel and exterminate Native peoples, Colonel William Crawford of the Continental Army met his much-ballyhooed demise. Because the wanton massacre at Goshchochking near Gnadenhutten by Colonel David Williamson's Pennsylvania militia on 8 March had caused no end of legal trouble and embarrassment to the Continental Congress, and in an attempt to prevent a repeat in the region, General William Irvine at Fort Pitt had Crawford take command of an ad hoc militia force. Entering Ohio on 24 May, Crawford led 480 men against Upper Sandusky, where 230 Indian troops and some British Rangers stood. Crawford's leisurely pace allowed 140 Shawnee to race north to join the defenders, increasing the Indian union numbers to 370, spooking the militias. Over 5 and 6 June 1782, Crawford was routed, as the militia undertook a wildly disordered flight. Williamson bolted along with his men, abandoning Crawford to capture as he tried to organize an honorable retreat.[76]

Taken on 6 June, Crawford was held responsible by the union of Ohio Indian nations for the militia massacre of the converts at Goshchochking, Ohio. Because Indian officials had actually been after Williamson, whom they knew perfectly well had led the massacre, the nations appointed the gifted and highly respected Katepakomen as Crawford's Speaker (lawyer) during his trial for the murders. Had Crawford simply held his tongue during the trial, he might have been spared execution, as he was not the target. Instead, he kept interrupting the proceedings with what he thought was a better case, appealing to those not conducting the trial, and generally bringing unnecessary attention to himself until Hopocan recognized him as having been on earlier, lethal campaigns. At that point, Katepakomen was shouted down and Crawford convicted and sentenced to death.[77]

The women carried out the execution. Tying a naked Crawford by a long line attached to a post atop a bed of hot coals, they had him shot

with ninety-six blanks (in honor of the ninety-six dead Lenape and
Mahican converts killed at Goshchochking). They then heaped hot coals
on him, periodically piling on more coals. It took most of the night of
11–12 June 1782 for Crawford to roast down to bones, but his story was
fanned into permanent life by the settlers, leading to lasting propaganda
against Indian War Women, even though it was the civil chiefs of the
mostly Wyandot, Lenape, and Shawnee there who had condemned
him—after a proper trial.[78] The names of the women who carried out
the sentence against Crawford were never recorded; they were simply
demeaned as "squaws," with one grandmother demoted to "old squaw
(whose appearance every way answered the ideas people entertain of the
devil)."[79] Crawford's death became a settler propaganda gift that kept on
giving, the subject of numerous paintings, including an amateurish rendering, *Execution of Crawford*, housed in the Seneca County Museum in
Tiffin, Ohio; a more polished illustration from 1887 in the *Ohio Archaeological and Historical Quarterly*; and the best-known rendering, Frank
Halbedel's *Burning of Colonel Crawford* from 1915.[80]

As Katherine McKenna observed in 2000, primary sources are sometimes almost impenetrable concerning Indian women due to the "crude
stereotypes" that still "dominate much thinking" about them in Western
histories, an observation that becomes only more true of Indigenous
Women Warriors.[81] To figure out who these women were and what they
did—whether winning in hand-to-hand combat against a man, surviving brutal cross-examinations, stealing a feared war chief's prize horse to
deliver important counterintelligence, or striding across a battlefield, de-
ploying their Women Warriors—is to turn to Indian lore, Indigenously
contextualized. There, free of European misperceptions and distortions,
researchers can seek what motivated these women to fight invasion until
they were dead and their bodies desecrated by men celebrating their demise. This much is clear: as what anthropologists call "honorary" men,
they fought on the same principle as all Young Men: Your cause is just,
and they can kill you only once.[82]

NOTES

1. "The immediate objects are the total destruction and devastation of their
    settlements and the capture of as many prisoners of every age and sex as
    possible." George Washington to John Sullivan, 31 May 1779, orders to at-
    tack Iroquois, in *The Writings of George Washington, Being His Correspon-
    dence, Addresses, Messages, and Other Papers, Official and Private, Selected*

and *Published from the Original Manuscripts*, ed. Jared Sparks (Boston: Russell, Odiorne, and Metcalf, and Hilliard, Gray, 1834–37), 6:264; full orders, 6:264–67.

2. David A. Bell, *The First Total War: Napoleon's Europe and the Birth of Warfare as We Know It* (Boston: Houghton Mifflin, 2007).

3. For my extended interpretation of the 1779 Sullivan-Clinton campaign, see Barbara Alice Mann, *George Washington's War on Native America* (Westport, CT: Praeger, 2005), 55–110.

4. William Leete Stone, *Life of Joseph Brant—Thayendenagea: Including the Border Wars of the American Revolution, and Sketches of the Indian Campaigns of Generals Harmar, St. Clair, and Wayne, and Other Matters Connected with the Indian Relations of the United States and Great Britain, from the Peace of 1783 to the Indian Peace of 1795* (New York: Alexander V. Blake, 1838), 1:71, 295; Isabel Thompson Kelsay, *Joseph Brant, 1743–1807: Man of Two Worlds* (Syracuse, NY: Syracuse University Press, 1984), 178. For the British "dirty trick" in gaining Indian allies, see Mann, *George Washington's War*, 13–14.

5. Barbara Alice Mann, *Iroquoian Women: The Gantowisas* (New York: Lang, 2000), 179–82.

6. Lucien Carr, "On the Social and Political Position of Woman among the Huron-Iroquois Tribes," Peabody Museum of American Archaeology and Ethnology, *Reports* 16–17, vol. 3, nos. 3–4 (1884): 211.

7. Joseph François Lafitau, *Mœurs des sauvages ameriquains, comparées aux mœurs des premiers temps* (Paris: Chez Saugrain l'Aîné, 1724), 1:72; Pierre-François-Xavier de Charlevoix, *A Voyage to North-America: Undertaken by Command of the Present King of France Containing the Geographical Description and Natural History of Canada and Louisiana with the Custom, Manners, Trade, and Religion of the Inhabitants; a Description of the Lakes and Rivers, with Their Navigation and Manner of Passing the Great Cataracts* (Dublin: John Exshaw and James Potts, 1766), 2:40.

8. Mann, *Iroquoian Women*, 239–41 (Atensic); James Mooney, "Myths of the Cherokee," in *Nineteenth Annual Report of the Bureau of American Ethnology, 1897–1898, Part 1* (Washington, DC: Government Printing Office, 1900), 242–49 (Selu); Thomas Wildcat Alford, *Civilization, as Told to Florence Drake* (Norman: University of Oklahoma Press, 1936), 63 (Kokomthena); Charles F. Voegelin, "The Shawnee Female Deity," in *Yale University Publications in Anthropology*, no. 10 (New Haven, CT: Yale University, 1936), 3–21 (Kokomthena); Mark Raymond Harrington, *The Indians of New Jersey: Dickon among the Lenapes* (New Brunswick, NJ: Rutgers University Press, 1966), 183. Harrington rendered Kahesana Xaskwim as "Kah-há sa-na Kaś-kweem."

9. For a heavily sourced summary of the First Epoch tradition of the Iroquois, including the female creators, see Bruce Elliott Johansen and

Barbara Alice Mann, *Encyclopedia of the Haudenosaunee (Iroquois Confederacy)* (Westport, CT: Greenwood Press, 2000), 83–97.

10. For the female twins, see Barbara Alice Mann, *Spirits of Blood, Spirits of Breath: The Twinned Cosmos of Indigenous America* (New York: Oxford University Press, 2016), 27, referencing John Napoleon Brinton Hewitt, "Iroquoian Cosmology, First Part," in *Twenty-First Annual Report of the Bureau of American Ethnology to the Secretary of the Smithsonian Institution, 1899–1900* (Washington, DC: Government Printing Office, 1903), 233. For Atensic misrepresented as "wicked," see James W. Herrick, *Iroquois Medical Botany*, ed. Dean R. Snow (Syracuse, NY: Syracuse University Press, 1995), 6, 11, and Barbara Alice Mann, "The Lynx in Time: Haudenosaunee Women's History and Traditions," *American Indian Quarterly* 21, no. 3 (1997): 427–28. For sex-change on Kokomthena, see Charles E. Voegelin and Erminie W. Voegelin, "The Shawnee Female Deity in Historical Perspective," *American Anthropologist* 46 (1944): 370–75, and Barbara Alice Mann, "'Where Are Your Women?' Missing in Action," in *Unlearning the Language of Conquest: Scholars Expose Anti-Indianism in America*, ed. Don Trent Jacobs (Austin: University of Texas Press, 2006), 125.

11. Lafitau, *Mœurs*, 1:72; Mann, *Iroquoian Women*, 236.

12. Mann, *Iroquoian Women*, 172, 178–79, 179–82; Pete Jemison, "Mother of Nations—The Peace Queen, a Neglected Tradition," *Akwe:kon* (1988): 68–70; Carr, "On the Social and Political Position of Woman among the Huron-Iroquois Tribes," 207–32.

13. Mann, *Iroquoian Women*, 182.

14. Lafitau, *Mœurs*, 1:72.

15. Charlevoix, *A Voyage to North-America*, 1:317.

16. Richard White, *The Middle Ground: Indians, Empire, and Republics in the Great Lakes Region, 1650–1815* (1991; New York: Cambridge University Press, 2011), 165, 165n32.

17. C[harles] C[hristopher] Trowbridge, *Meearmeear Traditions*, ed. Vernon Kinietz, Occasional Contributions from the Museum of Anthropology of the University of Michigan, No. 7 (1825 MSS; Ann Arbor: University of Michigan Press, 1938), 14.

18. Lafitau, *Mœurs*, 1:55.

19. Lafitau, *Mœurs*, 4:124.

20. Lafitau, *Mœurs*, 4:17–33. See the illustration of an execution, plate 14, facing 18.

21. Anthony F. C. Wallace, "Woman, Land, and Society: Three Aspects of Aboriginal Delaware Life," *Pennsylvania Archaeologist* 17, nos. 1–4 (1947): 27. For Western incomprehension, see John Heckewelder, *History, Manners, and Customs of the Indian Nations Who Once Inhabited Pennsylvania and the Neighboring States* (1820, 1876; reprint New York: Arno Press, 1971), xxvii–xxix, 70.

22. George Henry Loskiel, *History of the Mission of the United Brethren among the Indians in North America, in Three Parts*, trans. Christian Ignatius La Trobe (London: Brethren's Society for the Furtherance of the Gospel, 1794), part I, 125.

23. Wallace, "Woman, Land, and Society," 27.

24. For Gaihonariosk, see Lafitau, *Mœurs*, 1:93. For overthrow of the Mound Builders, see Barbara Alice Mann and Jerry L. Fields, "A Sign in the Sky: Dating the League of the Haudenosaunee," *American Indian Culture and Research Journal* 21, no. 2 (August 1997): 105–63; also Barbara Alice Mann, *Native Americans, Archaeologists, and the Mounds* (New York: Lang, 2003) 155–68.

25. Barbara Alice Mann, "Race, Ethnicity, and Culture," in *Race in America: How a Pseudo-Scientific Concept Shaped Human Interaction*, ed. Patricia Reid-Merritt (Santa Barbara, CA: ABC/CLIO-Praeger, 2017), 1:83–86.

26. James Adair, *The History of the American Indians: Particularly Those Nations Adjoining to the Mississippi, East and West Florida, Georgia, South and North Carolina, and Virginia* (London: Edward and Charles Dilly, 1775), 146.

27. For a chief in her own right, see Augustin Grignon, "Seventy-Two Years' Recollections of Wisconsin," in *Collections of the State Historical Society of Wisconsin*, ed. Lyman Draper (Madison: State Historical Society of Wisconsin, 1904), 3:210. For "queen," see Allie B. Busby, *Two Summers among the Musquakies, Relating to the Early History of the Sac and Fox Tribe, Incidents of Their Noted Chiefs, Location of the Foxes, or Musquakies, in Iowa, with a Full Account of Their Traditions, Rites and Ceremonies, and the Personal Experience of the Writer for Two and a Half Years among Them* (Vinton, IA: Herald Book and Job Rooms, 1886), 35, 213. For "daughter," see Makataimeshekiakiak ("Black Hawk"), *Life of Black Hawk: Ma-ka-tai-me-she-kia-kiak*, ed. Milo Milton Quaife (Chicago: Lakeside Press, 1916), 124. "Daughter" was probably used in Makataimeshekiakiak's memoir because his translator and editors supplied the term.

28. Edmund Bailey O'Callaghan, "Information Given by Severall Indians to the Governor at Albany," 6 August 1687, in *Documentary History of the State of New York* (Albany, NY: Weed, Parsons, 1850), 1:152.

29. Grignon, "Seventy-Two Years' Recollections," 207–10.

30. Charlevoix to Duchess of Lesdiguieres, 27 May 1671, in Charlevoix, *A Voyage to North-America*, 1:217. The old long "s," which appears similar to the letter "f," has been modernized to "s."

31. George R., "By the King, A Proclamation" (London: Mark Baskett, 1763), at "Royal Proclamation, 1763," Indigenous Foundations, 2009, https://indigenousfoundations.arts.ubc.ca/royal_proclamation_1763/; Colin Calloway, "The Proclamation of 1763: Indian Country Origins and American Impacts," in *Keeping Promises: The Royal Proclamation of 1763,*

Aboriginal Rights, and Treaties in Canada, ed. Terry Fenge and Jim Aldridge (Montreal: McGill-Queen's University Press, 2015), 33–48; Barbara Alice Mann, *President by Massacre: Indian-Killing for Political Gain* (Santa Barbara, CA: Praeger, 2019), 216–17, 219.

32. Mann, *George Washington's War*, 147–49.

33. Sudie Doggett Wike, *Women in the American Revolution* (Jefferson, NC: McFarland, 2018), 96.

34. Mann, *George Washington's War*, 67 (sixty towns); for entire expedition, 51–110.

35. Frederick Cook, ed., *Journals of the Military Expedition of Major General John Sullivan against the Six Nations of Indians in 1779* (Auburn, NY: Kapp, Peck and Thomson, 1887): Lt. William Barton, 9; Lt. Erkuries Beatty, 28; Maj. John Burrowes, 45; Dr. Jabez Campfield, 56–57; Lt. Col. Henry Dearborn, 73; Sgt. Moses Fellows, 89; Maj. Jeremiah Fogg, 96; Sgt.-Maj. George Grant, 111; Thomas Grant, 141; Lt.-Col. Adam Hubley, 158; Lt. John Jenkins, 173; Capt. Daniel Livermore, 186; Lt. William McKendry, 204; Lt. Charles Nukerck, 216; Maj. James Norris, 233; Sgt. Thomas Roberts, 244–45; Lt. Samuel M. Shute, 271; Lt. Rudolphus van Hovenburgh, 279; David Craft, 364; John Gano, *Biographical Memoirs of the Late Rev. John Gano, of Frankfort (Kentucky), Formerly of the City of New-York, Written Principally by Himself* (New York: Southwick and Hardcastle, 1806), 108.

36. Cook, ed., *Journals of the Military Expedition*, 28, 96. For analysis of "squaw" as a derogatory term related to a vulgar rendering of vagina, see Mann, *Iroquoian Women*, 19–22.

37. Cook, ed., *Journals of the Military Expedition*, 45, 57, 96.

38. Ibid., 100.

39. See, for instance, Sarah M. S. Pearsall, "Madam Sacho: How One Iroquois Woman Survived the American Revolution," *Humanities* 36, no. 3 (May–June 2015), https://www.neh.gov/humanities/2015/may june/feature/madam-sacho-how-one-iroquois-woman-survived-the -american-revolution.

40. Cook, ed., *Journals of the Military Expedition*, 364, 96, 111. For multiple dialects, see Nathan Davis, "History of the Expedition against the Five Nations Commanded by General Sullivan, in 1779," *Historical Magazine*, 2nd series, 3, no. 4 (April 1868): 201, full account 198–205.

41. Davis, "History of the Expedition," 201. For Davis as a private in the First New Hampshire Regiment during the expedition, see Cook, ed., *Journals of the Military Expedition*, 312.

42. Cook, ed., *Journals of the Military Expedition*, 271, 9, 100, 176, 273n.

43. Ibid., 186, 28, 100; Davis, "History of the Expedition," 204. Private Davis confused her with Grandmother Sacho, who was found alive but whom he thought was the dead woman ordered buried.

44. Cook, ed., *Journals of the Military Expedition*, 100.

45. Mann, *George Washington's War*, 31–32.

46. Cook, ed., *Journals of the Military Expedition*, 100.

47. For titles as unavailable to adoptees, see Tekahionwake [E. Pauline Johnson], "My Mother," in *The Moccasin Maker* (Toronto: Ryerson Press, 1913), 45.

48. Alison Duncan Hirsch, "'The Celebrated Madame Montour': 'Interpretress' across Early American Frontier," *Explorations in Early American Culture* 4 (2000): 83. For confusion about the Montour women, see Mann, *George Washington's War*, 187–88n120, 210n375.

49. Hirsch, "'The Celebrated Madame Montour,'" 81–82.

50. White, *The Middle Ground*, 36.

51. For Munsee, or "Minsi," as Lenape ("Delaware") Wolf Clan, see Heckewelder, *History, Manners, and Customs*, 52.

52. Paul A. W. Wallace, *Indians in Pennsylvania*, ed. William A. Hunter, 2nd ed. (1961; Harrisburg: Commonwealth of Pennsylvania and Pennsylvania Historical Museum Commission 2005), 164; George Patterson Donehoo, *Indian Villages and Place Names in Pennsylvania* (1928; reprint, Lewisburg, PA: Wennawoods, 1998), 122, 165, 202.

53. A recent book attempts to "clear" Egnohowin's (Esther's) name, doubting the stories of her war deeds, but reports are in line with the actions of female war chiefs. See Chad Anderson, *The Storied Landscape of Iroquoia: History, Conquest, and Memory in the Native Northeast* (Lincoln: University of Nebraska Press, 2020), 90–94.

54. Cook, ed., *Journals of the Military Expedition*, 5, 69, 85, 87, 151, 220, 229, 248, 260, 269, 270, 287; J. Niles Hubbard, *Sketches of Border Adventures in the Life and Times of Major Moses Van Campen*, ed. John S. Minard (Fillmore, NY: John S. Minard, 1893), 57–58, 64; Francis Whiting Halsey, *The Old New York Frontier, Its War with Indians and Tories, Its Missionary Schools, Pioneers and Land Titles, 1614–1800* (Port Washington, NY: Ira Friedman, 1901), 219; Louise Wells Murray, *A History of Old Tioga Point and Early Athens, Pennsylvania* (Wilkes-Barre, PA: The Raeder Press, 1908), 111–13.

55. Thomas Hartley to Pennsylvania Council (unclear), 10 August 1778, in *Pennsylvania Archives, Selected and Arranged from Original Documents, in the Office of the Secretary of the Commonwealth, Conformably to Acts of the General Assembly, February 15, 1851 to March 1, 1851*, ed. Samuel Hazard, 1st series (Philadelphia: Joseph Severn, 1853), 6:693.

56. Pennsylvania Council to Thomas Hartley, 15 August 1778, in Hazard, ed., *Pennsylvania Archives*, 6:705.

57. Samuel Hunter to George Bryan, 7 October 1778, in Hazard, ed., *Pennsylvania Archives*, 6:773.

58. For evacuations at the Sullivan-Clinton approach, see Mann, *George Washington's War*, 88–89.

59. For the Innocent, see Heckewelder, *History, Manners, and Customs*, 136, 136n1.

60. Cook, ed., *Journals of the Military Expedition*, 287.

61. John Bowman to George Rogers Clark, 13 June 1779, in *Collections of the Illinois State Historical Library*, ed. Clarence Walworth Alvord, Virginia Series III (Springfield: Trustees, Illinois State Historical Library, 1912), 8:332; "Bowman's Campaign of 1779," *Ohio Archaeological and Historical Publications* 22 (1913): 502–19; "Bowman's Expedition against Chillicothe, May–June 1779," *Ohio Archaeological and Historical Publications* 9 (1910): 446–59.

62. "Bowman's Campaign of 1779," 507; "Bowman's Expedition against Chillicothe," 457.

63. Mann, *George Washington's War*, 118–23.

64. John Heckewelder, *Narrative of the Mission of the United Brethren among the Delaware and Mohegan Indians from Its Commencement, in the Year 1740, to the Close of the Year 1808* (1820; reprint, New York: Arno Press, 1971), 284–89; Paul A. W. Wallace, ed., *Thirty Thousand Miles with John Heckewelder* (Pittsburgh: University of Pittsburgh Press, 1958), 133–34, 196. For the census of converts, see Mann, *George Washington's War*, 236n26. For Heckewelder's relationship with Brodhead, see Daniel Brodhead to John Heckewelder, 21 January 1781, and Heckewelder to Brodhead, 26 February 1781, in Louise Phelps Kellogg, *Frontier Retreat on the Upper Ohio, 1779–1780* (Madison: Wisconsin Historical Society, 1917), 321, 337–39. For Consul Willshire Butterfield on Brodhead's meeting with Heckewelder during the 1781 expedition against the Ohio union, see Kellogg, *Frontier Retreat on the Upper Ohio*, 378.

65. Heckewelder, *Narrative*, 257, 259; "Messengers of Peace," in Heckewelder, *History, Manners, and Customs*, 181, 182.

66. Wallace, *Thirty Thousand Miles*, 177; Heckewelder, *Narrative*, 269n.

67. For the Goshchochking Massacre, see Mann, *George Washington's War*, 156–65.

68. Katherine M. J. McKenna, "Mary Brant (*Konwatsi'tsiaienni, Degonwadonti*): 'Miss Molly,' Feminist Role Model or Mohawk Princess?" in *The Human Tradition in the American Revolution*, ed. Nancy Lee Rhoden and Ian Kenneth Steele (Wilmington, DE: Scholarly Resources, 2000), 198, 196, 191.

69. Ibid., 184, 198.

70. Mann, *George Washington's War*, 8.

71. John Norton [Teyoninkarawen], *Journal of Major John Norton, 1816*, ed. Carl F. Klinck and James J. Talman (Toronto: Champlain Society, 1970), 274.

72. Mann, *George Washington's War*, 12–13.

73. McKenna, "Mary Brant," 193.

74. Mann, *Iroquoian Women*, 178.

75. McKenna, "Mary Brant," 193.

76. "The Haldiman Papers," in *Collections and Researches Made by the Pioneer Society of the State of Michigan*, 2nd ed. (Lansing: Wynkoop Hallenbeck

Crawford, 1908), 10:577, 583, 595; John Rose to William Irvine, 17 June 1782; John Turney to Arendt de Peyster, 7 June 1782, in C[onsul] W[ilshire] Butterfield, *The Washington-Irvine Correspondence, the Official Letters* (Madison, WI: David Atwood, 1882), 118–19n3, 367–71, 368–69n3, 387n1. For the legal liability and black eye to Congress, see Mann, *George Washington's War*, 167–69.

77. Heckewelder, *History, Manners, and Customs*, 285–88; John Knight, "Narrative of Dr. Knight," in Archibald Louden, *A Selection, of Some of the Most Interesting Narratives, of Outrages, Committed by the Indians, in Their Wars, with the White People* (Carlyle, PA: A. Louden, 1808), 1:8; Thelma R. Marsh, *Lest We Forget: A Brief Sketch of Wyandot County's History* (Upper Sandusky, OH: Wyandot County Historical Society, 1967), 12–13.

78. Knight, "Narrative," 1:10–12; "From Fort Pitt," 23 July 1782, in Butterfield, *Washington-Irvine Correspondence*, 376n2.

79. Knight, "Narrative," 10, 12.

80. James Boroff, *Execution of Crawford* (photograph), undated, Tiffin-Seneca Public Library Postcard Collection, Seneca County Museum, Tiffin, Ohio, https://ohiomemory.org/digital/collection/p15005coll27/id/41523/; James H. Anderson, "Colonel William Crawford," *Ohio Archaeological and Historical Quarterly* 6 (1887): drawing, unattributed and untitled, plate facing 31; Frank Halbedel, *Burning of Colonel Crawford* (painting), 1915, Wyandot County Historical Society, Ohio History Connection, https://ohiomemory.org/digital/collection/p26740icoll36/id/2876/.

81. McKenna, "Mary Brant," 185.

82. George Stiggins, *Creek Indian History*, ed. Virginia Pounds Brown (Birmingham, AL: Birmingham Public Library Press, 1989), 124, 131. Stiggins was Muskogee, composing his manuscript in the 1830s. For anthropological usage of the term "honorary" man/woman, see, for instance, Michael W. Young, "Obituary: Marie Olive Reay, Born Maitland, NSW [New South Wales], Died Booragul, NSW, 16 September 2004," in Marie Olive Reay, *Wives and Wanderers in a New Guinea Highlands Society: Women's Lives in the New Guinea Highlands Society, Women's Lives in the Waghi Valley* (Canberra, Australia: Australian National University Press, 2014), appendix E, 191.

"A Shocking Thing to Tell Of"

Female Civilians, Violence, and Rape under British Military Rule

LAUREN DUVAL

—∿∿∿∿—

With regard to *the pollution of wives and daughters by the lustful brutality of the lowest of mankind,* I declare, that I do not recollect to have ever heard of more than one rape imputed to the soldiery. . . . The criminal was secured; an enquiry immediately took place; but the accuser refused to prosecute.

—General Sir William Howe, House of Commons, 29 April 1779

The Prisoner Lusty then came into the room, and laying hold of the Witness by the Arm, as she sat with the Child in her lap, swore that he would have his will of her, but she told him that if he did not let her alone, that she would tell his officers of him, upon which he said, *damn you and the officers too.* . . . The Prisoner Dunn then threw her on the bed; she hallowed and screamed, and they swore that if she did so, they would kill her; that Lusty then held her fast, whilst Dunn lay with her; and when he had done, he held her whilst Lusty lay with her; that her Daughter who is about 4 years old stood by, crying.

—Testimony of Elizabeth Johnstone, Newtown,
Long Island, September 1776

I N APRIL 1779, in the midst of the American Revolution, General Sir William Howe appeared before the House of Commons and vehemently refuted rumors of British soldiers' widespread rape of American women. Whether willfully ignorant or deliberately dishonest, Howe insisted that he knew only of a single accusation levied against a British soldier and that the victim had "refused to prosecute" the case.[1] Yet, despite Howe's insistence to the contrary, innumerable women endured sexual assault at the hands of British soldiers during the war. Most of these stories have been lost to history, yet some have been preserved in British courts martial records and the papers of the Continental Congress. In their depositions, American women testified to the brutal and agonizingly personal ways they experienced the American Revolution. For women like Elizabeth Johnstone, who was assaulted in her Long Island house by two British soldiers while her young daughter stood by crying, resistance to British authority was not an abstract concept or a political protest; it was immediately and deeply tangible, a traumatic invasion of her home and body that was indelibly entwined with the meaning and experience of the American Revolution.[2] Echoing down through the centuries, victims' voices starkly refute Howe's statements to the House of Commons and provide a rare glimpse into a wartime crime that is assumed to be widespread yet remains sparsely documented.[3]

During the American Revolution sexual violence took place in civilian homes and on city streets.[4] It occurred at isolated farms and during military raids. Anywhere soldiers went, women were vulnerable. No space was safe. Rape and the threat of rape structured women's daily experiences; it shaped how they traversed city streets and how they inhabited their houses.[5] Writing from British-occupied Philadelphia in 1777, Elizabeth Drinker confided to her diary that she was "often . . . afraid to go to Bed," remarking that "every noise now seems alarming, that happns in the Night."[6] To women feeling vulnerable and defenseless, every sound, every shadow held the threat of danger. This was, to some extent, true for women throughout the early modern world. Sexual consent and coercion existed along a continuum structured by intersections of gender, class, and race.[7] Yet occupying forces wielded a different kind of power than men did in peacetime. The institutional culture of the military, combined with the violence of war, fostered a group mentality that emboldened some soldiers and facilitated their ability to coerce sex.[8] Wartime conditions enlarged soldiers' power and gave them an increased license to rape—circumstances that informed the daily experiences of men and women alike during the American Revolution.

As is the nature of the crime and the stigma around it, incidents of rape during the American Revolution are sparsely documented. They appear as offhand allusions in letters and soldiers' diaries, as anonymous

accounts in newspapers, as rumors gleaned through hearsay and gossip.[9] Almost exclusively, these accounts decry the actions of British soldiers and their allies.[10] Yet accounts from Native nations suggest that
Continental soldiers also raped, especially those non-White female civilians identified as enemies.[11] As Sharon Block has argued, this archival
anomaly illustrates the politicization of rape discourses during the war.
Public outcry against British soldiers' rape of American women functioned as both a searing indictment of British tyranny and a "rallying cry"
for the revolutionary cause that exhorted men to defend their female relations from the ravages of British soldiers.[12] The history of sexual assault during the American Revolution, as Block puts it, is a story of "rape
without women."[13]

It is for this reason, that the handful of rape cases prosecuted in
British courts martial and a small collection of depositions submitted
to the Continental Congress between 1777 and 1779, primarily documenting women's experiences in New Jersey and Connecticut, offer a
much-needed corrective to narratives that decenter women's voices.[14]
These sources are notable for their frank discussion of wartime sexual
violence; they preserve these crimes in victims' own words, documenting women's voices as well as the witness testimonies of their household
and neighborhood communities. These sources are nevertheless unusual.
The Continental Congress depositions were intended to be circulated as
propaganda. Likewise, rape precipitated a small fraction of British military tribunals, and only the most egregious cases were prosecuted.[15] Unlike peacetime assaults, which were usually perpetrated by acquaintances
and veiled in the pretense of consent, the frequently public nature of
wartime rape closely adhered to cultural archetypes. Victims were more
likely to be assaulted by strangers (typically soldiers) and tended often
to be raped simultaneously by multiple assailants—circumstances that
permitted easier reporting and higher conviction rates than in peacetime.[16] There were exceptions, of course, especially among women and
children followers of the British Army, who were routinely abused by
acquaintances.[17] Rape prosecutions in British courts martial, not unlike revolutionary propaganda, provided a platform for British officers
to exhibit their paternalistic masculinity. In seeking justice for vulnerable
women, officers affirmed their own honor and reinforced a hierarchical
military culture in which superiors routinely regulated and intervened in
the sexual activity of enlisted men as a means of enforcing class distinctions.[18] Commanding officers had full discretion over prosecution, and
notably the defendants in all extant courts martials for rape were enlisted

men or loyalists. There is no evidence that a British officer was ever tried for the crime during the American Revolution.[19] As Emily Merrill has argued in her study of British military jurisprudence, only in the rare instances where the interests of officers and civilians "overlapped" were proceedings initiated and soldiers convicted.[20]

Parsing the layers of masculine performance that overlay rape testimonies, and in some instances facilitated them, women's depositions are nevertheless critical for excavating women's wartime experiences. In histories of the Revolution, too often rape has been lumped in with other forms of violence. And yet, sexual assault is distinct because it is at once gendered, racialized, and sexualized.[21] Women's depositions and testimonies elucidate these differences in vital ways by centering women's emotional trauma and demonstrating how rape defined women's spaces and movements during wartime. Violence, bloodshed, and terror were not confined to the battlefield; women faced these same threats in their homes and streets, as notions of safety eroded around them and the specter of sexual violence overshadowed their every interaction with soldiers.[22] By testifying about sexual assault in courts martial and depositions, victims contested their treatment and reclaimed agency in the aftermath of an event that fundamentally, if temporarily, deprived them of it.[23] Importantly, extant testimonies also reveal the networks that women relied on in wartime—relationships that illuminate the subtle ways that household and neighborhood communities collectively resisted soldiers' abuse.[24]

But as much as these depositions illuminate, it is also important to recognize their limits. In documenting moments of trauma and violence, they offer fleeting glimpses into individual lives and the horrors of war. Yet, there is much that remains hidden. Many of the women who appear in these records were poor and probably illiterate. Most of them left no other trace in the historical record. These women are known to history only because they were raped. We know their names and we can hear their voices only because they suffered traumatic violence. And because they chose to report it.[25]

On a cold December night in 1775, Anne Moore spent the evening in the Boston residence of Dr. Trotter Hill, the regimental surgeon for the British Army's 59th Regiment of Foot, organizing baggage for the doctor's upcoming trip. Around eight o'clock, Private Timothy Spillman, Hill's servant, arrived with some additional items. The two shared a drink to stave off the winter chill; Moore sipped tea and Spillman drank "some rum and water." They sat together for about half an hour before Anne retired. In the middle of the night, she "was awakened" by the "undrest" soldier climbing into her bed "and taking hold of her." She recalled that Spillman was irritated by "her resisting him, and refusing to gratify his desire." "He damned her, and said that she had disappointed him," and when Moore attempted to get out of bed, Spillman "prevented her and knockt her head against the Window," breaking four panes of glass. He beat her until she fainted. When Anne Moore regained conscious- ness, she "begg'd of him to let her alone, upon which he swore prodi- giously, and at last left the room." Without pausing to grab a cloak or a blanket, Moore fled, groggy, injured, and frightened into the frigid pre- dawn hours. Benjamin Hallowell, the Boston commissioner of customs, answered his door at five o'clock in the morning to find Anne Moore standing in her shift, "cruelly beaten, and . . . almost perished with Cold." Her injuries, as regimental surgeons would later attest, were severe—they believed her life to be in danger—and were inflicted "By a Man's fist," not, as Private Spillman feebly suggested during the court martial, by falling down the stairs.[26]

Anne Moore's assault illustrates the rapid and immediate dangers that occupying forces introduced into urban life.[27] For women of all social classes, daily routines and chores became precarious endeavors. Soldiers filled city streets. Patrols regularly circulated the city. Off-duty men took to taverns, playhouses, and brothels. In Charleston, Eliza Wilkinson described officers walking in groups of five or six, "hooking-arms."[28] In New York, Elizabeth Hunter recounted a sailor on the street grabbing her—twice—as she made her way to the Queen's Head Tavern for din- ner. Resisting his advances, Hunter told him "to go about his business, that she did not know him, and wanted nothing to say to him." The sailor refused to relent and the dispute ended with another sailor running the man through with a sword.[29] Holidays were particularly perilous for fe- male civilians, as drunken soldiers took to the streets, celebrating and carousing throughout the city.[30] Similar atmospheres prevailed when the troops were in winter quarters, where unfettered from the responsibili- ties of campaigning, soldiers indulged freely and frequently.

Although writing from Continental-occupied Newport, Rhode Is- land, the experience of loyalist Catherine Dudley reveals the dangers lurking in the streets, particularly for those women marked as political enemies. Walking home from the wharf in November 1775, Dudley encountered a group of about thirty men, two of whom "walk'd down to me watch'd me try'd to look under my Bonnet"—a subtle threat of their power to undress her elsewhere. Nervously making her way home,

Dudley realized that she was being followed as she "hurry'd thro'" the dark streets. "The fellow . . . was after me the whole way," Dudley recalled, his presence a menacing reminder that he could at any moment overpower her, and she "expect'd every moment, they wou'd have seiz'd me." Fearful, she sought shelter in a nearby house. "When I stop'd at Mr. P[ease]'s Door he said, Damn you; you bitch, you shall be mark'd as a Black Sheep, they were oblig'd to drag me in the Door, for I was unable to move Fear, Grief, Resentment, had got the better."[31]

The threat of rape was very real for women living in garrisoned cities. Women of the laboring class, and Black women in particular, were especially vulnerable. Typically responsible for running errands, these women were more likely to interact with common soldiers, who did not adhere to the same code of gentlemanly honor that pervaded the British officer corps (not that officers always acted accordingly).[32] Moreover, when laboring and enslaved women encountered soldiers who either legitimately or fraudulently presented themselves as military authorities, they lacked the status or the social connections to challenge them—and often had little choice but to engage with the men.

On 20 December 1777, a "frosty star-light Night," three men stopped two domestic servants, Catherine Stone, a White woman, and Isabella Mitchell, a Black woman, near the Southwark Theater on Fourth Street in Philadelphia.[33] One man was clearly a soldier, identifiable by the yellow facings on his jacket. The second man wore a blue coat, and the women were unsure if he was affiliated with the army. The third man wore "a kind of brown Jacket, and had more the appearance of a Sailor."[34] Claiming to be the patrol, the men insisted that the women accompany them to see the captain of the guard. The women must have expressed some hesitancy because in their respective testimonies, both Catherine Stone and Isabella Mitchell stated that the men physically "dragg'd them by force" and "carried them" to the Southwark Theater. Both women reported that the men beat them. And both women testified that they struggled, a requisite for rape convictions in eighteenth-century common law—although notably, the women charged the soldiers with the lesser crimes of robbery and ill-use, suggesting they had legal guidance from someone familiar with the military justice system.[35]

At the theater, the group separated. John Dillon, the man who looked like a sailor, forced Isabella Mitchell beyond the playhouse where, she testified, "throwing her down between two logs, he there ravished her." He then stole her cloak and went to find his companions, providing Mitchell with an opportunity to flee. The two other men, meanwhile, remained with Catherine Stone, attempting to force her into the playhouse cellar. During the struggle, Stone broke free and ran to a nearby house, but the owner refused to admit her, fearing "that she was some disorderly woman." The two men, at this point accompanied by Dillon, recaptured Stone and "again dragged her to the play-house," where they "beat her with a Stick," held her down, and covered her mouth while Robert Brown raped her. Stone recalled that "She screamed out and made all the resistance she could, but nobody came to her assistance." Following the assault, Stone learned that the men intended to "drag her elsewhere," presumably where they planned to assault her again, and Brown threatened "that if she said a word he would beat out her brains." But seeing a light in a nearby stable, Stone hazarded an escape. "Bloody her hair all dishevelled," and wearing only one shoe, she ran toward the light, where she found an officer and cried out, "for Gods sake, Sir, save me, save me."[36]

Revealing the vulnerability of women in occupied cities, particularly those of the "lower sort," this incident also, significantly, clarifies how race influenced contemporary perceptions of sexual assault.[37] In the subsequent court martial, Lieutenant Robert Douglas of the Royal Artillery, whose wife employed both women, admitted that his recollections of that night were muddled and that he had not been particularly interested in pressing the women for details. In fact, although he suspected it, Douglas never confirmed that Catherine Stone was raped, because he thought "she seemed desirous of concealing" it and so "he did not ask." Given these circumstances, Lieutenant Douglas's conclusions about what occurred on that cold December evening are themselves revealing, illuminating the gendered and racial contours that shaped his ideas about sexual assault. Although both women testified otherwise, Douglas identified John Dillon—the man described as looking like a sailor (and who raped Isabella Mitchell)—as Stone's assailant.[38] Likely drawing on stereotypes about sailors as uncouth, disorderly, and licentious, Douglas's assumption that the sailor assaulted Catherine Stone, a White woman, seemingly conflated his expectations about who was the worst of the men with what he deemed to be the more heinous of the crimes.[39]

Significantly, Douglas's testimony also omitted any reference to Isabella Mitchell's rape, situating her merely as a witness to Stone's assault.[40] Possibly Mitchell did not disclose that she had been raped; when she sought Douglas's assistance, the soldiers still held Catherine Stone captive. Or perhaps recognizing that sexual crimes against Black women were rarely punished, Mitchell assumed that the soldiers' assault on a White woman would be enough to condemn them—and chose to keep silent, only divulging that she had been raped once court martial proceedings were initiated.[41] Even so, signs of her struggle must have been evident when she arrived at the Douglas house "crying and in great distress."[42] Her clothes must have been rumpled and damp from the snowy ground; her hair wet and tangled. She was probably bloody and shaken from the traumatic assault. That Douglas failed to deduce the reason—as he did with Stone—suggests, at the very least, a mindset that privileged the safety of White women and ignored the plight of Black women as victims of sexual assault.[43]

The court martial proceedings replicated this inconsistent treatment between the two women, suggesting how race informed authorities' differentiated treatment of White and Black victims. The court's examination of Catherine Stone was noticeably longer and more in-depth than that of Isabella Mitchell. The court asked the former to account for numerous details: Was she forcibly dragged? How far? Were the men violent? Did she resist or make noise? For how long? How was she constrained? Was she raped more than once? What happened when she got home? How did she find the men again? In contrast, the court asked Mitchell only three brief questions.[44]

Despite this disparity, significantly, Isabella Mitchell did testify about her assault. She was the fourth person to take the stand during the trial and the first person to explicitly talk about the fact that she too had been raped.[45] Standing alone in front of thirteen British officers and the deputy judge advocate—in a foreign space and confronting unfamiliar pale male faces—she recounted the terror and violence of that night and asserted unequivocally that she had resisted her attacker. After asking Mitchell only two questions—had she resisted (yes); did she know the prisoner previously (no)—the court pressed her for additional details about Catherine Stone, asking if the soldiers had beaten her. Refusing to be so easily discounted, Isabella Mitchell inserted her own experiences into her answer, responding that "the Soldier struck them both." With her testimony, Mitchell, a Black woman who was probably illiterate and almost certainly poor, inscribed herself into the historical record—an enduring testament to her pain and her courage. Her testimony, along with Stone's, also had more immediate consequences. Both John Dillon and Robert Brown were found guilty; each man received one thousand lashes, was drummed through town "with ropes about their Necks," and turned out of the lines.[46]

NOTWITHSTANDING THE dangers of the streets, houses were not safe spaces either. Plunder was rampant, particularly when troops were on campaign. In July 1779, British forces under command of Major General

William Tryon launched a series of raids along the Connecticut coast. One Connecticut inhabitant recalled that "the Soldiers went where they pleased and did as they pleased without any Restraint." Fairfield resident Lucretia Radfield remembered that the soldiers were "abusive and insulting." They destroyed her furniture, tried to burn her house, "and attempted by with Threats and promises to prevail upon me to Yield, to their unchaste and unlawfull desires."[47] In New Haven, Tryon gave orders to fire the town, and British forces immediately began pillaging houses, beating men, and raping women. The nature of this raid was particularly cruel, intended to punish and frighten revolutionaries. Sarah Townsend recalled a chilling exchange in which she appealed to Sir George Collier of the Royal Navy for protection. Collier looked "at length" at the baby in her arms and sneered, "You have got a pretty Child there.... Are you willing that it should, be cut up, and made a Pye off, The Congress they say eat such Pies, and they are very good."[48]

Violence followed the British Army. Rural inhabitants residing near British encampments were particularly vulnerable to systematic plunder, resulting in bursts of intensified and unremitting ferocity, rather than the opportunistic crimes that occurred in cities where troops lived in close contact with civilian populations for extended periods of time. The British Army's 1776 capture of New York City, and the subsequent establishment of headquarters there, was particularly devastating for women in the surrounding areas, who were victims of what Mary Beth Norton has termed "a rampage of rape."[49] In December 1776, British soldiers plundered the New Jersey farm of Edward Palmer and raped his thirteen-year-old granddaughter Abagail. Abagail "Scream'd & beged," while her family pleaded for mercy. Ignoring their entreaties, "three of Said Soldiers Ravished her, and Likewise the next Day, & so on for three Days successively."[50] On the third evening, a group of soldiers again arrived at the Palmer house. One of the men raped Abagail in a back room while his companion assaulted her friend Elisabeth Cain. Another soldier attacked Elisabeth's older sister Sarah, placing "his Bayonet against her Breast" and threatening to "Run her thro the Heart" before "throw[ing] her upon the Floor" and raping her.[51] A fourth man found Abagail's aunt Mary Phillips hiding in the woods and forced her into the barn "& there had Carnal Knowlledge of her Body."[52] When the soldiers departed, they took Abagail Palmer and Elisabeth Cain with them back to camp, "where they was both Treated by some others of the Soldeirs in the same Cruel manner."[53]

Recognizing their vulnerability, some women took measures to avoid being alone with soldiers, although this strategy was negligible at best.

When British soldiers approached her father's New Jersey home in December 1776, Mary Campbell refused to go outside to speak to them, telling one of the men "he might speak to her in the House"—where her parents were—"if he had any thing to Say." Undeterred, the soldiers "Seiz'd hold of her Arms & drag'd" the pregnant Campbell to an "old Shop" nearby, where three soldiers raped in her succession.[54] Christiana Gatter of New Haven, conversely, managed to successfully thwart the British soldier who threatened to rape her at gunpoint in her garden. Feigning submission, Gatter "pretended to Comply" and directed the soldier to various spots around the property that she knew would be unsuitable for his proposed assault. She "flattered him along" until she caught sight of a neighbor and called for help.[55] Even so, Christiana Gatter's reprieve was temporary. That night, she, her husband, Martin, and their two young children "fastened the House and went to Bed," only to be awakened in the middle of the night by two soldiers breaking into their home. Martin fled through the backdoor "and hid in a Corn Field till Morning," while two soldiers raped Christiana, taking turns "whilst the other kept the Door."[56]

Not all domestic invasions took place in the context of military raids, however. Inhabitants routinely opened their doors to find soldiers requisitioning supplies or requesting refreshment. Civilians were hardly in a position to decline—and once inside, soldiers could wreak havoc. Under martial law inhabitants had limited capabilities to counter the brute force of these incursions. Many therefore turned to a more subtle form of interference to defend their families and homes from invading soldiers: they lingered in household spaces as deterrents to violence.

In the middle of a summer day in June 1778, Phebe Coe watched three soldiers approaching her Long Island house. Coe was a widow; she lived with her daughter, Abigail, who had been bedridden for nearly twenty years and suffered from lifelong fits. Two Black servants of uncertain freedom—a man named Mingo and an unnamed woman—were also working in the house that day.[57] The soldiers asked if Coe could spare some food and drink.[58] Agreeing, she went to prepare the food while Mingo remained with the men. Perhaps he and Phebe had briefly devised a plan as the soldiers approached the house. Perhaps their eyes met uneasily, and unspoken, they agreed to combat the invasion. Mingo lingered in the room where Abigail lay bedridden, and when the soldiers began drunkenly conversing with the Black woman, Mingo intervened and "bid her go up Stairs"—an action, Mingo noted, that "seemed to displease" the soldiers. It also, significantly, saved the woman from suffering the same fate as Phebe and Abigail. After the woman's departure, the soldiers turned their attention to Abigail Coe. Intervening again, Mingo explained that she was ill and "unequal" to conversation.[59] The soldiers seemingly dissuaded, Mingo went upstairs, presumably to talk with the unnamed female servant; possibly he encouraged her to hide, or to run for help. The nature of Mingo's relationship to the woman is uncertain but perhaps she was his primary concern in the moment.

In Mingo's absence, the soldiers acted quickly. They locked the upstairs door to trap Mingo above and turned Phebe out into the yard, bolting the door behind her. Two of the men began pillaging the house. To the mother's horror, as she peered through the window, she saw the third man, Bartholomew McDonough, "ravishing her Daughter." Distraught, she tried to reenter the house. Looking out the upstairs window, Mingo saw Phebe "crying and wringing her hands . . . [and] suspecting that something extraordinary must have happened," he "burst open the Door." Phebe rushed to her daughter's aid; Mingo went in search of assistance. When Phebe entered the room where Abigail lay, her daughter's assailant, Bartholomew McDonough, "laid violent hands on her [Phebe], threw her on the Bed, and there by force and against her Inclination, and notwithstanding she Urged everything she could to prevent him," raped her.[60]

The men finally departed—in part due to Phebe Coe's quick thinking in remarking on the imminent arrival of the neighbors—and Phebe set off for the British camp to make a complaint. On the road, she met an officer and "told him how her Daughter had been treated." Notably, Phebe remained silent about her own assault. When pressed on this point during McDonough's court martial, Phebe explained, "they did not ask her . . . and [she] thought it a shocking thing to tell of," and so "she only mentioned the Circumstance of her Daughter, for which alone she thought that he would suffer severely."[61]

Significantly, Phebe Coe's testimony and her initial silence about her assault provides insight into how women may have responded to being raped during the American Revolution. Women's reactions were, of course, deeply personal and individualized. They were also products of the times and cultures that these women inhabited. Yet, keeping these caveats in mind, the prudent application of contemporary psychological research on sexual assault aids understanding. As Phebe noted, she was hesitant to speak of her own trauma; it was "a shocking thing to tell of."[62] Rape is a notoriously underreported crime. Psychologists have demonstrated the "second rape" that victims endure in the courtroom, forced to confront their attackers and describe intense emotional and physical trauma to a room full of strangers. Moreover, any court in the eighteenth century—a court martial even more so—was inherently a masculine space.[63] Thirteen British officers, representing the power of the Crown and commanding the full authority of martial law, dressed in scarlet uniforms reminiscent of those worn by women's assailants, questioned victims about the details of intensely traumatic incidents. These circumstances produced unequal power dynamics between questioners and witnesses, dictated by gender, race, class, and status. Especially in instances where assailants raped multiple women, some victims may have remained silent about their own experiences, choosing instead to report only those incidents they deemed to be the most reprehensible—thus bringing their assailants to justice without having to publicly recount the trauma, and perhaps shame, they felt about their own assaults.

ALTHOUGH CONSTRAINED by the unequal power relations between soldiers and civilians, in some instances neighborhood communities banded together in attempts to protect women. Just before midnight on a snowy March evening in Philadelphia in 1778, inhabitants on Philadelphia's Front Street heard a woman cry out "Murder, Murder, a Rape a Rape."[64] Silver Crispin, a carpenter, and his wife, Sarah, were in their house awaiting supper. He recalled that his wife went to investigate and found their serving woman, Mary O'Hara, struggling with a British officer in the street.[65]

This portrayal of the event, however, oversimplifies the exchange and erases the networks and strategies that women relied on to protect one another in the occupied city. That evening, Patty Brockington, who lived in the apartment above the Crispins, was sitting by her window and "heard a Noise in the Street & on looking out of the Window she saw an officer lay hold of the Prisoner [Mary] O'Hara & she calling out." Recognizing Mary, Brockington alerted Sarah Crispin to her servant's distress. Sarah ran outside, insisting that Lieutenant Benjamin White leave the woman alone. In response, the officer "called her [Crispin] a whore & a Yankee." At this point, Silver Crispin emerged from the house to find his wife standing between Benjamin White and Mary O'Hara, "beg[ing] him not to hurt an old Woman, upon which Lieut. White push'd his Wife away, call'd her a whore & a rebel Bitch."[66] White's epithets sexualized Sarah Crispin's rebel politics by linking her supposed infidelity to the Crown to broader sexual promiscuity—attributes, White implicitly suggested, that justified his use of violence. He was not alone in such rationalization; men on both sides of the war used political labels to excuse violence, either sexual or otherwise, against American women.[67] Bristling at these insinuations, Silver Crispin intervened in the dispute, telling White that Sarah "was no whore, but his Wife," and "that was not proper Language to a married Woman." Lieutenant White drew his sword and the two men scuffled, falling into the snow. Mary O'Hara found a pair of tongs lying in the street and "struck Lieut. White with them." The incident ended when another officer arrived on the scene.[68]

Both Mary O'Hara and Silver Crispin were brought before a British court martial on the charge of knocking down an officer in the street. Significantly, testimonies during the trial reveal not only the gendered power dynamics of the occupied city but also the neighborhood networks that mobilized to protect Mary O'Hara from Lieutenant White's predations. Manipulating ideas about class and the propensity for crime, in his testimony White portrayed the incident as a failed robbery. He recalled that a woman had been running through the streets calling out murder and rape, and that on following her, he was immediately set upon by a man and a woman who began beating him with tongs. Silver Crispin's testimony, conversely, depicted himself heroically, defending his wife's honor and rescuing his servant from certain harm. Yet the testimonies of Sarah Crispin and Patty Brockington make clear that it was in fact the women themselves—their watchfulness, their networks of communication, and their swift mobilization—that successfully halted White's assault.[69]

This neighborhood mobilization, and women's actions in particular, are especially notable when juxtaposed with incidents in which neighbors declined to intervene. Fear permeated occupied regions, affecting individuals, communities, neighborhoods, and households. When faced with the British Army's martial authority and the threat of violence or impressment, many civilians prioritized their own safety over that of female acquaintances. Women thus fell victim not only to the depredations of the army but also the passivity of their neighbors. When British soldiers attacked Catherine Stone and raped her outside of Philadelphia's Southwark Theater, neighbors in a nearby house refused to offer her shelter. As they later explained, they feared "they might get themselves into a scrape" and so they "insisted upon her quitting the house immediately."[70] When Sarah Willis was raped at knifepoint in her house by Thomas Gorman, a mariner who gained entrance to her house pretending to be a press gang, she cried out for help. The walls were thin. Peter Leary, a laborer, heard her say "several times . . . *Let me alone.*" Sarah Willis even called out to him "saying Leary; take this Man out of my house." But Leary, "imagining that there was Press Gang in or about the house . . . was afraid to interfere." Likewise, William Anderson, another neighbor, testified that he had heard conversation and "a good deal of Scuffling on the floor, so much that it prevented him from Sleeping," but he declined to intervene and "what was said or done, he does not know."[71]

IN EARLY July 1779, on the day that Major General William Tryon launched his New Haven raid, Rose Luke and her husband returned home to find their house filled with British forces. Rose fled, but a British soldier caught her before she reached the door. Summoning her strength, she recalled, "I clenched my Hands in the place, where the Door latched, and held as fast, as I could, but the Soldiers used great Violence to get me loose." Rose's husband and a British colonel temporarily halted the attack, but after the colonel's departure, the plunder resumed. Wielding a cane, one of the soldiers forced Rose to a neighboring house, driving her like livestock. Once inside, the man directed her "up into the Chamber" and threatened to kill her if she refused. Grasping for an escape, Rose spied a Black female servant and "beged the other Woman" to accompany her upstairs, but the soldier threatened to kill the woman if she followed; she remained below. Rose recalled that the soldier "then laid fast hold of me, and carried me up in his Arms into the Chamber, and there was attempting to do violence to my Chastity, but I made all Possible Resistance by my struggles, and Cries untill an other person came up and saved me from his brutal Fury."[72]

Rose Luke's deposition illuminates the tangled strands that defined women's experiences under British military rule: invaded homes, the threat of sexual violence, household and neighborhood mobilization, and a forceful deposition that clarifies the gendered experience of war that women of all races and states of freedom confronted and endured during the American Revolution.

The testimonies of women like Rose Luke underscore the fact that for many American women the stakes of the American Revolution were agonizing and achingly personal. Integrating these experiences into narratives of the war provides new perspectives on how women experience war and what war does to women, by altering their relationships to spaces and safety. Rape and the threat of rape defined women's experiences under British occupation. It was a fear that overshadowed their daily lives. It was not abstract—it took form in the whispered experiences of their friends and neighbors, in cries echoing through their neighborhoods, in the sounds of crashing and weeping seeping through floorboards and walls, and in the heavy footsteps of soldiers traipsing through the streets. This history—embodied, aural, violent, and visceral—exists alongside but distinct from other types of wartime violence. It represents the lived experience of women who endured war on their doorsteps and in their homes, in city streets and rural farms. Women experienced war differently. Acknowledging this fact enriches our understanding of the American Revolution by exposing not only the gendered nature of the pervasive violence that saturated wartime life, and its traumatic effects, but also, significantly, women's courageous defense of their selves, their families, and their communities as their bodies became battlegrounds in the War for American Independence.

Notes

1. William Howe, *The Narrative of Lieut. Gen. Sir William Howe in a Committee of the House of Commons, on the 29th of April, 1779, Relative to His Conduct during His Late Command of the King's Troops in North America* (London: H. Baldwin, 1781), 59–60.
2. General Court Martial (hereafter GCM) of John Dunn and John Lusty, New Town, Long Island, 2–9 September 1776, WO 71/82, 413, film 675, reel 14, David Library of the American Revolution, Washington Crossing, PA, now at the American Philosophical Society, Philadelphia (hereafter DLAR).
3. Feminist scholars have demonstrated how sexual power is contingent on and replicates other forms of power—especially in wartime, when soldiers enact the subjugation of their enemies on the bodies of women. See Sharon Block, "Rape in the American Revolution: Process, Reaction, and Public Re-Creation," in *Sexual Violence in Conflict Zones from the Ancient World to the Era of Human Rights*, ed. Elizabeth D. Heineman (Philadelphia: University of Pennsylvania Press, 2011), 25. For an overview of feminist approaches to studying rape, see Ann J. Cahill, *Rethinking Rape* (Ithaca, NY: Cornell University Press, 2001).
4. Although most historians acknowledge that rape was pervasive during the American Revolution, only a few studies examine the topic. Sharon Block contends that the brutal and public nature of wartime rapes allowed women to more easily bring claims and convict their assailants, and that these narratives were reinterpreted in public discourse to delegitimize British rule. See Block, "Rape in the American Revolution," 25–38, and Block, "Rape without Women: Print Culture and the Politicization of Rape, 1765–1815," *Journal of American History* 89, no. 3 (December 2002): 849–68. Holger Hoock argues that rape testimonies demonstrate the "forensic" approach that the American Congress adopted to document

Britain's violation of the principle of just war; see Hoock, *"Jus in Bello, Rape and the British Army in the American Revolutionary War," Journal of Military Ethics* 14, no. 1 (2015): 74–97. Hoock likewise analyzes rape in the context of wartime violence but considers rape as only one manifestation of violence, rather than a sexually specific and gendered crime; see Hoock, *Scars of Independence: America's Violent Birth* (New York: Crown, 2017), 164–77. Emily Merrill's dissertation on the British Army offers a nuanced examination of rape and masculinity; see Merrill, "Judging Empire: Masculinity and the Making of the British Imperial Army, 1754–1783" (Ph.D. diss., University of Pennsylvania, 2015), 242–49. See also Mary Beth Norton, *Liberty's Daughters: The Revolutionary Experience of American Women, 1750–1800* (Ithaca, NY: Cornell University Press, 1980), 202–4, and Donald F. Johnson, *Occupied America: British Military Rule and the Experience of Revolution* (Philadelphia: University of Pennsylvania Press, 2020), 94–96. For more on rape and occupation, see E. Susan Barber and Charles F. Ritter, "'Unlawfully and Against Her Consent': Sexual Violence and the Military during the American Civil War," in Heineman, ed., *Sexual Violence in Conflict Zones,* 202–14; E. Susan Barber and Charles F. Ritter, "'Physical Abuse . . . and Rough Handling': Race, Gender, and Sexual Justice in the Occupied South," in *Occupied Women: Gender, Military Occupation, and the American Civil War,* ed. LeeAnn Whites and Alecia P. Long (Baton Rouge: Louisiana State University Press, 2009), 49–64; and Atina Grossmann, "A Question of Silence: The Rape of German Women by Occupation Soldiers," in *West Germany under Construction: Politics, Society, and Culture in the Adenauer Era,* ed. Robert G. Moeller (Ann Arbor: University of Michigan Press, 1997), 33–52. For rape in modern warfare, see Mary Louise Roberts, *What Soldiers Do: Sex and the American GI in World War II France* (Chicago: University of Chicago Press, 2013), 193–254; Cynthia H. Enloe, *Maneuvers: The International Politics of Militarizing Women's Lives* (Berkeley: University of California Press, 2000), 77–103; and Laura Sjoberg, *Gendering Global Conflict: Toward a Feminist Theory of War* (New York: Columbia University Press, 2013), 217–47. For the gendered nature of warfare and the value of feminist approaches to evaluating wartime experience, see Stephanie McCurry, *Women's War: Fighting and Surviving the American Civil War* (Cambridge, MA: Belknap Press of Harvard University Press, 2019); Enloe, *Maneuvers;* and Sjoberg, *Gendering Global Conflict,* esp. 248–78; see also Cynthia H. Enloe, *Bananas, Beaches and Bases Making Feminist Sense of International Politics* (Berkeley: University of California, 1990). For more on violence and archival production, see Marisa J. Fuentes, *Dispossessed Lives: Enslaved Women, Violence, and the Archive* (Philadelphia: University of Pennsylvania Press, 2016).

5. For sexual assault, urban space, and movement, see Cahill, *Rethinking Rape,* 158–61.

6. Elaine Forman Crane, ed., *The Diary of Elizabeth Drinker* (Boston: Northeastern University Press, 1991), 1:269 (22 December 1777), 1:264 (14 December 1777).

7. Sharon Block, *Rape and Sexual Power in Early America* (Chapel Hill: University of North Carolina Press, 2006), 240–41.

8. For more on these dynamics, see Block, "Rape in the American Revolution," 25–29.

9. For more on the "rhetoric of rape" in the American Revolution, see Block, "Rape in the American Revolution," 34–36.

10. This trend is also true for scholarship on rape in the American Revolution; see Block, "Rape in the American Revolution," and Hoock, "*Jus in Bello.*"

11. Maeve Kane, "'She Did Not Open Her Mouth Further': Haudenosaunee Women as Military and Political Targets during and after the American Revolution," in *Women in the American Revolution: Gender, Politics, and the Domestic World*, ed. Barbara B. Oberg (Charlottesville: University of Virginia Press, 2019), 92.

12. Block, "Rape without Women," 852–64, 862 (quotation); Block, "Rape in the American Revolution," 34–36.

13. Block, "Rape without Women," 852–64.

14. As Emily Merrill notes, these courts martial were "exceptional" because they were "very strong, unambiguous cases with multiple witnesses"; see Merrill, "Judging Empire," 247. I am not the first scholar to inspect these records: Mary Beth Norton examined them within the changing patterns of women's lives during the Revolution; Sharon Block analyzed them to uncover discourses of rape; Holger Hoock examined them as evidence of wartime violence. I analyzed these narratives to understand how wartime sexual violence and the threat of rape structured women's lives and altered their relationship to space. See Norton, *Liberty's Daughters*, 202–4; Block, "Rape in the American Revolution"; and Hoock, "*Jus in Bello.*"

15. Block, "Rape in the American Revolution," 27, 30–33; Merrill, "Judging Empire," 247.

16. Block, "Rape in the American Revolution," 25–30, 32; Merrill, "Judging Empire," 245–49. For rape in early America broadly, see Block, *Rape and Sexual Power*; Barbara S. Lindemann, "'To Ravish and Carnally Know': Rape in Eighteenth-Century Massachusetts," *Signs* 10, no. 1 (1 October 1984): 63–82; Cornelia Hughes Dayton, *Women before the Bar: Gender, Law, and Society in Connecticut, 1639–1789* (Chapel Hill: University of North Carolina Press, 1995), 231–84; Wendy Anne Warren, "'The Cause of Her Grief': The Rape of a Slave in Early New England," *Journal of American History* 93, no. 4 (March 2007): 1031–49; and Thomas Foster, *Sex and the Eighteenth-Century Man: Massachusetts and the History of Sexuality in America* (Boston: Beacon Press, 2007), 53–75. See also Anna Clark, *Women's Silence, Men's Violence: Sexual Assault in England, 1770–1845* (London: Pandora, 1987).

17. For children, see GCM of John Fisher, Philadelphia, 25 February 1778, WO 71/85, National Archives of the United Kingdom, Kew, England (hereafter NAUK); GCM of William Saunders, New York, 6–12 August 1778, WO 71/90, 85–88, film 675, reel 12, DLAR; and GCM of John Wilson, New York, 17–19 July 1781, WO 91/94, 253–60, film 675, reel 14, DLAR. I have found no cases of adult female camp followers prosecuting soldiers for rape, but for examples of marital violence, see GCM of Alexander Munroe, New York, 17–22 July 1780, WO 71/92, 217–22, film 675, reel 14, DLAR, and GCM of John Lindon, New York, 17–21 February 1781, WO 71/93, 196–98, film 675, reel 14, DLAR.

18. Merrill, "Judging Empire," 247. Strategically, it was also to the British Army's advantage to enforce discipline and cultivate amiable relations with civilians; see Hoock, "Jus in Bello," 84. For more on dynamics between officers and enlisted men, see Stephen Conway, "To Subdue America: British Army Officers and the Conduct of the Revolutionary War," *William and Mary Quarterly*, 3rd series, 43, no. 3 (July 1986): 381–407, and Conway, "'The Great Mischief Complain'd Of': Reflections on the Misconduct of British Soldiers in the Revolutionary War," *William and Mary Quarterly*, 3rd series, 47, no. 3 (1990): 370–90.

19. Hoock, "Jus in Bello," 79. For more on how race and class determined men's capacity to coerce sex, see Block, *Rape and Sexual Power*, 4, 63–80, 163–209.

20. Merrill, "Judging Empire," 247.

21. Cahill, *Rethinking Rape*, 27, 36, 48–49, 117–33. For early America specifically, see Block. *Rape and Sexual Power*, 7.

22. To be sure, flirtation and courtship were also prevalent in British-occupied cities. Although these interactions took place at all levels of society, contemporary observers often focused on interactions between British officers and elite White women, suggesting again how notions of class and race informed perceptions of social life under British rule. See Darlene Emmert Fisher, "Social Life in Philadelphia during the British Occupation," *Pennsylvania History* 37, no. 3 (July 1970): esp. 243–44, 246, and Serena R. Zabin, *The Boston Massacre: A Family History* (Boston: Houghton Mifflin Harcourt, 2020), 79–108. For backlash against this socialization, see Susan E. Klepp, "Rough Music on Independence Day: Philadelphia, 1778," in *Riot and Revelry in Early America*, ed. William Pencak, Matthew Dennis, and Simon P. Newman (University Park: Pennsylvania State University Press, 2002), 156–78. For gentility and British officers, see Judith L. Van Buskirk, *Generous Enemies: Patriots and Loyalists in Revolutionary New York* (Philadelphia: University of Pennsylvania Press, 2002), 73–105.

23. For testimonies as agency, particularly in regard to sexual coercion, see Terri L. Snyder, *Brabbling Women: Disorderly Speech and the Law in Early Virginia* (Ithaca, NY: Cornell University Press, 2003), 47, 49, 62–64. For testimonies as retaliation against terror and reaffirmations of women's

humanity, see Danielle L. McGuire, "'It Was Like All of Us Had Been Raped': Sexual Violence, Community Mobilization, and the African American Freedom Struggle," *Journal of American History* 91, no. 3 (December 2004): 906–31, esp. 907–8, 910. For more on the power of women's speech in early America, see Mary Beth Norton, *Founding Mothers and Fathers: Gendered Power and the Forming of American Society* (New York: Vintage Books, 1996), 253–69. For agency and subjectivity, see Cahill, *Rethinking Rape*, 13, 25–28, 109–42, esp. 130–32.

24. For community during the war, see Van Buskirk, *Generous Enemies*. For rape and community mobilization, see McGuire, "'It Was Like All of Us.'"

25. For more on archival silences and women who are made historically "visible through violence," see Fuentes, *Dispossessed Lives*, 124–43, 126 (quotation), and Warren, "'The Cause of Her Grief.'"

26. GCM of Timothy Spillman, Boston, 12–28 December 1775, WO 71/82, 250, 252, 251, 254, 253, 255–56, film 675, reel 8, DLAR. Spillman was found guilty and sentenced to receive one thousand lashes on his bare back with a cat-of-nine tails (256). Hill is listed in *A List of the General and Field-Officers, as They Rank in the Army; of the Officers in the Several Regiments of Horse, Dragoons, and Foot, on the British and Irish Establishments* (London: J. Millan, 1775), 113.

27. In many ways Anne Moore's experience was unusual for women during the American Revolution: she knew the British soldier who assaulted her and had previously interacted with him; see GCM of Spillman, WO 71/82, 252, DLAR. For more on these dynamics, see Block, "Rape in the American Revolution," 27–30.

28. Caroline Gilman, ed., *Letters of Eliza Wilkinson, during the Invasion and Possession of Charlestown, S.C., by the British in the Revolutionary War* (New York: Samuel Colman, 1839), 98 (Letter XI).

29. GCM of Thomas Bishop, New York, 16–24 November 1779, WO 71/91, 3, film 675, reel 13, DLAR.

30. Crane, ed., *Diary of Elizabeth Drinker*, 1:269 (24 December 1777), 1:289 (17 March 1778). See also Paul E. Kopperman, "'The Cheapest Pay': Alcohol Abuse in the Eighteenth-Century British Army," *Journal of Military History* 60, no. 3 (July 1996): 445–70.

31. Catherine Dudley to Charles Dudley, 19 November 1775, Dudley Papers, 1768–1837, Newport Historical Society, Newport, RI.

32. For errands, see Sarah Logan Fisher Diary, 31 January 1778, Historical Society of Pennsylvania, Philadelphia; Crane, ed., *Diary of Elizabeth Drinker*, 1:241–42 (9–11 October 1777); 1:246 (18 October 1777). For honor, see Arthur N. Gilbert, "Law and Honour among Eighteenth-Century British Army Officers," *Historical Journal* 19, no. 1 (1976): 75–87; Robert Shoemaker, "Male Honour and the Decline of Public Violence in Eighteenth-Century London," *Social History* 26, no. 2 (2001): 190–208,

and Michèle Cohen, "'Manners' Make the Man: Politeness, Chivalry, and the Construction of Masculinity, 1750–1830," *Journal of British Studies* 44, no. 2 (2005): 312–29.

33. GCM of Robert Brown and John Dillon, Philadelphia, January 7, 1778, WO 71/85, 207, NAUK. In the proceedings, Isabella Mitchell is referred to as both Isobel and Isabella. I use "Isabella" because it accompanies her own testimony. The lack of attention to her name is nevertheless suggestive of how the British Army regarded Black women and the racial dynamics of the courtroom.

34. GCM of Brown and Dillon, WO 71/85, 206, NAUK. These are Catherine Stone's descriptions of the men as related by Lieutenant Robert Douglas of the Royal Artillery (205).

35. GCM of Brown and Dillon, WO 71/85, 203, 209, 206–7, 204, NAUK. For the law, see Block, *Rape and Sexual Violence*, 128–42. For lesser charges, see Merrill, "Judging Empire," 242, and GCM of Brown and Dillon, WO 71/85, 203, NAUK.

36. GCM of Brown and Dillon, WO 71/85, 209, 203, 204–5, NAUK.

37. For the quotation, see Billy Gordon Smith, *The "Lower Sort": Philadelphia's Laboring People, 1750—1800* (Ithaca, NY: Cornell University Press, 1994).

38. GCM of Brown and Dillon, WO 71/85, 204, 206, 208–9, 207, NAUK.

39. For more on perceptions of sailors, see Paul A. Gilje, *Liberty on the Waterfront: American Maritime Culture in the Age of Revolution* (Philadelphia: University of Pennsylvania Press, 2004), 6–14.

40. GCM of Brown and Dillon, WO 71/85, 206, 209, NAUK.

41. For more on Black women, rape, and sexual coercion, see Block, *Rape and Sexual Power*, 67–74, and Warren, "'The Cause of Her Grief.'"

42. GCM of Brown and Dillon, WO 71/85, 205, NAUK.

43. This is the only incident I have discovered documenting soldiers' rape of Black women—a silence that in and of itself suggests the different treatment between White and Black victims. For more on these archival silences, race, and gender, see Fuentes, *Dispossessed Lives*.

44. GCM of Brown and Dillon, WO 71/85, 203–4, NAUK.

45. GCM of Brown and Dillon, WO 71/85, 203, NAUK. Although the men were charged with "ill using" both women, the entirety of the preceding trial focused on Stone's assault.

46. GCM of Brown and Dillon, WO 71/85, 209, 212, NAUK.

47. Deposition of Lucretia Radfield, Fairfield, CT, 21 July 1779, Papers of the Continental Congress, Papers and Affidavits Relating to the Plunderings, Burnings, and Ravages Committed by the British, 1775–84 (hereafter CC British Plundering), 244, M247, roll 66, National Archives and Records Administration, Washington, DC (hereafter NARA).

48. Deposition of Sarah Townsend, New Haven, 26 July 1779, CC British Plundering, 232, NARA.

49. Mary Beth Norton has suggested that this "rampage of rape" was perhaps a consequence of British frustration at Washington's successful escape into Pennsylvania, which prolonged the war and dispelled soldiers' illusions of a quick and easy victory. See Norton, *Liberty's Daughters*, 202–4, 202 (quotation).

50. Deposition of Abagail Palmer, Hunterdon County, NJ, 22 March 1777, CC British Plundering, 31, NARA. For more on the rhetoric and public depictions of rape during the war, see Block, "Rape in the American Revolution," 35–36; see also Block, "Rape without Women." For more on the congressional investigations of British rape, including the incident at the Palmer house, see Hoock, "*Jus in Bello*," 84–87.

51. Deposition of Sarah Cain, Hunterdon County, NJ, 22 March 1777, CC British Plundering, 35, NARA.

52. Deposition of Mary Phillips, Hunterdon County, NJ, 22 March 1777, CC British Plundering, 37, NARA.

53. Deposition of Palmer, CC British Plundering and Ravaging, 31, NARA; Deposition of Elisabeth Cain, Hunterdon County, NJ, 22 March 1777, CC British Plundering, 29, NARA.

54. Deposition of Mary Campbell, Hunterdon County, NJ, 22 March 1777, CC British Plundering, 33, NARA.

55. Deposition of Christiana Gatter, New Haven, CT, 26 July 1779, CC British Plundering, 237, NARA.

56. Deposition of Martin Gatter, CC British Plundering, 237, NARA; Deposition of Christiana Gatter, CC British Plundering, 238, NARA.

57. According to the 1790 census, Phebe Coe owned no enslaved servants and lived only with her daughter. A man identified as "free Mingo" lived in the household of Coe's neighbor Joseph Haviland, so perhaps this was the man present the day of the assault. See 1790 Census, New York, Queens County, Newtown Township, 19, Ancestry.com.

58. According to Coe, Abigail was "so helpless as not to be able to walk alone nor to dress or feed herself"; see GCM of Bartholomew McDonough, Brooklyn, NY, 24 July–1 August 1778, WO 71/86, 200, film 675, reel 10, DLAR.

59. GCM of McDonough, WO 71/86, 202, DLAR.

60. GCM of McDonough, WO 71/86, 201–2, 200, DLAR.

61. GCM of McDonough, WO 71/86, 200–202, DLAR. McDonough was found guilty and sentenced to death (206).

62. GCM of McDonough, WO 71/86, 201–2, DLAR.

63. Cahill, *Rethinking Rape*, 111; Rebecca Campbell, "The Psychological Impact of Rape Victims' Experiences with the Legal, Medical, and Mental Health Systems," *American Psychologist* 63, no. 8 (November 2008): 702–17.

64. For snow, see Crane, ed., *Diary of Elizabeth Drinker*, 1:287 (3 March 1778).

65. GCM of Silver Crispin and Mary O'Hara, Philadelphia, 6 March 1778, WO 71/85, 368, NAUK.

66. GCM of Crispin and O'Hara, WO 71/85, 368–70, NAUK.
67. For more on this, see Block, "Rape in the American Revolution," 28.
68. GCM of Crispin and O'Hara, WO 71/85, 368–69, NAUK.
69. GCM of Crispin and O'Hara, WO 71/85, 367, 370, NAUK. The charges against Silver Crispin and Mary O'Hara were ultimately dropped as "trifling, & frivolous."
70. GCM of Brown and Dillon, WO 71/85, 206, NAUK.
71. GCM of Thomas Gorman, Brooklyn, NY, 24 July–1 August 1778, WO 71/86, 173, film 675, reel 10, DLAR. Gorman alleged that the two were having an affair, that Sarah Willis "was as willing as he was," and that the press gang deception was Willis's idea. The rape charges, Gorman insisted, arose from her husband's jealousy (174). His testimony suggests the fine line between coercive sex and prostitution, noting that "he once gave her a Dollar & has always been welcome at the house." The court martial acquitted Gorman and found him not guilty (174). For more on coercion and consent, see Block, *Rape and Sexual Power*, 27–28.
72. Deposition of Rose Luke, New Haven, CT, 27 July 1779, CC British Plundering, 234, 235, NARA.

Neighbors, Land Ladies, and Consorts

New Jersey Women in the Midst of the Continental Army

STEVEN ELLIOTT

—◊◊◊◊◊◊—

Following the Battle of Princeton on 3 January 1777, General George Washington's forces marched northward to secure winter quarters in northern New Jersey and New York's Hudson Highlands. Continental Army officers and soldiers quartered on the inhabitants, filling civilian homes and public buildings with tired, sometimes undisciplined Continentals. The local families who hosted them, willingly or not, found themselves living in the midst of an army and engaged in civil-military negotiations sometimes complicated by gendered presumptions.

Susannah French Livingston, wife of William, New Jersey's Whig governor, experienced the complications firsthand. The British offensive had displaced the state's leading political family from their Elizabeth-town home. Like many refugees, Susannah moved in with a relative. Her brother-in-law Major General William Alexander (also known as Lord Stirling) of the Continental Army hosted her at his estate in Basking Ridge, New Jersey. Stirling, like many Jersey homeowners, also accommodated Continental soldiers and officers at his house.[1]

Susannah Livingston's stay at the crowded domicile in Basking Ridge lasted only until May and ended on a sour note. Stirling was a less than gracious host, and word had reached Washington. The commander in chief chided his subordinate for the latter's rude conduct and reminded him that gender and social rank mattered in these situations. Livingston's "character, connections, sex, and situation" entitled her, in Washington's mind, to "a degree of respect and consideration" that Stirling had denied her. Stirling retorted that Livingston's continued presence in his home greatly inconvenienced his family as well. Ultimately, the governor's wife found lodgings elsewhere in the state.[2]

A few months after Susannah Livingston's spat with Stirling, her daughter discovered how soldiers billeted in one's home could result in more than inconveniences. Catherine Livingston returned to her family's home in Elizabethtown in November 1777 to find it converted into a militia guard house. In the guards' six-week occupation of the home, she claimed they had "done ten times the mischief to the house than the Hessians." The militia had stripped the home of many of its valuables, and even panes of glass, wallpaper, furniture, and lead from the roof. They also burned the mahogany banisters and timber from the family property for firewood.[3] Together, the Livingston women's experiences encapsulated the many difficulties New Jersey civilians faced: displacement, residing in someone else's house, and living alongside an army. Even though the Livingston women came from an elite family, they suffered slights and abuses from Continental officers and plunder from soldiers.

How did women living in martial zones such as northern New Jersey contend with the difficulties that hosting, sometimes unwillingly, an army attended? What choices did they make when faced with soldiers' frequent disruptions to their daily lives? Historians of women in the American Revolution have commonly explored questions of women's service and motivation on what might be termed the home front. Away from the active combat theaters, women paraded and protested, contributed money and clothing to the cause, and bore the hardships of maintaining households while men were away fighting.[4] Other scholars have focused on the women who accompanied the army on campaign, filling roles as nurses, washerwomen, and domestic servants. Noncombatants who served alongside the army and fulfilled a vital role in keeping it in the field formed part of a "Continental community."[5] In between, and sometimes straddling defined military and civilian community lines, were the regions that experienced a prolonged military presence. One of those was northern New Jersey, which occupied a gray area between battlefront and home front.[6]

This essay focuses on the female inhabitants of that New Jersey "gray" area and explores how they responded to the intrusions of an ostensibly friendly army. Military necessities, and the behavior of its members, challenged amicable domestic relations. Women's experiences in wartime New Jersey's martial zone fell into three broad categories:

First were those of the landladies providing accommodations to officers and soldiers. Second were those of women who dealt with romantic and sexual advances and, occasionally, suffered attacks from service members. Third, nonelite women took an active role in sustaining the war effort by working at the various army depots and posts scattered throughout the region. Together, these women formed a group distinctly separate from the home-front women operating far from theaters of conflict or from the officers' wives and common camp followers that have been typically associated with women's military participation. They did not follow the army, but through strategic geography found themselves living with it.

This essay thereby pushes beyond earlier conceptions of women's support of the army centered on "camp followers," finding instead an extended Continental community that stretched into headquarters houses, garrison towns, and supply depots distant from the scenes of active campaigns. Furthermore, it confirms that Jersey women were not a monolith, and their experiences differed according to social standing and marital status. Their motivations likewise varied: some shared their homes and contributed their labor out of support for independence, but others displayed loyalist sympathies or no clear attachments to either side. Nevertheless, as landladies, consorts, and working neighbors, all faced a set of choices defined by their gender.

LANDLADIES

Along with their male counterparts, women homeowners faced the task of providing the Continentals with shelter. Early in the war, common soldiers frequently billeted with civilians while on campaign, especially during winter when the army tended to remain in place for up to six months. Homeowners consequently endured prolonged occupations of their houses. New Jersey witnessed widespread billeting in the first half of 1777. Plundering soon followed wherever soldiers quartered. Washington's army, led by inexperienced officers and exhausted from a long campaign, rapidly gave in to a marauding spirit that prevailed throughout the winter and spring.[7]

Civilians enjoyed few legal protections against quartering. As historian John Gilbert McCurdy has shown, while English law had restricted the presence of soldiers in private homes since the late seventeenth century, legislatures, courts, and military commanders contested the legal restrictions throughout the eighteenth century. No consensus on the legality of quartering developed by 1775, however, and populations in

different localities varied in their attitudes toward the presence of soldiers in civilian spaces.[8]

Eighteenth-century gender constructions identified the home as the
primary sphere of female duty in colonial America. Within this framework, the public sphere was a male domain while women toiled to maintain the household alongside their families. The Revolution complicated
this arrangement. Men departed their homes for military service, leaving behind women to manage the household alone as "deputy husbands."
Whether New Jersey women remained domestic managers attached to
their husbands or operated independently as deputy husbands, they
confronted a direct challenge to the domestic sphere whenever soldiers
sought billets.

Officers and their poorly disciplined men frequently ignored women's
authority in domestic spaces. Civilians suspected of sympathy for the
Crown faced particular distress. Catherine van Cortlandt, a loyalist
woman living in Hanover, New Jersey, strove to maintain the household
as a deputy husband while her partner lived in British-held New York.
She admitted, however, that the arrival of the patriot army in the region
in January 1777 "tested her resolution to its utmost strength." She suffered soldiers in her home and animal teams in her barn, "without even
the ceremony of asking liberty." While van Cortlandt conceded that some
officers proved hospitable, a New England company that lodged in her
home for a time struck her as "the dregs of the people."[9] Margaret Morris,
a loyalist-leaning Quaker widow living in West Jersey, experienced similar difficulties with soldiers staying in her home.[10] Yet even families with
impeccable Whig credentials suffered plunder, as Catherine Livingston's
account of depredations at the family estate in Elizabethtown reveal.

In 1782, the New Jersey government offered civilians the opportunity
to file claims for damages inflicted by both armies. Most claims filed by
Morris County residents reported plunder by patriot troops, most of it
occurring in 1777. Women's voices enter the historical record through
some of these documents. Phoebe Freeman, a Morris County resident,
filed claims for stockings, thread, yarn, an apron, silk gloves, and "a Barce-
lona handkerchief," taken by "the Continental Army, as they were quartered in the house at the time."[11] Sarah Dickenson filed a claim after the
war in the name of her deceased husband, Peter, for the loss of one "negro
man" valued at fifty pounds, along with a silver punch spoon, a horse,
and six hundred rails and one hundred posts for fences.[12] Phebe Budd
suffered plundering on four occasions between 1776 and 1782, losing an
assortment of clothing items and farm animals.[13]

Other women testified to bolster the claims of neighbors and family members. Abigail Fairchild supported Phineas Fairchild's claim for lost farm animals by reporting that she had seen plundered sheep near a Continental camp.[14] Susannah Marsh testified in support of a neighbor for loss of a calico curtain to "soldiers who frequented the house."[15] These accounts represent only those able and willing to make claims in 1782. Many other civilians suffered damages that went unrecorded. Overall, these women and their families do not stand out as either patriots or loyalists, indicating that soldiers' depredations transcended political fault lines.

Fortunately for homeowners, the Continental Army changed its quartering methods after 1777. During the 1777–78 winter, Washington eschewed billets for log huts. The transition from billets to huts derived from strategic and practical needs rather than concerns for civilian privacy.[16] Nevertheless, the new quartering policy led to a decline in the number of civilians suffering soldiers living in their homes. Some homeowners, however, continued to face requisitions of their houses for officers' quarters.[17]

Changes in civilian law and military practice altered the relationship between homeowner and tenant. In October 1777, the New Jersey legislature passed its first quartering laws. The laws stipulated fines for damages soldiers inflicted on civilian properties and emphasized public buildings such as inns and taverns as the state's preference for soldiers' quarters. Men could only billet in private houses with the approval of local justices of the peace.[18] Emboldened by the provisions of New Jersey's quartering laws, homeowners resisted the Continentals' use of their houses. In the war's early years, officers had claimed that the protection the army afforded homeowners balanced any inconvenience resulting from their presence. But, during the 1778–79 winter at Middlebrook, John Wallace demanded $1,000 compensation for hosting the commander in chief's headquarters. Major General Nathanael Greene, the army's quartermaster general, agreed to pay Wallace in this one instance but declared that a precedent had not been set.[19]

Nevertheless, under the terms of the new laws and standards for hosting officers, women operating as domestic managers sought to control the terms by which officers came into their homes. Since legally married women had no claim to property, wives had little power to influence housing decisions. Widows exercised more authority, and indeed several widow homeowners hosted Continental officers. Regardless of women's marital status, social conventions accorded them the position of domestic manager within the household. Consequently, every instance in which officers billeted in homes posed both a challenge and an opportunity for women. The state quartering laws provided a framework in which female householders could demonstrate their allegiance to republican ideals.

For women suspected of Tory sympathies, offering a home to Continental officers provided a way of protecting their property by exhibiting loyalty, or at least acquiescence, to the patriot cause. Theodosia Bartow Prevost administered her family's estate in Bergen County, New Jersey, while her husband served as an officer in the British Army. By 1778, hardening Whig attitudes meant Prevost faced the confiscation of her home by revolutionary authorities. In July of that year, she contacted George Washington and offered the general the use of her home as a headquarters while the Continental Army passed through the region after the Battle of Monmouth. Washington and his staff stayed at the home for only four days, but this was enough to garner Prevost support. She ultimately kept her house.[20]

Similar to Prevost's case, the experience of patriot homeowner Theodosia Ford illustrates the agency and limitations women encountered in quartering disputes. In late 1779, General Greene selected Ford's mansion on the edge of Morristown for Washington's headquarters. Theodosia's husband, Jacob, had died in 1777, and the family estate remained in the widow Ford's care until her adolescent sons reached maturity.[21] The mother of four therefore had full power to accede to or deny Greene's request. Hosting the commander in chief brought significant disruptions to the home, as the headquarters was also to house his five aides-de-camp, free and enslaved servants, Martha Washington, and other visiting dignitaries. Ford, her children, servants, and enslaved workers also remained in the home.[22]

Questions of status conjoined with practical concerns in the dialogue surrounding quartering. Theodosia Ford occupied a position at the top of the local social scene. Her husband had been a prominent iron forge operator and militia colonel while her father headed the town's Presbyterian church. Her close ties to the region's patriot community may have made it hard for her to say no for the risk of appearing unsupportive of the army. Washington's growing stature as a national hero, and his own reputation for gentlemanly conduct, made the prospect of billeting him and his staff less troublesome for Whig civilian hosts than it may have been for less renowned commanders. Considering Washington's status, Governor Livingston hoped Ford "will not resent that her house has entertained such a general."[23]

Theodosia Ford lacked the presumptions of equal authority that a male gentry homeowner would have carried into a negotiation with the army. Although a wealthy woman, she deferred to Washington's demands for rooms within her home. Washington and his staff thus occupied over half of the house, confining the Ford family and staff to the rooms of the house's kitchen wing. Washington's entourage took up residence in the majority of the home, while his guard camped on the Ford's property in front of the mansion.[24]

The widow Ford did not acquiesce to Washington's presence, however, without seeking compensation. Like many of her neighbors, she sought rent payments in the form of certificates that could hopefully be cashed in at a later date. In the army's haste to depart the home in June 1780, the Continentals failed to issue her such a document. In July, she contacted Colonel Richard Kidder Meade, one of Washington's aides-de-camp, requesting he "procure me a certificate from the general specifying the time how long and the number of rooms occupied."[25] Meade responded within the week with a certificate detailing the army's use of Ford's rooms and grounds. Ford had staked out a middle ground between unqualified support and resistance. This was probably the best she could have hoped for given the circumstances.[26]

By supporting the cause while curtailing military authority over civilian spaces, Ford also showed her allegiance to republican values. Several other area women did the same, acting as landladies and charging officers rent. Catherine Vanderveer charged Brigadier General Henry Knox for the use of her home by artillery staff during the 1778–79 winter.[27] At Morristown, quartermaster records list Hannah Morris and Abigail Whitehead receiving three and six pounds, respectively, for boarding officers.[28]

Women householders also fulfilled traditional roles as hostesses and caregivers for their officer tenants. At Middlebrook, Nathanael Greene's aides William Blodget, Richard Claiborne, and Robert Forsyth wintered in the home of a woman with whom they enjoyed a convivial relationship.[29] Henry Sewall, a Massachusetts lieutenant who spent much of the war encamped in the Hudson Highlands of New York, recorded a similar experience. While lodging with "the Widow Heights," Sewall wrote in his diary, "gratitude obliges me to rank this *woman* among the ranks of my friends. In distress she ministers unto me!"[30]

A more detailed view of women's roles as hostesses comes from the Pennsylvania Line's encampment outside Morristown during the 1780–81 winter. There, Lieutenant Enos Reeves lodged in the home of widow Mary Wick. On 26 December, Reeves spent the afternoon "with the fair sex, some of our agreeable neighbors Miss Wick, Miss Leddell or both." The Miss Wick referred to was Temperance, Mary Wick's twenty-two-year-old daughter. Reeves enjoyed a "pleasant chat" over tea with his companions, whom he described as "the agreeable young ladies."[31] In mid-January, Reeves complimented his hosts, having spent "time very agreeably in this very pleasant family in the constant company of the ever amiable and very agreeable Miss Betsy Leddell and very often with the additional happiness of Miss Wicks' company." Reeves proved loath to quit the company of the local families when his regiment relocated, lamenting "with regret I was forced to part with that agreeable family." Unlike Theodosia Ford, there is no record of Mary Wick seeking rent payments.[32]

CONSORTS

For unmarried officers, winter quarters provided an opportunity to indulge in flirtations with female inhabitants. As historian John A. Ruddiman has pointed out, socialization between Continental officers and women from prominent families helped to normalize connections between military and civilian society.[33] During winter quarters, elite young women and officers stood at the forefront of this normalizing process. Officers viewed social events as opportunities to bolster the army's image of respectability and sought to impress local women at such affairs.

New Jersey's cantonments provided officers ample prospects for socializing. The case of Nathanael Greene's young aides during the Middlebrook winter illustrates how recreation and refinement furthered the army's goal of projecting respectability. Greene's aide Major William Blodget viewed time in camp as an opportunity to mix with the inhabitants. In early 1779, he planned to invite "Mrs. Livingston, Miss Gilly (Lott), and Miss Cornelia Lott" to Middlebrook, along with Colonel William S. Livingston, and hoped to entertain them with a dance "in order to make camp more agreeable to them." Blodget viewed his conduct at the event as an extension of the army's respectable image. He promised to Greene that he and his associates would "do our possibles to make the department shine on the occasion."[34] One of Blodget's companions, Major Robert Forsyth, similarly viewed time in camp as an opportunity to court prominent local women. Forsyth, like Blodget, highlighted the presence of Livingston and the Lott sisters in camp, writing of Blodget's plans for a dance that "I imagine we shall make out very well."[35]

Grand assemblies provided the largest opportunities for socializing at winter quarters for gentlemanly officers and well-to-do women. At Morristown in February 1780, thirty-five officers including Washington, Greene, and their staffs agreed to pay four hundred dollars each to fund a dance assembly to be held in Morristown that month.[36] This idea apparently proved popular among officers and locals alike. By mid-February, 130 officers had subscribed to the assembly, as had 165 women.[37] A newly built house intended to hold the assemblies stood two stories tall, seventy feet long by forty wide, with a main hall and two drawing rooms.[38]

Continentals' diaries and private correspondence reveal that fraternization and projecting a virtuous image comprised only part of their motivations for socializing with local women. So too did loneliness and lust. Lieutenant Henry Sewall's diary indicates its author tended toward introversion, with numerous entries describing reading books rather than frolicking. Nevertheless, in March 1780 he spent the afternoon with the daughters of a local militia colonel while quartered in the Hudson Highlands. Sewall described this occasion as time spent "agreeably" and expressed particular pleasure that the women could "furnish subjects for conversation other than 'yes' or 'no.' And who are not ashamed to discourse with freedom on morality and religion."[39]

Officers did not stand alone in their pursuits of New Jersey's fairer sex. From Middlebrook, Sergeant Asa Worthington wrote that nearby New Brunswick was as "fruitful in good girls as any place I have ever been acquainted with." He described them as "sociable without affectation" and never transgressing the "strictest rules of decency." Worthington also highlighted their physical appeal. "Their beauty," he wrote, "is beyond description as is their wit."[40] But at least one common soldier at Morristown crossed the line from pursuit to assault. In May 1780, a brigade court martial found Private John de Armour guilty of "grossly abusing" local resident Katherine Slover and threatening to burn down her house. The court sentenced Armour to one hundred lashes.[41]

For some Continentals, the frequent moves that attended military service undermined their abilities to form liaisons. Captain Walter Finney of the 10th Pennsylvania Regiment proved particularly desirous for companionship. While stationed in Monmouth County during early 1779, Finney took up quarters in the home of John Little. Enjoying the status and freedom to socialize that came with such a billet, he attended at least three social engagements during his deployment.[42] In April, Finney declared himself "enamored with the ladies of that place." When recalled to Middlebrook that month, however, the Pennsylvania captain complained that just as he had begun to form attachments, the "striking of tents disappoints all our expectations." In sharp contrast to the frolics and flirtations headquarters staff enjoyed that winter, he described the Pennsylvanians' Middlebrook cantonment as the "male monastery on the Millstone." Officers in camp confines were "to live secluded from the enjoyment of the virtuous fair" sex. He joked to a fellow officer that Congress should provide officers with a wife in each state in addition to rations of rum, sugar, and tobacco.[43]

Finney's comment highlights the complicated attitudes patriot officers held toward civilian women. Officers especially carried expectations of gentlemanly conduct that demanded propriety in their interactions with women. Nevertheless, as Continentals passed tedious winter months in a largely male-only world, they experienced bouts of desire and frustration. Walter Finney may have joked when he proposed Congress provide wives in every state, but his equating of women to luxury consumer items such as sugar and tobacco nevertheless objectified them.

At least one Continental did record a New Jersey woman's rejection of an officer's advances. During early 1780, Captain Samuel Shaw sought numerous opportunities to socialize with local women; to his friend Captain Winthrop Sargent he wrote, "To be denied the pleasures we have promised ourselves in Jersey the ensuing winter would be a disappointment second to nothing but an exclusion from Heaven." The unfortunate Sargent had been sent to quarters in a smaller cantonment in the Hudson Highlands where he would not have the opportunity for flirtations with the opposite sex. Nevertheless, Shaw sought to arrange a courtship between Sargent and Cornelia Lott.[44]

During a March dance Shaw found himself paired with Lott, apparently the most sought-after young woman in New Jersey. Shaw used the opportunity to "be serviceable" in his mission for his friend Sargent. Unfortunately for Shaw's friend, Lott did not express any interest in pursuing a relationship with the captain stationed in the camp in the Hudson Highlands. Shaw believed she would remain "exceedingly on her guard in future" should he attempt to again play matchmaker.[45]

Extant sources provide mostly the male side of the story. Would women have found humor in Finney's proposal for congressionally funded concubines? Did the "good girls" of New Brunswick consider Sergeant Worthington as attractive as he did them? Did Henry Sewall's companions find that he furnished worthwhile subjects of conversation? Earlier studies of the war tended to romanticize the interactions between women and soldiers, as when historian Elizabeth Cometti wrote in 1947 that "marching soldiers never failed to bring women to the windows and fences."[46] The journal of Sally Wister, an adolescent Quaker living outside Philadelphia, records her mild flirtations with officers passing through her family's home during the Pennsylvania campaign.[47] And the continued presence of women at Continental balls indicates their interest in fraternization. Nevertheless, the loneliness evident in many officers' writings, and the outright rejection several experienced, shows that women set boundaries to these romantic advances.

Overall, the prolonged presence of the Continental Army near civilian populations fostered mixed-gender socialization. Traveling through New Jersey in 1781, the Marquis de Chastellux stopped at the home of Philip Van Horne near Middlebrook. Van Horne had frequently hosted Continental officers traversing the Raritan Valley. To Chastellux, Van Horne's daughter Harriet "appeared to be on terms of great familiarity with one of the young officers," but the marquis later discovered that despite their close contact, there was not "any idea of marriage between them." Chastellux shared this anecdote with his readers "only to show the extreme liberty that prevails in this country between the two sexes, as long as they are not married."[48] Despite Chastellux's observations, Continentals did marry local women. At the comparatively small and brief encampment at Redding, Connecticut, one local clergyman recorded eight marriages between Continentals and locals during early 1779.[49] In May 1781, Colonel Samuel Blachley Webb married Elizabeth Bancker, a resident of the Raritan Valley countryside adjacent to the Middlebrook encampment.[50] At least some women had proved open to romantic attachments with their military neighbors.

NEIGHBORS

Local women also worked for the army. The Continental Army's ongoing operations around New York led to a large-scale buildup of military infrastructure in northern New Jersey after 1778. Unlike the women throughout the colonies who contributed food, money, and clothing from a distance, female Jerseyans took part in a wider variety of tasks that facilitated military operations in the region. Cantonments, storehouses, hospitals, and artificers' camps all sprang up in the region stretching from the Delaware to the Hudson, drawing labor from surrounding civilian populations. Women appear occasionally in pay records of local quartermasters. Residents of a war-torn region, they may have worked to help families devastated by marauding armies or compensate for lost labor of male family members serving, wounded, or dead. Many may have similarly served out of allegiance to the revolutionary cause.

Women worked mostly in jobs traditionally ascribed to their gender. For example, Mary Delois served for four months in early 1779 as a cook for an artificers' regiment stationed at Morristown. Amanda Davis likewise cooked for the artificers in July. Sarah Meeker earned ten dollars in March 1779 for "keeping sick soldiers." Ann Davis was paid for washing army tents and "sundries" in May of that year, presumably in preparation for the army's departure from its log huts that June. Elizabeth Thompson, who was to serve as a cook for Washington's staff during his stay at the Ford House, received ninety dollars for similar work in August 1779, also for cooking for the artificers.[51]

Ladies from all over northern New Jersey contributed to the war effort by selling supplies and services. In 1781 and 1782, Ann Janney in Morris County received certificates for renting a room to a Continental storekeeper. Sarah Davis of Essex County, Elizabeth Pearson of Morris County, and Rebecca Hunnywell of Sussex each sold up to one ton of hay to the army. Rachel Morris of Hunterdon County sold "one fat sheep" in December 1780.[52] That quartermaster records identified women as the recipients of payment indicates that they likely operated independently. Numerous women may have also contributed their labor under the authority of male householders, but their work went unrecorded in army ledgers.

Women made their largest impact on clothing the army. The records of Commissioner of Clothing David Olden during 1777–79 include numerous payments to women. New Jersey's ladies provided blankets, cloth, stockings, hose, and thread. Sarah Davidson sold one pair of mittens in January 1778. In late July, Olden paid three women for making twenty-two shirts. In April 1779, he paid "Joseph Dennis' Wife" for six pounds of nails. Hannah Carman provided pewter and lead. Not all women's support came in the form of goods. Anne Hight was paid for "breaking linen" in May 1778. Twice in June she bleached thirty-five yards of cloth.[53]

In this manner, local civilian workers provided ancillary services to the army similar to those contributed by the community following the army. Nurses, sutlers, laundresses, and servants helped keep the Continentals in the field but moved with the army when it departed for its campaigns. Local women, by contrast, helped sustain the extensive military infrastructure undergirding the patriots' military. Rear-area duties and contributions of supplies formed another component of an extended Continental community.

WOMEN IN New Jersey's martial zones lived through the War for American Independence within the confines of gender roles that prescribed their opportunities to ameliorate its effects. They experienced wide-spread disruptions to the rhythms of domestic life and suffered the loss of property to marauding soldiers. Yet, as household managers, they stood at the forefront of disputes over quartering soldiers in houses and negotiated with military authorities to limit officers' access to homes and ensure financial restitution for the inconvenience of hosting. Some New Jersey ladies opened their homes as a form of political statement and contributed to the cause by playing an active role as hostesses. Others upheld republican values by charging rent and limiting military authority.

Throughout the war, women faced romantic and sexual advances of officers and enlisted men alike. Many of these seem to have occurred within a formalized framework of army-sponsored balls and other more personal social occasions, wherein, given the disappointment evident in some officers' writings, women exercised a degree of discretion in their choices of partners, just as they sought to do in sharing their homes. In a few cases, however, women faced violations of not just their homes but also their bodies. They dealt with threats as they contemplated opportunities.

Eighteenth-century gender conventions limited women politically and militarily, but they could, and many did, labor for Continental quartermasters and artificers. In recent decades, historians have highlighted the many ways in which women contributed to the war effort, as well as the impact the Revolution had on women's lives. The experiences of New Jersey women residing in the midst of a prolonged military occupation reveal the complexities of women's wartime challenges and contributions. As assertive landladies, discerning consorts, and supportive neighbors, they provided vital material and moral support to the Continental Army but sought to do so on their own terms.

NOTES

1. Susannah French Livingston to William Livingston, 7 February 1777, in *The Papers of William Livingston*, ed. Carl E. Prince and Dennis P. Ryan (Trenton: New Jersey Historical Commission, 1980), 1:218–19.

2. George Washington to Lord Stirling and Stirling to Washington, 6 May 1777, in *The Papers of George Washington, Revolutionary War Series*, ed. W. W. Abbot et al. (Charlottesville: University of Virginia Press, 1987–), 9:358–59, 359–60.

3. Catherine W. Livingston to Sarah Livingston and John Jay, 21 November 1777, in *In the Words of Women: The Revolutionary War and the Birth of the Nation, 1765–1799*, ed. Louise V. North, Janet M. Wedge, and Linda Freeman (New York: Lexington Books, 2011), 112–13.

4. For the broad categories of women's participation, see Elizabeth Cometti, "Women in the American Revolution," *New England Quarterly* 20, no. 3 (1947): 329–46. For works dealing with women's motivations and the impact of the Revolution on women's lives, see Linda K. Kerber, *Women of the Republic: Intellect and Ideology in Revolutionary America* (Chapel Hill: University of North Carolina Press, 1980), and Mary Beth Norton, *Liberty's Daughters: The Revolutionary Experience of American Women, 1750–1800* (Ithaca, NY: Cornell University Press, 1980).

5. Standard accounts of camp followers include Holly A. Mayer, *Belonging to the Army: Camp Followers and Community during the American Revolution* (Columbia: University of South Carolina Press, 1999), and Nancy K. Loane, *Following the Drum: Women at the Valley Forge Encampment* (Washington, DC: Potomac Books, 2009).

6. For more on this concept, see James J. Gigantino II, ed., *New Jersey in the American Revolution: Where the Battlefront Meets the Homefront* (New Brunswick, NJ: Rivergate, 2015).

7. For an overview of the campaign, see David Hackett Fischer, *Washington's Crossing* (New York: Oxford University Press, 2004).

8. John Gilbert McCurdy, *Quarters: The Accommodation of the British Army and the Coming of the American Revolution* (Ithaca, NY: Cornell University Press, 2019), 50–88.

9. H. O. H. Vernon-Jackson, "A Loyalist's Wife: Letters of Mrs. Philip Van Cortlandt, December 1776–February 1777," *History Today* 14, no. 8 (August 1964): 575–77.

10. Margaret Morris, *Private Journal Kept during a Portion of the Revolutionary War* (Philadelphia: Privately Printed, 1836).

11. Damage Claim of Phoebe Freeman, Revolutionary War Damage Claims, Morris County, New Jersey State Archives, Trenton.

12. Damage Claim of Sarah Dickenson, ibid.

13. Damage Claim of Phebe Budd, ibid.

14. Damage Claim of Phineas Fairchild, ibid.

15. Damage Claim of George O'Hara, supporting testimony, ibid.

16. For the debate before Valley Forge, see Wayne K. Bodle, "Generals and 'Gentlemen': Pennsylvania Politics and the Decision for Valley Forge," *Pennsylvania History* 62 (Winter 1995): 60–64, and Benjamin H. Newcomb, "Washington's Generals and the Decision to Camp at Valley Forge," *Pennsylvania Magazine of History and Biography* 117, no. 4 (October 1993): 313. For the winter encampment and the role of huts as housing instead of billets, see Jacqueline Thibaut, *In the True Rustic Order: Material Aspects of the Valley Forge Encampment, 1777–1778* (Washington, DC: National Park Service, 1980).

17. Carl Prince, *Middlebrook: The American Eagle's Nest* (Somerville, NJ: Somerset Press, 1957); Samuel Stelle Smith, *The Darkest Winter: Morristown, 1780* (Monmouth Beach, NJ: Philip Frenau Press, 1980).

18. *Journal of the Proceedings of the Legislative Council of the State of New Jersey* (Trenton, NJ: Isaac Collins, 1779), 18, 42; State of New-York, *An Act for Regulating Impress of Forage and Carriages, and for Billeting Troops within this State* (Poughkeepsie, NY: John Holt, 1778).

19. Nathanael Greene to John Wallace, 5 July 1779; Greene to Sidney Berry, 23 June 1779, in *The Papers of Nathanael Greene*, ed. Richard K. Showman, Dennis R. Conrad, and Roger N. Parks (Chapel Hill: University of North Carolina Press, 1976–2005), 5:205–6, 177–78.

20. Delight W. Dodyk, "Troublesome Times a-Coming: The American Revolution and New Jersey Women," in *New Jersey in the American Revolution*, ed. Barbara J. Mitnick (New Brunswick, NJ: Rivergate, 2005), 144–45.

21. Theodore Thayer, *Colonial and Revolutionary Morris County* (Morristown, NJ: Morris County Heritage Commission, 1975), 174.

22. Loane, *Following the Drum*, 38.

23. William Livingston to Timothy Johnes, 10 December 1779, in Prince and Ryan, eds., *Livingston Papers*, 3:256. For Washington's stay at the house, see Smith, *Darkest Winter*, 20–21. For Theodosia Ford and her family, see Jude M. Pfister, *The Fords of New Jersey: Power and Family during America's Founding* (Charleston, SC: History Press, 2010).

24. Thayer, *Colonial and Revolutionary Morris County*, 230–31.

25. Theodosia Ford to George Washington, 21 July 1780, George Washington Papers Online Edition, Library of Congress, Washington, DC, https://www.loc.gov/item/mgw424438.

26. Richard Kidder Meade to Theodosia Ford, 26 July 1780, in *The Writings of George Washington from the Original Manuscript Sources, 1745–1799*, ed. John C. Fitzpatrick (Washington, DC: U.S. Government Printing Office, 1931–54), 19:262.

27. Henry Knox, Purchases from Catherine Vanderveer, 4 June 1779, Henry Knox Papers, Gilder Lehrman Online Collection, New-York Historical Society, http://www.americanhistory.amdigital.co.uk.proxy.libraries.rutgers.edu/Documents/Images/GLC02437.08490/0.

28. Joseph Lewis, Return of Certificates Given in Specie, 1 May 1780, Lloyd W. Smith Collection, Morristown National Historical Park, Morriswn, NJ.

29. William Blodget to Nathanael Greene, 25 January 1779, in Showman, Conrad, and Parks, eds., *Greene Papers*, 3:181.

30. Henry Sewall Diary, 21 March 1780, Massachusetts Historical Society, Boston.

31. Enos Reeves to Unknown, 28 December 1780, in "Extracts from the Letter Book of Enos Reeves, of the Pennsylvania Line," *Pennsylvania Magazine of History and Biography* 20, no. 4 (1896): 472.

32. Enos Reeves to Unknown, 14 January 1781, in "Extracts from the Letter Book of Enos Reeves, of the Pennsylvania Line," *Pennsylvania Magazine of History and Biography* 21 (1897): 77, 80–81.

33. John A. Ruddiman, *Becoming Men of Some Consequence: Youth and Military Service in the Revolutionary War* (Charlottesville: University of Virginia Press, 2014), 130.

34. William Blodget to Nathanael Greene, 25 January 1779, in Showman, Conrad, and Parks, eds., *Greene Papers*, 3:181.

35. Robert Forsyth to Nathanael Greene, 25 January 1779, in ibid., 3:182.

36. Subscription List to Dance Assembly, n.d., in ibid., 5:408.

37. Ebenezer Huntington to Samuel B. Webb, 16 February 1780, in Samuel Blachley Webb, *Reminiscences of General Samuel B. Webb of the Revolutionary Army*, ed. J. Watson Webb et. al. (New York: Globe, 1882), 204–5.

38. Walter Stewart to J. M. Nesbitt, 1 February 1780, Walter Stewart Papers, Library of Congress.

39. Henry Sewall Diary, 21, 26 March 1780.

40. Asa Worthington to Ebenezer Foote, 28 May 1779, Sol Feinstone Collection, David Library of the American Revolution, American Philosophical Society, Philadelphia.

41. Brigade Orders, 26 May 1780, Stark's Brigade Orderly Book, Morristown National Historical Park.

42. Walter Finney, "The Walter Finney Diary," ed. Joseph Lee Boyle, *New Jersey History* 121 (2003): 46–47.

43. Walter Finney to William McPherson, 28 April 1779, McPherson Collection, Library of Congress.

44. Samuel Shaw to Winthrop Sargent, 17 November 1779, in Samuel Shaw, "Samuel Shaw's Revolutionary War Letters to Captain Winthrop Sargent," *Pennsylvania Magazine of History and Biography* 70, no. 3 (July 1946): 306–8.

45. Ibid.

46. Cometti, "Women in the Revolution," 341.

47. Albert C. Myers, ed., *Sally Wister's Journal: A True Narrative* (Philadelphia: Ferris and Leach, 1902), 76–77, 113–14.

48. Francois Jean, Marquis de Chastellux, *Travels in North America in the Years 1780, 1781 and 1782* (London: G. G. J. and J. Robinson, 1787), 1:79.

49. Charles Burr Todd, *History of Redding Connecticut* (New York: John Gray Press, 1880), 74.

50. Philip R. Griffin, "Samuel Blachley Webb: Wethersfield's Abelest Officer," *Journal of the American Revolution*, September 2016, https://allthings liberty.com/2016/09/samuel-blachley-webb-1753-1807/.

51. James Abeel Account Book, entries for 12 March, 27 July 1779, 5 August 1780, Society of the Cincinnati, Washington, DC.

52. Dorothy Agans Stratford and Thomas B. Wilson, *Certificates and Receipts of Revolutionary New Jersey* (Lambertville, NJ: Hunterdon House, 1996), 124, 160, 213, 236, 212.

53. Ibid, 183–94.

Betsey Loring

INVESTIGATING A WOMAN'S INFAMY
IN THE AMERICAN REVOLUTION

SEAN M. HEUVEL

—~~~~~—

O NE OF the most controversial and mysterious figures of the American Revolution was Elizabeth Lloyd Loring (1752–1831). Popularly labeled "Betsey," the loyalist wife of British Commissary of Prisoners Joshua Loring Jr. was the rumored mistress of General Sir William Howe and censured as such by critics on both sides of the War for Independence. While American critics snarked about Elizabeth Loring's supposed liaison to attack her virtue, and likely by extension that of other loyalist women, some loyalist and British critics faulted her for dampening Howe's desire to fight, thereby helping the Americans win the war. Other propagandists went further to assert that she was a covert revolutionary agent, intent on using her seductive charms to defeat the British. Loring's legend grew over time as she became a central character in everything from romance novels to comics. A lack of primary source materials abetted dramatic license as later authors interpreted her image and Howe's actions in order to titillate readers or school them in gendered civic or martial virtue.[1] Whereas some historical figures have been memorialized as heroes for readers to emulate, others have served as antiheroes (such as Benedict Arnold). Despite popular characterizations, Elizabeth Loring deserved neither appellation and thus her story—or stories—serve to illuminate not only the challenges she actually faced but also the difficulties of drawing history from contemporary gossip and later inventive chroniclers.

Social ambivalence and legal ambiguities over women's allegiances—political, personal, and even moral—affected how observers and writers interpreted Elizabeth Loring's position and actions during the war. Was she a femme fatale who seduced Howe from his duty? Was she a coquette who ultimately cuckolded her husband (which shamed both her and her husband)? Writers in the early republic used the label "coquette" to indicate "one of 'republicanism's stock villains' [a woman] associated in advice literature and fiction with self-interest, vice, and luxury— . . . the flaws of European patriarchy that republicans sought to avoid."[2] Or were her transgressions those of being a loyalist like her husband, taking refuge in an occupied city, and socializing as an elite provincial woman with a British general, thus being distrusted by one side and disparaged by the other?

Using never before published Loring family documents, this account challenges lore with a more balanced view of the *real* Elizabeth Loring and endeavors to answer those questions. In doing so, it provides a case study of gendered infamy: how gender dynamics appeared in wartime propaganda and postwar popular narratives. It provides insight into what can happen when a revolutionary-era woman's reputation and historical legacy is shaped more by propaganda and a resulting myth than by analysis that includes her own and her family's available records. It also sheds light on the cultural purposes of rumor, fiction, and myth during and beyond the revolutionary era, even as it also provides a more accurate portrait of Elizabeth, and in the process, offers guidance about how to navigate beyond or negate myths to find a more balanced interpretation in the study of other revolutionary-era women.

As CONTEXT helps bust myths, it is important to examine Elizabeth Loring's origins and the path she took that brought her to such a high degree of infamy during the American Revolution. Born to Nathaniel Lloyd and Elizabeth Davenport Lloyd, who had married at Boston in September 1751, the baby Elizabeth was christened on 15 October 1752 at St. George's Church in Huntington, New York—near the family estate at Lloyd's Harbor, Long Island.[3] Nathaniel, the son of Henry Lloyd, operated a profitable ship business while Elizabeth was the daughter of an Anglican minister.[4]

Tragedy struck the young Lloyd family about a month after Elizabeth's birth. Nathaniel, weakened by a recent bout with smallpox, was swept overboard by a violent gust in Boston Harbor while traveling to Long Island and was unable to save himself.[5] His body was never recovered. In November, Elizabeth's grandfather Henry Lloyd received the "Melancholy News," mourning "this awful striking affair. . . . Nat just past (happily) thro the smallpox . . . here preparing to sett out to you and his Deare Wife . . . was by a sudden & violent gust in an instant drowned."[6] Following her father's passing, Elizabeth and her mother were sent to live with Nathaniel's great-aunt Margaret Steel in Boston. Three years later, Elizabeth's mother married the wealthy and prominent Boston lawyer Nathaniel Hatch, with whom she would have seven more children.[7] Hatch, however, made it known that he did not want Elizabeth living with them, so she continued to live with her Aunt Margaret.[8] When Elizabeth was eight, she received a letter from her Grandfather Lloyd. Her response is one of the only known samples of her writing:

Honoured Sir,

I received your kind letter by Capt Wimble and am very much obliged to you for taking notice of a little girl and if you please to write to me often it will encourage me to try to improve in learning more than anything else, besides I shall know by your letters how you do. . . . Pray give my duty to Aunt Woolsey and Uncle Joseph. . . . I am Dear Grand Papa

> Your Dutiful
> Granddaughter
>
> Elizabeth Lloyd[9]

Little else is known about Elizabeth's childhood and adolescence before she reappeared in the historical record at age seventeen, when she married Joshua Loring Jr. on 19 October 1769 at the Hatch family estate in Dorchester, Massachusetts.[10] Joshua descended from a wealthy and distinguished Boston family. His father, Joshua Loring Sr. (b. 1716), began his career as a young tanner in Roxbury but the sea beckoned, and in 1744 he began operating as a privateer during King George's War.[11] He later found fortune and acclaim through service in the Royal Navy.[12] Following promotions to lieutenant in 1745 and captain in 1757, Joshua Sr. eventually served as a commodore during the Seven Years' War, commanding the British fleets at Lakes Champlain, George, and Ontario.[13] A serious wound suffered on 23 August 1760 during the Montreal campaign ended his naval career.[14] However, he quickly settled back into a comfortable life with his wife, Mary Curtis Loring, at their elegant Jamaica Plain estate in Roxbury and went on to serve as a mandamus counsellor for Governor Thomas Gage.[15]

His son Joshua Jr., born in 1744, followed a similar path of presti-
gious and lucrative service to the Crown. The younger Joshua was an
ensign and then lieutenant (August 1765) in the Royal Army's 15th Regiment of Foot.[16] He served at the siege of Havana (1762; then-Colonel
William Howe also participated), which may have led to the poor health
that later required a two-year convalescence in Europe before his return
to Massachusetts.[17] Following his departure from the army in 1768,
Joshua Jr. obtained a number of lucrative government posts, including
deputy surveyor of the king's woods in New Hampshire and high sheriff
of the province of Massachusetts.[18] He also became comptroller of the
port of Philadelphia in 1771, which entailed extensive travel among that
city, New York, and Boston.[19]

Elizabeth's marriage to Joshua was therefore a mutually beneficial arrangement, as she descended from a wealthy shipping family and stood to
inherit a fortune, while he had social prestige as well as excellent professional prospects.[20] Their future as a married couple among the elite looked
bright, but the onset of revolution turned everything upside down.[21]

The turn began when Joshua Sr.—the old commodore—decided to
stay aligned with the Crown, much to the chagrin of his neighbors in
Roxbury and even to his own extended family. He reportedly made this
decision "after serious consideration and consultation with friends," later
declaring, "I have always eaten the King's bread and I always intend to."
Consequently, after being "mobbed and otherwise ill-treated," Joshua Sr.
fled to Boston in summer 1774 and ultimately gave up his extensive land-
holdings, including his estate in Roxbury and elegant Boston mansion,
and so "for his loyalty he lost nearly everything." Joshua Sr. and his wife
later joined the British evacuation and traveled to Halifax before settling in London, where he died at Highgate in 1781.[22] By that time, his
granddaughter Eliza described him as being in a state of "second childhood."[23] Meanwhile, Joshua Sr.'s wife, Mary, reportedly regretted ever
leaving Massachusetts.[24]

The American Revolution posed similar difficulties to Joshua Jr. and
Elizabeth, but also opportunities. Like his father, Joshua Jr. had to flee
with his family to the protection of British forces at Boston. As some
of those forces marched on Lexington and Concord on 19 April 1775,
the Lorings abandoned their new country home built five miles from the
city, which was later burned down by angry rebelling colonists. According to Joshua Jr.'s daughter Eliza, his loyalism and position as high sheriff
made him a target "of vengeance to the rebels, he having firmly declined
all entreaties to join them." Joshua Jr. had continued in his duties and

issued proclamations to the resentment of the rebels. When General Sir William Howe arrived in Boston on 25 May 1775 to assume command, he was "agreeably surprised to recognize in the Sheriff his former very young lieutenant" from the siege of Havana. Thereafter, Joshua Jr.'s house became "the rendezvous of the two brothers Lord Howe and Sir William and the other superior officers." This would have likely been the point when Howe and Elizabeth first met. The Lorings remained in Boston until the British evacuation in March 1776, later following the army to Halifax and then New York, where Joshua Jr. assumed the post of commissary general of prisoners for the British Army.[25]

IN OCCUPIED New York City, the Lorings had power, position, and critics, which subjected them to wartime rumors and propaganda, which in turn led to the myths or quasi-historical "conduct-fiction," to borrow the concept from Sarah Emily Newton, of public memory. The history of Elizabeth became the "usable" tale of the infamous "Betsey," who provided a contrast to the ideal republican, that is, virtuous, wife and mother.[26]

The quasi-historical Betsey Loring flouted the paradigm, as she purportedly spent the bulk of her time outside of the domestic sphere engaging with Howe and his colleagues. The extremities of the Revolution's war tested her virtue—and by inference that of other men and women—and, according to patriot propagandists, by serving, or sleeping with, the enemy, she—and other loyalists—failed the test. In some respects, although a matron rather than maiden, this Betsey more resembled Hannah Webster Fowler's *The Coquette*, described by Kristie Hamilton as a young, middle-class woman torn between the republican expectation of marrying within one's socioeconomic class and the opportunities for upward mobility in late eighteenth-century urban America.[27] This juxtaposition between Betsey's alleged lifestyle and the new republic's ideals of virtuous womanhood may help explain the myth that grew quickly about her.

Yet British and loyalist observers were also critical of the Lorings. British observations or criticisms may have reflected a prejudice against or uneasiness over the loyalties of the provincials attached to the British Army, but both British and loyalist critics fretted most about a leader's personal affairs affecting military operations. The myth of "Billy Howe's Cleopatra" may have actually begun with their comments.[28]

By the time that Howe evacuated his army from Boston, Elizabeth—Betsey—was already supposedly his mistress.[29] According to historian David McCullough, while Joshua Jr. was listed among the loyalists departing Boston, his wife was not accounted for, suggesting that "she may have been provided with more comfortable accommodations abroad the flagship *Chatham* with General Howe." According to a contemporary loyalist wartime chronicler, "Joshua had a handsome wife. The general ... was fond of her. Joshua had no objections. He fingered the cash, the general enjoyed madam."[30] In this view, Joshua, ever mindful of where his bread was buttered, was quite willing to ignore where his wife was spending her nights in return for the prospect of satisfying his acquisitive instincts.[31] The *London Evening Post* even suggested that "Elizabeth Loring had been purchased from her husband in return for a contract, and that the country had to 'Pay the Piper for the Pimping.'"[32]

Thus, in return for his wife's favors, a grateful Howe appointed Joshua Jr. to the commissary general of prisoners position—a post that "promised a fortune in bribes from sellers of provisions."[33] Historian Edwin G. Burrows recounts that Joshua Jr. "possessed two unbeatable qualifications for the job: a settled conviction that men who took up arms against their sovereign deserved no mercy, and a beautiful wife, to whom the general had taken a fancy."[34] Joshua Jr.'s controversial tenure in that position could be the topic of another study. Some argued that he "became rich by feeding the dead (in charging for the provisions of dead prisoners of war) and starving the living," and Colonel Ethan Allen even referred to him as a "smiling monster."[35] However, other Continental Army and militia officers, including Captain Alexander Graydon and Brigadier General Gold S. Silliman, maintained that they were treated quite fairly as prisoners of war by Joshua Jr., so the truth is difficult to ascertain.[36]

While Joshua Jr. was busy tending to his duties, Betsey was allegedly living the good life with General Howe. First in Boston and then in New York, Howe "was openly enjoying himself . . . with his elegant dinners, extended evenings at the faro table, and conspicuously in the company of a stunning young woman about whom there was much talk."[37] Betsey regularly accompanied Howe to social occasions during this time, and British officers came to refer to her as "the Sultana."[38] Both appeared to share a taste for drinking and gambling, and Betsey reportedly squandered large sums of money at the gaming tables.[39] On one occasion in New York, Betsey was said to have lost three hundred guineas in one sitting.[40] Furthermore, as Howe displayed a certain sluggishness in mounting offensive operations throughout 1776 to capitalize on the tactical advantages he had over General George Washington, frustrated loyalists and British officers alike began to blame Betsey for his lethargic behavior.[41] One Englishman during the period wrote sarcastically that there would be fighting whenever Howe "shall think proper to leave Mrs. [Loring]."[42]

New York loyalist Thomas Jones went so far as to argue that Howe "neglected to win the war because he was more interested in her than in achieving victory."[43] Others soon echoed these sentiments and Betsey's alleged relationship with Howe came to be mocked in loyalist popular verse:

> Aware, arouse, Sir Billy,
> There's forage in your plain,
> Leave your little filly,
> And open the campaign.[44]

Betsey's notoriety reportedly even reached as far as England itself. In a conversation with none other than King George III, Lieutenant General Friedrich von Riedesel was surprised to learn how much His Majesty knew about the scandalous stories circulating around his commanders—particularly rumors about Howe's amorous escapades. The king's information source may have been a March 1778 handbill (originating as an anonymous letter from New York) that was delivered to both Houses of Parliament concerning Howe's failures to crush the rebellion. It stated that while General Washington's army was in its "wretched condition" at Trenton, "General Howe was at New York in the lap of ease; or rather, amusing himself in the lap of a Mrs. L——g, who is the very Cleopatra to this Anthony of ours." As historian and novelist Louise Hall Tharp noted, the reputation of the "beautiful golden-haired Mrs. Loring"—at least for a brief time—was indeed international.[45]

As the alleged romance continued between Betsey and Howe, the British press continued to speculate over additional details of the affair. Some sources maintained that Betsey had gone with the general to Philadelphia and resided with him at his elegant headquarters in Germantown. Another source even claimed that Betsey escorted Howe to his famed farewell celebration, known as the *Mischianza,* as the "General's Lady." However, in both cases there is no actual evidence to support either claim. All that is really known is that Elizabeth departed America for England at some point in 1778, thus likely ending whatever relationship she had with General Howe.[46] Meanwhile, General Howe went on to face a 1779 parliamentary inquiry along with his brother concerning the purported failures of their command. Elizabeth Loring's name did not appear to come up during the proceedings.[47] This suggests that post-1779, the alleged affair may have become more of a local or American tale than a transatlantic one.

Patriot propagandists picked up on the gossip and turned it to their purposes, which appears initially more to prick Howe than assault Elizabeth's, or her husband's, reputations. Although happy to take advantage of delayed actions, they mocked how "Betsey" was supposedly instrumental in contributing to the general's apparent languor as a military commander. For instance, a May 1777 American versifier lampooned Howe in a mythical scene where, accompanied by Betsey, he was addressing Tory troops about to strike out on a raid under General William Tryon:

> Without wit, without wisdom, half stupid and drunk
> And rolling along arm in arm with his punk,
> The gallant Sir William, who fights all by proxy,
> Thus spoke to his soldiers, held up by his doxy:
> "My boys, I'm a going to send you with Tryon,
> To a place where you'll get as groggy as I am."[48]

In a similar vein, Francis Hopkinson probably contributed the most famous patriot propaganda concerning the imagined relationship with Howe. After the revolutionaries in January 1778 sent kegs loaded with explosives down the Delaware River in an attempt to destroy British shipping, Hopkinson made light of the event in his famous "The Battle of the Kegs":

> Sir William he, snug as a flea,
> Lay all this time a snoring;
> Nor dream'd of harm as he lay warm
> In bed with Mrs. Loring.
> Now in a fright, he starts upright,
> Awaked by such a clatter;
> He rubs both eyes, and boldly cries,
> "For God's sake, what's the matter?"[49]

Ultimately, many on both sides were puzzled as to why General Howe consistently failed to take the strategic initiative and win the war when all of the odds were in his favor. According to the aforementioned loyalist Thomas Jones, the general had evacuated Boston and later rested indolent on Staten Island for a couple of months after allowing the whole rebel army to escape him on Long Island. Jones also argued that Howe had countless additional opportunities to defeat the Continental Army decisively throughout 1776 and 1777 but failed to act on them. Shocked that Howe had been knighted for his services in America, Jones concluded that "had the General been properly rewarded for his conduct while Commander-in-Chief in America, an execution, and not a mischianza, would have been the consequence."[50] In the view of Jones and many other of his contemporaries, Howe's preoccupation with Mrs. Loring—Betsey—must have been the cause for what they saw as nonsensical and unexplainable behavior.

In fairness to Howe, modern historians have argued that he probably had other, more valid reasons for his inaction, and that the supposed affair with Betsey was more a consequence of the situation than its cause. For instance, Joseph P. Cullen argued that after the bloody Battle of Bunker Hill, Howe was likely cautious to commit his troops to additional, high-risk frontal assaults. In addition, with an eye toward possibly brokering a peace with the revolutionaries alongside his brother, Admiral Lord Richard Howe, Howe may have been reluctant to escalate the fighting any more than absolutely necessary. Ultimately, the main reason for Howe's inaction, according to Cullen, may have been the result of his military training and experience. During that era, the philosophy of warfare centered on campaigning by maneuvering for position and forcing the enemy to retreat and abandon important territory—not on fighting costly battles with troops who were expensive to raise, train, and transport.[51] Thus, Howe may have been set on a well-intentioned yet flawed strategy of trying to defeat the Americans while expending the least amount of human and material capital possible.

Regardless of Howe's true military strategy and the actual role that Elizabeth played in executing it—or not—her legend continued to grow within the realm of popular literature. One reason, already mentioned, may have been its application within the "conduct" genre of American literature that instructs readers, generally young ones, in "a code of ethical behavior that delineates approved gender roles."[52] The other reason stemmed from the scandalous nature of the story, which ensured listeners and readers.

Examples of sensationalist writing continued into the twentieth century, as historical fiction authors took what shreds of truth that did exist about Mrs. Loring and twisted and exaggerated them until Betsey bore little resemblance to Elizabeth. They also often created portrayals of Betsey that contradicted one another. For instance, as the chronicler Philip Young ably synthesized, in Kenneth Roberts's novel *Oliver Wiswell*

(1940), she was depicted as a "pouty, baby-talking flirt" totally incapable of the accomplishments with which other writers credited her. Expanding on this flirtatious portrayal, Roberts described Betsey as "promisingly arrayed in a gown that would become embarrassing 'if she'd coughed unguardedly,'" and as having "a suggestion of indecencies in her voice." A contemporary novel to *Oliver Wiswell* painted Betsey in a much different light. In E. Irvine Haines's *Exquisite Siren* (1938), Betsey, referred to in the book as the "haughty beauty . . . Jane Lloyd Loring," was depicted as a trusted and faithful agent of George Washington himself![53] In this interpretation, Betsey was a cunning and shrewd patriot agent who almost singlehandedly won the war for the revolutionaries by distracting Howe from his duties. While this depiction of Betsey was patently absurd, it is interesting nonetheless in that it attempted to cast her in the role of a heroine. Furthermore, it attempted to suggest that there may have been a worthy motive for Betsey's supposedly scandalous behavior with Howe.

While Roberts's and Haines's characterizations of Betsey may have represented two behavioral extremes, Christine Blevins's more modern interpretation in *The Tory Widow* (2009) is closer to the accepted, conventional view of Betsey and her supposed personality. In Blevins's work, Betsey is portrayed as a cold and calculating operator taking maximum advantage of the situation that was presented to her by Howe and his affections. Blevins writes, "Unprincipled as she may be, Howe's mistress [Betsey] was by any standard a striking beauty. Provincial sensibilities were shocked by the arrangement the general had come to in procuring his bed and gaming companion. But wagging tongues did not stop Mrs. Loring from fully enjoying her position as consort to the most powerful man on the continent."[54]

Of the various fictional depictions of Betsey, Blevins's may possibly be the most realistic and plausible.[55] As a high-society woman whose family had lost everything and been driven from their home, perhaps Elizabeth sought the protection that Howe could provide her and her family as a way of grasping for a sense of security in the midst of a chaotic war. Through her affiliation with Howe, she and her family could continue to live in the lifestyle to which they were accustomed, despite having lost their own fortune. An issue, however, remains: who was the real Elizabeth Loring, and what was her history beyond the assault on her character?

THE POPULAR image of Elizabeth "Betsey" Loring as merely Howe's "sultana," or as a coquette or cunning femme fatale, is challenged by at least three important yet little known facets of her life that are rooted in the historical record. First, in all the coverage of Elizabeth and her rumored affair with Howe, few writers or scholars mention that during that time, Elizabeth was a young mother experiencing profound personal loss. By spring 1775, Elizabeth was the mother of three small children—Elizabeth ("Eliza") Loring, born in 1771, and the twins John Wentworth and Joshua Loring, born in October 1773.[56] However, as private family accounts reveal, Elizabeth was separated from her two infant sons in spring 1775.[57] According to her daughter, Eliza, this came about as rebels retaliated against Joshua Jr. after he refused their entreaties to join them. Describing the scene, Eliza wrote, "They immediately burnt down [our] new house in the country. My father was at his post in Boston; the war had not yet begun when my father sent for my mother wishing to give her some directions. She took me with her into Boston for the drive, but never could return to the country house. My two brothers Wentworth and Joshua, both babies, were seized by the rebel party before they burnt the house."[58]

In what is likely one of the only known samples of her writing as an adult, Elizabeth also recounted this alarming situation as she mentioned how she visited her baby sons against all odds. She obtained the help of a relative by marriage, "whom I had never met with until she had the humanity greatly to relieve the anxiety of my mind by taking me beyond the military lines, and in disguise, to see my poor infant boys."[59] Young Joshua died, after which, according to Eliza, the problems then centered on "how to recover Wentworth . . . [which] was managed sometime afterwards by arrangement between Generals Gage and Washington."[60] These insights reveal a side of Elizabeth as a caring and focused mother that contrasts with her image as a flirtatious adulteress focused solely on debauchery.

Another challenge to the conventional stereotypes about Elizabeth is that there is evidence to suggest that she and Joshua Jr. continued to share a marital life together throughout the war and beyond. This stands in stark contrast to the image of an adulterous "Betsey" who focused her time and attention exclusively on General Howe while Joshua Jr. was always elsewhere. A pair of wartime letters from Joshua Jr. help to shed light on this revelation. Joshua wrote his "Dear Betsey" sometime in 1776 or 1777:

> Don't be alarmed at a report of the Rebels being landed on Long Island which prevents my returning tonight as I promised the General. I would not go out of town, should it prove true I shall be obliged to go to Long Island in the morning to take up all the Rebel Officers, in

that case will send you word. My trunk of papers and your plate you will bring to town with you should I send out for you to come to town, let Othello come back with Cornelius on one of the General's horses, and I'll send him out to you early in the morning when I have seen the General—keep everything I have wrote you a profound secret.

> Yrs most affectionately
> J. Loring[61]

Thus, while there certainly could have been an affair between Elizabeth and Howe, this letter suggests that she and Joshua Jr. remained in regular communication for much of the war—even when they were physically apart. It therefore challenges the notion that Joshua Jr. was somehow out of circulation completely during the time that Elizabeth and Howe were supposedly together. In a similar vein, a 24 March 1782 letter from Joshua Jr. to his "Dear Daughter" Eliza sheds further light on their internal family dynamic during the war. At the time, Elizabeth, Eliza, and Wentworth were in England while Joshua Jr. remained in New York:

> How could you think I had forgot you who I know professes one of the best hearts and most excellent understanding of any little girl on Earth. Cultivated and improved in the highest manner by the abilities and great attention of a fond Mother, who is entirely devoted to you and your brother's good. . . . Do honor to the pains she is bestowing on you; you will not only lay up a treasure of knowledge of virtue and religion, but you will secure the affections of a fond father. . . . As to your education I have entrusted it entirely to her care. . . . Follow strictly her commands in all things and you cannot fail of possessing a warm share in my heart.

> Love, advise and assist
> your brothers and be
> assured of the regard of
> your affectionate father,
> J. Loring.[62]

While it is problematic to generalize too much from a pair of letters, they do suggest the possibility that Elizabeth was an active mother and wife who was devoted to her family. Moreover, it is worth noting that following their move to England, Joshua Jr. and Elizabeth went on to have three more children together—Henry, William, and Robert Loring.[63] Thus, the pair continued married life together, even if there had been a brief affair with Howe. Again, this all challenges the traditional stereotype of Elizabeth as the uncaring sultana so common in both war-time propaganda and later fictional accounts.

A third facet further supports this assertion. Few, if any, of the writers and historians who have chronicled Elizabeth's alleged affair with Howe have discussed Elizabeth's postwar life in England, where she ultimately raised a family of five children by herself. Following Joshua Jr.'s move to England around 1783, he was beset with health problems that compromised his ability to work. Thus, while influential friends promised him lucrative government or diplomatic posts, Joshua Jr. was often too ill to pursue those opportunities.[64] Most of his time was spent petitioning the government for either assistance or repayment of salary for posts that he once held in America.[65] He died on 18 September 1789 in Berkshire, England, at the age of forty-four, leaving Elizabeth to fend for herself.[66]

Shortly after Joshua Jr.'s death, Elizabeth petitioned the government for assistance, arguing that by his death "the principal support of his family, a widow and five children, three of whom are infants, is also lost, and they must sink into the most distressing state of poverty unless relief is extended to them."[67] In this, Elizabeth stands as a representative of other loyalist women who ended up in England with little or nothing.[68] Interestingly, General Howe endorsed the petition, adding, "I certify to the facts as stated in this petition relative to the late Mr. Loring's loyalty, to the widow's present distressed circumstances, and to the affluent income Mr. Loring enjoyed in America.—W. Howe." As historian Eva Phillips Boyd noted, "Certainly a weight of sorrow and humiliation had fallen between Howe and Elizabeth Loring since they had danced too often together in America and these days fourteen years later which find her appealing for help."[69]

While the government did issue Elizabeth a small allowance, which she received until her death in 1831, it did not make the process or costs of raising five small children much easier. Somehow, she secured the funds to move her family to Reading, where she enrolled her eldest son, John Wentworth Loring, in the local grammar school. Wentworth went on to become his mother's partner in supporting their family. Anxious to redeem the family's name and societal station, he entered the Royal Navy and quickly climbed the officer ranks, with some initial support from his uncle Captain John Loring. During his early years as a young officer, Wentworth sent most of his earnings home to support his mother and siblings. He went on to become one of the Royal Navy's top frigate captains during the Napoleonic Wars and ultimately became a full admiral, earning knighthoods from both King William IV and Queen Victoria.[70] Elizabeth's eldest child—daughter Eliza—was probably active in helping raise the family as well, which may explain why she never married herself. Elizabeth's other sons went on to highly successful careers in both the military and the church. Henry Lloyd Loring later served as the first archdeacon of Calcutta, while his brothers William and Robert Roberts served as officers in the British Army during the Napoleonic Wars.[71]

These details pertaining to Elizabeth's later life and to the professional success of her children are significant as they provide another important glimpse into her full persona. Undoubtedly, Elizabeth must have possessed certain strength of character to raise a family of five children as a cash-strapped widow in a seemingly foreign land. It is debatable whether the self-obsessed, debauchery-loving sultana as Elizabeth is often portrayed could have endured under such circumstances. So, ultimately, who was the real Elizabeth Loring? Did she really have a notorious affair with General Howe that helped shape the course of the American Revolution? What do the stories say about her and about those who wrote them? Due to a frustrating lack of unbiased primary source materials, a fully accurate examination of events has likely been lost to history. Interestingly, neither Elizabeth nor her children ever mentioned such an affair or anything close to it in any of their known writings. It could be that they decided collectively to put that episode in their family's history behind them. Alternatively, the relationship with Howe may have just been an innocent, wartime flirtation that went a bit too far, resulting in rampant speculation, gossip, and exaggeration from curious observers.

What is clear based on surviving primary source evidence is that the situation was likely more complicated than how it was depicted by the wartime propagandists and romance novelists. This demonstrates that context matters, and that dismissing Elizabeth as a coquette or a femme fatale does a disservice to her story and, by extension, a proper historical accounting. An observer's or writer's position and purpose must be considered in interpretations. Elizabeth may have actually been a pragmatist who was trying to find a way to protect her family during a time of war. Such an assertion echoes historian Donald F. Johnson, who wrote that revolutionary-era "people living under military rule made pragmatic, calculated decisions to ensure their survival, protect loved ones, and safeguard property."[72] Thus, perhaps Elizabeth Loring's search for security did lead to an adulterous affair with General Howe, but perhaps it did not. Regardless, her story serves as a case study of what can happen when legend outgrows what is factually known about an individual. Future evidence will hopefully shed additional light on this historical mystery. In the meantime, we may reflect on how Elizabeth Loring's story reveals political and gendered propaganda, and the effect on histories, both past and present.

NOTES

1. For examples of scholarship examining historical women's actions being used to embody preferred values and engender emulation, see Paula D. Hunt, "Sybil Ludington, the Female Paul Revere: The Making of a Revolutionary War Heroine," *New England Quarterly* 88, no. 2 (June 2015): 187–222, esp. 188–89, 221–22, and Katherine Brackett, "Remembering the Nancy Harts: A Female Militia, Gender, and Memory," *Georgia Historical Quarterly* 102, no. 4 (2018): 303–37, esp. 305.

2. Kristie Hamilton, "An Assault on the Will: Republican Virtue and the City in Hannah Webster Foster's *The Coquette*," *Early American Literature* 24, no. 2 (1989): 138, including quotation from Jan Lewis's "The Republican Wife: Virtue and Seduction in the Early Republic," *William and Mary Quarterly*, 3rd series, 44, no. 4 (October 1987): 720.

3. Philip Young, *Revolutionary Ladies* (New York: Knopf, 1977), 76: As Young's *Revolutionary Ladies* is the most comprehensive biographical treatment of Elizabeth Loring to date, it is utilized extensively in this essay.

4. Quentin Decker, "A Defense of Joshua Loring, Jr.," unpublished manuscript, 2019, 16, copy in author's possession.

5. Dorothy C. Barck, ed., *Papers of the Lloyd Family of the Manor of Queen's Village, Lloyd's Neck, Long Island, New York, 1654–1826* (New York: New-York Historical Society, 1927), 513; Decker, "A Defense of Joshua Loring, Jr.," 16.

6. Quoted in Young, *Revolutionary Ladies*, 76.

7. Decker, "A Defense of Joshua Loring, Jr.," 16; Young, *Revolutionary Ladies*, 76.

8. Decker, "A Defense of Joshua Loring, Jr.," 16.

9. In Young, *Revolutionary Ladies*, 77.

10. Ibid., 77. According to family tradition, Elizabeth's guardians gave consent to the marriage on the condition that Joshua Jr. sold out of the army.

11. Charles Henry Pope, *Loring Genealogy* (Cambridge, MA: Murray and Emery, 1917), 78.

12. Eva Phillips Boyd, "Commodore Joshua Loring, Jamaica Plain by Way of London," *Old-Time New England*, April–June 1959, n.p., republished by Jamaica Plain Historical Society, 14 April 2005, https://www.jphs.org/people/2005/4/14/commodore-joshua-loring-jamaica-plain-by-way-of-london.html, 2.

13. Pope, *Loring Genealogy*, 78. Joshua Sr.'s official title was "Commodore and Commander of Naval Ships on the Lakes."

14. Boyd, "Commodore Joshua Loring," 4. A cannon ball tore Joshua Sr.'s right calf during a battle.

15. Pope, *Loring Genealogy*, 78. The author is a second cousin nine times removed of Mary Curtis Loring.

16. E. Alfred Jones, *The Loyalists of Massachusetts: Their Memorials, Petitions, and Claims* (1930; reprint, Baltimore, MD: Genealogical Publishing, 1995), 200; Decker, "A Defense of Joshua Loring, Jr.," 7. Brother Benjamin Loring graduated second in Harvard's class of 1772, when class placement was ranked in order of family prestige.

17. Decker, "A Defense of Joshua Loring, Jr.," 7; Elizabeth Loring, "Loring Family Sketch," 1854, 1, Loring Family Papers, private collection in author's possession.

18. Loring, "Loring Family Sketch," 1. For his military services Joshua Loring Jr. was granted twenty thousand acres of land in New Hampshire.

19. Young, *Revolutionary Ladies*, 69.

20. Decker, "A Defense of Joshua Loring, Jr.," 7–8.

21. Barck, ed., *Papers of the Lloyd Family*, 503.

22. Pope, *Loring Genealogy*, 78; Young, *Revolutionary Ladies*, 68. Many of Mary Curtis Loring's relatives—including her brothers—were prominent patriots.

23. Loring, "Loring Family Sketch," 2.

24. Pope, *Loring Genealogy*, 79.

25. Loring, "Loring Family Sketch," 1, 2; Jones, *The Loyalists of Massachusetts*, 200; Thomas B. Allen, *Tories: Fighting for the King in America's First Civil War* (New York: Harper, 2010), 171.

26. Sarah Emily Newton, "Wise and Foolish Virgins: 'Usable Fiction' and the Early American Conduct Tradition," *Early American Literature* 25, no. 2 (1990): 140. The Elizabeth Loring of legend is identified here as "Betsey" as it is still unclear how much of this myth applied to the life of the actual individual.

27. See Hannah W. Foster, *The Coquette: The History of Eliza Wharton* (Boston: William P. Fetridge, 1855), and Hamilton, "An Assault on the Will," 135–36. See also Sarah Emily Newton's summary of the moral lesson in the tale of Flavia, raised "right" in a good, rural, i.e., republican, household but seduced by "fashionable life," i.e., urban or British/loyalist society, compared to Foster's *The Coquette*, in Newton, "Wise and Foolish Virgins," 156–57.

28. For references to "Billy Howe's Cleopatra," see David McCullough, *1776* (New York: Simon and Schuster, 2005), 75, and Thomas Fleming, *1776: Year of Illusions* (New York: Norton, 1975), 63.

29. Andrew Jackson O'Shaughnessy, *The Men Who Lost America: British Leadership, the American Revolution, and the Fate of the Empire* (New Haven, CT: Yale University Press, 2013), 97; Allen, *Tories*, 171. General Howe's wife, Frances, remained in England for the duration of the war.

30. McCullough, *1776*, 103, 75.

31. Fleming, *1776: Year of Illusions*, 63.

32. O'Shaughnessy, *The Men Who Lost America*, 97.

33. Allen, *Tories*, 171. During this time, Joshua Jr. and a brother-in-law also operated a company that sold wine and spirits to royal officers and troops; see John R. Alden, *A History of the American Revolution* (1969; reprint, New York: Da Capo Press, 1989), 504.

34. Edwin G. Burrows, *Forgotten Patriots: The Untold Story of American Prisoners during the Revolutionary War* (New York: Basic Books, 2008), 10.

35. Alden, *A History of the American Revolution*, 504; Jones, *The Loyalists of Massachusetts*, 200.

36. Alden, *A History of the American Revolution*, 504. The American commissary general of prisoners, Elias Boudinot, was also satisfied with the work of his counterpart, Joshua Loring Jr.

37. McCullough, *1776*, 75.

38. O'Shaughnessy, *The Men Who Lost America*, 97.

39. Alden, *A History of the American Revolution*, 504; O'Shaughnessy, *The Men Who Lost America*, 97.

40. Young, *Revolutionary Ladies*, 60.

41. George Athan Billias, ed., *George Washington's Generals and Opponents: Their Exploits and Leadership* (1964, 1969; reprint, New York: Da Capo Press, 1994), 49.

42. Quoted in Young, *Revolutionary Ladies*, 60.

43. Noted in Alden, *A History of the American Revolution*, 504.

44. As quoted in O'Shaughnessy, *The Men Who Lost America*, 97; Joseph P. Cullen, "Not a Better Soldier in the Army: General William Howe," *American History Illustrated*, December 1972, 31.

45. Excerpted and including Tharp's interpretation in Young, *Revolutionary Ladies*, 62.

46. Ibid., 78.

47. For discussion of the parliamentary inquiry, see Ira D. Gruber, *The Howe Brothers and the American Revolution* (1972; reprint, New York: Norton Library, 1975), 338–49.

48. Recorded in Alden, *A History of the American Revolution*, 303; Young, *Revolutionary Ladies*, 64.

49. In Alden, *A History of the American Revolution*, 303; Young, *Revolutionary Ladies*, 65.

50. Quoted in Alden, *A History of the American Revolution*, 305.

51. Cullen, "Not a Better Soldier in the Army," 29.

52. Newton, "Wise and Foolish Virgins," 139–40.

53. All noted in Young, *Revolutionary Ladies*, 79–80.

54. Christine Blevins, *The Tory Widow: A Novel* (New York, Berkeley Books, 2009), 254–55.

55. Other modern fictional depictions of Betsey appear in Laura Innes's *The Dreamer* comic book series (San Diego: IDW, 2009), where she is portrayed in a manner similar to *The Tory Widow*, and Noelle Donfeld's book/play *The Revolution of Betsey Loring* (2020), http://noelledonfeld.com/shows/betsy-loring, where she is depicted as a patriot. Betsey is also mentioned in the 2000 A&E film *The Crossing*, where it is surmised that General Howe's preoccupation with her was the main reason he had not destroyed the Continental Army by late 1776.

56. Pope, *Loring Genealogy*, 17.

57. Elizabeth Lloyd Loring, "Family History," 1833, 1, Loring Family Papers; Eliza Loring, "Family History," 1854, 1, Loring Family Papers.

58. Eliza Loring, "Family History," 1.

59. Elizabeth Lloyd Loring, "Family History," 1.

60. Eliza Loring, "Family History," 1.

61. Letter quoted in Young, *Revolutionary Ladies*, 83.

62. Ibid., 83–84.

63. Eliza Loring, "Family History," 2; Pope, *Loring Genealogy*, 137. Henry Lloyd Loring was born in 1784, William in 1785, and Robert Roberts in 1789.

64. Eliza Loring, "Family History," 2.

65. Boyd, "Commodore Joshua Loring," 15.

66. Eliza Loring, "Family History," 2.

67. Boyd, "Commodore Joshua Loring," 15.

68. For more information about the experiences of loyalist women in England, see Mary Beth Norton, "Eighteenth-Century American Women in Peace and War: The Case of Loyalists," *William and Mary Quarterly*, 3rd series, 33, no. 3 (July 1976): 386–409.

69. Boyd, "Commodore Joshua Loring," 15.

70. Sean M. Heuvel, "Admiral Sir John Wentworth Loring, KCB, KCH," *Trafalgar Chronicle*, no. 24 (2014): 146–47.

71. Eliza Loring, "Family History," 2.

72. Donald F. Johnson, "Ambiguous Allegiances: Urban Loyalties during the American Revolution," *Journal of American History* 104, no. 3 (December 2017): 610.

Killed, Imprisoned, Struck by Lightning

SOLDIERS' WIVES ON CAMPAIGN WITH THE BRITISH ARMY

DON N. HAGIST

———~~~~~~———

"A VERY REMARKABLE event happened that Night, which was: A Woman's shift being burnt upon her body, lying in a Birth on board a Transport, and she a Sleep, by a Flash of Lightning, without the least damage to her skin or Flesh."[1] This incident was recorded by a British soldier on a ship bound for Head of Elk, Maryland, on 17 August 1777. It is the only account of the event and gives no indication of the woman's identity. We do not know her name or anything about her other than this frightening experience.

The presence of women with eighteenth-century armies, and in particular with the British Army during the American Revolution, is well known, albeit often overlooked in traditional military histories, because there are no clear instances where the presence, or absence, of women affected an army's operations. This is not to suggest that soldiers' wives were irrelevant. Early works that discussed wives of British soldiers presented them as problematic, including Walter Hart Blumenthal's almost absurd characterization in his 1952 work *Women Camp Followers of the American Revolution*, which drew heavily on earlier work that characterized the entire British military system of the era as flawed and quirky.[2] Three decades later, Paul Kopperman took a more scholarly approach but nonetheless focused on problems caused by British Army wives.[3]

More recent works have demonstrated that, rather than a problem to be solved (but which was inexplicably never solved), army wives were a part of the military infrastructure, part of an established system of civilians providing vital services that were a century away from being handled by military organizations. Washing clothes, nursing in hospitals, and sutling (selling food and drink, mostly alcohol) were regular, paid activities of British Army wives in America, as were occasional tasks such as producing supplemental military clothing, gathering hay, and cutting turf for fuel.[4] While the contributions of these wives to the military infrastructure is finally apparent, there remains a lack of detail about their actual lives and experiences, with studies instead attempting to characterize individual lives in terms of common factors across centuries-long timespans.[5] Although such histories incorporate examples of women's lives in the army, they generally do so over such a broad scope that the specifics of a particular location and time are lost: is it safe to say that the experiences of a soldier's family in the Venetian army in the 1620s and that of a British soldier in Spain in 1809 fully reflect those of an army family in Boston in 1775?[6] Large-scale histories reveal connections or patterns but often at the expense of illuminating the reality of diverse experiences. Digging out the accounts of individuals fosters comparisons that test general conclusions both in military and in gendered histories.[7]

The lack of detailed literature, including familial demographics, specific to the British Army in the American Revolutionary War reflects the great difficulty of studying the wives of the soldiers serving in it. Their presence was pervasive, they were an integral part of the military infrastructure, and yet as individuals we know almost nothing about them. The names of most British soldiers survive on muster rolls that allow us to trace their careers, and other sources provide many of their ages, places of birth, and similar details. About one in eight of these soldiers had a wife with him in garrison or on campaign, many with children in tow—between five and ten thousand women altogether, and a similar number of children.[8] Some soldiers brought their wives with them from Europe, while others married women in America. These wives endured more than just the dangers of the voyage, often accompanying their husbands on campaigns and even in captivity.

Only recently have a few works attempted to look at British soldiers' wives as people who were part of a community defined by a particular time and place, a population of individuals with diverse backgrounds, everyday lives and responsibilities, and stories only visible in fragments.[9] Yet there is far more information available than has been assimilated and assessed. This essay presents some new material in its examples of the hazards British soldiers' wives encountered within the eight years of warfare in America from 1775 through 1783. A compilation of examples from a narrow period is important because it demonstrates that the "Mysogyny in the Corps" discussed by Jennine Hurl-Eamon and others was likely not the prevailing attitude, or at least that such an attitude is not apparent in the way that military personnel wrote about army wives at that time.[10]

Furthermore, this essay challenges misleading multi-century overviews on the numbers of wives who accompanied the British Army in America. A review and revision of the numbers and resulting statistics in conjunction with the qualitative sources promotes a better understanding of the demands women placed on the army and the utility they provided it. John A. Lynn, a distinguished historian of early modern European warfare, asserts that "British troops fighting in North America at this time were allowed but six women per hundred."[11] That figure, widely repeated in various accounts with the exception of "per company" instead of "per hundred," is accurate only in a very specific context, the space allowed on transports that brought troops to America. The British government allocated shipping for sixty wives to accompany each British infantry regiment, which typically consisted of about five hundred men—though strength varied during the course of the war—sent to America.[12] These were wives of the soldiers—the sergeants, corporals, drummers, fifers, and privates. Once posted in America, the numbers changed. Soldiers married women they met locally, resulting in widely varied numbers of wives with each regiment; typical numbers were about one for every eight men, roughly 25 percent more than the number that had been allowed on the voyage to America. When armies went on campaign, such as General John Burgoyne's army setting out from Canada toward Albany in June 1777 or General William Howe's army embarking in New York to sail toward Philadelphia the following month, commanders limited the number of wives allowed to accompany the campaign army; others remained behind in garrison. But in every location, women formed part of the infrastructure that allowed the army to take the field while facing dangers often equal to those of the soldiers, sometimes narrowly escaping death, other times succumbing to it. The attrition caused by these hazards means that the sixty women who embarked with a regiment sailing for America in 1775 were not the same sixty that returned to Great Britain with the regiment in 1783.

Following a soldier husband meant traveling far more extensively than most people of the era. The journey from Great Britain to America could be anywhere from eight to sixteen weeks on board a ship tossed by storms and threatened by disease—a facet of military life not shared by most European armies that focused their activities on the continent. The number of women that embarked with each regiment was usually recorded but not the number that disembarked; it was not unusual for a few soldiers to die during ocean voyages, so probably some wives and children did as well. But while muster rolls enumerate the soldiers' deaths, records of women who died at sea are scarce. Elizabeth Sennett is one of the few named. She boarded the schooner HMS *Savage* in New York in December 1782 to travel home with her daughter Margaret and her fifty-five-year-old husband, Patrick, a twenty-six-year veteran being discharged because of wounds. She died a month later of unknown causes, still at sea but only days away from England's shore.[13] On 23 December 1775, the *Marquis of Rockingham,* a transport carrying three companies of the 32nd Regiment from England to Ireland to replace troops sent to America, was dashed on the rocks of the Irish coast. "Upwards of 90" soldiers drowned, as did every single woman and child on board, a number not published, probably around thirty.[14] On 22 April 1779, the *Mermaid* transport foundered near Egg Harbor, New Jersey. One hundred and thirteen men of the 82nd Regiment were lost; the thirty-five men who survived were listed by name in a newspaper account of the tragedy. None of the dead were named, including all thirteen wives and seven children on board who perished.[15]

On shore, army wives lived in the same barracks, tents, huts, and outbuildings as the soldiers when space permitted, and found their own quarters when it did not. When away from the frontlines, there were dangers nonetheless. In September 1779, a soldier's wife perished when the boat carrying her and three others from New York City to Sandy Hook overturned. Her name is not given in the only record of the incident, a newspaper advertisement placed by the owner of the boat seeking its return.[16] Two years later, a British barracks in Charleston, South Carolina, burned down, and "a woman in childbed died in the blaze."[17]

Domestic strife could endanger any woman anywhere, and the army was no exception; indeed, it may have escalated it. On Staten Island in 1776, Sarah Norrington of the 40th Regiment was stabbed with a bayonet—but not fatally—by her husband after he saw her assaulted by another soldier—whom he stabbed to death—while she was asleep after being "very drunk."[18] Sergeant Alexander Monroe of the 76th Regiment came home one afternoon in New York in 1780 to find his wife very drunk—and drinking with another man, he claimed, but no one else corroborated that detail—and beat her. She died of a bayonet wound. On trial for murder, he claimed that his bayonet had fallen from its scabbard as he struggled with her, and she fell on it accidentally. With no definitive evidence that he had stabbed her intentionally, he was convicted of manslaughter rather than murder.[19] William Whitlow of the 44th Regiment stabbed his wife with a rusty bayonet in September 1779 on board a transport carrying the regiment from New York to Quebec. Even though "there was not a happier Couple in the Regiment," Whitlow was prone to erratic fits caused, it was said, by a fall from a wall when he was a child. It was during one such fit that he "seemed Crazy and like a Madman," accusing his wife of infidelity and appearing "staring and wild." Several people saw him poke her chest with the bayonet, a wound that seemed superficial but which caused her death four days later. On trial for murder, he had no recollection of the event and was acquitted because "he was in a State of Lunacy at the time."[20]

There was no acquittal for John Lindon of the 22nd Regiment. His wife, an army nurse, refused to live with him. In August 1780, he went to the hospital where she worked and confronted her in front of several onlookers. They argued. She told him to go away and not make a disturbance in the hospital. He said he would not go until he had "his right." She asked what that right was, and he replied, "herself was." She asserted that she "would never live with him or any one else," to which he retorted, "if she would not live with him she should not live with any one else." He turned as if to leave but instead picked up his musket, leveled it at her chest, and fired at point-blank range. She died within hours. At his murder trial, John Lindon testified that his wife's "repeated ill behaviour exasperated him in such a manner, that at times he was not sensible and could not be accountable for his Actions." The court did not accept this rationale and convicted him. He was hanged in March 1781. Were it not for his trial record, nothing at all would be known about his wife; no one at the trial even mentioned her first name.[21]

Lynn argues that pillage was a common motive driving women to marry into European armies.[22] This may be true of some women who married when war was imminent or in progress, especially before the eighteenth century, but this motive is questionable after the advent of standing armies when soldiers could spend entire careers without setting foot in hostile territory. Many British Army wives had been in America well before war broke out in 1775, whether they came from Great Britain with their regiments—some of which arrived as early as 1767 for routine garrison duty—or were already in America when they found their soldier husbands. They cannot be assumed to have married on the hope that war would eventually break out and afford an opportunity for spoils.

Even after hostilities began, British troops came to America to quell a rebellion, not to conquer a foreign power, making plunder an unlikely motive, especially for American-born women, to marry into the army. That
said, laying aside premeditation, there is no question that moving from
place to place, combined with wartime conditions, turned army wives
into resourceful opportunists, some of whom turned to dishonorable
ways to supplement their existence.

Armies going on campaign were accompanied by different numbers
of wives at the discretion of local commanders—sometimes four per
company (of about fifty soldiers), sometimes two, sometimes no specified number, the remainder staying behind in garrison. Some of those
who went on campaign participated in the rampant plunder that plagued
British Army operations in America. A British newspaper report on operations in New Jersey in 1777, compiled from letters recently arrived
from America, reported, "As to the plundering, there is nothing so common as to see the soldiers wives, and other women, who follow the army,
carrying each three or four silk gowns, fine linen, etc. etc. which have
been stolen by the soldiers from different houses in their march."[23] In an
effort to curtail such pillaging, women were often ordered to march with
the baggage of the army and forbidden from straying or straggling. That
such orders were repeated suggests that they were not strictly followed,
even after threats of being "punished on the Spot, in the most Exemplary
Manner." In early 1781, company commanders campaigning in the Carolinas were ordered to "cause an immediate Inspection of the Articles of
Cloathing at present in the possession of the women in their Companies," and to inspect them again periodically to ensure that nothing new
was illicitly acquired. This, it was hoped, would "prevent these Women
(Suppos'd to be the Source of the most infamous Plundering) from evad-
ing the purport of this order." It was nonetheless necessary only a week
later to order women to attend all roll calls and to drum out any who
were absent.[24] No record has been found of whether any women actually were drummed out on this campaign.

As Ruma Chopra points out in her study of loyalist women in the
city of New York, a "disorderly camp required disciplinary measures."[25]
Those included summary penalties when the army was on the march and
more formal, court-ordered punishments in garrison. Records of both
suggest a distinction between how the army perceived and responded to
plundering as compared to theft in garrison. Three wives were tried by
general court martial during the war for theft or receiving stolen goods.
Others may have been tried by lower courts for which no records survive,
but given the overall number of women in America during the eight-year

war, there is not enough evidence to argue that "wives' efforts to subsist often led to theft or squabbling, which put them at risk of criminal punishment."[26] The cases described below are not a few examples to illustrate a pervasive problem but rather are the only presently known examples during the entire war.

Anne Hennessey and her husband, John, a soldier in the 52nd Regiment of Foot, went to trial in Boston in December 1775 for harboring stolen goods. She lived in a rented apartment, and military officials found the goods in other parts of the building; lacking any evidence that the couple knew of the stolen items, the court acquitted them.[27] That same month, Thomas and Isabella McMahon of the 43rd Regiment stood trial for "receiving Sundry stolen goods knowing them to be such." In this case, one of the thieves confessed and testified against the others, leaving no doubt that Isabella McMahon had been involved in dividing and selling the stolen clothing and fabric. The court sentenced her "to receive one hundred lashes on her bare back at the Cart's tail in different portions in the most conspicuous parts of the town, & to be imprisoned for three months." It is not known whether the sentence was carried out or remitted.[28] Eleanor Webb was an American woman who had married Edward Webb of the British Foot Guards in Philadelphia in 1778. The following year in New York, a court martial tried her for receiving stolen goods. When she was found guilty, her sentence was to be "drummed out of the lines with a rope around her neck." Her husband was also involved and sentenced to five hundred lashes; he nonetheless stayed in the army until 1796, when he received a pension after twenty-four years of service, and he did further stints in British garrison corps until 1807.[29] Whether he ever saw Eleanor again after she was drummed out remains unknown; there is no record of her after her trial proceedings.

Followers faced not only military discipline but also hazards on campaign, which ranged from comic to tragic. A soldier in the 33rd Regiment remembered a raid to destroy enemy stores at Bedford, New York. Amid other destruction, the soldiers broke open hogsheads of molasses. "A soldier's wife went to dip her camp-kettle in," he wrote, "and while she was stooping in order to fill her kettle, a soldier slipped behind her and threw her into the hogshead: when she was hauled out, a bystander threw a parcel of feathers on her, which adhering to the molasses, made her appear frightful enough." At the unnamed woman's expense, "This little circumstance afforded us a good deal of amusement."[30] In Yorktown, Virginia, in August 1781, "thunder and Lightning & rain" killed two soldiers and a woman of the 43rd Regiment of Foot, the men's names traceable through muster rolls, the woman a nameless fatality.[31]

One ordeal of campaigning was particular to women. Roger Lamb, a soldier in the 9th Regiment of Foot, was traveling alone in 1777 from General Burgoyne's army at Fort Miller on the Hudson River to Fort Ticonderoga, a distance of about sixty miles. Stopping at a house for the night, he discovered the wife of a sergeant in his regiment in the throes of childbirth. She had been left at Ticonderoga when the army moved south toward Albany, but unwilling to be away from her husband, she set out on her own toward the frontlines. The homeowners found her in the woods, in labor, and took her in. The intrepid woman gave birth to a daughter, with whom she set out the very next day to catch up with the army. They apparently fared well, for decades later Lamb met the daughter in Dublin.[32] When Burgoyne's soldiers were being marched as captives over the Green Mountains toward Boston in November 1777, a soldier's wife gave birth to a child "in the midst of the heavy snow-storm, upon a baggage cart, and nothing to shelter her from the inclemency of the weather but a bit of an old oil-cloth." In spite of the harsh conditions, they arrived at the Prospect Hill barracks where "she and the infant are both well." The officer who recorded this pointed out that "it may be said, that women who follow a camp are of such a masculine nature, they are able to bear all hardships; this woman was quite the reverse, being small, and of a very delicate constitution."[33] Lamb wrote in turn that the sergeant's wife "gave an instance of the strength of female attachment and fortitude, which shews that the exertions of the sex are often calculated to call forth our cordial admiration."[34] But neither author thought to mention the names of these admirable women.

As soldiers became prisoners of war, so too did their wives. American forces surprised the tiny garrisons of Fort Ticonderoga and Crown Point in May 1775. They took forty-nine sergeants, drummers, and privates of the 26th Regiment of Foot and sent them into captivity in Connecticut. With them were thirty-four women and children.[35] Toward the end of that year, American forces moving toward Quebec captured most of the 7th and 26th Regiments at posts along the Richelieu River. Several hundred soldiers, with over seventy wives, went into captivity in a barracks in Lancaster, Pennsylvania.[36] The British Army that surrendered at Saratoga in October 1777 went into barracks outside of Boston. A return of those troops at Prospect Hill, which included only the British soldiers (the German soldiers were at Winter Hill), included 2,616 noncommissioned officers and privates and 211 women.[37]

The prisoners held on Prospect Hill were being fed, but this was not the case for all imprisoned wives. The garrison captured at Stony Point on the Hudson River in July 1779 was marched to Philadelphia and held in jails there. On 10 August, one of the captive soldiers, William Dinsmore of the 71st Regiment, wrote a petition to the American commissary of prisoners explaining "that your Petitioner is a Married Man has his Wife and two Children with him in the Goal. That the rations allowed, is not Sufficient, to maintain or support them. That he has no money or any thing to raise money in order to purchase any thing for his Family." He continued that although wives were allowed out of jail to find work, Mrs. Dinsmore had been unable to "get any Family that would admit her with the trouble of her, with her two Children, as She can do very little more than take care and attend her own Children." He therefore sought permission to be released to work at his own trade, rope-making, to support his family.[38] The following week, Hannah Norman, wife of Sergeant William Norman of the 17th Regiment of Foot, penned her own letter to the commissary of prisoners. "During the time of my Confinement in the New Prison," she wrote, "I have been very much afflicted with Sickness, but being something recovered I beg your honour wou'd be pleased to grant my Liberty to walk out once or twice a week that I may be more capable of procuring some nourishment, which, at this time, I am not able to provide." She signed her name "Hannah Norman, 17th foot."[39]

The prisoners taken at Saratoga in October 1777 remained interned until the end of the war, and although the majority absconded, a return from June 1781 suggests that married men were much more likely to remain imprisoned than escape. In January 1778, there were 211 wives with the British prisoners at Prospect Hill. In June 1781, those prisoners were at Lancaster, Pennsylvania; less than one-third of the soldiers remained but there were 174 with wives present.[40] Lacking names from 1778, it is not possible to determine whether some men had married while prisoners, nor are there comprehensive records to reveal what became of the women who were no longer among the prisoners. One of them, Mary McCarthy, wrote a petition describing her remarkable story. She had married into the 9th Regiment of Foot when her former soldier-husband in the 7th Regiment died in Canada early in the war. She followed her new husband on campaign to Saratoga, where he was captured. When the prisoners were moved from Prospect Hill to Virginia in 1779, her husband attempted to escape while crossing the Hudson River but was recaptured. Mary McCarthy, with three children in tow, spent a year in the Hudson Highlands before getting an unusual opportunity to go down river to British-held New York City. Benedict Arnold, then an American general, gave her a pass to carry dispatches to his British correspondents in New York. She made the journey on 4 September 1780, delivering coded letters that finalized the terms of Arnold's treasonous attempt to surrender the post at West Point, a plot that was foiled three weeks later. She never did connect with her husband again, and in 1783 petitioned the British military government in New York for permission to relocate to Nova Scotia.[41]

Mary Driskill's ordeal also began in 1777 but further south in early December when the British Army sent a foraging expedition out from Philadelphia into the Pennsylvania countryside. In fighting around Whitemarsh, her husband, Cornelius Driskill, a grenadier in the 10th Regiment of Foot, was wounded and left for dead on the battlefield; she was taken prisoner and put into jail in Trenton, New Jersey. She escaped but was caught and imprisoned once again, this time in Lancaster, Pennsylvania. She escaped, this time with three soldiers. Caught once more, she was "cast into Carlisle Prison." At some point during her repeated imprisonments, she gave birth to twins. She and two other women managed to escape from Carlisle and cross the Susquehanna River in a canoe. After days of "lying in the Woods with her Two Twins" and "many other hardships," she got into New York City with her children. By this time, her regiment had returned to Great Britain, and she found herself with no support in a city crowded with refugees. In November 1779, she wrote a petition for relief, explaining that she was "in a Very Disconsolate Condition, having by means of Lying in the Woods with her Two Twins, lost her hearing, and has nothing to Support herself and Children, nor a house to shelter her and little Ones, from the Inclemency of the Weather."[42] Like so many determined British Army women, Mary Driskill's fate is not known. Her husband, meanwhile, had not died on the battlefield but recovered from his wounds in Philadelphia and in 1778 was sent with another regiment to the West Indies; he returned to Great Britain, was discharged from the army in 1792, and received a pension, but there is no record of whether he was ever reunited with his wife or the two children he had never met.[43]

Mary Driskill was captured because she was close to the fighting, rather than because her garrison or the field army as a whole was captured. Other unnamed women also had this experience. During the siege of Boston on the night of 7 January 1776, "about 150 of the Rebels came over to the out posts of Charles Town set 2 old houses on fire, took a Sergt & 4 men & a woman (who contrary to orders lay in these out houses) prisoners."[44] Being among the men on the front lines put countless wives in danger, of whom we have records of only a few. Fredericka Riedesel, wife of a German general, spent several days in a basement with a few other women when Burgoyne's army was besieged at Saratoga in 1777. She recounted, "Because we were badly in need of water, we finally found the wife of one of the soldiers who was brave enough to go to the river to fetch some. This was a thing nobody wanted to risk doing, because the enemy shot every man in the head who went near the river. However, they did not hurt the woman out of respect for her sex, as they told us themselves afterwards."[45]

Random shots knew no respect for gender. In a skirmish in New Jersey on 22 June 1777, "where the Quibbletown Road meets and turns into the Amboy Road" in New Jersey, American musketry "killed and wounded about 20 Soldiers and a Woman a Grenadiers Wife."[46] During the siege of Newport, Rhode Island, in August 1778, American mortar bombs arced into encampments behind British lines. A town resident wrote in his diary that "the cannonading continues briskly; 1 soldier and 2 women were killed in the camp by the bursting of a bomb; a child was killed in its mother's lap by a cannon-ball."[47] They remain unnamed wives of unnamed soldiers with unrecorded stories who met untimely deaths on American battlefields.

Throughout the entire eighteenth century there are a few documented cases of women disguising themselves as men and serving as British soldiers, none of which pertain to the American Revolution.[48] British newspapers, however, reported several incidents of women trying to enlist, only to be discovered. Five anecdotal accounts appeared in British newspapers between January and April 1776, all pertaining to the 71st Regiment of Foot that was being raised in the Scottish Highlands for the war in America. None are corroborated by other sources, and although similar, each has distinctive details. A "good-looking girl" attempted to enlist due to "a quarrel with her father, whose cloaths she had absconded in."[49] "A stout woman dressed in mens clothes" enlisted but was soon identified by a man who "claimed her as his wife." "A young woman in Glasgow, of the name of Gardener, having got herself equipped in the Highland dress," enlisted but was discovered. "A servant maid, disguised in men's apparel" received enlistment bounty money from a recruiter, then was given leave to return home; "she paid off some debts, and then fled the country." "A young woman of the name of Black, enlisted herself for a soldier" and served for five weeks, until "a woman in a house which she sometimes frequented became amorous of the supposed handsome young lad, and made such advances as brought on a discovery of the recruit's sex."[50] Some, if not all, of these stories may be permutations of the same rumor, and all may be nothing more than romantic hearsay

at a time of vigorous recruiting for the American war. Yet the fact these
vignettes, true or not, were reported in newspapers shows the persistence
of the "warrior women" in popular culture that Lynn demonstrates existed at least as early as the 1620s.[51]

Here and there, women did fight. A British officer wrote of an alter-
cation outside of Boston between the wife of a British prisoner of war
and an American guard. Wives had been allowed to leave and reenter
the prison area, but "an old man upon guard" one day refused a woman
this privilege. They argued, and she "displayed much of the Billingsgate
oratory," that is, used the sort of foul language made famous in London's
Billingsgate fish market. Irritated by this, the guard pointed his musket
at her, but being "a true campaigner," she grabbed the firearm from him,
"knocked him down, and striding over the prostrate hero, in the exulta-
tion of triumph, profusely besprinkled him." She stood over her antago-
nist, wielding his weapon, until a party of guards came to free him.[52]

If the British Army had a Margaret Corbin or a Molly Pitcher, it
would be the wife of John Middleton of the 47th Regiment of Foot. He
was in the Battle of Trois Rivières, which took place along the St. Lawrence River between Quebec and Montreal on 8 June 1776. While he was
engaged in the fighting, Mrs. Middleton went "for some Milk to carry to
her Husband." She found a house a quarter mile from the river, but upon
opening the door she was startled to discover six rebel soldiers inside. She
summoned the courage to lash out at them, saying, "Ay'nt ye ashamed of
yourselves ye villains to be fighting against your King & Countrymen!"
They looked at her sheepishly, so she proclaimed that they were her prisoners and demanded their firearms, which they gave over to her. Standing between them and their weapons, and keeping an eye on two other
rebel soldiers outside, she called to some sailors at the river who came
to her aid, taking the two men outside and receiving her prisoners from
her.[53] She had single-handedly captured six men and caused the capture
of two more, with only her strong will as a weapon.

Her husband, Robert Middleton, was born in the early 1730s in Carlow, Ireland. He had been a tailor before joining the army and stood five
feet seven, with gray eyes, light brown hair, full face, and a fresh complexion. Like most British soldiers, he had enlisted in his early twenties. He
received an army pension when he was discharged in 1785 after twenty-
nine years of service, then spent several years in the Carlow militia. He
was still alive in 1800 and could not write his own name.[54] All this can be
determined from carefully kept army records, but there is no indication
that he distinguished himself in any way during almost four decades as a

soldier. His wife took six prisoners during the American Revolution, but the writer who left the single record of her achievements did not even give her name, referring to her only as "the wife of Middleton Soldier in the 47th Regt." and mentioning that she was "a very modest, decent well looking Woman."[55]

This is the legacy of the American Revolution's British Army wives. We can estimate that between five and ten thousand were with their soldier husbands during the American Revolution, but a precise number is not known. The names of about eight hundred have been found, probably only about 10 percent of the total; of those, the first names of fewer than half are recorded.[56] For most, there is only a single record of their existence, with no indication of age, background, how long they followed the army, or how long they lived. As John Lynn astutely points out, "there is more to the story of women in the campaign community" than simply tallying their numbers.[57] There is also more to the lives of the women who served with the British Army in America during this war than can be discerned by a few surveys. Throughout the American Revolution, the participation of wives in every aspect of military activity, not just in supporting roles, is apparent in both personal and military writings. In all cases where writers mentioned soldiers' wives by name, and in many cases where they related an experience of an unnamed wife, they mentioned the regiment in which she served, a strong indication of the wives' connection not just to a man but to a military organization.[58] Were it not for occasional passing mentions, there would not be any record of their incidents and exploits. And yet they supported operations and endured the rigors of campaigns, gave birth and cared for children, suffered captivity, sustained wounds, died on battlefields, and sometimes performed acts of bravery and feats of endurance equal to any soldier.

NOTES

1. Journal of Thomas Sullivan, 973.3.SW5, American Philosophical Society, Philadelphia.
2. Walter Hart Blumenthal, *Women Camp Followers of the American Revolution* (Philadelphia: G. S. Macmanus, 1952); Henry Belcher, *The First American Civil War* (London: Macmillan, 1911).
3. Paul Kopperman, "The British High Command and Soldiers' Wives in America, 1755–1783," *Journal of the Society for Army Historical Research* 60 (1982): 14–34.
4. For details on these roles, see Don N. Hagist, "The Women of the British Army during the American Revolution," *Minerva Quarterly Report on Women and the Military* 13, no. 2 (Summer 1995): 29–85.

5. See, for example, Veronica Bamfield, *On the Strength: The Story of the British Army Wife* (London: Charles Knight, 1974), and Noel T. St. John Williams, *Judy O'Grady and the Colonel's Lady: The Army Wife and Camp Follower since 1660* (London: Brassey's Defence, 1988).

6. See Jennine Hurl-Eamon, *Marriage and the British Army in the Long Eighteenth Century: "The Girl I Left Behind Me"* (New York: Oxford University Press, 2014), and John A. Lynn, *Women, Armies, and Warfare in Early Modern Europe* (New York: Cambridge University Press, 2008).

7. Although not a microhistory, this essay reflects some of its ideas. For a description of microhistory, see "What Is Microhistory," The Micro-Worlds Lab: A Humanities Unbounded Collaborative Project in History at Duke University, https://sites.duke.edu/microworldslab/what-is-microhistory/.

8. These figures are deduced from a wide assortment of military returns throughout the war. See Hagist, "The Women of the British Army during the American Revolution," 29–40.

9. Notably, Serena Zabin, *The Boston Massacre: A Family History* (Boston: Houghton Mifflin Harcourt, 2020).

10. Hurl-Eamon, *Marriage and the British Army*, 124–31.

11. Lynn, *Women, Armies, and Warfare*, 13.

12. The established full strength of a British infantry regiment changed several times during the war; five hundred men, not including officers, is a good figure for making generalities.

13. Muster book, HMS *Savage*, ADM 36/10223; Out Pension Admission Books, WO 116/8, entries for 31 March 1783 (for Patrick Sennett), National Archives of the United Kingdom, Kew, England (hereafter TNA). Note that the voyage from America to Great Britain usually took only about a month.

14. *Edinburgh Advertiser*, 9 January 1776. It was typical to embark six women per company, and a similar number of children, so we can estimate eighteen wives and ten to twenty children for three companies.

15. *Edinburgh Advertiser*, 18 June 1779.

16. *New York Gazette and Weekly Mercury*, 27 September 1779.

17. "Valentin Asteroth's Diary of the American War of Independence, 1776," in *Diary of A Hessian Chaplain and The Chaplain's Assistant*, trans. Bruce E. Burgoyne (Scotland, PA: Johannes Schwalm Historical Association, 1990), 17–60.

18. Trial of William Norrington, WO 71/82, 377–88, TNA.

19. Trial of Alexander Monroe, WO 71/92, 217–22, TNA.

20. Trial of William Whitlow, WO 71/90, 397–405, TNA.

21. Trial of John Lindon, WO 71/83, 196–98, TNA.

22. Lynn, *Women, Armies, and Warfare*, chap. 3.

23. J. Almon, *The Remembrancer; or, Impartial Repository of Events, for the Year 1777* (London: J. Almon, 1778), 154.

24. Orders for 27 December 1780, 28 February, 2 March 1781, in "A British Orderly Book, 1780–1781," ed. A. R. Newsome, *North Carolina Historical Review* 9, no. 1 (January 1932): 57–78.

25. Ruma Chopra, "Loyalist Women in British New York City, 1776–1783," in *Women in Early America*, ed. Thomas A. Foster (New York: New York University Press, 2015), 22.

26. Hurl-Eamon, *Marriage and the British Army*, 136.

27. Trial of John and Ann Hennessey, WO 71/82, 235–40, TNA.

28. Trial of Thomas and Isabella McMahon, WO 71–82, 207–10, TNA.

29. Park M'Farland Jr., *Marriage Records of Gloria Dei Church* (Philadelphia: M'Farland & Son, 1879), 76; Trial of William Grinsell, Edward Webb, and Eleanor Webb, WO 71–91, 47–51; Discharges of Edward Webb, WO 121/13/11 WO 121/116/36, WO 121/145/497, WO 121/156/113, TNA.

30. Don N. Hagist, *British Soldiers, American War* (Yarley, PA: Westholme, 2012), 25.

31. Notebook of daily operations against the Americans in the War of Independence, written by an officer of the 76th Regiment, Robertson of Kindeace Papers, GD146/18/6, National Archives of Scotland, Edinburgh.

32. Roger Lamb, *Memoir of His Own Life* (Dublin: J. Jones, 1811), 182–83, 189.

33. Thomas Anbury, *Travels through the Interior Parts of America, in a Series of Letters* (London: W. Lane, 1789), 2:24.

34. Lamb, *Memoir*, 189.

35. Total number of prisoners sent into New England from the two garrisons, Thomas Gage Papers, American Series, vol. 129, William L. Clements Library, University of Michigan, Ann Arbor.

36. John B. Linn and William H. Egle, eds., *Pennsylvania Archives*, 2nd series (Harrisburg: State Printer, 1879), 1:411–20.

37. Return of the British Troops Who Draw Provision, Prospect Hill, 5 March 1778, Musters and Payrolls, vol. 9, Massachusetts Archives, Boston.

38. William Dinsmore to Thomas Bradford, 10 August 1779, Collection No. 1676, series 3, box 22, vol. 2, p. 53, Thomas Bradford Papers, Historical Society of Pennsylvania, Philadelphia.

39. Hannah Norman to Thomas Bradford, 18 August 1779, Collection No. 1676, series 3, box 22, vol. 2, p. 57, Thomas Bradford Papers.

40. "List of British Prisoners Brought to Lancaster by Major Baily the 16th of June 1781," Peter Force Papers, series 9, reel 106, pp. 675–85, Library of Congress, Washington, DC.

41. John C. Fitzpatrick, ed., *Calendar of the Correspondence of George Washington* (Washington, DC: Government Printing Office, 1906), 1504; Petition of Mary McCarthy, PRO 30/55/8798, TNA.

42. Petition of Mary Driskill, WO 30/55/2452A, TNA.

43. Discharge of Cornelius Driskill, WO 121/11/316, TNA.

44. "Bamford's Diary," *Maryland Historical Magazine* 27, no. 4 (December 1932): 242.

45. Marvin L. Brown Jr., *Baroness von Riedesel and the American Revolution: Journal and Correspondence of a Tour of Duty, 1776–1783* (Chapel Hill: University of North Carolina Press, 1965), 60.

46. C. Willcox, ed., *Major André's Journal* (Tarrytown, NY: William Abbatt, 1930), 30.

47. "Newport in the Hands of the British: A Diary of the American Revolution," *Historical Magazine* 4 (1860): 106.

48. For the several known cases, see Elizabeth Ewing, *Women in Uniform through the Centuries* (London: B. T. Batsford, 1975).

49. *Middlesex Journal, and Evening Advertiser* (London), 4 January 1776.

50. *Edinburgh Advertiser,* 19 January, 2 February, 22 March, 5 April 1776.

51. Lynn, *Women, Armies, and Warfare,* 166–72.

52. Anbury, *Travels,* 2:81–82.

53. "Letters to Lord Polwarth from Sir Francis-Carr Clerke, Aide-de-Camp to General John Burgoyne," *New York History* 79, no. 4 (October 1998): 413.

54. Out Pension Admission Books, WO 116/9, entries for 8 November 1785, TNA; Discharge of Robert Middleton, WO 121/149/63, TNA. Note that Middleton was discharged from the 8th Regiment of Foot, into which he had transferred from the 47th. Muster rolls, 47th Regiment of Foot, WO 12/5871, TNA.

55. "Letters to Lord Polwarth," 413.

56. The author has compiled names of British soldiers' wives from myriad sources and found fewer than eight hundred at this writing. Many documents give phrases like "John Wilson and wife" or "Mrs. Johnston" rather than recording full names; other references are passing mentions, such as depositions in which soldiers mention having wives. More names will certainly turn up, but there is no comprehensive record of wives even from a single regiment.

57. Lynn, *Women, Armies, and Warfare,* 89.

58. This connection is explored in some detail in Hurl-Eamon, *Marriage and the British Army,* chap. 4.

Catharine Greene's War
for Independence

MARTHA J. KING

—◇◇◇◇◇—

ONE EARLY September day in 1782 in the waning months of the American Revolution, Lewis Morris wrote to his commander, General Nathanael Greene, at his South Carolina headquarters. He offered news of the general's wife, Catharine Littlefield Greene, and described life on Kiawah, a sea island fourteen miles off the coast of Charleston, where she and several officers of the Southern Army had gone to recuperate from malarial fevers. Morris flattered, "We are much indebted to Mrs Greene for her vivacity and good humor" as she kept them "all in good spirits" and helped drive away the "blue divils" of depression. The island adventures of Catharine and her coterie filled pages of Morris's correspondence to his betrothed as well. He described efforts to restore their health and "laugh away the fever" by filling their mornings with reading and conversation, afternoons with "riding upon an extensive beach, gazing at the wide ocean and plunging into its waves." Evenings were chock-full of songs, stories, backgammon, and cigar smoking. Catharine and her "little society," with Morris as its designated caterer, feasted on duck, chicken, beef, crab, fish, potatoes, coffee, and wine. Catharine sent her husband some of the island's seafood bounty. The general, in turn, shipped flour, spirits, sugar, peaches, paper, quills, wax, and even a spyglass.[1]

With such good living, Morris concluded to his general, "Your lady has got her Block Island complexion and looks as she used to do." He then tattled, "But I am afraid her dress is too thin." Thinking that Nathanael could exert influence over his wife's wardrobe from his headquarters more than twenty miles away, but overestimating Greene's powers, Morris subtly queried, "Would it not be right, as the weather is growing cooler, and she wears no stays, to send her a flannel vest and recommend her to put it on?"[2] Despite his aide's concern, the forty-year-old Nathanael Greene was hardly inclined to tell his twenty-seven-year-old free-spirited wife of ten years what to wear and how to wear it. This general's wife and mother of four, unencumbered by clothes, children, or kin, discovered freedom in her travels to the Carolina Lowcountry. Paradoxically, Catharine Greene experienced more leisure, liberty, and tranquility during the War for Independence and battled more in peacetime when she later fought with Congress to indemnify her late husband's debts and clear his reputation.

Catharine Greene's travels to South Carolina, where her husband had assumed command of the Southern Army in 1780, were fraught with risk but also opportunity. Three major factors fostered her enhanced mobility and ensuing freedom. Foremost, she had a large kinship network in the couple's native Rhode Island—including her husband's brothers and her own family on Block Island—to raise her children. Second, her status as the wife of a general afforded her escorted passage, special treatment, and preferential accommodation both en route and in camp that other soldiers' wives and followers did not receive or expect. Finally, she had been inoculated for smallpox, providing her with a degree of immunity to venture forth from the confines of her New England home.[3] She was free to express her status, sociability, even sexuality while senior officers concomitantly vied for her attention and the approval of her husband, to whom they reported and depended for back pay, promotions, and potential postwar opportunities. She experienced liberation in assuming her identity as Lady Greene and the perks that came with being the general's wife, even as her husband worried about how to exact supply quotas from the southern legislatures to feed and clothe his troops.[4] Caty Greene, meanwhile, could choose to be nearly naked or fashionably attired. Just as she discarded the stays and sartorial strictures in the sultry heat of summer on Kiawah Island, she also cast off the associated expectations of proper behavior for her class and status, relishing her chance to play the part—or not—at times when it most suited her.

Carefree living and abundant provisions were not what most women experienced during the Revolution. War could be brutal for those who either chose direct involvement, were recruited into it, or were inadvertently caught in its crosshairs. Recent scholarship has defined and enriched our understanding of the American Revolution and the women whose experiences of war were as myriad as the unique individuals who endured it.[5] Women's wartime existence varied by region, class, age, race, and whether they remained at home or their homes and communities became combat zones or occupied territory.[6]

Catharine Littlefield Greene's activities provide another lens with which to view women's actions, agency, and influence in the American Revolution. Unlike the correspondence of other elite compeers who were often separated from spouses (like Martha Washington, Abigail Adams, and Lucy Knox), no letters written to her husband exist.[7] Her letters to other contemporaries and their words about her, fortunately, do survive. This evidence reveals that war offered Catharine Greene experiences beyond the home front that shed new light on the nature of marriage, the meaning of independence, and the choices women faced as they exercised gendered power in the midst of armed conflict. Catharine Greene's story conveys how seemingly contradictory experiences could coexist—that there could be leisure and freedom even in the midst of fighting, that not all White women were shouldering "deputy husband" duties when their spouses went off to war, that occupation could be opportunity, that allegiances were rarely clear-cut but were often ambiguous.[8] This is not to diminish the very real worries, sacrifices, and suffering that were almost constant for wives of enlisted soldiers and officers. Nor is it to mitigate the grim atrocities of guerilla warfare, partisan fighting, and privation in the Revolutionary South. Rather, this story of the war as it was winding down offers another perspective to enrich and complicate our understanding of women's lived realities during war.

The Americans achieved victory at Yorktown in October 1781 before Catharine Greene's southern sojourn in 1782–83, but the war that dominated the couple's marriage was still far from over. Throughout the Greenes' twelve-year marriage, Catharine spent much of her time en route to or visiting with her husband at his camps despite the dangers of wartime travel, the responsibilities of a growing family, and sometimes her husband's admonitions for her personal health and safety. She proved to be an important social mediator, a bridge between polite society and the harsh and brutal realities of war. For her husband she was a distraction and a reminder of domestic felicities. As hostess, raconteur, morale booster, and matchmaker, Catharine played an important though often under-recognized role in the Continental Army's community. At balls, parties, teas, and other social events, Catharine relished the attention and new acquaintances from her visits to her husband in camp, and she reveled in her celebrity status and the community she fostered.

Catharine Littlefield was born in 1755 on Block Island, Rhode Island. After her mother died, she was raised by a maternal aunt, Catharine Ray

Greene, the wife of William Greene Jr., who later became governor of Rhode Island.[9] She married the Quaker anchor-smith and merchant Nathanael Greene in 1774.[10] Shortly thereafter, her husband chose a military career, despite his Quaker upbringing, as the best way to secure his economic and political future; he rose through the ranks from the local militia and Kentish Guards to service as a general in the Continental Army. His appointment in the regular army included duty as quartermaster general and a very short-lived command at West Point until George Washington ordered him south in the autumn of 1780.[11]

Personal hardships, long separations, and fluidity of plans were the yoke of wartime service for military families, but Catharine often joined her husband in camp, including at Cambridge, Valley Forge, Brooklyn, and Morristown. Thus, war did not always mark the end of her domestic happiness; rather, it created new social opportunities and popularity for her.[12] She befriended other generals' wives and enjoyed her husband's wartime acquaintances and comrades including Washington, Alexander Hamilton, Anthony Wayne, Henry Knox, Baron von Steuben, and the Marquis de Lafayette. Squabbles with her in-laws, who managed her absent husband's affairs and helped care for their children, made Nathanael's invitations to visit him very appealing. While her husband was busy with the army, Catharine enjoyed a more independent, carefree social life in camp. Being present to or in proximity of the general meant she stayed current on intelligence and helped ease her burden of not knowing if her husband were safe or well. While devoted to her children, her maternal bonds and concerns about their upbringing paled in comparison to the immediacy of spousal connection. Certainly, the couple expressed their longing to be together when apart, and passionate reunions punctuated their marriage.

Catharine proudly acted the role of a general's wife on visits to her husband in his headquarters where the welcome sometimes included dinner invitations and dances in her honor as well as preferential housing, where she extended hospitality to junior officers.[13] The performative nature of her role created a public display of her marriage—her own theater of operations—as well as a more private opportunity for intimacy away from extended family. But these conjugal visits came at a price and frequently meant traveling while pregnant, nursing, or weaning an infant. Sometimes childbirth itself happened in camp, as it did for many other camp followers, but under much better care and conditions for a general's wife.[14] Wartime visits might have relieved Catharine of productive labor on the home front, but she never escaped the possibility of reproductive labor that came from being with her husband.

Many people tried to discourage Catharine from going to her husband in South Carolina by using some familiar tropes of home as a woman's proper sphere. Military aides and even her husband himself repeatedly advised Catharine not to undertake such a journey.[15] In March 1781, Nathanael cautioned that the war in the South would present her with "rude manners" and "shocking scenes" to which a lady was unaccustomed.[16] "My dear you can have no Idea of the horrors of the Southern war."[17] He wrote her from the High Hills of the Santee in mid-July 1781, "South Carolina and Georgia have been the seat, and are still, of a hot and bloody war. Therefore you would have had no resting place in this Country on this side Pennsylvania. Besides the hot season of the year would have made sad havock with your slender constitution."[18]

George Washington extended an invitation to Catharine to come to camp only if her husband deemed it wise.[19] But Nathanael knew the true power dynamic in their marriage and realized she alone would ultimately make the choice. He expressed to Henry Knox his wife's independence in the decision to travel, painting "the dangers and difficulties in such strong colours. However I left her at liberty to follow her own inclinations, and perhaps her wishes has got the better of her prudence."[20] Her husband knew she would be better off, although less content, at home. Nathanael, ever the martial strategist, also mastered the marital tactic of keeping silent and losing the battle to win the war, or rather keep the peace, thereby honoring his promise to leave her at liberty to make up her own mind.

Several reasons prompted Catharine to make the long journey. In the spring of 1781, she had been involved in an emotional gossiping feud with Deborah Olney, the wife of one of her husband's relatives, and a southern trip might have been a welcome respite from rumor mills in Rhode Island social circles.[21] Loneliness, depression, and even jealousy of others might account for her feeling "in a widowed state far from most all my friends," as she expressed it a few months later to a friend in Connecticut.[22] Catharine did not, however, lack for familial support, enslaved labor, and servant help during her husband's deployments. She moved from Coventry, Rhode Island, with the children to Nathanael's farm in Westerly. Her brother-in-law Jacob and his wife, Margaret, managed the Coventry house during the war and assumed the extra burden of watching their children.[23] Years earlier, before setting off for war, Nathanael directed her to follow his brothers' advice, "unless they should so far forget their affection for me as to request anything unworthy of you to comply with. In that case, maintain your own independance untill my return."[24] It seems plausible that Catharine did not enjoy being managed by her husband's five brothers and their wives or being indebted to them financially.

With her mind made up to travel south, Catharine arranged for the care of their "dear little Pledges of conjugal affection," as Nathanael was wont to call his children.[25] She placed the three youngest with relatives and readied her oldest, almost six-year-old son George Washington Greene, for the long journey. In November 1781, Catharine and her son, accompanied by her husband's aide, set out from Rhode Island in a two-horse phaeton for the four-day ride to Philadelphia. Necessity, social opportunity, routine repairs, weather delays, and the generosity of friends slowed their travel. During an extended layover in Philadelphia in November, Catharine enjoyed the attention of polite society including the hospitality of Colonel Clement Biddle and his wife.[26] She also visited with the Washingtons, who were then residing in Philadelphia and who invited her to stop at Mount Vernon along the way. George Washington remarked in a letter to Nathanael in mid-December that Mrs. Greene "is in perfect health and in good Spirits," and that he would gladly "strew the way over with flowers" during her journey.[27] Martha Washington (for whom the Greenes' eldest daughter was named) and Catharine Greene had been friends since their days spent together visiting their husbands at the Cambridge, Massachusetts, headquarters of the Continental Army in the winter of 1775–76. Catharine was now able to provide some comfort to the grief-stricken Lady Washington, who was mourning the loss of her only son, John Parke Custis, who had contracted a fever and died a few days after the siege of Yorktown.[28] Catharine's friendship also deepened with his widow, Eleanor Calvert Custis, whom she had known since the winter in Cambridge when they were both young brides, with the two exchanging gossip and accounts of balls and society ever since.[29]

Catharine's other friends from her extended stay in Philadelphia, from late November 1781 to mid-January 1782, also prevailed on her to leave her young son George behind in the care of Colonel Charles Pettit, who attended to the boy's education and eventually took him to Princeton where he studied under Reverend John Witherspoon of the College of New Jersey.[30] Once free of her parental duties, Catharine continued on her journey south accompanied by another aide, Major Ichabod Burnet, and a Mrs. Kingston.[31] Snowstorms and iced roads delayed their departure from Philadelphia until February. But Burnet reported to his commanding general that despite it all, "Mrs Greene bears all the fatigue and delay with her usual fortitude and cheerfulness."[32]

Catharine exercised much independence in her social choices along the way. She and her "suite" arrived in Fredericksburg, Virginia, on 4 February and stayed about a week, hosted by General George Weedon and his wife, Catherine Gordon Weedon, who gave a ball in Greene's honor on 8 February. A few days later was the celebration of Washington's birth-day, and Catharine "suffered herself to be prevailed upon to stay till that time." In a brilliant crowd of more than sixty couples, Catharine danced with General Alexander Spotswood while Major Burnet "personated General Greene and danced with Mrs. Spotswood."[33] Even in her hus-band's absence, she was able to invoke his presence to afford her social status by association.[34]

Catharine's trip assumed heightened urgency as she made her way fur-ther south, hoping to reach her husband's headquarters by spring. When she passed through Richmond, one officer reported that Mrs. Greene "flew by us with the wings of impatience."[35] Yet she conveyed a sense of social and military protocol in her wish to be met at least five miles out from camp.[36] On 25 March 1782, the joyful day of their reunion, Na-thanael exceeded her expectations and greeted her twelve miles from his Dorchester, South Carolina, headquarters.[37]

After almost two years apart, General Greene reported his happiness on his wife's arrival: "She is in better health and spirits than I could have expected after such a disagreeable journey. She is kinder to me than I am just to her. To come a eleven hundred miles to visit me through such a variety of difficulties and dangers claim a grateful and generous return."[38] Her demeanor was a temporary distraction for her husband from wor-ries about supplying the troops, restoring civil order, convening the South Carolina Assembly at nearby Jacksonborough, and planning for the British evacuation of Charleston. Nathanael reported that despite such concerns, he was "as happy as my little Chatty Girl can make me."[39] "Her flowing tongue and chearful countenance quite triumphs over my grave face," he later remarked.[40] Although she suffered from bouts of colic, Catharine's main preoccupations were matchmaking, dancing, and various social pleasantries with the senior officers of the Southern Army. Adapting to the rhythms of marriage once again, Nathanael bemusedly wrote to his friend George Weedon, "Have you learnt to bow properly? I have been so long in the woods that Mrs Greene says I have the graces to study anew. . . . you see after all my labours I am under petticoat Govern-ment still."[41]

Nathanael seems to have reveled in Catharine's popularity with his fellow officers. Each spouse may have enjoyed the increased social sta-tus that the other's presence legitimated and created but looked askance at their flirtations with others.[42] Peter S. DuPonceau recalled her from Valley Forge as a "handsome, elegant, and accomplished woman" who spoke French and was well-versed in French literature, thereby charming foreign officers who felt welcome at her residence.[43] Catharine appeared "as elegant in her manners as in her person" by wearing a military jacket and skirt and traveling on horseback with a large retinue. "Her decorations were richly plaited" and were very stylish, remarked one commentator recalling how she presented herself in the South.[44] Nathanael boasted to a friend, "They call her the french Lady in Charlestown."[45] Her expensive fashion predilection also set the general's wife apart in Charleston, although it might not have endeared her to Greene's bedraggled rank and file.

Soldiers in the Southern Army knew privation and experienced first-hand what one doctor later observed about Carolina being "in the spring a paradise, in the summer a hell, and in the autumn a hospital."[46] In the sweltering summer and early fall of 1782, Nathanael grew gravely concerned about malarial fevers. In "the sickliest season known this thirty years," he lamented the tragic loss of soldiers' lives not on the glorious field of battle but in the lonely beds of pestilential camp hospitals.[47] He banned all funeral marches so as not to further depress his sickly troops.[48] By the second week in September, an estimated half of the men in camp were ill. General Anthony Wayne, who had joined Greene in South Carolina shortly after the British evacuation of Savannah, suffered a near fatal fever. Malaria led to the deaths of almost one hundred men in September.[49] Many of the new draftees were ill and unfit for service. Even with her earlier smallpox inoculation, Catharine's health was also of tantamount concern to the southern commander.

Nathanael tried to drum up much-needed recreational opportunities for his lagging officers, whose failing health and homesickness seemed to worsen as they awaited back pay and the British evacuation of Charleston. When her husband obtained permission for his recuperating senior officers to travel under a flag of truce to Kiawah Island, Catharine wanted to go.[50] She too stood to benefit from a salubrious stay on the island, its social opportunities, and its less costly lifestyle than in urban, British-occupied Charleston as she and her fellow travelers would live off the land and the marine bounty while her husband remained behind in camp.

In late August 1782, the small party of about a half-dozen members boarded boats to make the brief passage. Catharine found Kiawah an inviting place with its southern border on the Atlantic Ocean, its moderate climate, and its abundant natural resources.[51] Among the crew accompanying her were Dr. Robert Johnston, the purveyor for hospitals of the Southern Department who was himself recovering from fevers;

Colonel William Washington and his new wife, Jane Elliott Washington; Colonel Lewis Morris Jr.; Major William Pierce; Captain Nathaniel Pendleton Jr.; and his brother Judge Henry Pendleton.[52] Mordecai Gist, the brigadier general from Maryland who had commanded the remnants of Lee's Legion and served with Greene in the summer of 1782, joined the Kiawah Island group later in September.

Nathanael kept abreast of the activities and health of the island sojourners through correspondence with his aides. He wrote Lewis Morris Sr. and passed on comforting news about the benefits of "a change of air, diet, and exercise" and described their surroundings—the fine beach, fine fish, wild game, and fresh fruit that promised to restore them to health.[53] Lewis Morris also regaled his father and future bride, the wealthy plantation heiress Ann (Nancy) Elliott, with idyllic accounts of their indulgent island life of rest and recuperation.[54] Morris reported on the group's plan to remain at Kiawah possibly until the evacuation of Charleston and offered reassurance that they were secure from plundering "as Gen Leslie has pleased to favor us with protection."[55]

In their relaxed environment, Catharine befriended some of her husband's fellow officers and served as matchmaker, encouraging them in their romantic pursuits.[56] As raconteur, she delighted them with her amusing tales. For female companionship, Catharine, "a great favorite even with the ladies," relied on young Charlotte Fenwick, the daughter of a South Carolina planter and future wife of William Pierce.[57] Nathanael remarked on the lighthearted activities of the group who were engaged in singing, dancing, and learning "the rules of gallantry by heart in french and English."[58] Both Catharine and her husband advised securing one's financial future through marrying well. As matriarch, not by age but by position, of the transplanted army and as the general's wife, Catharine needed an escort on social occasions and thereby provided the young officers with practice in social deportment so crucial for courtship in southern society.[59] They in turn vied for her attention, whether smitten by her charms or hoping to make a favorable impression to be reported to her husband that could possibly advance their careers.

The group apparently stayed at the Gibbes plantation on the island. At first, their hosts seemed "infinitely obliging." But then Nathaniel Pendleton wrote to Greene berating the lack of hospitality and shortage of wine from their host, Robert Gibbes, a loyalist and Charleston merchant.[60] Pendleton also complained that Gibbes forbade them to use the Black oarsmen or to take forage from the island: "The washwoman is taken from Mrs Greene and none but the fisherman remains."[61] A few

days later, Pendleton described that although they were "extreemly cautious" of Gibbes's property, their host seemed to think "we have made too
free with it," and perhaps they did. Despite previous offers of assistance,
Gibbes had ordered all "his Negroes into the field, & the wench home."
Pendleton regretted that they were obliged to use Gibbes's enslaved laborers to bring them fresh water each day from Johns Island. When William Washington asked to borrow a cart to transport his baggage, Gibbes
replied that his oxen were too fatigued to make another journey to Kiawah.[62] At first glance it might seem strange that the commander of the
Continental troops in the South would send his wife and fellow senior
officers to a plantation owned by a known loyalist. But Greene was a
pragmatic general who knew that adaptability to changing circumstances
was essential for survival and perhaps recognized the same in Gibbes.
He likely acknowledged the pragmatic choices Gibbes had made earlier
in the war to keep his plantation from being burned by the British or
confiscated by the Continentals in this delicate dance of accommodation
and ambiguous allegiances.[63]

Uncertain of their precise lodgings or the duration of the island ex-
cursion, Nathanael initially doubted his wife would stay a fortnight.[64]
Morris and Catharine did soon return, she presumably to tend to her
husband's health when he succumbed to fevers in September.[65] Once
confident, however, that Nathanael was on the mend, Catharine returned to Kiawah, and his aide William Pierce kept him informed of
the island party's "delights" and occasions for philosophic solitude and
contemplation. Pierce wrote caricatures of each of his island compatriots
and concluded, "Mrs Greene who is the very picture of health, sits, ob-
serves, and laughs at all about her."[66] General Mordecai Gist, an island
late-comer, reported Mrs. Greene's "immoderate passion for Gaming at
BackGammon" and the losses that altered her temper and disposition
as a result. On one such occasion, when Catharine had lost a considerable sum of money to Gist, "she in a very revengeful manner threw both
Dice & Men at my Head. I lodge this report against her, that she may be
recalld, brought to trial, and justice done me for the Insult."[67]

Around mid-November, the island group disbanded and departed
from the comforts of Kiawah. The British evacuation of Charleston was
imminent. It was a proud day for both Lady Greene and her general on
14 December 1782, when the last British soldier left town. And fashionable Caty Greene played the part. Lewis Morris asked his fiancée to assist in procuring a small pair of gold epaulettes for his commander's wife,
who had "so much the spirit of the military about her." "As she is the better

part of the General himself, and has a claim to equal rank," he explained, she was "determined to be in uniform with her husband and therefore prefers deep blue with yellow buttons and buff facings."[68] Obviously Ann Elliott was obliging, for a few weeks later Morris reported, "Mrs Greene will be quite militaire with her fine epauletts, and you must not be surprised if she should mount her Bucephalus and enter the Town at the head of the army."[69] The American forces followed quickly on the heels of the British in the peaceful changeover. Anthony Wayne moved toward the British works leading four companies of light infantry, a detachment of Lee's Legion, and two artillery pieces. By three o'clock that afternoon, Greene, the governor, his council, and other prominent citizens rode in a triumphant procession into Charleston. The streets and balconies were crowded with cheering well-wishers.[70]

Lady Greene, in a ceremonial combination of military, political, and social display, was certainly among those overjoyed at the reoccupation of the city by the Americans. She exercised a class imperative to see and be seen, embodying and asserting the merits of privilege. She and Nathanael established residence in former Governor John Rutledge's "very elegant" house in Charleston. In a letter to her cousins in Rhode Island she recounted,

> The Gen writes his letters I suppose are well stored with Politicks; so I shall say nothing upon that subject—I must however tell you that we have got possession of Charlestown or rather Jerusalem for it is all in all with this country—Now *we* have drove all the lobster backs out of this country—indeed I know not what we should have done this winter without Charlestown—for you know the country is not the place for amusement and as the army has gone through so many distresses and fatigues I think a little relaxation is but just and proper.[71]

They did more than relax. Nathanael expected "a great frolick" terminating with a fine ball to mark the British evacuation, and noted that "Mrs Greene has set her heart upon it."[72] Catharine, partnering with George Washington, had danced "upwards of three hours without once siting down" during a stay at Middlebrook, and she recalled such occasions with playful pride.[73] She planned an even more memorable ball in Charleston on 2 January 1783, and with the help of Thaddeus Kosciuszko, decorated a ballroom with magnolia leaves and paper flowers.[74] The Greenes also expected the ball would "equal a Connecticut thanksgiving," implying much free-flowing rum and spirits, as Kosciuszko and other officers awaiting a return to civilian life made the most of the social whirl.[75]

But by spring 1783 and more than a year since she left Rhode Island, Catharine had grown restless. While her husband and others awaited confirmation of the peace treaty recognizing American independence and worried about their postwar livelihoods and whether to return home or perhaps pursue a planter lifestyle in the South, Catharine wondered about her children. She decided it was time to head for home. On 6 June she boarded the ship *Christiana* for Philadelphia, not feeling well enough to make the entire journey by coach. The trip from Charleston to Cape Henlopen, Delaware, took four days during which Catharine, Kosciuszko, and other travelers found themselves queasy from the rough waters and winds.[76]

Philadelphia, the city that had been so graciously hospitable to her a year earlier, repeated the welcome. More balls, parties, and renewed friendships with Wayne, Jeremiah Wadsworth, and others greeted Catharine at every turn.[77] She stayed with family friends, the Biddles, and was "pestered to death with ceremony and civility."[78] Knowing his wife's enjoyment of the social scene and male attention, Nathanael wrote ahead to Gouverneur Morris of his wife's visit: "On her arrival in Philadelphia you'l exhibit against her articles of impeachment for such high misdemeanors as her conduct may merit. I leave her to answer for her self."[79] And this went for her spending habits as well.

Catharine spent money compulsively and conspicuously on clothes and carriages as she tried to maintain the image of a successful general's wife.[80] Nathanael worried that he could not make good on all the debt she was accruing, including a new phaeton, constructed at the cost of seven hundred dollars. Before she left Philadelphia in early August, her husband was in debt nearly six hundred pounds for her additional purchases. Nathanael, who was surprised by these bills, later complained of his wife, "She is a little extravagant; but she spends money very good Naturedly."[81] What bothered him more though was that she had not written. Annoyed at her husband's attempt to rein her in, Catharine responded with cold silence. After a brief stay in New York where she saw Alexander Hamilton, she traveled to Rhode Island by water.[82]

Nathanael did not leave South Carolina until mid-August 1783. In dramatic contrast to his wife, who left by ship in June, Nathanael traveled to Philadelphia by horseback, careful of costs to counter wartime and wifely debts.[83] Whereas Catharine purchased silks, Nathanael purchased slaves.[84] Worries about how he would make his southern plantations economically viable and profitable preoccupied him as he saw the poverty and devastation of the postwar states on his trip home. He did, however, enjoy the honors and gratitude bestowed on him as commander of the Southern Army as he passed through Richmond, Fredericksburg, Alexandria, Annapolis, and Baltimore.[85] After arriving in Philadelphia in early October, he sailed on, reaching Newport in late November. While he was en route, peace commissioners signed the treaty in Paris marking the official end of a long and bloody war and the beginning of his return to civilian life.

Upon her return home, Catharine once again took up domestic burdens with children to care for, reduced mobility, limited landscapes, and reinforced roles and gender constraints.[86] When Nathanael returned, he was alarmed by his wife's advanced pregnancy and his correspondence from as early as March 1784 repeatedly shows that he believed that she would be brought to bed at any moment.[87] Catharine gave birth to her fifth child, Louisa, on 17 April 1784, slightly more than ten months after she had left South Carolina and her husband's bed. No explanation of the baby's belated birth appears in the correspondence, and Nathanael probably opted for pragmatic acceptance. He did delay business trips and visits with his brothers during his wife's lying in, and three months after she delivered, he sailed back to Charleston where he ostensibly tended to unsettled financial matters for four months. He may also have been stewing over possible infidelity. Rumors swirled that Nathanael would divorce his wife because she had been unfaithful to his bed. Isaac Briggs, a Quaker surveyor and engineer who traveled widely in the South, investigated the claim in 1785 among the general's friends in Newport and concluded it had no basis in truth but that others were envious of a woman who thought and acted as she pleased.[88] Catharine had two more pregnancies: in Newport she gave birth in August 1785 to a daughter who died shortly thereafter, and in early April 1786, just two months before Nathanael died, she fell and lost another baby.

In the autumn of 1785, the Greene family moved from Rhode Island to Mulberry Grove outside Savannah. This two-thousand-acre confiscated loyalist plantation estate boasted some of the best rice lands in the South, and Georgia gifted it to Nathanael in recognition for his wartime service. Nathanael also acquired Cumberland Island, off of Georgia's southern coast, for his island-born wife. Even with the potential value in these lands, huge financial burdens filled the Greenes' postwar years. Those burdens included the wartime debts he had incurred by signing guarantees to John Banks and other contractors to provision the Southern Army. Congress, who voted against reimbursing his use of his private funds and business profits to procure desperately needed supplies for his troops, claimed his business dealings had been unauthorized and conducted secretly.[89]

After her husband's death from a presumed heat stroke on 19 June 1786 at Mulberry Grove, Catharine tried to get an indemnity petition for Nathanael's wartime debts. The campaign for financial independence and debt liberation was a long-fought battle. At the same time, she championed her husband's good name and reputation as well as her own as the general's wife while seeking to secure his family's fortune.[90] She felt triumphant when in April 1792, Congress awarded her $47,000 to be paid in installments. In 1796, in the presence of George and Martha Washington, Catharine married her children's Yale-educated tutor, Phineas Miller, who had been hired by Nathanael eleven years earlier and who had been a witness to the general's will. Catharine spent her later years managing a large plantation and providing financial support and patronage to Eli Whitney, who had joined them on the estate and who received Catharine's encouragement in his invention of the cotton gin. In 1814, a twice-widowed Catharine died at the age of fifty-nine on her Cumberland Island plantation.[91]

The constraints in the waning months of the war coupled with the Greene family's postwar personal financial crises provide a sharp contrast to the island leisure, freedom, and abundance that Catharine had experienced in September, October, and November 1782 during her southern sojourn. In comparison to Martha Washington and Lucy Knox, whose visits to husbands in their winter encampments seemed more grounded in patriotic duty, Catharine relished how such duty allowed her to act as if she were important and provided an acceptable occasion to exercise some independence that she lacked in Rhode Island where she could not really act as mistress of her own estate.

Camp visits during the War for Independence provided Catherine Greene with some of her happiest times and most liberating moments. She exerted her social capital as the general's wife while he spent—and lost—his economic capital in a quest to become a successful planter. Without disregarding her love for her children or her sacrifices during the military campaigns, one could interpret Catharine's life as the most engaged and independent in wartime camps and the most confined and dependent when at home, either under the watchful eyes of her brothers-in-law or in her postpartum/post-camp blues.

Because of her rank, race, and class, she was privileged with choices that other military spouses simply did not have. Some historians argue that the Revolution was not liberating for women as a whole or

that a woman gained only temporary domestic autonomy in her husband's absence.[92] Perhaps expanded definitions of independence are thus
merited, or at least more attention needed to where and when gendered
power is exercised in individual lives. For Catharine, the proclaimed
peace after the Revolution brought in its wake her own war to restore
her husband's name and reputation. As she fought for her family's financial solvency, she sought to obtain freedom *from* debt and exercise her
freedom *to* manage a plantation in the southern slave economy. Ironically,
the invention of the cotton gin, which Catherine Greene promoted and
hoped would secure her independence, further entrenched a system that
denied enslaved men and women from achieving their own freedom.[93]

Notes

1. Lewis Morris Jr. to Nathanael Greene (hereafter NG), 4 September 1782,
   and NG to Morris, between 1 and 4 September 1782, in *The Papers of
   General Nathanael Greene*, ed. Richard K. Showman et al. (Chapel Hill:
   University of North Carolina Press, 1976–2005), 11:627, 624–25 (hereafter
   NGP); Lewis Morris to Ann Elliott, 1 September 1782, in "Letters from
   Col. Lewis Morris to Miss Ann Elliott," *South Carolina Historical and Genealogical Magazine* (hereafter *SCHGM*) 40, no. 4 (1939): 133.
2. Lewis Morris Jr. to NG, 4 September 1782, in *NGP*, 11:627–28. Morris
   may also have been trying to impress his general with a classical allusion,
   "*Cois tibi paene videre est ud nudam.*" See Horace's Satire, book 1, satire 2,
   lines 101–2, in H. Rushton Fairclough, *Horace: Satires, Epistles, and Ars
   Poetica* (Cambridge, MA: Harvard University Press, 1929), 26, 27.
3. Elizabeth A. Fenn, *Pox Americana: The Great Smallpox Epidemic of 1775–82*
   (New York: Hill and Wang, 2001), 32, 98–101. For Catharine Greene's
   inoculation, see John F. Stegeman and Janet A. Stegeman, *Caty: A Biography of Catharine Littlefield Greene* (Athens: University of Georgia Press,
   1985), 23.
4. NG to Peter Horry, 8 June 1782, in *NGP*, 11:306. See also Malcolm Bell Jr.,
   Major Butler's Legacy: Five Generations of a Slaveholding Family (Athens:
   University of Georgia Press, 1987), 42–43, and John S. Pancake, *This Destructive War: The British Campaign in the Carolinas, 1780–1782* (Tusca-
   loosa: University of Alabama Press, 1985), 237–38.
5. Holly A. Mayer, *Belonging to the Army: Camp Followers and Community
   during the American Revolution* (Columbia: University of South Carolina Press, 1996); Carol Berkin, *Revolutionary Mothers: Women in the
   Struggle for America's Independence* (New York: Random House, 2005);
   Susan Branson, "From Daughters of Liberty to Women of the Republic: Women in the Era of the American Revolution," and Betty Wood,

"Southern Women of Color in the American Revolution, 1775–1783," in *The Practice of U.S. Women's History*, ed. S. Jay Kleinberg, Eileen Boris, and Vicki L. Ruiz (New Brunswick, NJ: Rutgers University Press, 2007), 50–66, 67–82; Holly A. Mayer, "Wives, Concubines and Community, Following the Army," in *War and Society in the American Revolution: Mobilization and Home Fronts*, ed. John Resch and Walter Sargent (DeKalb: Northern Illinois University Press, 2007), 235–62; Holly A. Mayer, "Bearing Arms, Bearing Burdens: Women Warriors, Camp Followers and Home-Front Heroines of the American Revolution," in *Gender, War and Politics: Transatlantic Perspectives, 1775–1830*, ed. Karen Hagemann, Gisela Mettele, and Jane Rendall (London: Palgrave Macmillan, 2010), 169–87; Nancy K. Loane, *Following the Drum: Women at the Valley Forge Encampment* (Washington, DC: Potomac Books, 2009); Tom Foster, ed., *Women in Early America* (New York: New York University Press, 2014); Barbara B. Oberg, ed., *Women in the American Revolution: Gender, Politics, and the Domestic World* (Charlottesville: University of Virginia Press, 2019).

6. See the excellent overviews by Kate Haulman, "Women, War and Revolution," in *The Oxford Handbook of American Women's and Gender History*, ed. Ellen Hartigan-O'Connor and Lisa G. Materson (New York: Oxford University Press, 2018), 551–69, and Gregory H. Nobles, "Historians Extend the Reach of the American Revolution," in *Whose American Revolution Was It? Historians Interpret the Founding*, ed. Alfred F. Young and Gregory H. Nobles (New York: New York University Press, 2011), esp. 224–55. For Charleston, see Lauren Duval, "Mastering Charleston: Property and Patriarchy in British-Occupied Charleston, 1780–82," *William and Mary Quarterly*, 3rd series, 75, no. 4 (October 2018): 589–622.

7. For Martha Washington, see Joseph E. Fields, ed., *"Worthy Partner": The Papers of Martha Washington* (Westport, CT: Greenwood Press, 1994), and the Martha Washington Papers Project, http://gwpapers.virginia.edu/martha-washington-papers-project/. For Abigail Adams, see Margaret A. Hogan and C. James Taylor, eds., *My Dearest Friend: The Letters of Abigail and John Adams* (Cambridge, MA: Belknap Press of Harvard University Press, 2007). For Lucy Knox, see Phillip Hamilton, *The Revolutionary War Lives and Letters of Lucy and Henry Knox* (Baltimore: Johns Hopkins University Press, 2017).

8. Donald F. Johnson, "Ambiguous Allegiances: Urban Loyalties during the American Revolution," *Journal of American History* 104 (December 2017): 610–31.

9. The only full-length biography of Catharine Greene is Stegeman and Stegeman, *Caty*. For her family background, see also *NGP*, 1:19n, 65–66, and "Nathanael Greene's Letters to 'Friend Sammy' Ward," *Rhode Island History* 16 (1957): 83. For a briefer interpretation of her life, see Catherine A.

Allgor, "Greene, Catharine Littlefield (1755–1814)," in *Women in World History: A Biographical Encyclopedia,* ed. Anne Commire (Waterford, CT: Yorkin, 2002), 6:494–99.

10. *NGP,* 1:32n.

11. NG resigned as quartermaster general on 26 July, briefly led the army in late September during Washington's absence, and commanded West Point from 8 to 17 October 1780 after Benedict Arnold's treason; see *NGP,* 6:xlv–xlvi.

12. For generals' wives, see Mayer, *Belonging to the Army,* 146–52, and Berkin, *Revolutionary Mothers,* 67–91. For NG's admission "How unfriendly is war to domestic happiness," see NG to Catharine Greene (hereafter CG), 15 or 16 October 1780, in *NGP,* 6:397–98.

13. NG invited army officers to dine in rotation with him and CG; see Francis T. Brooke, *A Narrative of My Life for My Family* (Richmond, VA, 1849), 40. For preferential housing, see Mayer, *Belonging to the Army,* 148–49, and NG to CG, 20 May 1777, in *NGP,* 2:86.

14. Several of CG's children were conceived or born in camp. George Washington Greene was born in late January or early February 1776 and was christened in camp. Presumably he was born in Rhode Island before CG set out for Cambridge on 20 February. Catharine visited NG in the summer of 1776 and gave birth to Martha Washington Greene in mid-March 1777. Her third child, Cornelia Lott, born 23 September 1778, was named for the daughter of family friends and their hosts at Morristown. Nathanael Ray Greene, the fourth child, was born at camp in Morristown on 31 January 1780. Louisa, the fifth child, was born in April 1784. *NGP,* 1:188n; 2:xxxix, 86n; 5:xxxvii; 13:xxxvii.

15. NG to CG, 18 November 1780; 23 June 1781, in *NGP,* 6:482–83; 8:443–44.

16. NG to CG, 30 March 1781, in *NGP,* 8:7.

17. NG to CG, 23 June 1781, in *NGP,* 8:443–44.

18. NG to CG, 18 July 1781, in *NGP,* 9:35–36.

19. George Washington to CG, 22 March 1781, in *The Writings of George Washington,* ed. John C. Fitzpatrick (1937; reprint, Westport, CT: Greenwood Press, 1970), 21:352–53.

20. NG to Henry Knox, 10 December 1781, in *NGP,* 10:27.

21. See the exchange of letters between CG and Deborah Olney in Marian Sadtler Hornor, "Notes and Documents: A Washington Affair of Honor," *Pennsylvania Magazine of History and Biography* 65 (July 1941): 362–70.

22. CG to Jeremiah Wadsworth, 11 September 1781, quoted in Stegeman and Stegeman, *Caty,* 90. For similar expressions of the "widowed state," see Alisa Wade's essay in this volume.

23. See Jacob Greene to NG, 4 May 1783, in *NGP,* 12:640–44.

24. NG to CG, 2 June 1775, in *NGP,* 1:82. NG was one of six sons born to Nathanael Greene Sr. and his second wife, Mary Mott. See also NG

to Christopher Greene, 20 January 1777, in *NGP*, 2:9. In addition to sharing parental responsibilities for the Greene children, NG's brothers were
involved in a family forge and business partnership that suffered financial
setbacks.

25. See, for example, *NGP*, 2:86.

26. Clement Biddle to NG, 11–18 November 1781; Charles Pettit to NG,
    14 December 1781, in *NGP*, 9:587–88; 10:55–57.

27. George Washington to NG, 15 December 1781, in *NGP*, 10:63.

28. Custis served as his stepfather's civilian aide during the Battle of York-
    town. See Custis to NG, 8 October 1781, in *NGP*, 9:437. See also Fitzpat-
    rick, ed., *Writings of Washington*, 23:392.

29. Eleanor Calvert Custis to Catharine Littlefield Greene, 23 March 1782,
    Historic Manuscript Collection, box 7, folder A-371, Fred W. Smith Na-
    tional Library for the Study of George Washington at Mount Vernon,
    Mount Vernon, VA.

30. For correspondence about George Washington Greene's schooling, see
    NG to Charles Pettit, 14 August 1782; Pettit to NG, 19 August 1782; John
    Witherspoon to NG, 19 August 1782; NG to Witherspoon, 28 August
    1782; Witherspoon to NG, 23 October 1782, in *NGP*, 11:540–41, 561–63,
    563–64, 586–88; 12:102–4.

31. Ichabod Burnet to NG, 22 November 1781, in *NGP*, 9:608–9.

32. Ichabod Burnet to NG, 5 February 1782, in *NGP*, 10:317–19.

33. *Maryland Gazette*, 24 March 1782, in *NGP*, 10:319n. Washington's birth-
    date on the old-style or Julian calendar was 11 February 1732; see also Alex-
    ander Spotswood to NG, 13 February 1782, in *NGP*, 10:362.

34. For the ways balls functioned to maintain elite identity, see Samantha Sing
    Key, "Aristocratic Pretension in Republican Ballrooms: Dance, Etiquette,
    and Identity in Washington City, 1804," *Early American Studies* 16 (2018):
    460–88, and Lynn Matluck Brooks, "Emblem of Gaiety, Love, and Legisla-
    tion: Dance in Eighteenth-Century Philadelphia," *Pennsylvania Magazine
    of History and Biography* 115, no. 1 (January 1991): 63–87.

35. William Davies to NG, 14 March 1782, in *NGP*, 10:502.

36. John Mathews to NG, 24 January 1782, in *NGP*, 10:259.

37. Theodore Thayer, *Nathanael Greene: Strategist of the American Revolution*
    (New York: Twayne, 1960), 399. Thayer says that NG set out from camp
    on 5 April to meet CG. Ichabod Burnet to Charles Pettit, 12 April 1782, in
    NGP, 11:38, suggests an earlier reunion. See also Burnet to NG, 21 March
    1782, in *NGP*, 10:259, 262, 529–30.

38. NG to Henry Knox, 14 April 1782, in *NGP*, 11:60–62.

39. NG to Jeremiah Wadsworth, [after 1 July? 1782], in *NGP*, 11:389–90.

40. NG to Charles Pettit, 29 August 1782, in *NGP*, 11:593.

41. NG to George Weedon, 22 April 1782, in *NGP*, 11:99–100. It is likely that
    Nathanael was familiar with "petticoat government" from reading the

popular and widely reprinted essays in the *Spectator* by Joseph Addison and Richard Steele suggesting that women reigned over the domestic sphere while their husbands were more suited for the outside or public sphere. See Mary Beth Norton, *Separated by Their Sex: Women in Public and Private in the Colonial Atlantic World* (Ithaca, NY: Cornell University Press, 2011), 76–104, 144–74.

42. For an example of the passionate nature of their marriage, which seemed to thrive on separations, reunions, and flirtations with the opposite sex, see NG to CG, 30 March 1777, in *NGP*, 2:50.

43. Peter S. DuPonceau, "Autobiographical Letters of Peter S. DuPonceau," *Pennsylvania Magazine of History and Biography* 40, no. 2 (1916): 181.

44. Joseph Johnson, *Traditions and Reminiscences Chiefly of the American Revolution in the South* (Charleston, SC: Walker and James, 1851), 469. For a discussion of visual characteristics used to convey a person's social standing and worth, see Robert V. Wells, *Revolutions in Americans' Lives: A Demographic Perspective on the History of Americans, Their Families, and Their Society* (Westport, CT: Greenwood Press, 1982), 203–5.

45. NG to Otho H. Williams, 6 June 1782, in *NGP*, 11:299–301.

46. Attributed to German physician Johann David Schoepf (1784) in Jennie Holton Fant, ed., *The Travelers' Charleston: Accounts of Charleston and Lowcountry South Carolina, 1666–1861* (Columbia: University of South Carolina Press, 2016), 39.

47. NG to Charles Pettit, 2 November 1782, in *NGP*, 12:136–37.

48. NG's orders, 26 August 1782, in *NGP*, 11:576.

49. Joseph Lee Boyle, ed., "The Revolutionary War Diaries of Captain Walter Finney," *South Carolina Historical Magazine* 98, no. 2 (1997): 143–45; Mary C. Gillett, *The Army Medical Department, 1775–1818* (Washington, DC: Center of Military History, U.S. Army, 1981), 124.

50. NG to Alexander Leslie, 20 August 1782, in *NGP*, 11:564–65.

51. George C. Rogers Jr., Alexander Moore, and Lawrence S. Rowland, *The History of Beaufort County, South Carolina*, vol. 1, *1514–1861* (Columbia: University of South Carolina Press, 1996), 171. For the ownership and history of early Kiawah, see Michael Trinkley, ed., *The History and Archaeology of Kiawah Island, Charleston County, South Carolina* (Columbia, SC: Chicora Foundation, 1993), 50–56, and Ashton Cobb, *Kiawah Island: A History* (Charleston, SC: History Press, 2006), 40–49.

52. For Robert Johnston, see *NGP*, 11:324–25, 622, 660. William Washington, of Stafford County, Virginia, and second cousin once removed of George Washington, had been captured after the battle at Eutaw Springs and was recuperating from a bayonet wound and a fall from his horse. While a British prisoner in Charleston for almost a year, he courted Jane Elliott, the daughter of Charles and Jane Stanyarne Elliott, who inherited the family's large rice plantation at Sandy Hill. She married Washington on 21 April 1782, and they remained in South Carolina where he became a planter,

state legislator, and civic leader. Suzanne Cameron Linder, *Historical Atlas of the Rice Plantations of the ACE River Basin—1860* (Columbia: South Carolina Department of Archives and History, 1995), 126; Stephen E. Haller, *William Washington: Cavalryman of the Revolution* (Bowie, MD: Heritage Books, 2001), 1, 56, 145, 147, 149–51, 157; William Washington to NG, 8 September 1781, in *NGP*, 9:306. Brevet Lieutenant Colonel Lewis Morris, son of Lewis Morris Sr. (a signer of the Declaration of Independence), graduated from the College of New Jersey in 1774 and served as aide-de-camp for NG from 1779 to 1782. Linder, *Historical Atlas*, 251. Nathaniel Pendleton was a lieutenant in the 11th Virginia Continental Regiment in 1776 at Fort Washington when it was captured. He later joined NG as an aide-de-camp in November 1780 and remained with him until the end of the war. *NGP*, 4:51n; 5:110n; 6:472n, 523n. His brother Henry Pendleton, a lifelong bachelor, was a member of the Charleston bar and served as a judge from 1776 until his death in 1788. NG had requested his parole from General Alexander Leslie, who found him "so very obnoxious" and hoped he would not stay in South Carolina. Pendleton was released with parole. See Henry Pendleton to NG, 10 May 1782; Leslie to NG, 27 June, 4 July 1782, in *NGP*, 11:179n, 377, 394–95.

53. "Letters to General Lewis Morris," *Collections of the New-York Historical Society for the Year 1875* 8 (1876): 506; NG to Lewis Morris Sr., 26 August 1782, in *NGP*, 11:577.

54. Lewis Morris and Ann-Barnett Elliott married on 23 January 1783 at her family home at Accabee near Charleston. NG, who approved of the match, wrote to Morris's father that Elliott was a "mistress of a fortune, not in expectancy but in possession, of at least 25,000 pounds sterling." NG to Lewis Morris Sr., 26 August 1782, in "Letters to General Lewis Morris," 8:506; *NGP*, 11:577. Lewis Morris developed Hope Plantation with almost four thousand acres and hundreds of enslaved persons, served five terms in the South Carolina State House of Representatives and one term as lieutenant governor, and inherited his family estate of Morrisania in Westchester County, New York. Linder, *Historical Atlas*, 252–54, 575.

55. Lewis Morris Jr. to Lewis Morris Sr., "Letters to General Lewis Morris," 8:507. See also Lewis Morris to Ann Elliott, 24 August 1782, in "Letters from Col. Lewis Morris to Miss Ann Elliott," *SCHGM* 40 (1939): 122–36; 41 (1940): 1–14.

56. NG to Otho H. Williams, 12 November 1782; NG to Williams, 17 September 1782, in *NGP*, 12:175; 11:671. For NG's general advice to bachelors, see Thomas Richardson to NG, 7 December 1782, in *NGP*, 12:270.

57. NG to Charles Pettit, 29 August 1782, in *NGP*, 11:593.

58. NG to Lewis Morris Jr., between 1 and 4 September 1782, in *NGP*, 11:625.

59. Lewis Morris was to escort CG to Accabee and the Elliott estate earlier in July. Morris to Ann Elliott, 15 July 1782, in "Letters from Col. Lewis Morris to Miss Ann Elliott," *SCHGM* 40 (1939): 123.

60. Nathaniel Pendleton to NG, 2 September 1782, in *NGP*, 11:621–22. Robert Gibbes's daughter Mary had a life estate in southern Kiawah. She married Thomas Middleton in 1774 but died in childbirth the following year. On her death, Robert Gibbes likely resumed operation of the plantation, which he held in trust for his granddaughter Mary. Michael Trinkley contends that the officers of the Southern Army assumed Robert Gibbes to be the owner of the Kiawah estate where they stayed. Gibbes was known to have British loyalties, which may explain why his plantation remained unscathed while another on the island's northern end was burned by the British in 1780. Trinkley, ed., *History and Archaeology of Kiawah Island*, 57–58.

61. Nathaniel Pendleton to NG, 16 September 1782, in *NGP*, 11:666.

62. Nathaniel Pendleton to NG, 20 September 1782, in *NGP*, 11:682–84.

63. Rebecca Brannon, *From Revolution to Reunion: The Reintegration of the South Carolina Loyalists* (Columbia: University of South Carolina Press, 2016); Donald F. Johnson, "Forgiving and Forgetting in Postrevolutionary America," in *Experiencing Empire: Power, People, and Revolution in Early America*, ed. Patrick Griffin (Charlottesville: University of Virginia Press, 2017), 171–88; Dennis M. Conrad, "General Nathanael Greene: A Reappraisal," in *General Nathanael Greene and the American Revolution in the South*, ed. Gregory D. Massey and Jim Piecuch (Columbia: University of South Carolina Press, 2012), 7–28.

64. NG to Charles Pettit, 29 August 1782, in *NGP*, 11:593.

65. Lewis Morris to Ann Elliott, 27 September 1782, in "Letters from Col. Lewis Morris to Miss Ann Elliott," *SCHGM* 40 (1939): 136.

66. William Pierce Jr. to NG, 14 September 1782, in *NGP*, 11:659–61.

67. Mordecai Gist to NG, 16 October 1782, in *NGP*, 12:67–68.

68. Lewis Morris to Ann Elliott, 29 October 1782, in "Letters from Col. Lewis Morris to Miss Ann Elliott," *SCHGM* 41 (1940): 5.

69. Lewis Morris to Ann Elliott, 19 November 1782, in "Letters from Col. Lewis Morris to Miss Ann Elliott," *SCHGM* 41 (1940): 8–9.

70. Hugh F. Rankin, *Francis Marion: The Swamp Fox* (New York: Thomas Y. Crowell, 1973), 288–89; Joseph W. Barnwell, "The Evacuation of Charleston by the British in 1782," *SCHGM* 11 (1910): 1–26; George Smith McCowen Jr., *The British Occupation of Charleston, 1780–82* (Columbia: University of South Carolina Press, 1972).

71. CG to Samuel Ward and Celia Greene, 23 December 1782, in *Rhode Island History* 17, no. 1 (January 1958): 19. Celia Greene, CG's cousin, was the sister of Ward's wife Phebe; see *NGP*, 12:328n.

72. NG to Otho H. Williams, 12 November 1782, in *NGP*, 12:175.

73. NG to Jeremiah Wadsworth, 19 March 1779, in *NGP*, 3:354.

74. Alexander Garden, *Anecdotes of the American Revolution* (Brooklyn: Union Press, 1865), 3:168; Miecislaus Haiman, *Kosciuszko in the American*

Revolution (Boston: Gregg Press, 1972), 125–26, 138–41. Thaddeus Kosciuszko joined NG as chief engineer in 1780. In 1782, he was stationed near Charleston according to the *Dictionary of American Biography*, ed. John H. Finley (New York: Charles Scribner's Sons, 1928–58), 10:497–98; George W. Kyte, "Thaddeus Kosciuszko at the Liberation of Charleston, 1782," *South Carolina Historical Magazine* 84 (1983): 11–21. See also Thaddeus Kosciuszko to Otho Williams, 1782, Otho Williams Papers, MS 908, #172, Maryland Historical Society, Baltimore.

75. NG to Jeremiah Wadsworth, 21 December 1782, in *NGP*, 12:326.

76. William Pierce Jr. to NG, 19 June 1783, in *NGP*, 13:40.

77. Jeremiah Wadsworth was in Philadelphia at this time before departing for Europe in late July. A recuperating Anthony Wayne arrived in the city in August and was lionized for his service in Georgia. Wayne toasted the city's "winter amusements" and enjoyed visiting "the Ladies at all hours" and going "to routs Balls Assemblies, &ca." so that "the body & mind are kept in such a whirl of pleasure dissipation & Intoxication as almost to preclude every Serious Idea." Quoted in Paul David Nelson, *Anthony Wayne: Soldier of the Early Republic* (Bloomington: Indiana University Press, 1985), 197; Mary Stockwell, *Unlikely General: "Mad" Anthony Wayne and the Battle for America* (New Haven, CT: Yale University Press, 2018), 147–49, 198, 233–34, 240, 288–91.

78. William Pierce, Jr. to NG, 19 June 1783, in *NGP*, 13:41.

79. NG to Gouverneur Morris, 3 April 1783, in *NGP*, 12:561–62.

80. CG acquired silk for herself and also delivered to George Washington a "Green silk embroidered pattern for a waistcoat" from the West Indies. NG to George Washington, 5 June 1783, in *NGP*, 13:24. On bills for her carriage purchases, see NG to Charles Pettit, 22 April 1784, in *NGP*, 13:297–98. For her expenses earlier in the war, see *NGP*, 13:720–22.

81. NG to Charles Pettit, 4 August 1783, in *NGP*, 13:84–85.

82. Alexander Hamilton to NG, 1 October 1783, in *NGP*, 13:134. CG remained on friendly terms with Alexander Hamilton, who on at least one occasion loaned her money; see CG to Hamilton, 10 May 1794; Catharine [Greene] Miller to Hamilton, 3 December 1796, in *Papers of Alexander Hamilton*, ed. Harold C. Syrett et al. (New York: Columbia University Press, 1961–87), 16:401–2; 20:419.

83. Thayer, *Nathanael Greene*, 421, 436. A congressional committee headed by Thomas Jefferson found that NG had overdrawn $6,000 on his allowance for personal expenses while in South Carolina. The committee recommended that in consideration of the high prices in the South at the time, the debt should be canceled. This was not done, and NG eventually received a bill, with the option to dispute charges, from the comptroller's office for $6,229 in specie. Congress canceled the debt except for $319 in September 1786, after NG's death. NG to CG, 4 August 1783, in *NGP*, 13:83.

84. See James Penman to NG, 1 October 1783, in *NGP*, 13:135–36. For NG and slavery, see Gregory D. Massey, "Independence and Slavery: The Transformation of Nathanael Greene, 1781–1786," in *General Nathanael Greene and the American Revolution in the South*, ed. Gregory D. Massey and Jim Piecuch (Columbia: University of South Carolina Press, 2012), esp. 246–62.

85. For NG's travels home, see *NGP*, 13:122–31.

86. Writing to Henry Knox on 12 March 1786, NG described his wife, "She is transformed from the gay Lady to the sober house wife." *NGP*, 13:669.

87. For CG's departure, see Boyle, ed., "Revolutionary War Diaries of Walter Finney," 152. See NG to Henry Knox, 4 and 25 March 1784; NG to Joseph Reed, 14 May 1784, in *NGP*, 13:252–53, 275–77, 311–13. For concerns about CG's pregnancy, see Jacob Greene to NG, 3 April 1784, in *NGP*, 13:283–84. NG remarked to Charles Pettit on 22 April 1784, "Mrs Greenes not getting to bed as early as she expected prevented my setting out for the Southward.... Mrs Greene is in bed and in a good way of recovery. I expect she will be about the house in ten days or a fortnight." *NGP*, 13:297–98. CG sailed from Charleston to Philadelphia with William Pierce, Thaddeus Kosciuszko, and Alexander Garden Jr. Accompanied by Garden, CG left Philadelphia for New York on 3 August. William Pierce to NG, 19 June 1783; NG to Charles Pettit, 4 August 1783, in *NGP*, 13:40–42, 84–85.

88. See Isaac Briggs to Joseph Thomas, 23 November 1785, in "Three Isaac Briggs Letters," *Georgia Historical Quarterly* 12, no. 2 (June 1928): 177–84; Ella Kent Barnard, "Isaac Briggs," *Maryland Historical Magazine* 7 (1912): 409–19. See also Jeremiah Wadsworth to George Washington, 1 October 1786; Washington to Wadsworth, 22 October 1786, in *Papers of George Washington, Confederation Series*, ed. W. W. Abbot et al. (Charlottesville: University of Virginia Press, 1992–97), 4:282–85, 298–99; and NG to Charles Pettit, 22 April 1784, in *NGP*, 13:298n.

89. Paul David Nelson, "Nathanael Greene," in *American National Biography*, ed. John A. Garraty and Mark C. Carnes (New York: Oxford University Press, 1999), 528–30; Savannah Unit Georgia Writers' Project, Work Projects Administration of Georgia, "Mulberry Grove from the Revolution to the Present Time," *Georgia Historical Quarterly* 23 (December 1939), 315–36; *NGP*, 13:ix–xiii.

90. See CG to John Adams, 14 March 1796, RG 46, Records of the Senate, National Archives of the United States, College Park, MD; Report on the Petition of Catharine Greene, 26 December 1791, in Syrett et al., ed., *Papers of Alexander Hamilton*, 10:406–68; CG to Thomas Jefferson, 24 April 1792; Jefferson to CG, 25 April 1792; Phineas Miller to Jefferson, 3 May 1793; Miller to Jefferson, 27 May 1793; Petition from Eli Whitney, 20 June 1793, in *Papers of Thomas Jefferson*, ed. Julian P. Boyd et al. (Princeton, NJ: Princeton University Press, 1950–), 23:457, 462–63; 25:644–45;

26:134, 334. For examples of the financial and legal difficulties CG faced, see CG to Jeremiah Wadsworth, 18 April 1789, in *Documentary History of the First Federal Congress, 1789–1791*, vol. 15, *Correspondence—First Session: March–May 1789*, ed. Charlene Bangs Bickford et al. (Baltimore: Johns Hopkins University Press, 2004), 280–81; and Peter Anspach to Alexander Hamilton, 2 July 1790, in *Documentary History of the First Federal Congress, 1789–1791*, vol. 7, *Petition Histories—Revolutionary War—Related Claims*, ed. Kenneth R. Bowling, Charles DiGiacomantonio, and Charlene Bangs Bickford (Baltimore: Johns Hopkins University Press, 1997), 492–96.

91. Stegeman and Stegeman, *Caty*, 124–210 *passim*.
92. See, for example, Elaine F. Crane, "Dependence in the Era of Independence: The Role of Women in a Republican Society," in *The American Revolution: Its Character and Limits*, ed. Jack P. Greene (New York: New York University Press, 1987), 257; Linda K. Kerber, *Women of the Republic: Intellect and Ideology in Revolutionary America* (Chapel Hill: University of North Carolina Press, 1980); Mary Beth Norton, *Liberty's Daughters: The Revolutionary Experience of American Women, 1750–1800* (Ithaca, NY: Cornell University Press, 1980); and Rosemarie Zagarri, *Revolutionary Backlash: Women and Politics in the Early American Republic* (Philadelphia: University of Pennsylvania Press, 2007). For an interpretation of CG's postwar life, see Larry E. Tise, *The American Counterrevolution: A Retreat from Liberty, 1783–1800* (Mechanicsburg, PA: Stackpole Books, 1998), 161–201.
93. Edward J. Cashin, "Three Officers and a Lady: The Hudson Highlands and Georgia during the Revolution," *Hudson River Valley Review* 21, no. 2 (March 2005): 30.

Eliza Lucas Pinckney

Female Fortitude and the Revolutionary War

LORRI GLOVER

—◦◦◦◦◦◦—

IN POPULAR imagination, the story of the American Revolution centers on the "founding fathers," elegantly clad in velvet knee-britches and powdered wigs, gathered in legislative halls writing the creeds of a nation. Patriotic statues and paintings make the creation of the American Republic appear reasoned, peaceful, admirable, and, inevitably, about White men. The War for Independence conjures up similarly romantic masculine images: tricornered capped state militiamen and Continental soldiers valiantly engaged in battles, facing down British Redcoats.[1]

Eighteenth-century Anglo-American culture and law prohibited women's direct involvement in governance and constitution-making. While White women participated in resistance campaigns against imperial taxation policies in the 1760s and early 1770s, they could not attend the meetings in which White men designed new state governments and declared independence from Great Britain. Nor were they present at the various congresses that governed the fledging republic, or participants in the conventions that drafted and ratified the Constitution. While many and diverse people created the new United States' culture and economy, the lawgivers were White men of rank and power.

The war was another matter: it was undiscriminating in its volatility and violence. The Revolutionary War was waged not only—or even primarily—by soldiers in pitched battles but also by civilians, who often contested the war's meanings and purposes. As the vicious conflict raged across North America, the home front and frontlines blurred beyond distinction, so that the eight-year-long contest touched—and transformed—virtually everyone in North America. Enslaved people, members of Native nations, and White women suffered displacement, brutalization, disease, and devastating financial and familial losses, but they also seized opportunities to secure independence—on their own terms. Their stories are central to fully understanding the Revolutionary War: the history beyond the imagined heritage.

Women's biographies hold great promise for correcting these distortions by illuminating the complex nuances of the revolutionary era and highlighting the centrality of women and families to the War for Independence. Depicting the imperial crisis and war from the point of view of female participants not only balances the historical record; the shift in perspective complicates longstanding assumptions about gender in the eighteenth century and the nobility of the patriot cause. To that end, this essay joins a growing number of scholarly biographies that dive into the lives of individual women who survived the guerilla, civil war of 1775–82.[2]

SOUTH CAROLINIAN and longtime planter-patriarch Eliza Lucas Pinckney (1722–1793) was neither a silent witness to the nation-making of self-styled gentlemen nor newly empowered by newfound independence. The most well-documented woman from the revolutionary-era South, she endured the most violent phase of a pervasively violent war. Her focus before, during, and after the brutal contest remained unchanged: the wealth, stability, and prominence of her family—priorities to which Pinckney devoted her life. But the war was far from an aside or an afterthought for her; it was immediate, long, chaotic, and cruel. What she endured turns our focus from men to women, from seats of power to the countryside, and from high-minded political theories to the hard realities of war.

Despite her gender, Eliza Lucas Pinckney had been an independent planter and head of household for much of her adult life: a quintessential eighteenth-century patriarch in nearly every way save for her gender. Historians are unaccustomed to imagining colonial women as patriarchs. But Eliza met the responsibilities, exercised the racial power, and enjoyed the community respect that came with the role, even when her hold on her family wealth and power was sometimes tenuous and anxiety-producing, as it was during the Revolutionary War.[3]

Starting in 1739, while still a teenager Eliza Lucas managed her father's properties in the South Carolina Lowcountry. The ambitious and formidable young planter partnered with established men to produce indigo, which soon became a cornerstone of South Carolina's economy. She commanded enslaved people on three plantations and conducted the international business associated with commodities production. She even studied legal treatises and wrote wills for some of her poorer neighbors.

In 1744, Eliza married the much older, wealthy widower Charles Pinckney and transitioned into a more traditional lifestyle, bearing four children in rapid succession. Eliza happily moved to England with Charles and her three surviving children in the early 1750s. When Charles died during a return trip to South Carolina in 1758, Eliza was devastated. But she had children to raise and a complicated estate to rescue from the shoddy management, she said, of "ignorant or dishonest Over Seers."[4] Eliza willed herself to climb out of the grief of widowhood and resolved to right her family's rocky finances and create a lasting legacy for her children, Charles Cotesworth, Harriott, and Thomas.

In his will, Charles left everything—and everyone—he owned to Eliza and their underage children. Charles also named Eliza his executrix. She managed the estate and the children's inheritances, numerous houses, thousands of acres of land, and scores of enslaved people. Eliza did not even bother to prove Charles's will. There was, she saw, "no body to call me to account."[5]

Eliza intended to keep that independence. "A second marriage never once entered into my head," she insisted.[6] Instead, Eliza embarked on a second, fifteen-year-long stint as a Lowcountry planter-patriarch. A savvy, conscientious businesswoman, she diversified her investments, purchasing, she explained, "different kinds of property, and in four or five different parts of the Country."[7] By 1774, her grown children had taken responsibility for their shares of a family estate that she had set on a rock-solid foundation. Eliza, in her fifties and a grandmother, felt secure in her wealth and status and proud of the highly accomplished children she had raised as a single mother. She expected to grow old in ease and comfort.

THE REVOLUTIONARY War upended Eliza Lucas Pinckney's privileged, predictable life and compounded her responsibilities as a planter-patriarch. She worked to keep her family united despite separations, exile, and divided loyalties. She tried to keep them safe during waves of violence, sickness, predations, and death. Her efforts and those of other women on behalf of their families and the patriot cause extended and, in some instances, deepened the brutality of the war. As the conflict dragged on, Eliza lost her homes, her livelihood, her wealth.

Eliza's wartime travails began soon after the outbreak of fighting in Massachusetts in the spring of 1775. Her sons, Charles Cotesworth and Thomas, immediately joined the military along with Daniel Horry, the husband of Eliza's daughter, Harriott. With the men immersed in the burgeoning war effort, Eliza Lucas Pinckney and Harriott Pinckney Horry assumed day-to-day responsibilities for the numerous Pinckney and Horry estates and business interests. Eliza lost friends, loyalists who fled back to the metropole, as severed allegiances and trade networks rocked the family finances.[8]

The war reached Eliza's hometown in June 1776. Carolinians mustered forces in a makeshift fort on Sullivan's Island, at the entrance to Charles Town harbor. Outgunned and outmanned, the Carolinians held one key if unanticipated advantage: they built their bastions using palmetto trees. The soft, spongy wood kept Britain's cannonballs from causing much damage. British commanders, stunned at their failure to break through the fortifications, gave the ceasefire order just after nightfall. The Carolinians—stunned themselves—had managed to prevail. This unexpected triumph emboldened reluctant Carolinians to embrace the still-radical idea of American independence. The fiasco at Sullivan's Island left a mark on the British too. Commanders refrained from undertaking another major incursion into South Carolina until late 1779.[9]

The three-year absence of pitched battles did not mean that Eliza and her family enjoyed peace. Thomas, Charles Cotesworth, and Daniel remained in their military appointments, which frequently carried them away from home and into harm's way. They balanced those perilous duties with onerous political offices as the new state of South Carolina and the young republic struggled to create viable governments. No one knew when the British might strike the Lowcountry again. Just days after the Second Continental Congress declared independence, Eliza asked Charles Cotesworth where she should move to keep safe. He could not say: "It is so uncertain when the Enemy will renew their attack."[10] Rumors ran like wildfire—about the size of Britain's forces, the timing of an invasion, the cruelty of soldiers. Some of it was true, much false. Fear of an assault on Charles Town traumatized people long before the war reached them.

Despite Eliza's and Harriott's diligence, the family finances suffered under the growing weight of embargos and inflation. For South Carolinians, the economy constituted the most chaotic and painful part of the Revolutionary War between 1776 and 1779. British blockades collapsed the Lowcountry export markets and fueled staggering inflation. Charles

Town, "once the seat of pleasure and amusement" for the Pinckneys, endured "almost total stagnation of every kind of business." What few items residents could import cost a fortune. Export profits could scarcely keep pace with tax obligations.[11]

Fearful of an invasion, Eliza, Harriott, and Harriott's children evacuated Charles Town for Ashepoo, one of Thomas's plantations fifty miles southwest of the city, part of a large exodus of White patriots and the beginning of a years-long pattern of fear and flight. Among their greatest fears: the rebellion of enslaved Carolinians on whose labor the Pinckneys' wealth depended. Eliza and Harriott soon moved again, with family friends, then with extended kin.[12]

Everyone in the family grew weary of these wartime disruptions. Eliza tried to take comfort in her deep religious faith. She kept repeating to herself and her children aphorisms about providential design and God's omnipotence. "I exert my utmost resolution," she said. Still, she found it "impossible not to be anxious."[13] And the worst was yet to come.

FRANCE'S ENTRY into the American conflagration in early 1778 widened the theater of war and forced Britain to recalibrate its strategy, sending troops into Central America, the Caribbean, West Africa, and India while fearing an invasion of the metropole. Concerned about their lucrative Caribbean holdings, the British decided to shore up the mainland southern provinces. South Carolina moved into Britain's crosshairs.

With the long-dreaded invasion imminent, Eliza retreated with Harriott to Harriott's principal residence, a plantation called Hampton, thirty-five miles northeast of Charles Town and far from the expected route of invading British forces. In the spring of 1779, Charles Cotesworth's wife, Sally Middleton Pinckney, and a half-dozen other women and their children moved in with Harriott and Eliza. Across the state, White women holed up together, seeking emotional and physical security in numbers. From reports out of New England and the mid-Atlantic, they had heard about sadistic British soldiers who waged war on the countryside and communities, violating women's homes and bodies. They knew they needed to rely on each other for protection, as the war effort consumed the attention of their male kin.

The Pinckney brothers along with Daniel Horry joined an expedition heading south to try and wrest Savannah from the British. The British stayed one step ahead, marching forces north in a bid to seize Charles Town. British soldiers inflicted tremendous damage as they made their way through the countryside. In early May 1779, a detachment raided

Thomas's Ashepoo plantation, which Eliza and Harriott had once envisioned as among the family's safest properties. The soldiers slaughtered Thomas's livestock, drank his liquor, burned down his house, and rode off on his horses. Nineteen enslaved people left with the British soldiers. The rest of the African Americans, Thomas complained to Eliza, "are now perfectly free & live upon the best produce of the plantation."[14]

General Sir Henry Clinton, British commander of the southern campaign, set out for South Carolina just after Christmas 1779, convinced that "this is the most important hour Britain ever knew."[15] By winning back the southern provinces—including capturing the largest city and most important port south of Philadelphia—he could save his country's claim over North America and, at last, break the Continental Army. The strategy was precise, the force designed to overwhelm. By March 1780, as far as Charles Town residents could see, British warships filled the sea. At least one hundred vessels under the command of Admiral Marriot Arbuthnot trained their weapons on the city. The mistakes of June 1776 would not be repeated. General Clinton, leading an army of ten thousand men, moved relentlessly up the southern coastline. General Benjamin Lincoln of the Continental Army, trying to defend Charles Town with no more than five thousand troops, found himself cut off by land and sea.[16]

When the Carolinians refused to accept reality and surrender, on 9 May 1780 Clinton and Arbuthnot unleashed the full force of their military might on the city. Two hundred cannon fired at once. As General William Moultrie of the Continental Army watched the bombardment, it appeared to him "as if the stars were tumbling down."[17] There was no relief from the whizzing cannonballs, concussing mortars, exploding magazines, and raging fires. Patriot forces fought all night, in vain. Britain held all the advantages. Dawn revealed the carnage: mutilated bodies riddled the streets with random limbs scattered about and "people burnt beyond recognition, half-dead and writhing like worms."[18]

Charles Town fell in less than forty-eight hours. The surrender, on 11 May 1780, marked Britain's greatest triumph of the war and the patriots' most devastating loss. Lincoln turned over his entire army: thousands of soldiers with all their weapons and supplies, seven generals, and nearly three hundred officers.[19]

Eliza grieved for her sons, who had been commanding soldiers in the futile defense of Charles Town, and for her collapsing family fortune. British forces confiscated her city house, along with everything else the family owned in Charles Town. The Pinckneys numbered among scores of Carolinians who lost their houses and plantations: the British seized over one hundred estates and five thousand enslaved people.[20] Commanders of the occupying forces set up their offices in the most majestic residence in town, owned by Rebecca Brewton Motte, another powerful Lowcountry woman, a friend of Eliza's, and the mother-in-law of Thomas Pinckney. Thomas's wife, Elizabeth "Betsey" Motte Pinckney, was with her mother and two sisters when British soldiers unceremoniously moved in. From Rebecca Brewton Motte's parlor, General Clinton assumed he had conquered South Carolina. He offered pardons to residents who reaffirmed their allegiance to George III and soon departed, leaving Lieutenant General Earl Cornwallis in command and charged with the seemingly minor matter of subduing the countryside.[21]

General George Washington knew what he had lost with the fall of Charles Town. But he also understood two fundamental truths about the war that Clinton and Cornwallis missed. First, occupation of cities did not equal victory. Second, a protracted contest worked in the patriots' favor; the money and manpower required to hold South Carolina would tax British resources and, in the long term, advantage the Americans.[22]

This was the Continental Army's wager: South Carolinians would provoke and endure unspeakable carnage to bleed the British into surrender. The home front became the frontlines.

In 1780–82, Eliza Lucas Pinckney and the women of South Carolina lived through a guerilla civil war marked by staggering viciousness. Resentments over the British occupation fueled vengefulness, which begat cruelty. British commanders also openly advocated a war of attrition and wholesale destruction, waging war on South Carolina's economy and environment, not simply the opposing military. Near-total anarchy disrupted households, communities, and institutions. Lawlessness became the new normal. Nothing was sacred: combatants slaughtered surrendering opponents and left their corpses to rot.[23]

The majority of people suffering on the home front/frontlines were civilians, and most of them women and children. Deployments and wartime deaths made South Carolina's White households decidedly female-centered even before the fall of Charles Town. Then, thousands more soldiers became prisoners of war. As the war spiraled into women's homes, communities felt at once absent of and overrun by men: too few protectors and too many predators. With kinsmen dead or away from home, or suffering physically and psychologically from their service, many women struggled to run family farms and businesses, to protect their houses, even to feed their families.[24] Gardens and livestock became spoils of war. Rivaling forces turned elites' homes into field hospitals and barracks. The ensuing chaos brought both disruptions and opportunities to Black families. Thousands of enslaved Carolinians saw in the advancing British troops a chance to escape bondage, and they took it. Some Black men joined the fighting, others found themselves forced to labor in the occupied city. Parents carried their children into a warzone because it was a safer choice than the estates of their enslavers. In one example from the Pinckney plantations, thirty-six-year-old Dinah fled with a child in her arms and a thirteen-year-old daughter, Phillis. Dinah was also "big with Child when she went away."[25]

This women's war, even for elites like Eliza Lucas Pinckney and Harriott Pinckney Horry, was defined by scarcity and deprivation, disease and violence, occupation and exile. Soldiers took over women's homes, pillaged with impunity, wantonly slaughtered livestock, and burned farmland as they left. Commanders likened the insurgents to "beasts of prey."[26] Raids to destroy crops, livestock, and other vital resources were not simply a consequence of the war but an intentional policy. British occupying troops tried to break the will of patriot women and, by extension, men. They threatened and terrorized women who stood fast in their convictions. In one macabre spectacle, when a woman refused to cooperate with the British, soldiers forced her and her children to watch as they exhumed her husband's body.[27]

As the home front turned into the frontline of the war, women feared being raped. As early as 1777, the Continental Congress called for a report of rapes occurring in the war, but few women would come forward. Rumors abounded, however, about sexual assaults against women and girls, and rape as a tactic of war.[28]

Harriott Pinckney Horry's namesake daughter, Harriott Horry Jr., lay sleeping in her Grandmother Eliza's bed one night when Mary Motte, Betsey Motte Pinckney's sister, ran screaming into the room, chased by soldiers who had come to Hampton searching for patriot combatants. Eliza jumped from the bed and hid Mary under her covers. As Harriott Jr. later remembered the story, Eliza stood up to the soldiers, and they "shrank abashed" before her. Perhaps. Or that might be a sanitized account so as to both honor and obscure what happened to women in the extended Pinckney family in the middle of war.[29]

Between episodes of plunder and violence, women managed households, farms, and family businesses, operating outside their normal roles and without their male kin. Many men remained away from home in military or political service. Others were held as prisoners of war or forced into exile. Some returned home physically and psychologically debilitated. And many women buried their husbands, fathers, and sons. As women took over the responsibilities of their absent kinsmen, they had to do so without the security of familiar domestic spaces and under the weight of chronic deprivation and dread. Most of those women were far less experienced with running plantations and farms than Eliza and Harriott. Women beset by the war turned to female kinship and friendship networks to protect themselves and their family assets. The Pinckney women, for example, secreted away everything from horses to gold.[30] But the war disrupted those support systems too, deepening women's anxiety. This forced entry into unfamiliar responsibilities was not about the occasional outlier. Changes in women's roles went far beyond temporary oversight to build a society-wide, years-long pattern: independent women operated as farmers, business managers, planters, and heads of households. Some women, of course, including Eliza and Harriott, had been doing that for a long time—though never in a warzone.

By holding on to farms, businesses, and plantations and keeping them even sporadically functioning, White property-owning women—old hands and newcomers alike—undercut Britain's campaign to control the countryside, which extended the war's cruelties.

OVER THE course of the long war, Eliza lost nearly everything. Like many well-to-do Americans, the war collapsed the value of her careful investments. Her estate, she complained, was "shatter'd and ruin'd."[31] British forces seized her lavish home in Charles Town and her country estate, Belmont, as well as all her rental properties. Raiders confiscated her livestock, ransacked her stores, chopped down her timber. The people she enslaved—who constituted her most valuable "property"—fled, refused to work, joined the British, and were impressed into public works. By 1782, she could not pay a modest sixty-pound bill. "A strange concurrance of circumstances must happen," Eliza observed, "before a person so situated, as I was, should become thus destitute of the means of paying a small debt."[32] But there she was.

Besides the loss of her homes, investments, farmland, financial stability, and personal security, Eliza grieved for her children, each of whom faced their own tribulations during the war. Her inability to end their misery weighed heavy on Eliza and felt like a failing. But she did succeed in keeping the four of them a tight-knit group, determined to weather the war together.

As Charles Town fell, Charles Cotesworth Pinckney bore the humiliation of surrendering and became a prisoner of war. When he refused to renounce his patriot allegiance, British soldiers were dispatched to his East Bay home to evict his wife and children, ages six, four, and one.[33] Then, Charles Cotesworth's infant son and namesake got sick. Imprisoned with his letters screened and his visits restricted, Charles Cotesworth relied on Eliza for updates about the boy's worsening health. "I am anxious, exceedingly anxious about the fate of my poor Child," he wrote his mother. Until the baby recovered, Charles Cotesworth wanted candid updates from Eliza at least once a day. He knew his mother: "You who are the most affectionate of Parents, will easily account for my anxiety." Certainly she could. Eliza understood exactly how it felt to watch, helplessly, as a precious baby suffered. She had lost an infant son in 1747. Although well-versed in medical treatments, Eliza could not save her grandchild and spare her son the grief she knew too well: Charles Cotesworth Pinckney Jr. died in early 1781.[34]

Through these ordeals, Charles Cotesworth followed the example of fortitude his mother had set for him her whole life: "I entered into this Cause after much reflection, & through principle," he said. Nothing he endured changed his mind about the righteousness and the necessity of the patriot cause: "My heart is altogether American."[35]

Harriott Pinckney Horry's troubles during the 1780–82 occupation were of a different sort entirely. After Charles Town fell, her husband got to come home to Hampton Plantation because he renounced his allegiance to the American cause. He was hardly alone; nearly two thousand Charles Town residents signed oaths of allegiance to Britain.[36] Still, Daniel put Harriott in an uncomfortable position: one brother imprisoned and the other still fighting while he took the easy way out. Harriott's brothers seemed reluctant to criticize Daniel, likely to avoid worsening their sister's situation.[37]

Eliza was less forgiving of her son-in-law's vanishing patriotism. She had been quite pleased when Harriott and Daniel married in 1768 and soon came to think of Daniel as one of her children. But after 1780, she rarely mentioned him in any of her letters, even when she was often living with him and Harriott at Hampton. In letters to her sons, Eliza always sent her and Harriott's love, usually adding greetings from her grandchildren, but not Daniel. In fact, he dropped out of nearly all the family correspondence. Were they embarrassed? Angry? No one said. But Eliza and her sons clearly kept Daniel at arm's length.[38]

In a convenient departure from the doubtlessly tense scene, Daniel left South Carolina in 1781 to take his son to England so that the boy could pursue his formal education. The longer Carolinian soldiers suffered in British prison camps and lived in exile, the more relatives left behind looked askance at those who cast off their allegiances in exchange for an easier life. Men who, as one refugee put it, "thro' fear, or Self Interest, have meanly submitted," deserved the scorn of their neighbors.[39]

Unlike with Charles Cotesworth's heartbreak over losing his son, Eliza had no experience to draw on for counseling Harriott. She and her husband, Charles, never faced a serious disagreement, and he had certainly never done anything to embarrass her or alienate her from her family and friends.[40]

Harriott's troubles deepened after the war, when Daniel paid the price, literally, for his waffling allegiances. As the British evacuated, state leaders confiscated the property of some loyalists and imposed steep fines on many others.[41] With her husband standing to lose everything, Harriott wrote to state officials: "If Mr. Horry is so guilty as to deserve this forfeiture," she reasoned, "I hope it will be remember'd that it is impossible to separate him from the many innocent ones connected with and who must suffer with him." Sequestering Daniel's assets would, she explained, only add to "the many Injuries and mortifications which myself, my Mother and brothers with their Families have suffer'd . . . from our attachment to our Country."[42]

Thanks to Harriott's appeal and family name, Daniel forfeited only 12 percent of the estate. Prominent men in Charles Town gossiped about Daniel's embarrassment while noting, "Had it not been for the many Virtues of the Pinckneys, his Estate would have unquestionably been confiscated."[43]

Thomas Pinckney, Eliza's youngest child, fought during the 1780 siege of Charles Town and managed to get around British lines before the city fell. He raced into the backcountry, British soldiers in pursuit. "The trial is at present rather severe," he confessed. Still, he remained resolute. Like Charles Cotesworth, Thomas vowed to stand firm in his principles, "let my fate be what it may." Thomas planned to head north and join the Continental Army. In mid-July, Betsey Motte Pinckney assumed that her husband was encamped with George Washington. But Thomas never made it out of South Carolina.[44]

Thomas's tribulations were likely another reason why Eliza lost respect for her wobbly son-in-law, Daniel Horry. In August 1780, she heard from Thomas that while fighting in the Battle of Camden he got shot in the leg. Thomas, the bones of his leg shattered, nearly bled to death as the British routed the Americans. Amazingly, one of Thomas's English schoolmates, Charles McKenzie, saw Thomas lying among the wounded rebels and convinced British surgeons to operate on him.[45]

Thomas's ensuing medical treatment reflected another critical role that women played during the war: providing health care. After surgery, Thomas moved into the Camden home of Ann Legardere Clay, where a group of her female kin were running a makeshift hospital.[46] Thomas remained bedfast at the Clay house for weeks. By September, Thomas confided to Harriott that he looked like a skeleton: "My Legs are literally no thicker than a Stout Man's Wrist." Thomas had inherited his mother's optimism. Despite the grievous, painful injury, he reported good news: "I have hopes of retaining my Leg."[47]

Betsey Motte Pinckney was nine months pregnant with her first child when her husband was shot. After the triage in Camden, she became Thomas's nurse while caring for her infant, Thomas Jr. The caretaking was so grisly that Betsey fainted one day while trying to pull bone splinters out of Thomas's leg.[48]

When Thomas was strong enough to travel, Betsey moved him to one of her mother's plantations, Mount Joseph. Rebecca Brewton Motte had relocated the women in her family to Mount Joseph after British troops forced her out of her Charles Town mansion. Like Ann Legardere Clay, Rebecca turned her home into a provisional hospital, staffed by female kin.[49] It was a common pattern in war-torn South Carolina: women gathered for protection from the raging war took care of patriot soldiers either paroled or too sick for transport to military prisons in British-occupied Charles Town. Thomas's trip to Mount Joseph was excruciating, and he arrived too weak even to sit upright. The women gave him great care. Still, to escape deadly infections during his long recovery was a minor miracle. A year later, Thomas's leg remained too weak for him to mount his horse. His mother's son, he took it all in stride. After he relocated to his mother-in-law's house, Thomas started corresponding with his ten-year-old nephew Daniel Horry. "I suppose you are curious to know the Situation of my Leg," Thomas wrote the boy. So, he mailed him one of the bone fragments that Betsey had removed.[50]

Eliza did all she could for Thomas from afar. He refused her overtures to come to Camden, insisting it was too dangerous for her to travel to "such a place of sickness, filth and wretchedness."[51] If Eliza fretted over being excluded from her son's day-to-day care, she did not show it. She sent medical advice and loving letters to Thomas and Betsey. She also coached Betsey about dealing with the overwhelming situation. She offered her daughter-in-law timeless wisdom: "The greatest favor you can do him, will be to take care of your self, and bear with an equal mind your present trials."[52]

Then, just as Thomas began to recover some strength, Betsey got sick, and both the Pinckneys and the Mottes feared she might die. Besides grieving for Betsey's suffering, Eliza agonized over what losing her might do to Thomas. She knew the devastation of burying a beloved mate and prayed Thomas might be spared that ordeal. Thankfully, Betsey recovered, and within a few months she got pregnant again. The war did not stop the rhythms of life. She delivered a daughter, named Elizabeth Brewton Pinckney, in 1781, the fourth of five members of the next generation of Pinckneys born in war.[53]

THE WAR forced the Pinckney family to stay on the move. In the summer of 1781, it was Thomas and Charles Cotesworth's turn to become exiles. They left South Carolina for Philadelphia as part of a prisoner exchange. Exiles and refugees spilled across North America and the Atlantic World during the war years. Charles Cotesworth and Thomas joined a large contingent of South Carolinians exiled to Philadelphia. By the end of 1781, 570 Carolinians—two-thirds of them women and children—moved there. Unlike Daniel Horry, in the eyes of patriots those families refused to "Sully their honour & Conscience by taking protection."[54]

The Pinckneys were hardly refugees in the twenty-first-century sense of the word. Eighteenth-century values called for very different treatment of high-ranking officers than ordinary soldiers and sailors. Charles Cotesworth and Thomas had to leave South Carolina, but they did so in the style befitting gentlemen. The two brothers sailed with their wives and children, joined by Charles Cotesworth's brother-in-law Edward Rutledge and his family. (Sally Middleton Pinckney's sister Henrietta was married to Edward.) A rich friend loaned the South Carolinians a house, where they lived together while socializing with local elites. The Pinckney brothers remained in Philadelphia for most of the rest of the war, shielded by their wealth and rank from the worst of the conflict.

Wealth did not buy women on the home front/frontlines nearly as much ease. Sometimes it made them bigger marks. Because women nursed, supplied, and spied for the rebels, they became legitimate targets in Britain's campaign to subdue South Carolina. Also, British forces knew that otherwise resolved patriots might be cowed—or at least shamed—to learn how much their kinswomen suffered. The tactic should have felt familiar to slaveholders: they routinely brutalized the wives, daughters, and mothers of defiant Black men.

Eliza, nearly sixty years old, could have evacuated with her sons. But she stayed behind with Harriott to weather waves of danger, depredation, and indignity. She found herself unable to describe "the deplorable state of our Country." Combatants continued to take whatever they wanted, whenever they wanted. In 1782, a band of British soldiers demanded Harriott's jewelry, among the last things she had kept from raiders. Eliza condemned the "insolence of power, and wanton cruelty" inflicted on her family. And there seemed no bottom to the financial collapse. When Thomas and Charles Cotesworth left, the Continental dollar had already fallen in value to the British pound from 125:1 to 700:1.[55]

"FORTITUDE," ELIZA proclaimed in the middle of it all, "is as much a female as a masculine virtue."[56] Throughout the long war and occupation, she often felt afraid and exasperated at having to sacrifice so much of what she had spent her life creating. But Eliza never lost confidence in the American cause or resolve to restore her family legacy. By early 1782, she could see the tide had turned in the patriots' favor, and she began thinking about the future, after the British left. Although Cornwallis's surrender at Yorktown did not stop the fighting in South Carolina, British forces controlled less and less of the state. By the spring of 1782, they barely held Charles Town and that, as George Washington had predicted, required massive, unsustainable expenditures. Instead of subduing the rebels, Britain's total war campaign hardened the patriots' resolve to win independence at any cost.

When Eliza calculated a way out of her family's financial free-fall, she, like many other once-wealthy White Americans, decided the answer was slavery, though it would take time to reassert mastery. Thousands of enslaved men and women had fled South Carolina for freedom, and those who remained would continue to fight for their independence. Without a hint of awareness of her hypocrisy, Eliza complained that people she had enslaved "behaved so infamously" in order to become "quite their own masters."[57] But she was a patient woman who believed the Americans would prevail, and when they did, she and people of her rank would be able to reassert their racial power and rebuild their wealth.

She was right, about her own family and about the American republic. Reflecting a widespread attitude, Eliza refused to allow her new allegiance to the United States to compromise her old reliance on slavery. Instead, she and her children joined prominent Americans across the southern states in perpetuating slaveholding to reclaim their wealth and power. Charles Cotesworth and Thomas became national leaders, charged in the 1790s with the top diplomatic assignments in Europe. By 1790, Harriott numbered among the wealthiest people in South Carolina.[58] And Eliza Lucas Pinckney got to live out her last years, as she said, under her "own vine and fig tree." She survived another decade and watched her descendants prosper in a new country that felt comfortably familiar to the aged patriarch.[59]

NOTES

1. There have been numerous scholarly challenges to this national creation story including, most recently, Holger Hoock, *Scars of Independence: America's Violent Birth* (New York: Crown, 2017). He persuasively argues, "For over two centuries, this topic has been subject to whitewashing and selective remembering and forgetting. While contemporaries experienced the Revolution as frightening, messy, and divisive, its pervasive violence and terror have since yielded to romanticized notions of the nation's birth." Hoock, *Scars of Independence*, xii. See also Rebecca Brannon, *From Revolution to Reunion: The Reintegration of the South Carolina Loyalists* (Columbia: University of South Carolina Press, 2016), 12–13, and Jim Piecuch, *Three Peoples, One King: Loyalists, Indians, and Slaves in the Revolutionary South, 1775–1782* (Columbia: University of South Carolina Press, 2013), 55–57.

2. Foundational works on women in the revolutionary era include Carol Berkin, *Revolutionary Mothers: Women in the Struggle for America's Independence* (New York: Knopf, 2005); Linda K. Kerber, *Women of the Republic: Intellect and Ideology in Revolutionary America* (Chapel Hill: University of North Carolina Press, 1980); Cynthia A. Kierner, *Beyond the Household: Women's Place in the Early South, 1700–1835* (Ithaca, NY: Cornell University Press, 1998); Mary Beth Norton, *Liberty's Daughters: The Revolutionary Experience of American Women, 1750–1800* (Ithaca, NY: Cornell University Press, 1980); and Rosemarie Zagarri, *Revolutionary Backlash: Women and Politics in the Early American Republic* (Philadelphia: University of Pennsylvania Press, 2007). For individual women's experiences in the war, see the essays in Barbara B. Oberg, ed., *Women in the American Revolution: Gender, Politics, and the Domestic World* (Charlottesville: University of Virginia Press, 2019), especially Ami Pflugrad-Jackisch, "'What Am I but an American?': Mary Willing Byrd and Westover Plantation during the American Revolution," 171–91, and Martha J. King, "'A Lady of New Jersey': Annis Boudinot Stockton, Patriot and Poet in an Age of Revolution," 103–27. See also Patricia Cleary, *Elizabeth Murray: A Woman's Pursuit of Independence in Eighteenth-Century America* (Amherst: University of Massachusetts Press, 2000), chap. 5; Elaine Forman Crane, ed., *The Diary*

of Elizabeth Drinker: The Life Cycle of an Eighteenth-Century Woman, abridged ed. (1994; Philadelphia: University of Pennsylvania Press, 2010), 55–94; Alexis Jones Helsley, "Rebecca Brewton Motte," in *South Carolina Women: Their Lives and Times,* ed. Marjorie Julian Spruill, Valinda W. Littlefield, and Joan Marie Johnson (Athens: University of Georgia Press, 2009), 1:109–26; and Charlene Boyer Lewis, "Most Troublesome Female Loyalist: Peggy Shippen Arnold and the Treason at West Point," conference paper (2019), copy in author's possession.

3. For Eliza and her daughter Harriott Pinckney Horry in the war, see also Cokie Roberts, *Founding Mothers: The Women Who Raised Our Nation* (New York: HarperCollins, 2004), 1–11, and Constance B. Schulz, "Eliza Lucas Pinckney and Harriott Pinckney Horry: A South Carolina Revolutionary-Era Mother and Daughter," in Spruill, Littlefield, and Johnson, eds., *South Carolina Women,* 1:79–108. For biographies illuminating the disruptions of the war in other women's lives, see Patricia Brady, *Martha Washington: An American Life* (New York: Penguin, 2005), chaps. 6–7; Cleary, *Elizabeth Murray,* chap. 5; Crane, ed., *Diary of Elizabeth Drinker,* 55–94; Woody Holton, *Abigail Adams, A Life* (New York: Free Press, 2009), chaps. 8–13; and Rosemarie Zagarri, *A Woman's Dilemma: Mercy Otis Warren and the American Revolution,* 2nd ed. (1995; New York: Blackwell-Wiley, 2015), chap. 4.

4. Eliza Lucas Pinckney to George Morley, 14 March 1760, in *The Letterbook of Eliza Lucas Pinckney, 1739–1792,* ed. Elise Pinckney (1972; reprint, Columbia: University of South Carolina Press, 1997), 144 (hereafter *Letterbook*).

5. Eliza Lucas Pinckney to George Morley, 14 March 1760, in *Letterbook,* 144.

6. Eliza Lucas Pinckney to Wilhelmina-Catharine King, 27 February 1762, in *Letterbook,* 176. For insight into widows' decisions about remarriage, see Vivian Bruce Conger, *The Widows' Might: Widowhood and Gender in Early British America* (New York: New York University Press, 2009), 26–45. For the importance of marriage to South Carolina gentry society, see Lorri Glover, *All Our Relations: Blood Ties and Emotional Bonds among the South Carolina Gentry* (Baltimore: Johns Hopkins University Press, 2000), and Cynthia M. Kennedy, *Braided Relations, Entwined Lives: The Women of Charleston's Urban Slave Society* (Bloomington: Indiana University Press, 2005), chap. 4.

7. Eliza Lucas Pinckney to Alexander Garden, 14 May 1782, in *The Papers of Eliza Lucas Pinckney and Harriott Pinckney Horry: Digital Edition,* ed. Constance Schulz, http://rotunda.upress.virginia.edu/PinckneyHorry (hereafter Digital Edition).

8. Many prominent Lowcountry families fractured along political lines with some loyalist members fleeing in fear for their fortunes and lives. Over two hundred Lowcountry families relocated to the metropole by 1778. For the flight of families, see Cynthia A. Kierner, *Southern Women*

in Revolution, 1776–1800: Personal and Political Narratives (Columbia: University of South Carolina Press, 1998), 95, and Edward McCrady, *The History of South Carolina under the Royal Government, 1719–1776* (New York: Macmillan, 1899), 557–58. The South Carolina government passed stricter prohibitions against loyalism in 1778. See Piecuch, *Three Peoples, One King,* 96. For South Carolina loyalist families, see Brannon, *From Revolution to Reunion,* 5–22, and Kennedy, *Braided Relations, Entwined Lives,* chap. 2. For the exodus of loyalists generally, see Maya Jasanoff, *Liberty's Exiles: American Loyalists in the Revolutionary World* (New York: Knopf, 2011), and Mary Beth Norton, *The British Americans: Loyalist Exiles in England, 1774–1789* (New York: Little, Brown, 1972). For the tenuous commitments of loyalists in occupied cities, see Douglas F. Johnson, "Ambiguous Alliances: Urban Loyalties during the American Revolution," *Journal of American History* 104, no. 3 (December 2017): 610–31. Barbara L. Bellows sees Eliza Lucas Pinckney as slower to support the patriot cause. Bellows, "Eliza Lucas Pinckney: The Evolution of an Icon," *South Carolina Historical Magazine* 106, nos. 2–3 (April–July 2005): 159–61. For women's growing political consciousness in the revolutionary era, see Berkin, *Revolutionary Mothers,* chap. 2; Kierner, *Beyond the Household,* chap. 3; Kerber, *Women of the Republic,* chap. 3; and Norton, *Liberty's Daughters,* chap. 6. For women's political engagement and identity into the early republic, see Zagarri, *Revolutionary Backlash.*

9. For a vivid description of the Sullivan's Island episode, see William R. Ryan, *The World of Thomas Jeremiah: Charles Town on the Eve of the American Revolution* (New York: Oxford University Press, 2010), 146–51. For the American transformation from resistance to British policies to independence, see T. H. Breen, *The Marketplace of Revolution: How Consumer Politics Shaped American Independence* (New York: Oxford University Press, 2004); Pauline Maier, *From Resistance to Revolution: Colonial Radicals and the Development of American Opposition to Britain, 1765–1775* (New York: Knopf, 1972); and Maier, *American Scripture: Making the Declaration of Independence* (New York: Knopf, 1997).

10. Charles Cotesworth Pinckney to Eliza Lucas Pinckney, 7 July 1776, Digital Edition.

11. Charles Pinckney to Eliza Lucas Pinckney, 24 February 1779, Digital Edition. This Charles Pinckney was Eliza's nephew. For Eliza and Harriott's correspondence about family finances, see, for example, Eliza Lucas Pinckney to Harriott Pinckney Horry, 28 May 1778, Digital Edition. For Eliza's oversight of rice production, see Thomas Pinckney to Harriott Pinckney Horry, 23 May 1779, in "Letters of Thomas Pinckney, 1775–1780," ed. Jack Cross, *South Carolina Historical Magazine* 58 (1957): 234. For South Carolina's economy, see Kinloch Bull Jr., *The Oligarchs in Colonial and Revolutionary Charleston: Lieutenant Governor William Bull II and His Family*

(Columbia: University of South Carolina Press, 1991), 196–203; Walter J. Fraser Jr., *Patriots, Pistols, and Petticoats: "Poor Sinful Charles Town" during the American Revolution*, 2nd ed. (1976; Columbia: University of South Carolina Press, 1993), 49–65; Piecuch, *Three Peoples, One King*, 16–17; and Ryan, *The World of Thomas Jeremiah*, 39–43, 137–39. According to Walter J. Fraser Jr., an item costing one shilling in 1777 could cost sixty-one shillings by 1780. Fraser, *Patriots, Pistols, and Petticoats*, 100.

12. For early movements, see Harriott Pinckney Horry to Elizabeth Trapier Martin, 28 November 1775; Charles Cotesworth Pinckney to Eliza Lucas Pinckney, 7 July 1776, Digital Edition.

13. Eliza Lucas Pinckney to Harriott Pinckney Horry, 8 June 1778; Eliza Lucas Pinckney to Harriott Pinckney Horry, 28 May 1778, Digital Edition. See also Eliza Lucas Pinckney to Harriott Pinckney Horry, 12 May 1778, Digital Edition.

14. Thomas Pinckney to Eliza Lucas Pinckney, 17 May 1779, Digital Edition. See also Harriott Horry Ravenel, *Eliza Pinckney* (New York: Charles Scribner's Sons, 1896), 168, and Marvin R. Zahniser, *Charles Cotesworth Pinckney, Founding Father* (Chapel Hill: University of North Carolina Press, 1967), 58. For the flight of enslaved people in the war, see Kennedy, *Braided Relations, Entwined Lives*, chap. 2, and Piecuch, *Three Peoples, One King*, 158–72, 214–27.

15. Clinton quoted in Fraser, *Patriots, Pistols, and Petticoats*, 114.

16. Fraser, *Patriots, Pistols, and Petticoats*, 129; Carl P. Borick, *Relieve Us of This Burthen: American Prisoners of War in the Revolutionary South, 1780–1782* (Columbia: University of South Carolina Press, 2012), 4. For overviews of the war in South Carolina, see Brannon, *From Revolution to Reunion*, 3–33; Fraser, *Patriots, Pistols, and Petticoats*, chaps. 3–4; Hoock, *Scars of Independence*, 299–321; Jack Kelly, *Band of Giants: The Amateur Soldiers Who Won America's Independence* (New York: St. Martin's Press, 2014), 171–94, 211–12; Kierner, *Southern Women in Revolution*, 11–20; and Robert Olwell, *Masters, Slaves, and Subjects: The Culture of Power in the South Carolina Low Country, 1740–1790* (Ithaca, NY: Cornell University Press, 1998), 221–70.

17. William Moultrie, *Memoirs of the American Revolution* (New York: David Longworth, 1802), 2:96.

18. Joseph P. Tustin, ed., *Diary of the American War: A Hessian Journal, Captain Johann Ewald* (New Haven, CT: Yale University Press, 1979), 238–39 (quotation); Moultrie, *Memoirs of the American Revolution*, 2:97. For the destruction of Charles Town, see Emma Hart, *Building Charleston: Town and Society in the Eighteenth-Century British Atlantic World* (Charlottesville: University of Virginia Press, 2010), 186–88.

19. Scholars' estimates of the number of soldiers captured varies. See, for example, Borick, *Relieve Us of This Burthen*, xi, 46; Fraser, *Patriots,*

Pistols, and Petticoats, 131; Kelly, *Band of Giants,* 174; and Andrew Jackson O'Shaughnessy, *The Men Who Lost America: British Leadership, the American Revolution, and the Fate of the Empire* (New Haven, CT: Yale University Press, 2013), 230–31.

20. George C. Rogers Jr., *Charleston in the Age of the Pinckneys* (1969; reprint, Columbia: University of South Carolina Press, 1980), 124; Jasanoff, *Liberty's Exiles,* 74. Lauren Duval puts the number of confiscated estates higher in "Mastering Charleston: Property and Patriarchy in British-Occupied Charleston, 1780–82," *William and Mary Quarterly,* 3rd series, 75, no. 4 (October 2018): 598–622.

21. The house is widely admired as one of the finest examples of Georgian architecture in North America. The British did not expect to engage in long-term occupation. They assumed loyalists were in the majority in the southern provinces and would rally to the British cause. For fuller discussions, see Duval, "Mastering Charleston"; O'Shaughnessy, *The Men Who Lost America;* and Piecuch, *Three Peoples, One King.*

22. George Washington to Jonathan Trumbull, 11 June 1780, in *Writings of George Washington from the Original Manuscript Sources, 1745–1799,* ed. John C. Fitzpatrick (Washington, DC: U.S. Government Printing Office, 1931–44), 18:509–10.

23. See, for example, descriptions in Moultrie, *Memoirs of the American Revolution,* 2:354–55, and Caroline Gilman, ed., *Letters of Eliza Wilkinson, during the Invasion and Possession of Charlestown, S.C., by the British in the Revolutionary War* (New York: Samuel Colman, 1839), 46.

24. For the Revolution as a civil war and women's involvement, see Berkin, *Revolutionary Mothers,* chap. 3; Kerber, *Women of the Republic,* chap. 2; Norton, *Liberty's Daughters,* chap. 7; and Roberts, *Founding Mothers,* chap. 3. For families, see Lorri Glover, *Founders as Fathers: The Private Lives and Politics of the American Revolutionaries* (New Haven, CT: Yale University Press, 2015), and Phillip Hamilton, *The Making and Unmaking of a Revolutionary Family: The Tuckers of Virginia, 1752–1830* (Charlottesville: University of Virginia Press, 2003).

25. Thomas Pinckney advertisement, 1 December 1779, in *The Papers of the Revolutionary Era Pinckney Statesmen Digital Edition,* ed. Constance Schulz (Charlottesville: University of Virginia Press, Rotunda, 2016), https://rotunda.upress.virginia.edu/founders (hereafter Revolutionary Statesmen Digital Edition). For context, see Daina Ramey Berry, *The Price for Their Pound of Flesh: The Value of the Enslaved from Womb to Grave, in the Building of a Nation* (Boston: Beacon Press, 2017), and Erica Armstrong Dunbar, *Never Caught: The Washingtons' Relentless Pursuit of Their Runaway Slave, Ona Judge* (New York: Atria, 2017).

26. George Washington Greene, *The Life of Nathanael Greene, Major-General in the Army of the Revolution* (New York: Hurd and Houghton, 1871), 3:226.

27. Hoock, *Scars of Independence*, 312. For the near-total anarchy, see Kennedy, *Braided Relations, Entwined Lives*, 30. For intentional shortages to break civilians' wills, see Berkin, *Revolutionary Mothers*, 27. For the deprivations and dangers women endured, see Duval, "Mastering Charleston," 591, 606–7; Kennedy, *Braided Relations, Entwined Lives*, chap. 2; and Roberts, *Founding Mothers*, 83–84.

28. For rape fears and rape victims, see Berkin, *Revolutionary Mothers*, 39–41; Hoock, *Scars of Independence*, 163–74, 312; Kerber, *Women of the Republic*, 46–47; and Norton, *Liberty's Daughters*, 208–9.

29. Ravenel, *Eliza Pinckney*, 286. Harriott Jr. is an author designation, intended to help curtail confusion for modern readers. She was not called Harriott Jr. in the family.

30. Betsey Motte Pinckney and Harriott Pinckney Horry worked together to hide horses. Sally Middleton Pinckney's sister, Henrietta Middleton Rutledge, hid gold for Charles Cotesworth Pinckney. See Elizabeth Motte Pinckney to Eliza Lucas Pinckney, 17 July 1780; Charles Cotesworth Pinckney to Thomas Pinckney, 9 June 1780, Digital Edition. For the effect of the war on women, see Berkin, *Revolutionary Mothers*, 11, 149; Duval, "Mastering Charleston," 595; Kennedy, *Braided Relations, Entwined Lives*, 30–31; Kerber, *Women of the Republic*, 120–21, 147–49; and Norton, *Liberty's Daughters*, 195–224. For the similar experiences of the most well-known woman in this era, see Holton, *Abigail Adams*, 143, 155, 178, 185.

31. Eliza Lucas Pinckney to Daniel (Charles Lucas Pinckney) Horry, 7 August 1783, Digital Edition. This Daniel Horry was Harriott's son and Thomas's nephew. Later in life, Daniel Horry changed his name to Charles Lucas Pinckney Horry to honor his mother's family.

32. Eliza Lucas Pinckney to Alexander Garden, 14 May 1782, Digital Edition.

33. For his experiences, see Philander D. Chase et. al., eds., *The Papers of George Washington, Revolutionary War Series* (Charlottesville: University of Virginia Press, 1985–), 10:188; Rogers, *Charleston in the Age of the Pinckneys*, 124; Charles Cotesworth Pinckney to Harriott Pinckney Horry, 8 October 1780, Smythe Family Papers, South Carolina Historical Society (hereafter SCHS); and Zahniser, *Charles Cotesworth Pinckney*, 65. For an overview of prisoners of war during the southern campaigns, see Borick, *Relieve Us of This Burthen*.

34. Charles Cotesworth Pinckney to Eliza Lucas Pinckney, 22 October 1780; Charles Cotesworth Pinckney to Eliza Lucas Pinckney, 16 October 1780, Digital Edition. For Charles Cotesworth's anguish about his son in conversations with his mother, see also Charles Cotesworth Pinckney to Eliza Lucas Pinckney, 10 November 1780, 5:00 p.m.; 10 November 1780, 10:00 p.m.; 13 November 1780; 15 November 1780; 25 November 1780; 28 November 1780, Digital Edition. The exact date of the boy's death is unclear.

35. Charles Cotesworth Pinckney to John Money, 30 June 1780, Revolutionary Statesmen Digital Edition.

36. Johnson, "Ambiguous Allegiances," 614. For the language of those oaths, see 620–21.

37. For Thomas's response, see Thomas Pinckney to Eliza Lucas Pinckney, 11 June 1780, Digital Edition.

38. Eliza Lucas Pinckney to Harriott Pinckney Horry, c. May 1774, Digital Edition. There were earlier hints at difficulties in the Horry marriage. Harriott quit having children in 1770 at age twenty-two. Perhaps she learned to control reproduction through her extensive knowledge of botany. Or, she and Daniel might have had troubles before the Revolutionary War.

39. Mabel L. Webber, ed., "Josiah Smith's Diary, 1780–1781," *South Carolina Historical and Genealogical Magazine* 34, no. 2 (April 1933): 78.

40. For Eliza's love and respect for Charles, see Eliza Lucas Pinckney to Charles Pinckney, [1744]; Eliza Lucas Pinckney to Fanny Fayerweather, [1744]; Eliza Lucas Pinckney to Mary (Polly) Lucas Atkinson, 3 October 1758, Digital Edition; Eliza Lucas Pinckney to Charles Cotesworth and Thomas Pinckney, August 1758, in *Letterbook*, 95.

41. South Carolinians called those fines "amercements." For a list of estates confiscated and amerced, see Mabel L. Webber, ed., "Josiah Smith's Diary, 1780–1781," *South Carolina Historical and Genealogical Magazine* 33, no.4 (October 1933): 194–99. For the process, see Brannon, *From Revolution to Reunion*, 8, 49–51, and Kierner, *Southern Women in Revolution*, 95–98.

42. Harriott Pinckney Horry to Unknown, c. 1782, Digital Edition. The posture adopted by Horry in her appeal matched the pattern uncovered by Cynthia Kierner in her study of women's postwar petitions, *Southern Women in Revolution*. For the plight of loyalist wives, see Kerber, *Women of the Republic*, chap. 4. For loyalist petitions, see also Brannon, *From Revolution to Reunion*, 66–72.

43. Edward Rutledge to Arthur Middleton, 26 February 1782, Digital Edition.

44. Thomas Pinckney to Harriott Pinckney Horry, July 1780, in Cross, ed., "Letters of Thomas Pinckney," 239 (quotation); Elizabeth Motte Pinckney to Eliza Lucas Pinckney, 17 July 1780, Digital Edition.

45. Eliza Lucas Pinckney to Thomas Pinckney, August 1780, Digital Edition. For the Battle of Camden, see Kelly, *Band of Giants*, 175–80, and O'Shaughnessy, *The Men Who Lost America*, 257–59.

46. Eliza Lucas Pinckney to Thomas Pinckney, 13 September 1780, Digital Edition.

47. Thomas Pinckney to Harriott Pinckney Horry, 26 September 1780, in Cross, ed., "Letters of Thomas Pinckney," 242; Thomas Pinckney to Horatio Gates, 18 August 1780, in *The State Records of North Carolina*, ed. Walter D. Clark (Goldsboro, NC: Nash Brothers, 1886–1907), 14:560. See

also Charles Cotesworth Pinckney to Harriott Pinckney Horry, 24 September 1780, Smythe Family Papers, SCHS.

48. Charles Cotesworth Pinckney, *Life of General Thomas Pinckney* (1895; reprint, Memphis: General Books, 2012), 20; Thomas Pinckney to Daniel (Charles Lucas Pinckney) Horry, 26 October 1780, Digital Edition.

49. Thomas told his nephew, "The House has been really an Hospital for some time past." Thomas Pinckney to Daniel (Charles Lucas Pinckney) Horry, 26 October 1780, Digital Edition. For the women-centered household at Mount Joseph, see Eliza Lucas Pinckney to Thomas Pinckney, 4 October 1780, Digital Edition.

50. Thomas Pinckney to Daniel (Charles Lucas Pinckney) Horry, 26 October 1780, Digital Edition. The details of Thomas's travels from Ann Legardere Clay's house to Mount Joseph are unclear. Some family memories reported Betsey going to Camden to care for him. Others had Betsey sending a cousin to transport Thomas to her mother's house. Ravenel, *Eliza Pinckney*, 295; Pinckney, *Life of General Thomas Pinckney*, 20.

51. Eliza Lucas Pinckney to Thomas Pinckney, August 1780, in "Letters of Eliza Lucas Pinckney, 1768–1782," ed. Elise Pinckney, *South Carolina Historical Magazine* 76, no. 3 (July 1975): 159.

52. Eliza Lucas Pinckney to Elizabeth Motte Pinckney, 18 June 1780, Digital Edition.

53. Eliza Lucas Pinckney to Thomas Pinckney, 28 November 1780, Phoebe Caroline Pinckney Seabrook, SCHS; Charles Cotesworth Pinckney to Eliza Lucas Pinckney, 1 December 1780, Digital Edition.

54. Mabel L. Webber, ed., "Josiah Smith's Diary, 1780–1781," *South Carolina Historical and Genealogical Magazine* 33, no. 2 (April 1932): 78. For the list of Carolinians in Philadelphia, see 78–83. For another South Carolina family enduring separation and losses in the war, see Joanna Bowen Gillespie, *The Life and Times of Martha Laurens Ramsay, 1759–1811* (Columbia: University of South Carolina Press, 2001). For women in New England, see Catherine A. Brekus, *Sarah Osborn's World: The Rise of Evangelical Christianity in Early America* (New Haven, CT: Yale University Press, 2013), chap. 10, and Elaine Forman Crane, "Religion and Rebellion: Women of Faith in the American War for Independence," in *Religion in a Revolutionary Age*, ed. Ronald Hoffman and Peter J. Albert (Charlottesville: University Press of Virginia, 1994), 52–86.

55. Eliza Lucas Pinckney to Rebecca Raven Evance, 25 September 1780 (first quotation); Harriott Pinckney Horry to Elizabeth Blake Izard, 16 April 1782; Eliza Lucas Pinckney to Daniel (Charles Lucas Pinckney) Horry, 7 August 1783 (second quotation), Digital Edition. For inflation, see O'Shaughnessy, *The Men Who Lost America*, 247.

56. Eliza Lucas Pinckney to Elizabeth Motte Pinckney, 18 June 1780, Digital Edition.

57. Eliza Lucas Pinckney to Rebecca Evance, 25 September 1780, Digital Edition.

58. According to the first U.S. Census in 1790, Harriott held 340 enslaved people at Hampton. That made Hampton one of the largest commercial agricultural enterprises in the South and Harriott the fourth largest slaveholder in South Carolina. 1790 Census, Department of Commerce and Labor Bureau of the Census, *Heads of Families at the First Census on the United States Taken in the Year 1790, South Carolina* (Washington, DC: Government Printing Office, 1908), 37. Thomas served as minister to Great Britain. Charles Cotesworth served as minister to France.

59. Eliza Lucas Pinckney to Daniel (Charles Lucas Pinckney) Horry, 7 August 1783, Digital Edition. This phrase was commonly invoked by powerful eighteenth-century planter-patriarchs such as George Washington, Thomas Jefferson, and George Mason to reflect their desire to retire from political office to their plantation estates.

A Black Loyalist's Liberty

How Lucy Banbury Took Back Her Freedom

CARIN BLOOM

—◊◊◊◊◊◊—

W HEN LORD Dunmore's Proclamation offering freedom to the enslaved made its way through the colonies in late 1775, networks of communication between enslaved populations were already well-established. Although the royal governor aimed his proclamation primarily at Virginians, and although similar proclamations offering freedom to the enslaved who chanced escape to British lines and military service were later broadcast elsewhere in the American War for Independence, probably none had the impact that Dunmore's did among those held in bondage by rebel slaveholders.[1] Word reached South Carolina quickly, alarming slaveholders and likely spurring action by the enslaved, for many of the latter, John Banbury among them, are recorded in the *Book of Negroes* as having fled slavery there in 1776.[2] A year later, John's wife Lucy slipped away, following him north to the British Army and to freedom. Though no direct link of causation can be drawn between Dunmore's Proclamation and John and Lucy Banbury's escapes, the timing of their self-emancipation could reflect arrival of news from Virginia.

The Banburys declared independence by emancipating themselves from Declaration of Independence signer Arthur Middleton. It is unclear from which of the twenty plantations owned by the Middleton family that John and Lucy escaped, but Middleton Place Foundation has begun research into the scarce documentary evidence in an attempt to trace Lucy's—and John's—journeys for liberty. It does so somewhat in response to Cassandra Pybus's work to uncover the stories of individuals who emancipated themselves.[3] Both she and Betty Wood recount tales of enslaved women of color who acted individually and with their own myriad concerns—most often involving families and children. While Wood focuses exclusively on women's choices, Pybus shares stories of enslaved parents of both genders, but each emphasizes considerations surrounding children and family. Wood's "Southern Women of Color and the American Revolution, 1775–1783," offers a few scenarios that run the gamut from women escaping and leaving children behind to women choosing to stay bound in order not to leave their families.[4] Conversely, Pybus's *Epic Journeys* offers multiple examples of not only mothers self-emancipating with children in tow but also fathers with children and entire nuclear families running away. Records have not yet revealed whether Lucy and John had children—one ledger suggests that Lucy may have escaped with one—yet we can be sure that consideration of their choices' effects on any family they did have would have factored into their decision-making.

Middleton Place Foundation's researchers also rely heavily on studies produced about Black loyalists throughout the colonies that likely parallel the environments, dangers, social pressures, and possible benefits that Lucy encountered. Many such works focus on men. Just as Dunmore offered freedom to escaped men who bore arms to support royal authority, modern-day authors tend to focus on the men who fought or, as was more often the case, labored with British forces. But women too acted on the promise and labored for liberty, and thus researchers also search for evidence of enslaved women taking action on behalf of themselves. Ira Berlin in *Many Thousands Gone* presents a framework that traces the social networks of enslavement in the Lowcountry, which suggests how, why, and with what Lucy considered her options. Berlin argues that enslaved peoples' perspectives of the American Revolution would have differed with their localities: those in bondage in cosmopolitan urban locations seeing and confronting different opportunities and risks than those enslaved on the plantations in the countryside.[5] Using the above studies, along with Darlene Clark Hine and Kathleen Thompson's *A Shining Thread of Hope*, helps researchers deduce and construct pieces of Lucy's story. In their case study of Charleston, Hine and Thompson enumerate not only the physical labor demands that an enslaved woman such as Lucy likely would have faced but potential punishments and abuses as well, which surely would have influenced her choices.[6] Additionally, in her seminal work *Revolutionary Mothers*, Carol Berkin points out that in the face of a mass exodus, remaining in bondage may not have been the safer choice: "On South Carolina plantations, where desertions ran high, there were not enough field hands to plant or harvest crops.

Food grew scarce, and it was 'the poor Negroes' who remained behind who starved."[7] Lucy's mental and emotional states and physical situation as she made the decision to self-emancipate are lost to time, but outlining the complex social forces and frayed webs—or loosened shackles—of political and legal authorities in the early years of the American Revolution illuminate how, when, and why she could and did act to gain and maintain her freedom.

People in British North America's enslaved communities had limited avenues by which to acquire freedom before war broke out between the colonies and the government of King George III. Some colonies offered choices for both slaveholders and enslaved persons to pursue emancipation, including purchase and petition, but southern ones, with their greater enslaved populations, were more restrictive. South Carolina enacted draconian slave laws following the tumultuous years in the early half of the eighteenth century, which included violent revolts such as the Stono Rebellion in 1739. Revolts, which required common action, ended in extreme punishments and escalated repression. Running away, which could entail one or more enslaved persons of color, was always a risk, for failure could entail a heavy price. The price—punishments by whip or sale among others—was endorsed by the law and authorities.[8]

The American rebellion undermined, at least in the short term, the political power structures that supported the institutions of slavery. Dunmore cracked the structure in November 1775 by sanctioning what had been an illegal act—escape or stealing one's self—in response to an even greater unlawful act—rebellion.[9] When Dunmore proclaimed a path to guaranteed freedom, he offered a new option with better odds. Although he saw his invitation as simply a means to the greater end of reasserting imperial control, the enslaved population saw freedom as the greater end. His offer was too enticing to pass up for a tremendous number of enslaved persons. That engendered anger among the White population in South Carolina as they perceived oppression by the Crown and feared potential large-scale slave revolt. Actions and perceptions led to reactions. After South Carolinians executed Thomas Jeremiah, a free Black seaman and pilot convicted for plotting insurrection and to help Royal Navy vessels enter Charles Town harbor in August 1775, numerous Blacks—five hundred were documented—escaped to Sullivan's Island to join the British.[10] If Jeremiah was used as a scapegoat, whose story fed patriots' anti-imperial and pro-enslavement sentiments, then it is no wonder that the knowledge of Dunmore's Proclamation moving fast through enslaved communities only fanned the flames of fear in the slave-owning South. Wood posits that "by early 1776, well before the [broader 1779] Phillipsburg Proclamation, the notion of the British as potential liberators had also taken deep root in the South Carolina and Georgia Lowcountry."[11]

Dunmore and his commanders worked diligently to collect Black loyalists, forming an Ethiopian Regiment—a fighting force made up of former slaves and numbering around three hundred. There is some dispute as to whether that regiment's companies were engaged at what became the Battle of Great Bridge, Virginia, on 9 December 1775, but it appears Black soldiers participated. Dunmore's Ethiopian Regiment and other freedmen certainly had additional opportunities to serve in combat or other roles. Dunmore's subordinates took their cue from him and created companies of support and construction workers, the "Black Pioneers."[12] Each of these companies' successes varied by degrees, but stories of their endeavors might have spread, much like the news of the proclamation. Conversations between John and Lucy Banbury on the Middleton plantation at night after their work was complete could have included discussion of these new and daring opportunities for a life of freedom. How might they have balanced the practical logistics of attempting such a feat against the psychological toll of taking their lives into their own hands? How many times was the idea dismissed as a fantasy, and how many times was it more empowering than frightening to consider? Wood considers these questions as well, and as they applied to Black persons weighing their options with the American or British sides, though she acknowledges that they still cannot be answered directly: "Could enslaved men belonging to Patriot owners trust their promise of eventual freedom in exchange for military service? Ought those belonging to Loyalist owners to ignore it? Was it worthwhile to run the many physical risks entailed in trying to reach British lines and the certainty of brutal punishment if caught by the Patriots? What would be the British reaction to the arrival not just of would-be slave soldiers but also of their wives and children?"[13] The outcome for John and Lucy (and thousands of others) suggests that not only did they deem it worthwhile to take a risk but it was more practicable for them to do so separately.

The stories of men escaping to the British Army are fairly easy to follow. Although the men are not usually individually detailed, their service is documented in the lists of the Black loyalist regiments. Furthermore, the duties and service of those regiments are documented. Even George Washington recognized the military threat to his cause that raising Black loyalist regiments presented, and although he never fully sanctioned the recruitment of escaped enslaved men into the Continental Army, he and some other commanders accepted Black recruits to supplement regiments.[14]

Integrating Black soldiers into established regiments was one thing; raising African American regiments another. John Laurens, son of rich slave trader and Continental Congress president Henry Laurens, was one of the most vocal abolitionists in the patriot cause. Although his own wealth stemmed from his father's slave trading, John remained adamant that raising entire Black regiments would significantly affect the outcome of the war in the revolutionaries' favor. He continually appealed to his father for an inheritance of slaves, rather than money, so that he might create his own force to oppose Dunmore's growing numbers.[15]

Many of the movers and shakers of the Continental cause were aware of the moral objection to holding humans in bondage, but awareness was one thing, action another. Forcing servitude on others due to their continent of origin and color of their skin went against Enlightenment ideals that informed some of the formative principles of the United States' republic. George Mason and Alexander Hamilton, one a slaveholder from Virginia and the other an immigrant abolitionist, both rejected the practice of enslavement, and both espoused ideas about eventual emancipation. Mason found maintaining the institution a corrupting force that at its best affected the abilities of an individual to function in civilized society, and at its worst brought such widespread corruption that the result was downfall, as with the Roman Empire.[16] During the Revolutionary War, Hamilton wrote to his close friend John Laurens to support Laurens's attempts to raise a Black Continental regiment, though he did not expect success. Hamilton cited "prejudice and private interest" as hindrances to what "public good" might come of such an action: "Even the animated and persuasive eloquence of my young Demosthenes will not be able to . . . dissolve the fascinating cha[racter] of self interest."[17] Mason, at the conclusion of the War for Independence, refused to sign the Constitution that extended the practice into the next twenty years. For Hamilton's part, he proposed an eventual phasing out of the practice in New York as the new republic put down roots.[18] Neither would see their ideas realized in their lifetimes.

Hamilton was right about the power of prejudiced interests, and resistance to the formation of a Black Continental regiment in the South was an obstacle never surmounted. The North offered other options, and some of the self-emancipated men who enlisted for the American cause with the same hopes for independence as their loyalist counterparts were the longest-serving members of the Continental forces. Alan Gilbert relates an estimate of 225–50 Black soldiers in the First Rhode Island Regiment, whose "average term of service in the regiment was three years. Many served for five." They served with distinction in the North, as at the Battle of Rhode Island, as well as in the South, maintaining a presence at the siege and subsequent surrender of the British at Yorktown.[19]

As the American War for Independence progressed, the British recruitment strategy improved. Gilbert acknowledges that the devoted attention that the British Army gave to encouraging self-emancipation of enslaved people in the South was less out of moral obligation and more out of a pragmatic understanding of the effects these Black loyalists would have on fragile American forces. Lord Dunmore's tactics were noticed and adopted by Lieutenant Colonel Moses Kirkland, a provincial loyalist, and Lieutenant Colonel Archibald Campbell of the British Army, who began recruiting as a means to devastate southern supply lines. The British commanders correctly identified the southern colonies' economy as wholly dependent on the enslaved labor force; those colonies would be hamstrung from providing aid to the rebellion if the numbers of laborers were reduced by half or more. The southern patriot response to this strategy was given to occasional mania, whereas the southern loyalist response was to feel caught between a rock and a hard place. Although the potential loss of enslaved labor to self-emancipation was ever-present, there was also an added concern that enslaved people would be confiscated as property in the service of the king, or that social pressure would dictate that a holder of enslaved workers "willingly" offer them for service. Knowing that signing over enslaved laborers to the service of the British Army was a way to prove allegiance to King George as rightful monarch in America, loyalist slaveholders could hardly protest their forcible seizure either, even as it meant those slaveholders would be unable to maintain their own livelihoods.[20]

Most of the units created from escaped and seized enslaved men were Black Pioneers—construction crews digging trenches or building earthworks; others were scouts and guides for the British Regulars to navigate the treacherous landscapes of the southern colonies, and some were foragers and service workers—domestic servants, porters, and so on.[21] To what unit did John Banbury run? Was he, in fact, part of the army? A number of men recorded in the *Book of Negroes* have not only their names, ages, and physical descriptions listed but also what service they performed on behalf of the Crown. Some historians suggest that British ship captains would not have accepted petitions to sail to Nova

Scotia from runaways who had not served. John Banbury ran away in 1776 but does not reemerge in the records until 1783 in New York City, reunited with Lucy. John appears in the *Book* but has no accompanying service recorded. The initial returns from the British Army are spotty at best, and most refer to regiments formed starting in 1778, well after both John and Lucy had escaped.[22]

Alongside such evidence and while awaiting more, the *Book of Negroes* remains the prime source, and it is also where there are records of women in service to the army. Women followed both the British and the American armies out of necessity. Both offered work to women of color whether enslaved, formerly enslaved, or free. That leads to a probable part of Lucy's story, for she is not only listed in the *Book of Negroes* but also in the 1784 Muster Roll of Port Roseway Associates in Nova Scotia, and in the "List of the Blacks in Birch Town Who Gave Their Names for Sierra Leone in November 1791."[23] Such records may indicate services rendered to the British Army from Lucy of her own accord, rather than being a follower of her husband, who filled a laborer niche. Unfortunately, like the nature of John's service during the war, Lucy's affiliation is not specifically recorded. From the research work of Ruth Holmes Whitehead on the *Book of Negroes*, the best that can be said is that both John and Lucy are recorded as having "escaped to the British Army."[24] Like her White counterparts, it is most likely that Lucy was a laundress, a seamstress, or a nurse. It is also possible that she was employed by an officer as a cook or a lady's servant for that officer's wife.[25]

The services of women were recorded and preserved in some instances just like those of men in the returns of the British Army, some of which were produced prior to the *Book of Negroes*. These records not only speak to former slaves' occupations; they also describe the sheer numbers of soldiers, workers, and followers that would have augmented British forces. For example, a military return at New York in November 1779 that counted 101 members (45 of them women and children) in "Stuart's Black Company" probably included other Black soldiers—and Black followers—in "mixed" companies. The amalgamated return, which added up to 22,401 soldiers, 3,347 women, and 3,163 children, indicates hundreds and infers perhaps thousands of Black soldiers, followers, and refugees were already with the British forces at that time and place.[26]

A number of questions arise when piecing together what life might have looked like for Lucy and John upon their arrivals behind British lines. The first among them might be: how did they get there in the first place? It is unknown when the two encountered the British—but it was lucky for them that they ran away from Arthur Middleton early. In the opening days of the war, when the majority of the battles and skirmishes were up North, the southern colonies were in social upheaval. Upheaval provided openings, the British Army a place to go, and, as the outlook for British victory seemed initially favorable, the possibility that service with it would confirm independence. As the years progressed and the theater of war moved south, however, the numbers of runaway enslaved people grew, and British control faltered. In his study of Black loyalists, James Walker suggests that as the British began to lose influence and loyalty in the southern colonies, accompanied by a more tenuous and therefore constrained authority, the enslaved workers who sought freedom were aware of the weakening: "In one district of Charleston . . . black outnumbered white by 520 to 418. Here were concentrated the largest number of blacks within British lines, and already problems had been met in trying to feed and organize them."[27] This rapid overpopulation of escaped enslaved individuals caused General Sir Henry Clinton to issue orders against receiving any further petitions for refuge.

Along with the diminishing British presence came a demand from the revolutionaries who considered escaped enslaved people to be their lost property—and with every battle won by those Whigs, there came a cry to restore said lost property. Many British officers were faced with the decision of upholding their word and honor as gentlemen to self-emancipated persons or following the proper conduct of war including the return of stolen property. Had Lucy and John waited another four years or so, they might never have gained the relative safety and employment afforded by the Crown in the first place, nor subsequent passage to Nova Scotia.

As the nature of the conflict changed, so too did the consistency with which the British kept their promises. In 1779 at New York, General Clinton issued the Phillipsburg Proclamation, which largely echoed the earlier Dunmore document but promised freedom to all those escaping rebel slaveholders in the colonies and offering formerly enslaved people the opportunity to choose their own occupations within British lines. By 1780, however, Clinton's policy had become more detailed and nuanced. As Walker summarizes, "Slaves seized in war became public property and were to be put to work to serve the public good. A commission established to manage sequestered estates was authorized to employ all available slaves to keep the plantations working."[28] That meant little leverage to choose one's occupation after all. This policy, coupled with personal decisions by some British officers to resell enslaved people to loyalist claimants, made for volatile situations. Not every enslaved worker who escaped or was "liberated" was actually freed. Whether Lucy and John knew about these potential hazards and policy differences, or whether they simply saw an early chance and took it, the decision to leave at the start of the war might have made the difference in terms of their success.

There is not much recorded in the British documents, which are mostly ledgers and lists, that illuminate the experience of escape to British lines. Since the Banburys escaped separately from one another, it is conceivable that each of them met up with soldiers in different places. The most likely scenario for John was an escape behind the lines right in Charleston; even as the British lost the Battle of Fort Sullivan in June 1776, there were other Lowcountry battles and skirmishes that year which ended favorably for them. Lucy's journey to freedom a year after her husband's escape could have mirrored John's, though that is not necessarily a given.

By 1777—the year of Lucy's escape—the British had a score of Cherokee allies in the Upcountry, but Cherokee raiding was unsuccessful against Whig militia. Eventually, the Cherokee War—a conflict that ensued concurrent with the American Revolution—ended in an American victory, and the Cherokee Nation entered into the Treaty of DeWitt's Corner in May 1777. The terms of the treaty resulted in the Cherokee ceding most of their remaining land to the South Carolina government.[29] This effectively curtailed a major British presence in the South until that army captured Savannah in December 1778. It is likely then that Lucy had to travel further from her state of bondage to find the safety of the British Army. It also leaves many unanswered questions about when and where she and John were able to reunite. Was she able to find the unit to which he was attached as a laborer shortly after her escape, or did they not see each other again until sometime closer to 1783, when they were both inspected in New York City for transport to Nova Scotia?

Another consideration about the difficulty of reuniting includes the hazards that Lucy and John might have encountered—though Lucy's journey was probably more affected if she did indeed have to travel farther. The potential pitfalls included the same environmental hazards that enslaved people encountered daily in bondage: from heat and humidity taking their tolls on the body, to standing water and its associated diseases—foot rot, typhoid, and dysentery among them—to the malaria spread by mosquitos, to the wildlife in the marshes and fields including alligators, all manner of snakes, and mammals that prowl at night. It is plain that the odds were stacked against escaped persons of color who traveled with little but the clothing they wore. Traveling together would have been helpful, but groups walked a fine line between having enough people to share the burdens and too great a number that would catch the unwanted attention of slave catchers, angry Whig plantation owners, or opportunistic British soldiers looking to sell someone back into slavery. As Walker details, "They swam, they hiked, they stowed away in boats and wagons, they carried each other to safety with the Redcoats."[30] Through this glimpse into the physical environment, Lucy's likely travails come more clearly into focus. It does not require an especially creative mind to conjure the courage, determination, and resilience a person like Lucy needed to survive, even as the world she knew devolved into chaos.

The chaos created by ongoing war manifested in a variety of ways, including in 1781, when Charles, Earl Cornwallis, recognized the multitudes of former enslaved people as a weapon of sheer volume and considered mobilizing them as an agent of that chaos. That may have fit with weaponizing disease, leveraging the smallpox that plagued scores of the self-emancipated into a sort of biological warfare by General Cornwallis against southern revolutionaries. While there is debate about the intentionality of creating newly free Blacks as an army of disease-spreaders, the transmission of smallpox throughout Virginia and the Carolinas among the ranks of newly freed Blacks is recorded.[31] Captain Johann Ewald, a Hessian, described a baggage train following the British Army as a "swarm of locusts."[32] And Brigadier General Charles O'Hara described "the hundreds of wretched Negroes, that are dying by scores every day."[33] In short, each compounding circumstance that escaped former slaves encountered in the South affirms the good fortune that Lucy and John had in acting on their bold decision early.

Whether she was making her way to the British in the neighborhood (a small presence after the 1776 defeat at Fort Sullivan, before reappearing in 1779), or taking a longer route north, Lucy persevered through all potential setbacks to find herself, and her husband, in New York City. Records are spotty between Lucy's escape in 1777 and her inspection for the ship to Halifax in 1783. It is unknown whether she met up with John prior to her arrival in New York or with whom she traveled. Ruth Whitehead has examined various copies of the *Book of Negroes*, and there is a suggestion from one of them that Lucy and John may not have been the only escaped members of the Banbury family. Tom Cain and his wife, Silla, listed as Sella Banbury in one copy, are the entries just under John and Lucy. Although Tom and Silla are documented as having escaped in 1776 (were they traveling with John?), all four sailed together for Nova Scotia from New York. We know then, at least by 1783, that Lucy was reunited not only with her husband but with possible kin as well.[34]

Lucy and John Banbury, and Tom and Silla Cain, all sailed from New York on the British ship *L'Abondance*, commanded by a Lieutenant Phillips. Lucy and John are listed as having been "inspected" on the same day—31 July 1783—at Fraunces Tavern in New York City, a historic site that is still actively engaged in telling its own history. The muster lists of the ships that sailed for Nova Scotia, eventually compiled into what is known as the *Book of Negroes*, were a direct result of Sir Guy Carleton's address of the Provisional Agreement signed at the end of the Revolutionary War in 1782. Article VII of that document details the return of property to Americans upon the departure of British forces; it was left to General Carleton to interpret what that meant, especially the provision that "his Britannic Majesty shall, with all convenient speed, & without causing any Destruction of carrying away any Negroes, or other Property of the American Inhabitants withdraw all his Armies Garrisons and Fleets from the said United States and from every Port, Place, and Harbour within the same."[35] Patriot enslavers petitioned Carleton and his board of enquiry to reclaim their lost "property," but it determined that "refugees who had resided within British lines at least 12 months were free to depart." Further, Carleton determined that Blacks "who were already with the British before 30 November 1782 and who claimed freedom by the proclamations were technically free and therefore could not be considered as American property on that date." Even as Carleton came to his decisions, he was receiving pushback from the most powerful American in the land—George Washington argued that all runaway persons of color who had been enslaved were still considered property. None was eligible to depart.[36] As political leaders discussed ratification of the treaty ending America's War for Independence, Washington and Carleton negotiated the return of posts, prisoners, and runaways from enslavement. After some correspondence, they met on 6 May at Orangetown, New York, where Washington started their conference by stating that Congress wanted the return "of all Negroes & other property of the Inhabitants of these States in the possession of the Forces or subjects of, or adherents to his Britannic Majesty."[37]

Carleton responded that he had already allowed the departure of a number of Blacks among the six thousand or more people eligible for evacuation. Washington thought that action contrary to the stipulations in the treaty and showed bad faith. Carleton replied,

That by Property in the Treaty might only be intended Property at the Time, the Negroes were sent off—That there was a difference in the Mode of Expression in the Treaty; Archives, Papers, &c., &c.,

were to be restored—Negroes & other property were only not to be destroyed or carried away. But he principally insisted that he conceived it could not have been the Intention of the B. Government by the Treaty of Peace, to reduce themselves to the necessity of violating their faith to the Negroes who came into the British Lines under the proclamation of his Predecessors in Command— ... that delivering up the Negroes to their former Masters would be delivering them up some possibly to Execution, and others to severe punishments, which in his Opinion would be a dishonorable violation of the public Faith, pledged to the Negroes in the proclamations.

Washington did not fully accept this, as he again "observed that he conceived this Conduct on the part of Genl. Carleton, a Departure from both the Letter and the Spirit of the Articles of Peace." Carleton parried with his interpretation: "that by the Treaty he was not held to deliver up any property but was only restricted from carrying it away."[38]

Although Carleton did not acquiesce to Washington's wishes, it must have been an intense moment to be a Black loyalist. Twice-escaped Boston King described the experience of waiting to hear whether Carleton would return the formerly enslaved: "This dreadful rumor filled us all with inexpressible anguish and terror, especially when we saw our old masters coming from Virginia, North Carolina, and other parts, and seizing upon their slaves in the streets of New York, or even dragging them out of their beds. Many of the slaves had very cruel masters, so that the thoughts of returning home with them embittered life to us. For some days we lost our appetite for food, and sleep departed from our eyes."[39] Surely Lucy and John Banbury, Tom and Silla Cain, and many others—recorded and unrecorded—experienced similar trepidation and sleepless nights. Imagine their relief to finally board *L'Abondance* and sail for Nova Scotia.

Whatever sense of relief Lucy might have felt was short-lived, however. The voyage lasted just over a month, beginning on 2 August 1783 and ending with all passengers discharged on 3 September into what was soon called Birchtown, Nova Scotia. The ship's first stop, however, was Shelburne, where the log references that many of the Black loyalist passengers aboard had fallen ill. A temporary tent hospital was set up on shore, and fifty-three sick persons were sent to it on Monday, 18 August; their names are unrecorded. Whether Lucy and/or John were among them is unknown, but all passengers, including the ill who recovered, were eventually brought to Birchtown. Those who never took ill remained aboard *L'Abondance* until her final port of call on the 3rd.[40]

If potential illness was not enough to cause consternation, there was the matter of unfulfilled promises from the Crown and the discrimination against free Blacks that Lucy and John surely encountered the moment they came ashore. Walker suggests that the original intention of the British government was to provide loyalists with compensation for their losses and provisions to sustain them as they grew their farms, preventing the need for anyone to become a wage-laborer; there is no mention of a racial distinction among said loyalists being made. Unfortunately, problems of land and provision shortages arose in mid-1783 before Lucy and John even arrived, and much like the country they had just left, preferential treatment was given to White loyalists. Because it was determined that those who were perceived to have lost the most when departing for Nova Scotia should be landed and provisioned first, often there was little or nothing left for Black loyalists, even those arriving in the early waves of 1783.[41]

Due to the continued presence of the institution of slavery in Nova Scotia, Lucy and John arrived into another unpredictable scenario. Sentiments against freedom for people of African descent continued, probably due to a long-ingrained understanding of American slavery as a means to exploit humans for work and economic gain: people of color "were usually considered to be nothing but a source of labor."[42] John, described in the "Muster Book of the Free Black Settlement of Birchtown" as a laborer, surely fell into the trap of being a construction worker or wage-laborer, precisely the employment which the Crown promised would not be necessary upon gaining freedom. Yet free and still-enslaved Blacks could mingle at will, and enslavers quickly lost their holds on their human property, both physically and psychologically. It was difficult for slaveholders to maintain a mental system of oppression on a people in bondage when those enslaved saw others around them who looked similar and yet were free.[43]

When, how, and whether Lucy and John received acreage and provisions from the government is a mystery, but eventually they did own land in Birchtown, one of three all-black settlements in Nova Scotia. The average land grant that Black loyalists were supposed to receive was 50 acres, in contrast to the 160-plus acres recommended, or the 204 acres actually occasionally given by Crown surveyors to White loyalists. Whether Lucy and John received all fifty and sold some, or whether they saved money from their labors to purchase their own plot, by 1791 they had ten acres, part of which was "improved by the Government."[44] November 1791 is when we pick up Lucy's trail again, this time without John. His year of death is not recorded, but by the time Lucy applied for removal to Sierra Leone, she was alone.

"The List of the Blacks in Birch Town Who Gave Their Names for Sierra Leone" reveals the final leg of Lucy's journey. After living in Birchtown for eight years and presumably creating a life both with and then without her husband, Lucy applied to be removed to Africa and was granted passage. The list offers some of the few known details of Lucy's life, including an age discrepancy. In 1783, the *Book of Negroes* listed Lucy as aged forty years, but eight years later she is recorded as forty-three. Bad bookkeeping or not knowing her true age notwithstanding, one of the most interesting and pertinent pieces of information disclosed is her birthplace. Lucy identified herself as having been born in Africa, meaning the application for removal to Sierra Leone was a decision to go home. One can imagine many thoughts and emotions that might have accompanied pursuit of this opportunity for a self-emancipated woman who likely thought she would never set foot on her native continent again. Details that are arguably less important but useful for developing the richness and complexity of Lucy's life include the minutiae of her occupation and belongings, listed out in the form of a ledger. Lucy is described as a farmer who owned one axe, one hoe, a "10-acre lot part improv'd Government," a chest, two other pieces of portable property or luggage, and a certificate of "Good Character."[45]

Lucy embarked for Africa with the company enumerated in the list, and her last known whereabouts sailed with her. To date, Middleton Place Foundation has neither found nor received a record of those who successfully landed in Sierra Leone in 1792, but there is little reason to doubt that Lucy, whose lifetime of arduous travels took her thousands of miles by land and sea, would have arrived safely. It is left to the imagination to consider what her first steps in Sierra Leone must have felt like, and whether she found peace on home soil, even if she never returned to her specific country of origin. As Walker notes, "Land, independence and security, had in fact been among the chief attractions drawing the fleeing slaves to the British during the American War." After still feeling the bonds of servitude as laborers, indentures, or share-croppers in Nova Scotia, removal to Sierra Leone might have seemed like the ultimate opportunity for formerly enslaved people to accomplish these simple, yet difficult and elusive goals. The fact that Lucy already owned land of her own makes her application all the rarer, and her desire for independence in a place she had strong emotional ties to all the more likely. As Walker eloquently states, "[The British abolitionist and founder of Freetown,

Sierra Leone, John] Clarkson offered not only land, but the Promised Land. A farm in Nova Scotia was no substitute for an entire country in Africa."[46] We can only imagine if that was how Lucy felt in making her decision, but we may certainly hope that the result was worth all of her sacrifices.

NOTES

1. Michael A. McDonnell discusses the proclamation's cause and effects in Virginia in *The Politics of War: Race, Class, and Conflict in Revolutionary Virginia* (Chapel Hill: University of North Carolina Press, 2007), 133–43, and Sylvia R. Frey notes expansion of effects to other colonies in *Water from the Rock: Black Resistance in a Revolutionary Age* (Princeton, NJ: Princeton University Press, 1991), 63–66.

2. The British iteration of the *Book of Negroes* is in the Sir Guy Carleton Papers, National Archives of the United Kingdom, Kew, England, and available at https://novascotia.ca/archives/Africanns/BN.asp, whereas the American version is at the U.S. National Archives and Records Administration, Washington, DC. See also Graham Russell Hodges et al., *The Black Loyalist Directory: African Americans in Exile after the American Revolution* (New York: Garland, 1996).

3. Cassandra Pybus, *Epic Journeys of Freedom: Runaway Slaves of the American Revolution and Their Global Quest for Liberty* (Boston: Beacon Press, 2006), xvi–xvii.

4. Betty Wood, "Southern Women of Color and the American Revolution, 1775–1783," in *The Practice of U.S. Women's History*, ed. S. Jay Kleinberg, Eileen Boris, and Vicki L. Ruiz (New Brunswick, NJ: Rutgers University Press, 2007), 67–82, esp. 73.

5. Ira Berlin, *Many Thousands Gone: The First Two Centuries of Slavery in North America* (Cambridge, MA: Belknap Press of Harvard University Press, 1998), 154–75.

6. Darlene Clark Hine and Kathleen Thompson confront the questions of physical punishment and sexual abuse suffered by enslaved women at the hands of their enslavers—a subject often glossed over—in *A Shining Thread of Hope: The History of Black Women in America* (New York: Broadway Books, 1998), 42–50.

7. Carol Berkin, *Revolutionary Mothers: Women in the Struggle for America's Independence* (New York: Vintage Books, 2005), 126. Berkin not only gives an excellent overview of the plights of the enslaved as they struggled to self-emancipate during the chaos of the Revolution through the loyalist removal to Canada; she also traces a number of individual stories of women powerfully exercising their agency in chapter 8, "The Day of Jubilee Is Come."

8. Peter H. Wood says repression was so great in South Carolina after the Stono Revolt that the enslaved could not "take advantage of the libertarian rhetoric" of the Revolution in *Black Majority: Negroes in Colonial South Carolina from 1670 through the Stono Rebellion* (New York: Norton, 1975), 320–26, but Ira Berlin notes how quickly slaves in the Lower South acted to gain liberty in *Many Thousands Gone*, 291–94.

9. For more on the ramifications of Dunmore's Proclamation, see Woody Holton, *Forced Founders: Indians, Debtors, Slaves, and the Making of the American Revolution in Virginia* (Chapel Hill: University of North Carolina Press, 1999), 136–37, 152–61.

10. Alan Gilbert, *Black Patriots and Loyalists* (Chicago: University of Chicago Press, 2012), 37, 39, 45.

11. Wood, "Southern Women of Color," 70.

12. Virginia Humanities, "Battle of Great Bridge," AfroVirginia, http://afrovirginia.org; Gilbert, *Black Patriots*, 27.

13. Wood, "Southern Women of Color," 69–70.

14. Gilbert, *Black Patriots*, 63.

15. Ibid., 80.

16. Ibid., 53.

17. Alexander Hamilton to John Laurens, 11 September 1779, in *The Papers of Alexander Hamilton*, ed. Harold C. Syrett (New York: Columbia University Press, 1961), 2:165–69.

18. Gilbert, *Black Patriots*, 57, 92.

19. Ibid., 101–2. For other information, see Judith L. Van Buskirk, *Standing in Their Own Light: African American Patriots in the American Revolution* (Norman: University of Oklahoma Press, 2017).

20. Gilbert, *Black Patriots*, 117.

21. James W. St. G. Walker, *The Black Loyalists: The Search for a Promised Land in Nova Scotia and Sierra Leone 1783–1870* (1976; reprint, Toronto: University of Toronto Press, 1992), 5.

22. Gilbert, *Black Patriots*, 123, 122.

23. "Muster Book of the Free Black Settlement of Birchtown, Muster 3d & 4th July 1784," Heritage Canadiana Digital Archive, 2019, image 89 (pp. 132–33), http://heritage.canadiana.ca/view/oocihm.lac_reel_h984/89?r=0&s=1; "List of the Blacks in Birch Town Who Gave Their Names for Sierra Leone in November 1791," Black Loyalist Digital Archive, 2019, http://www.blackloyalist.info/source-image-display/display/111.

24. Ruth Holmes Whitehead, *The Shelburne Black Loyalists: A Short Biography of All Blacks Emigrating to Shelburne County, Nova Scotia after the American Revolution 1783* (Halifax: Nova Scotia Museum Manuscript, 2000), 68.

25. Gilbert, *Black Patriots*, 123.

26. Ibid., 123–24. As Gilbert indicates, pioneer or service companies like Stuart's (or Stewart) noted more African American members than regular

units. That, in addition to his assumptions about followers, raises questions about some of his extrapolations.

27. Walker, *The Black Loyalists*, 9.
28. Ibid., 2, 6.
29. "Treaty of Dewitt's Corner between the Cherokee Nation and South Carolina, 1777," 2009, Teaching American History in South Carolina Project, https://digital.scetv.org/teachingAmerhistory/lessons/treatyof dewittscorner.htm.
30. Walker, *The Black Loyalists*, 3–4.
31. Ruth Holmes Whitehead, *Black Loyalists: Southern Settlers of Nova Scotia's First Free Black Communities* (Halifax: Nimbus, 2013), 116–17.
32. Johann Ewald, *Diary of the American War: A Hessian Journal* (New Haven, CT: Yale University Press, 1979), 305.
33. Charles O'Hara, "the hundreds of . . . ," cited in Whitehead, *Black Loyalists*, 117.
34. Ibid., 50–51.
35. Preliminary Articles of Peace, November 30, 1782, The Avalon Project: Documents in Law, History and Diplomacy, Yale Law School Lillian Goldman Law Library, 2019, https://avalon.law.yale.edu/18th_century/prel1782.asp.
36. Walker, *The Black Loyalists*, 10, 11.
37. "Account of a Conference between Washington and Sir Guy Carleton, 6 May 1783," Founders Online, National Archives, https://founders.archives.gov/documents/Washington/99-01-02-11217.
38. Ibid.
39. Boston King, "This dreadful rumor . . . ," cited in Whitehead, *Black Loyalists*, 139. For more on the evacuations and eventual migrations of Black and White loyalists at war's end and beyond, see Maya Jasanoff, *Liberty's Exiles: American Loyalists in the Revolutionary World* (2011; reprint, New York: Vintage, 2012).
40. Whitehead, *Black Loyalists*, 150–51.
41. Walker, *The Black Loyalists*, 43.
42. Ibid., 42.
43. "Muster Book"; Walker, *The Black Loyalists*, 41.
44. Walker, *The Black Loyalists*, 29; "List of the Blacks in Birch Town."
45. "List of the Blacks in Birch Town."
46. Walker, *The Black Loyalists*, 125, 127.

In Reduced Circumstances

LOYALIST WOMEN AND BRITISH
GOVERNMENT ASSISTANCE, 1779–1783

TODD W. BRAISTED

—⁓⁓⁓—

THE AMERICAN War for Independence, like all wars, affected combatants and noncombatants alike. The nature and expanse of the conflict, combined with an over-stretched British Army in America, left only a small portion of territory under actual Crown control, which saddled loyalists in the countryside with difficult circumstances and choices. British authority could not be restored in America without the occupation of great swaths of territory with forces adequate to support and protect those professing loyalty to the Crown. The absence of such support, due to limited troops in America, put most loyalists amid neighbors generally hostile to their politics. Whether or not they chose to continue active support of British authority, they often paid a steep price. Such was the case, as an example, for one South Carolinian, Anne Carrol, who not only suffered loss of property and family but was herself injured while en route for aid. Loss of property, income, and opportunities to secure them, often combined with the absence or death of a spouse, guaranteed a continual flood of refugees to British-controlled areas such as Charleston, New York, and Quebec. Usually destitute and often suffering from illness, the refugees desperately needed assistance, but diverting limited resources in aid, such as food, money, and fuel, could defeat a force, in this case the British Army with its three-thousand-mile supply train. Pushing loyalists, including thousands of women and children, to British lines put immense pressure on British logistics and was thereby another way for Americans to wage war against their enemies.

*   *   *

THE REFUGEE crisis was particularly acute in New York City. Women's needs were especially extensive, as most arrived without money and often alone or with dependent children or aged parents. Many of these women had no choice but to leave the rebel countryside due to property confiscation or decrees by civilian authorities enforced by militias. These victims of civil war, whether widows or wives with absent husbands, became heads of households, needing to provide food, clothing, and shelter for themselves, children, parents, and occasionally injured or wounded spouses. One acute need was shelter, but that was not easily supported. Large parts of the city were reduced to ashes in the spectacular fires of September 1776 and August 1778, making it difficult to house the city's residents, military members, and the newly arrived refugees. Refugees faced an indeterminate future of living among the rubble or sharing quarters, either with others in similar situations or squeezing in with residents who did not always welcome them. Mary Van Gorden, a widow from Catskill, New York, faced such challenges. Her loyalist husband, Benjamin Van Gorden, had joined the British Army at New York City on 16 March 1778, enlisting as a private soldier in the 2nd Battalion, New Jersey Volunteers.[1] It would have taken a considerable time before Mary at home on the farm learned her husband had been killed at the Battle of Monmouth, New Jersey, on 28 June 1778.[2] That was one blow; the next was eviction. Turned out by a local committee in October 1780, she and her two children, with only the clothes on their backs and six days' worth of food, sought refuge in crowded New York City. Applying for rations on her arrival, she was refused, but authorities allowed her a room with a fellow refugee, a Mrs. McCarthy, who had arrived two months or so earlier. Upon a representation of the expense of rations and firewood for herself and family, she was authorized two months' worth of food. Whether she renewed the request afterward is unknown.[3]

In the early years of the war, the trickle of refugees into New York was manageable. Large-scale property confiscations by the states had not yet taken place, nor had the war delivered the number of widows that grew with each passing year. With no standardized method of requesting aid, refugees petitioned the senior commander on site and requested whatever appropriate assistance to which they felt entitled or necessary. One early and interesting pair needing help were Margaret Brush, widow of Vermont loyalist Crean Brush, and her daughter Frances Buchanan, widow of Captain John Buchanan of the Queen's American Rangers. Crean Brush had been an early foe of Ethan Allen, declaring in early 1776 that the rebellion was being fomented by the "unweared Assiduity of an artful ambitious Confederacy," which he sought to help crush.[4] His only action in this regard seems to have been making off with a large number of linen and woolen goods during the evacuation of Boston. A privateer, however, quickly captured Brush's ship and returned him to Boston, where he was jailed. Margaret Brush arrived in Boston a year later in 1777 under a flag of truce. About seven months after her arrival, Crean escaped on 5 November. Amid allegations that Margaret had aided his escape, possibly through costuming him in women's attire, she herself was jailed until "the Jayl Keeper, and others exacted large sums of money from her," after which she returned to New York City. As Crean had died after his arrival at New York, his widow petitioned for any back pay that might have been due him for his services to the Crown in the hopes of obtaining some means to support herself. Her daughter Frances, in turn, requested a pension for being the widow of an officer who died in September 1777, a gratuity not yet formally established for provincial officers and their widows. Both women requested rations be given them.[5]

Margaret and Frances were in the vanguard of what would eventually become a flood. In July 1778, forty women without husbands present were among those being provisioned at New York. As this number included several women connected to absent British regiments, they were not all refugees per se.[6] That soon changed. With the continued influx of refugees from the countryside, Sir Henry Clinton looked to bring them all into some sort of order under one administrator. His choice was Roger Morris, a British colonel on half-pay (i.e., retired) who lived in New York. Morris had solicited for some sort of employment in September 1778 but was not entirely eager to return to a military career; he preferred something akin to a civil occupation to maintain his family.[7] By January 1779, Clinton had appointed him inspector of refugees at New York and laid out the guidelines to be followed for all those taking refuge in New York and seeking assistance.

NOT ALL loyalists were considered equal, at least not by the British government. Morris was to determine each person's "station in life" and give them aid according to a four-tiered ranking system, with assistance ranging from a dollar a day with rations down to just rations. These tiers, not particularly specified, were probably tied to a refugee's known social and economic standing. This would determine what each would receive, that is, those of the first class or tier would be issued one dollar per day plus rations; those of the second class, one half-dollar per day and rations;

those of the third, one shilling and rations; and those at the bottom just rations. No "able bodied Single man," or other men fit to work unless ill, was to receive rations. Anyone falsifying their situation or "of suspected Character or disorderly Behavior" would be cut off from rations and/or confined in the provost. Finally, Clinton utilized his authority as commander in chief to give Morris the sole power to admit "none, but zealous Friends, to His Majestys Government, and giving the higher Pay only to Persons of Orders of Life, above Labor and Handicraft Trade."[8] It was later proposed to create "a Board of Commissioners" to examine and inquire into the petitions of refugees and to make recommendations, but there is no evidence any such body was ever appointed.[9]

Given Morris's power to discriminate, there is little wonder why the loyalists of the lower sorts fumed. By January 1782, displeasure reached such a degree that over three hundred refugees signed a petition against Morris, accusing him of being ignorant, cruel, inhumanly austere, and "extremely obnoxious." The petitioners begged Clinton to remove Morris, asserting his conduct had "a baneful effect on Loyalty, & Prejudices his Majesty's Interest" in America.[10] Sir Henry, who had laid down the rules by which Morris operated, was hardly sympathetic with the "fourth class" of refugees, and therefore Morris remained in his position. Hundreds of petitions passed through Morris's hands over the four years he held the inspector's position, many with direct orders from staff or general officers to place individuals on the rations list. Morris's discretion was not always universal, with both men and women seemingly denied by whim.

THE RATIONS refugees received were drawn from the Commissary General's Department, one of the civil branches of the army. It issued a full ration for men, a half-ration for women, and just a quarter ration for children. Each ration generally consisted of what a soldier got: pork or beef, bread or flour, rice, peas, butter, and perhaps oatmeal, rum, and beer.[11]

Not everyone receiving rations at New York did so for an unlimited time. Morris's office constantly culled rolls, looking for those who had found employment, recovered health, or in the case of some women, married or had a husband return from captivity. While the number of people receiving assistance could go up or down, the number of people receiving provisions from one source or another never dropped but simply shifted from one account book to another. That may have been the case when some refugees who had been out of work and drawing rations eventually found employ in a corps of wood cutters commanded by Major Thomas Ward. The corps started in April 1780 with about 100 men, but by 4 March 1782 it drew rations for 313 men, 53 women, and 109 children.[12]

THE MONETARY cost of support was something that affected both sides in the conflict, but with different outcomes. Garritie Maybee of Bergen County, New Jersey, was left at home with two children when her loyalist husband joined the British. Major John Mauritius Goetschius of the county's militia feared that she did not have the means to support herself, which meant that "she being very Poor and must of course (this winter) fall upon the Public for support." The solution was the confiscation of her home by the state and having her sent with her bed, bedding, and some "trifling Houshold furniture" to the British in New York, where presumably her husband, and by extension the British administration, would take care of her.[13]

The continuous arrival of displaced loyalists ensured no meaningful reductions could ever take place. Each year of warfare increased the number of widows and of the dispossessed. The civil authorities of each state continued to confiscate loyalist properties every year. Time served the establishment of American power, which in turn challenged the British pocketbook: it added to the number of mouths being fed at New York. Even after striking some refugees from aid, a return of 15 May 1782 at New York showed 199 men, 250 women, and 534 children on the refugee rolls drawing provisions. Of the women listed, 119 were single or widowed. The combined number of those then receiving aid added up to a daily consumption of 457½ rations, roughly the equivalent of that being consumed by a British regiment of infantry at the time.[14]

WIDOWS OF Provincial officers killed in action were initially provided for on an ad-hoc basis. Mary Barnes of Trenton, New Jersey, was the widow of Major John Barnes of the New Jersey Volunteers, who had been mortally wounded repulsing Sullivan's Raid on Staten Island in August 1777. New Jersey confiscated his estate in Trenton after his death and compelled Mary "to seek Protection within his Majesty's Lines, having Nothing left her in New-Jersey to subsist on, and bringing with her a Daughter of uncertain and precarious Health."[15] Sir Henry Clinton on 13 August 1778, presumably after Mary Barnes arrived in New York and nearly a year after her husband's death, awarded her one year's full pay according to her husband's rank, which was £273.15.0.[16] Each successive commander followed that example, and so the number of gratuities grew with the increasing number of recipients. By early 1780, Barnes was one of five widows of slain provincial officers petitioning Clinton to extend further benefits.[17] The same five widows also took their case over the commander in chief's head, petitioning Lord George Germain, asking that he "lay their distress before His Majesty from whose great Goodness they can alone hope for Relief."[18] The relief was indeed extended to quarterly allowances and made inclusive to any provincial widows, regardless of the cause of death.[19]

If a loyalist volunteer had not yet received an officer's commission, the widow had little hope of receiving anything more than rations. Such was the case of Elizabeth Marsh, whose husband, Henry Marsh, was slated to be confirmed the captain-lieutenant of the 4th Battalion, New Jersey Volunteers, and was acting in that capacity when he was shot and killed in a raid near Newark, New Jersey, in April 1777.[20] An officer's commission was his legal authority for rank and pay, without which he could only be considered a volunteer. Commissions for provincial officers, which had to be signed by the commander in chief, often took a while to obtain. Such was the case, unfortunately, with Henry Marsh. With her home in Bergen County confiscated, and what was left of her cash seized by a fellow officer to whom her husband was indebted, Elizabeth finally applied for aid in May 1783, being "reduced to great Want."[21] Despite testimonials of several officers on her behalf, she was not added to the list of widows receiving allowances.

Not all of the women requesting aid were helpless or sat idle as the conflict raged around them. It would be an injustice not to mention the risks undertaken by some who sacrificed much while eventually asking for a little recognition and recompense in return. One such woman was Ann Nevil of Sussex County, New Jersey. Nevil, believed to be a single woman, took it on herself to guide escaped prisoners from what was known as the Convention Army, the troops that had surrendered with General John Burgoyne at Saratoga in October 1777. The Convention Army had been marched under guard from the neighborhood of Boston to prison camps in Pennsylvania, Maryland, and Virginia, losing a number of men along the way, both by escape and acceptance of employment by commissaries and local authorities to fill shortages of labor. Those that escaped were strangers in a foreign land and had to utilize an "underground" network to obtain food, shelter, and guides to return to the British at New York. This was the role Ann Nevil fulfilled, leading a number there in December 1778, shortly after the troops had passed through her neighborhood. "Suspected by the Rebels to be the most Notorious Malafacter Imaginable," those rebels confined her in the Sussex County jail. Released after two months, she arrived in New York in 1779, "in a most deplorable Condition not able to Assist herself."[22] She received rations and money from the British for the rest of the war.

Hannah Tomlinson of Bucks County, Pennsylvania, was even more daring in her assistance efforts and also found herself in need as a result. As part of the refugee network, Hannah and her husband, Joseph, had hidden away, by their claim, one hundred officers and men who had escaped from prison. Making the dangerous trek from Bucks County to New York in June 1780, Hannah related to Major General James Pattison, commandant of the city, that the constant aid provided the prisoners "reduc'd myself & Family to a very low ebb."[23] There is no record of what aid she received, if anything. Supplying them with food, shelter, and guides, the Tomlinsons and other such civilians put their property and lives at risk for little or no reward. Sergeant Cornelius Crowley of the 47th Regiment of Foot named seventy-eight such people, men and women, in just Delaware and Maryland alone in aiding his escape to New York City.[24] It is unknown exactly how many women risked their freedom in such a manner, and it is certain not all were successful. In September 1780, while George Washington's army was encamped in Bergen County, New Jersey, desertion to neighboring New York was a serious concern. A major in the New Jersey State Troops reported to Washington about the area known as Schraalenbugh: "Six deserted through that Naughbourhood from the Pensilvania line one of them my men Got, him I have sent to his Ridgment under Gaurd together with his Pilote being a Refugees wife from New York."[25]

THE STORY of people of color seeking assistance is often hard to ascertain because so few recorded their trials and tribulations. The most immediate assistance often came from the Royal Navy. Enslaved men and women, most typically in the South, aimed for the Royal Navy warships prowling the coasts to escape their masters and get on board. Besides facilitating their freedom, the ships would feed any and all who made it on board. The ship muster book of HMS *St. Lawrence*, for example, recorded that on 29 March 1776, it had picked up escapees known only as Luno, Lucy, Susan, Sarah, Bess, Charlotte, and Flora, all in the Savannah River. These women were kept on board until other arrangements could be made for them, some being sent to St. Augustine in East Florida and others onto the packet ship *Glasgow*, where they were presumably given further assistance.[26] The exact number of refugees from slavery who made their first contact and gained assistance from the British in this manner is unknown but certainly exceeded a thousand.

Not all people of color were enslaved at the time of the Revolution, so for them there was a real choice whether or not to support the British or take part in the rebellion. That faced the Holmes family in New Jersey. A native of Hackensack, Bergen County, Elias Holmes was described as a five-foot-eleven-inch-tall mulatto, born about 1744.[27] Joining the British forces on the family's arrival at Fort Lee in November 1776, Holmes served as a wagoner, carting baggage for the 71st Highlanders as a member of the Quarter Master General's Department.[28] Wishing for a more active role in the conflict, he joined up with a refugee corps known as the King's Militia Volunteers, under the command of Captain David Peak. Wounded in three places and taken prisoner, most likely in a small raid in Bergen County, Holmes was imprisoned on 15 October 1778 in the jail at Hackensack, where he remained until he escaped with three other loyalists on 10 May 1779.[29] For bearing arms with the British, the county court indicted him for high treason and authorized confiscation of his property. When he finally hobbled into New York, Elias Holmes was admitted to the College Hospital where he lay incapacitated for months. For his family, there was little choice but to seek shelter with the British and request assistance. Arriving in New York City that summer, Catrena Holmes, Elias's wife, sought the assistance of Captain Peak, New York City mayor David Mathews, New Jersey royal governor William Franklin, and one other loyalist in requesting rations for herself, her four children, "and an Old Mother" who had no way to earn a living.[30] Among the property confiscated at their home was "one Loome and Tackling," which was no doubt used by Catrena.[31] Despite three petitions over a four-month period by such officials as Governor Franklin and Mayor Mathews, there is no evidence any aid was then provided. By 1782, however, the family, which had increased by a fourth child, was receiving 2¼ rations a day and an annual allowance £67.10.0 for living expenses. By way of comparison, that was over nine times the annual pay for a private soldier serving in the army, before deductions for rations.[32]

NEW YORK was not the only refuge. While refugees trickled toward the British Northern Army in Quebec throughout the war, the winter of 1777–78 saw a great influx of displaced loyalists. Grace Clarke lived on five hundred acres of land in New York's Mohawk Valley, "happy & Comfortable" with her husband, James, before he set off in 1777 to join Burgoyne's army advancing from Canada toward Albany. Turned "out doors" by her neighbors, she followed her husband, who had probably joined one of the loyalist units then being raised. By the time Burgoyne's army had surrendered at Saratoga on 17 October 1777, James was dead, killed in battle. His widow then trudged to Quebec with the other defeated loyalists under the terms of the Convention of Saratoga, "destitude of all the necessarys of Life."[33] Refugees to Canada would find themselves not only in the major cities of Montreal and Quebec but also in the lesser posts of Vercheres, Machiche, Isle aux Noix, St. Jean, Chambly, Yamaska, and others.[34]

The Northern Army in Canada was far behind that in America in establishing regulations for civilian refugees, but it did find more innovative ways to deal with the challenges. Instead of simply allowing rations, it herded those who were infirm, sick, or women with children to be housed together, where they could be easily fed and receive medical care. While there, they would be employed by the government in making blanket coats and leggings for the military "at a Fixt & Cheaper Rate than the Canadians [charge]."[35]

NOWHERE WAS the war more costly or destructive to families than in South Carolina from 1780 to 1782. While the British remained in the field, most loyalists stayed in the countryside, serving in the militia and tending to their families. Reverses of fortune and a lack of manpower forced the British to retire to the outskirts of Charleston by the end of September 1781, shortly after the Battle of Eutaw Springs. Without the protection of British arms, the proverbial floodgates opened and refugees by the thousands came within the lines. One of the startling differences looking at the requests for aid between New York and Charleston was the large number of widows at the latter. Loyalist men had died by the hundreds in militia service, either falling in combat or by murder at the hands of their neighbors. Illness swept through the ranks of those who were spared the bullet and bayonet.

Tending to the needs of those distressed refugees huddled around Charleston were Paymaster and Colonel Robert Gray of the loyalist militia, and his immediate superiors, city commandants Lieutenant Colonel Nisbet Balfour and his successor, Lieutenant Colonel Isaac Allen. Each refugee received rations and cash, five dollars per adult, two dollars for each child. By 26 May 1782, the British were feeding a small army of 1,165 men, 1,062 women, and 822 children. Only 782 of the number were serving as militia, the rest of the men being aged or infirm.[36] More came in every day, primarily from the Ninety Six District. In July 1782, Colonel John Hamilton of the Ninety Six Militia reported on the new arrivals from his district in need of assistance, amounting to 35 men, 74 women, and 250 children, 10 of the latter being orphans from 4 families. The overall number would have been higher, but two men and two wives died before the report was made.[37]

Nearly half of the women refugees huddled at Charleston were widows, among them Martha Snead.[38] Martha remained at home while her husband served as a captain in the militia under the British. After the defeat of the loyalists at King's Mountain in October 1780, Snead's home was plundered and local authorities gave her four days to remove to Charleston, along with four other women in like circumstances. She remained at Charleston until her husband died, when she attempted to return home. Being refused the right to live again in Ninety Six, she once more returned to Charleston, probably in July 1782, when Colonel John Hamilton made his report on new arrivals.[39] Martha Snead was well-off when compared to the likes of Anne Carrol, described as an old woman from Little Saluda, South Carolina. In 1781, Carrol's house was plundered, and she was exiled to Charleston, where her militiaman son was badly wounded in the hospital. On the way to Charleston on 8 September 1781, the day of the Battle of Eutaw Springs, a wagon ran over her, leaving her greatly bruised. Being "almost distracted with her situation" and waiting in various officer's offices for several days, she was given two guineas and sent on her way.[40] Janet Read was a widow with two children from Ninety Six District. She had lost her husband to wounds in the general hospital. Her aid was "14 yards of Linnen, a Camp Kettle and a little tea and Sugar."[41] Similar stories filled three volumes of records by the end of 1782.

NOT ALL requests for aid were confined within America during the course of the war. Some refugees, perhaps with family ties or whose station in life necessitated considerable financial support, chose to go to England and plead directly with the government in London for aid. Loyalist emigration to England continued throughout the war. Enough were living in London in September 1779 that they offered to form themselves into a military company in the event of a French invasion.[42] As the war was still in progress, and Britain assumed it would be victorious, these England-based claims became known as "temporary support" and were made to provide immediate relief until the claimant could return to America at the war's (presumed successful) conclusion.[43] While there is no complete record of how many of these wartime refugees made their way to London, documents in various files indicate that some were women, most notably widows. Among them was Jane Constable, widow of Captain Alexander Constable of the 2nd Battalion, DeLancey's Brigade. Captain Constable had been captured at sea on his passage from New York to Savannah in 1779 and jailed in irons in Charleston, South Carolina. The British released him from confinement when they captured that city in May 1780. Plagued by "distempers" after his liberation, he died five months later, leaving Jane a widow. Seeking compensation for (unspecified) property losses from the rebellion, Jane embarked for England on board the ship *Mary & Charlotte*, which sank on the passage. Another ship saved the passengers and crew, but Jane lost all her worldly possessions, valued at four hundred pounds. On her arrival in London in April 1781, she applied directly to Lord Germain for compensation for her losses. Germain, the secretary of state for American affairs, had his undersecretary recommend her case to the Treasury, which he accordingly did.[44] Despite testimonials attesting to her situation and hiring a person to lobby on her behalf at the Treasury, she conceded it was "all to no purpose," possibly because of the vague nature of her actual losses and no official guidelines yet having been established in England for compensation.[45] Prior to an act of Parliament in 1783 that established commissioners to enquire into the losses and services of loyalists, all claims in England were handled on an ad-hoc basis at the discretion of the Treasury.

It is difficult to put a complete price tag on the cost of refugees during the war, even at places such as New York and Charleston, which had dedicated inspectors to administer funds. Rations, firewood, quarters, monetary allowances, and sundries came from several sources and thus were not recorded on one ledger. Allowances to widows of provincial officers were on the books of the Provincial Forces' inspector general's office, while firewood came through the Barrack Master General's Department. Looking specifically at the accounts of Colonel Roger Morris between the period January 1779 and May 1783, the British expended through his hands alone a total of £25,655.6.7, which included the salary of himself and his staff.[46] Refugee lotteries, established at New York and Charleston, provided additional funds for the poor, but only a fraction of what the government could provide.

It is even harder to ascertain Colonel Robert Gray's expenditures at Charleston. Gray was inspector of both militia and refugees. While the costs were in separate accounts, many widows stayed with the militia regiments in which their late husbands had served, and consequently their expenses were noted on those accounts. The cost of just the refugee account, however, for the period 1781–82 was £11,272.15.0⅔.[47] Thousands more pounds were spent by various individuals on behalf of refugees and on a variety of services, such as for tailor Hugh Ross, who was paid two pounds and change "making Clothes for distressed refugees."[48] The auditing of all these accounts continued into the next two decades.

SARAH WINSLOW, sister of Massachusetts loyalist and Provincial Muster-Master General Edward Winslow, probably spoke for many loyalists, male and female, when writing to her cousin Benjamin Marston in Nova Scotia, a place she would soon call home. Sarah was still in New York City in April 1783 when the preliminary articles of peace arrived from England, acknowledging the independence of the United States. She and other refugee women had waged war in their day-to-day requests for aid, but now she and other loyalists had to contend with peace. The loyalists could attempt to go home, recover property, or find friends and relatives in the country willing to support them. The other option, chosen by many, was to leave the new United States and start their lives over again, either in England or, more typically, in what remained of British North America, particularly Nova Scotia and Upper Canada (Ontario). Hannah Tomlinson and her husband, Joseph, chose the latter as they traded the comforts of Pennsylvania for the wilderness of Beaver Harbour, New Brunswick.[49] That process, and new requests for aid, were still in the future for Sarah Winslow and her fellow loyalists. In April 1783, Winslow could only lament the hardships and losses of the past eight years:

> Was there ever an instance, my dear Cousin, can any history produce one, where such a number of the best of human beings were deserted by the government they have sacrificed their all for? The open enemys of Great Britain have gained their point, and more than ever they could have had impudence to have asked for—while their brave, persevering Noble Friends, who have suffered and toiled for years, and whom they were bound by every tie of honour and gratitude to assist, are left without friends, without fortune, without prospect of Support but from that Being who has hitherto supported us, and upon whom We must rely for further protection. This "peace" brings none to my heart.[50]

NOTES

1. Return of Three Recruits Enlisted in the 2nd Battalion, New Jersey Volunteers, New York, March 1778, Ward Chipman Papers, MG 23, D 1, series 1, vol. 30, part 2, p. 444, Library and Archives Canada, Ottawa (hereafter LAC).
2. Muster Roll of Major John Antill's Company, 2nd Battalion, New Jersey Volunteers, New York, July 1778, RG 8, "C" Series, vol. 1854, p. 20, LAC.

3. Memorial of Mary Van Gorden to Sir Henry Clinton, New York, 18 February 1781, Headquarters Papers of the British Army in America, PRO 30/55/3345, National Archives of the United Kingdom, Kew, England (hereafter TNA).

4. Margaret Brush to Lord George Germain, Boston, 10 January 1776, Colonial Office, Class 5, vol. 115, ff. 187–188, TNA.

5. Memorial of Margaret Brush and Frances Buchanan, Widows, to Sir Henry Clinton, 20 February 1778, Sir Henry Clinton Papers, vol. 31, item 21, William L. Clements Library, University of Michigan, Ann Arbor (hereafter CL).

6. "List of Refugees and Others Provisioned by Order of the Commander in Chief and Others, New York, 27 July 1778," Sir Henry Clinton Papers, vol. 38, item 5, CL.

7. Roger Morris to Lord Amherst, New York, 24 September 1778, War Office, Class 34, vol. 145, ff. 469–469v, TNA.

8. "Instructions for the Inspector of Refugees," c. 1779, Sir Henry Clinton Papers, vol. 225, item 12, CL.

9. Proposal to Create a Board of Commissioners, unsigned, c. 1779, Sir Henry Clinton Papers, vol. 229, item 49, CL.

10. Petition of Captain Edward Stow et al. to Sir Henry Clinton, New York, 17 January 1782, Sir Henry Clinton Papers, vol. 190, item 30a, CL.

11. "Abstract of Provisions Issued from the Deposit at Marstons Wharf from 23rd June & 27th June 1777," Seth Norton Papers, L 83.2.3, Nassau County Museum, Roslyn Harbor, NY.

12. "Provision Return for the Loyal Refugees on Bergen Neck Commencing the 4th March and Ending 23 Day March [1782] Both Days Inclusive," Sir Henry Clinton Papers, vol. 191, item 23, CL.

13. John Mauritius Goetschius to Brigadier General Anthony Wayne, Schraalenburgh, 8 December 1779, Wayne Papers, vol. 9, f. 64, Historical Society of Pennsylvania, Philadelphia.

14. "A List of the Names, of the Refugees, &c. Who Receive Provisions, New York 15 May 1782," War Office, Class 60, vol. 33, part 2, TNA.

15. Memorial of Mary Barnes to Sir Guy Carleton, New York, c. 1782–83, Headquarters Papers of the British Army in America, PRO 30/55/6621, TNA.

16. List of Warrants Granted and Paid by Sir Henry Clinton between 1 July 1778 and 30 September 1778, Treasury, Class 64, vol. 109, ff. 53–61, TNA.

17. Frances Dongan, Mary Barnes, et al. to Sir Henry Clinton, New York, 14 February 1780, Sir Henry Clinton Papers, vol. 85, item 19, CL.

18. Frances Dongan, Mary Barnes, et al. to Lord George Germain, New York, 14 February 1780, Sir Henry Clinton Papers, vol. 97, item 20, CL.

19. Quarterly Allowance to Widows of Provincial Officers, 1 January–1 April 1783, Headquarters Papers of the British Army in America, PRO 30/55/6890, TNA.

20. *Pennsylvania Evening Post* (Philadelphia), 17 April 1777.

21. Elizabeth Marsh to Sir Guy Carleton, New York, 22 May 1783, Headquarters Papers of the British Army in America, PRO 30/55/10108, TNA.

22. Petition of Ann Nevil to Sir Henry Clinton, New York, June 1779, Headquarters Papers of the British Army in America, PRO 30/55/2097, TNA.

23. Hannah Tomlinson to James Pattison, New York, 13 June 1780, Headquarters Papers of the British Army in America, PRO 30/55/2823, TNA.

24. Intelligence Report of Sergeant Cornelius Crowley, c. 1780–81, Sir Henry Clinton Papers, vol. 136, item 33, CL.

25. Major John Mauritius Goetschius to Washington, Closter, 10 September 1780, George Washington Papers, series 4, General Correspondence, 1697–1799, MSS 44693, reel 070, Library of Congress, Washington, DC.

26. Muster Book of HMS *St. Lawrence*, 1 March–30 April 1776, Admiralty, Class 36, vol. 8434, TNA.

27. Advertisement by Sheriff Adam Boyd for Arrest of Elias Holmes and Others, Bergen County, 11 May 1779, *New Jersey Gazette* (Trenton), 19 May 1779.

28. Petition by Captain Samuel Peeck and Others on Behalf of Elias Holmes, New York, 29 November 1779, Headquarters Papers of the British Army in America, PRO 30/55/2456, TNA.

29. Petition by Captain David Peak and Others on Behalf of Elias Holmes, New York, 17 September 1779, Headquarters Papers of the British Army in America, PRO 30/55/2305, TNA.

30. Memorial of Captain David Peak and Others on Behalf of Catrena Holmes, New York, 20 July 1779, Headquarters Papers of the British Army in America, PRO 30/55/2133, TNA.

31. Memorial of Elias Holmes to the Commissioners for American Claims, Sorel, c. 1784, Audit Office, Class 13, vol. 18, f. 248, TNA.

32. The daily pay for a provincial soldier was 6 pence a day, from which was deducted 2½ pence for provisions. The annual pay of a private, before that deduction, was £9.2.6 sterling. See "Abstract of Subsistence for the Non Commission Officers, Drummers and Private Men of the New York Volunteers from 25th October 1778 to 24th December 1778 Following," Chancery, Class 106, vol. 90, part 1, bundle 1, TNA.

33. Memorial of Grace Clarke to the Commissioners for American Claims, Halifax, 8 March 1786, Audit Office, Class 13, vol. 25, ff. 110–11, TNA.

34. For an example of the numbers of soldiers and refugees fed at the different Canadian posts, see "Monthly Return of the Number & Denominations of People Victuall'd & Number of Rations Drawn between April 25th & May 24th 1778 Inclusive, & the Provisions Remaining in the Different Magazines in Canada on the 24th of May 1778," Additional Manuscripts, no. 21853, folio 2, British Library, London. For more on the refugee experience with the Northern Army, see Gavin Watt's *Loyalist Refugees: Non Military Refugees in Quebec, 1776–1784* (Milton, ON: Global Heritage

Press, 2014), and Janice Potter-MacKinnon's *While the Women Only Wept: Loyalist Refugee Women in Eastern Ontario* (Kingston, ON: McGill-Queen's University Press, 1995).

35. Regulations for Royalist Refugees, Montreal, 6 March 1782, Additional Manuscripts, no. 21825, ff. 5–6, British Library.

36. "Return of the Number of Persons Victualed from His Majesty's Stores in South Carolina, 26 May 1782," War Office, Class 60, vol. 32, part 2, bundle 6, TNA.

37. "Report of Distress'd Refugees from Ninety Six Dist . . . Charles Town July 1782," Treasury, Class 50, vol. 4, ff. 274–75, TNA.

38. Ibid.

39. Memorial of Martha Snead to the Commissioners for American Claims, c. 1786, Audit Office, Class 13, vol. 25, ff. 459–60, TNA.

40. Report of Colonel Robert Gray to Nisbet Balfour on Distressed Refugees, Charleston, 22 September 1781, Treasury, Class 50, vol. 4, ff. 116–18, TNA.

41. Report of Colonel Robert Gray to Nisbet Balfour on Distressed Refugees, Charleston, 12 October 1781, Treasury, Class 50, vol. 4, ff. 130–31, TNA.

42. Memorial of Forty-Nine Americans under Chairman John Randolph to Lord George Germain, c. September 1779, Colonial Office, Class 5, vol. 80, ff. 1–2, TNA.

43. For a fuller account of the system in place in Britain, see Eugene R. Fingerhut, "Uses and Abuses of the American Loyalists' Claims: A Critique of Quantitative Analysis," *William and Mary Quarterly*, 3rd series, 25, no. 2 (1968): 245–58.

44. Benjamin Thompson to Sir Guy Cooper, Whitehall, 10 April 1781, Audit Office, Class 13, vol. 73, f. 384, TNA.

45. Memorial of Jane Constable to the Commissioners for American Claims, No. 2 Inn Temple Lane, c. 15 March 1784, Audit Office, Class 13, vol. 73, ff. 380–81, TNA.

46. Declared Account of Colonel Roger Morris, 1 January 1779–31 March 1783. Audit Office, Class 1, vol. 850, roll 1, TNA.

47. Declared Account of Paymaster Robert Gray, 1781–82, Audit Office, Class 1, vol. 326, roll 1291, TNA.

48. Declared Account of Deputy Paymaster Josiah Paul Collin, 1781–82, Audit Office, Class 1, vol. 326, roll 1292, TNA.

49. Memorial of Joseph Tomlinson to the Commissioners for American Claims, c. 1786, Audit Office, Class 13, vol. 21, ff. 423–25, TNA. For a detailed look at the diaspora of the loyalists at the end of the American Revolution, see Maya Jasanoff's *Liberty's Exiles* (New York: Knopf, 2011).

50. Sarah Winslow to Benjamin Marston, New York, 10 April 1783, in *Winslow Papers, A.D. 1776–1826*, ed. W. O. Raymond (Saint John, NB: Sun Printing, 1901), 78–79.

Complicated Allegiances

Women, Politics, and Property in Post-Occupation Charleston

JACQUELINE BEATTY

———∿∿∿∿∿———

T HE BRITISH occupied the city of Charleston (Charles Town) from the spring of 1780 until the summer of 1782. Once Whigs regained control of the region, Americans—women and men—had to account for their behavior during the two years of tension, violence, and suffering that the cities' inhabitants had endured. Women in particular had to come to terms with their own complicated political and social allegiances during the British occupation when they often had to make choices about whether (and how) to prioritize their families or their politics. After the occupation, they faced the consequences of these choices as the revolutionary state began to expel alleged loyalists and seize their estates. In this process, women purposefully constructed a particular persona in petitions to the South Carolina General Assembly.

Some women continued to suffer—or perhaps suffered even more—after the British retreated from the peninsula, and thus sought clemency and relief by petitioning the assembly. Sarah Scott, for example, attempted to account for her husband John's alleged disloyalty to the American cause. She noted that John had served in the militia in Charleston, but that the British had imprisoned him once they captured the city. They subsequently forced John, in her view, to sign a congratulatory address applauding Lord Cornwallis's victory at Camden. Sarah insisted that John had felt compelled to do so or risk losing the home in which they and their child lived. This was "the effect of necessity, not of choice"; knowing "the distresses of his family being then exceedingly great," she insisted, John signed the address, as it was, in her view, the only means of "alleviating the wants of his family." Moreover, Sarah maintained that General William Woodford of the American forces had vouched for her husband's kindness and patriotism, Woodford having written a letter of John's "friendly disposition" toward an American officer during the conflict. In closing, Sarah beseeched the assembly to "relieve the misery and distress in which she and her innocent child are involved."[1] If the assembly did not heed Scott's plea, both she and her child would be innocent victims of the destruction wrought by a war begun and waged primarily by men.

Women like Sarah Scott employed the language of well-worn tropes of White femininity: dependence, helplessness, and vulnerability, which appear especially striking relative to men's strength and independence. Scott's expressions of dependence on her husband are both implicit and explicit in her plea. She implied that her family's survival was contingent on John's safe return and the return of his property, subtly yet deftly demonstrating her reliance on him. In providing justification for her husband's seemingly treasonous actions as valiant acts of a devoted spouse and father, however, she signaled that her dependence was the cause of John's political malfeasance. It was Sarah's and her child's dependence on John that forced the man's hand, compelling him to acquiesce to British demands and subsequently necessitating his violation of the Confiscation Act of 1782. The power of Sarah's language was in her exploitation of the tropes of femininity but also of husbandly duty to wife and child; a husband, after all, was socially and legally obligated to care and provide for the dependents under his care. Sarah's narrative was evidently persuasive to the committee despite John's ostensible disloyalty; Scott achieved her goal, though her husband was politically neutered in the process.[2]

Petitions like Scott's, though brief, illuminate much about the complicated and often malleable prescriptions of gender in wartime. Scholars of revolutionary-era women's history have studied women's petitions with an eye toward gender in order to understand the social, economic, and political lived experiences of the war. Beginning with the pioneering work of Linda K. Kerber and Mary Beth Norton, women's and gender historians have excavated these sources and found similar linguistic patterns.[3] Yet the incredible power inherent to women's status as wives and mothers within their dependent status has been understudied. In the wake of the evacuation of British troops from Charleston, women used the legislative petition to seek clemency from the newly reempowered Whig government, and did so within the confines of White femininity as it was constructed for middling and elite Anglo-Americans.

Linguistic performances of femininity (and masculinity) were critical tools for families in arguing for clemency, repatriation, relief, or restoration of property from the South Carolina General Assembly. Women's linguistic focus on their helplessness, vulnerability, powerlessness, and apolitical nature demonstrates their familiarity with tropes of femininity, and their shrewd understanding that this language held strategic value for their—and their families'—survival.

Women's wartime experiences shaped both their petitioning strategies and expectations about their relationship to the state.[4] When they criticized the state and their husbands for failing to uphold their paternal—and patriarchal—duties, they often did so carefully. By submitting petitions to the legislature, women acted as political beings while performing an ignorance or distance from politics. Their petitions from this period demonstrate the powerful constraints on women's behavior, while also underscoring how the disruptions of wartime allowed for women to subtly subvert traditional tropes of femininity, often to their advantage.

Recently, scholars have delved into the complex nature of urban occupation during the American Revolution, particularly as it pertains to the toll it took on women.[5] Historians have likewise dedicated increasing study to the subject of loyalism, political allegiances, and the loyalist diaspora.[6] But as Rebecca Brannon notes, few historians have paid close attention to loyalists (or those Whigs defined as loyalists) who decided to *stay* in the United States after occupation and after the war.[7] Importantly, the vast majority of those classified as "loyalists" remained in the new United States, which certainly merits a closer study of their experiences. What scholars have paid even less attention to is the role women played in the reconstruction of society and their families when the British evacuated American cities.[8] It was women's unique position as *women*, as wives and mothers, as supposedly helpless and vulnerable apolitical victims of this vicious civil war, that provided them with the room, the justification, and the opportunity to make such assertive arguments in defense of themselves and their families in claims to the legislature which merits further study by historians.

Repatriation and Repatriarchalization

After the British evacuated Charleston, Whig leadership expelled a number of alleged Tory sympathizers from South Carolina and confiscated their property. In the wake of this wave of banishments, many women

were left to mend their broken families. Some used this moment to present sympathetic narratives to the state legislature.[9] White male officials
in the assembly accepted the gendered paradigm of women's need for
protection, because sympathy for others was a social obligation in the
eighteenth century, especially for elite, White men in positions of power.
Women, then, held power in their subordinate status and exploited this
new emotional paradigm to suit their particular needs as women. The
rhetorical tool of sympathy provided them with one outlet to escape
their difficult situations. Women who petitioned their state legislatures
for various forms of relief themselves were able to capitalize on this "renewed communalism," this emerging sense of obligation that elite White
legislators expressed toward their social dependents. Women—wives
and mothers in particular—garnered special attention as the "epitome of
pity," eliciting "indulgence with their woes."[10] Women thus adeptly tar-
geted the sympathetic language of their petitions to their audience: the
paternalistic, patriarchal state.

This language served to persuade legislators of the worthiness of
women's cases. Some women, for instance, acquiesced to the understanding that they were dependent on men for financial support while
simultaneously undermining other tropes of masculinity. Mary Peronneau, widow to the late Arthur, sought mercy for her brother-in-law
Robert, whom the legislature had banished and whose property was
seized with the 1782 Confiscation Act. Robert had been "warmly attached to the Cause of his Country"; so "eager to take an active part" in
the war, Robert traveled from Britain to the United States in 1778 despite
"numberless appeasing difficulties."[11] He served nobly, she insisted, until
Charleston fell into British hands.

Like many others in her situation, Mary Peronneau argued that
circumstances—rather than political ideology—coerced Robert to sign
the Congratulatory Address to Lord Cornwallis on the general's victory
at Camden. It was in "an unguarded moment," she insisted, and at the
urging of friends that he acquiesced to the British loyalty oath. Mary
was convinced that the stress of this ordeal had caused his health to decline, which, as a result, caused trouble for herself and her children. With
her husband, Arthur, deceased, Mary and her children found themselves
wanting and "in a great measure" still "dependent on [her brother-in-law]
for support."[12] Without Robert, Mary and her children had nowhere to
turn; she insisted that she was incapable of providing for her family without his assistance, painting herself—likely accurately—as the consum-
mate pitiable figure.

It was in this emphasis on her dependence and helplessness—particularly in financial matters—that Mary Peronneau found a legitimate reason to petition her government for leniency in Robert's case. Her argument was clearly convincing, as the legislature granted her petition.[13] Peronneau's situation, though, was not unique. A number of women faced similar hardships in the wake of the British retreat from Charleston, and the vast majority repeated gendered tropes of female helplessness and vulnerability. In so doing, however, they managed to reassert a bit of power and agency over their lives, through ironically emphasizing this very powerlessness.

Mary Peronneau's petition likewise highlights the ways in which women's language emasculated men and undermined their patriarchal authority while elevating women's domestic and even political roles. Mary crafted an image of her brother-in-law as her sole source of financial support but also as a powerless stooge who bowed to the whims of Tory authorities and peer pressure, thus abandoning his political convictions when they became inconvenient or threatened his status. The Robert of 1782 was not the man of principle of 1778. His declining health also spoke to the physical weakness of his constitution, unable to cope with the consequences of his actions. Her request for "compassion to her & a large family, who have suffered much in these calamitous times" met the gendered expectations of White femininity, though Robert failed his family in the process.[14] Women's language implicitly illustrated that they had the strength to hold fast to expectations of gendered comportment in wartime, even when the men around them did not.

In their petitions for clemency and for their husbands' and other family members' repatriation, women had to address these men's alleged disloyalty while not explicitly usurping the masculine role in the family and state. Many chose to present their respective husbands' decisions to sign oaths of loyalty during the British occupation of Charleston as an extension of their husbandly and fatherly roles. These men, they admitted, abdicated their duty to the state of South Carolina, but they did so to protect their wives and children from the calamities of war. In some cases, women themselves encouraged this choice. In their petitions, women continued to perform the role of vulnerable, defenseless wives, enabling them to justify their husbands' behavior and see these men (and their property) returned to them.

Other women were able to explain their husband's shifting political allegiances in a way that at least attempted to retain the veneer of masculine honor. Mary Brown suggested that prior to the occupation of

Charleston, her husband, Archibald, "was amongst the foremost at the Post of Danger," acting as "a zealous and active Friend in the Cause of his Country." He fought for the British only after the fall of the city, when he believed the cause had been lost. When he took command of the Goose Greek Company, he did so out of a sense of "Duty, to keep the Peace of the Town as he had formerly done under the American Government," and linked his allegedly treacherous behavior with that of "a Multitude of other Inhabitants."[15] Archibald abandoned his political principles, Mary insisted, to protect the people of Charleston.

Importantly, women's position as apolitical actors allowed them (and their narratives) to soften the effect that such a rebuke of Whig leadership might have had were the critique to have come from men. Mary Brown's implicit suggestion that she understood the political machinations of men was couched in her role as a wife and was therefore more palatable to the assembly. Throughout her petition, Mary continued to cite the numerous ways in which her husband had been an advocate for American interests. She cited Archibald's record as a member of the American militia and as an agent to France, and reminded the legislature of the injuries he had sustained at Port Royal and Savannah, which he had borne "in the Cause of his Country."[16] Archibald had established a long history of active military service, having sacrificed his body in service of his political principles, and only abdicated his position when the war, and his ideals, seemed lost.

But Mary could not ignore the specter of the loyalty oath Archibald had signed. The only "excuse" she could offer was that her husband was taken by "that kind of Contagion which spreads on such occasions, from the force of Examples set before him." Up to this point, Mary had portrayed her husband as a strong man, one willing to put his life on the line for his beliefs. The only way she could explain away his behavior, though, was to describe this moment of weakness as his having succumbed to a "contagion," a disease of the mind in this case, which compelled him to waver. Yielding to this metaphorical weakness, he signed the oath because it was his only option, according to Mary, and as the only way to protect his "many near Connexions who have much dependence on him."[17]

Although she presented a snapshot of a moment of weakness for her husband, Mary's humility and powerlessness was the focal point of her narrative. She admitted discomfort in interjecting herself in the political and military affairs of men. She was "loath to bear testimonies" of her husband's conduct yet felt compelled to do so out of her love for him and the well-being of her family.[18] Mary's petition had wandered into the affairs of men but only insofar as it was an extension of proper feminine comportment—or so she presented her case that way. She was justified in challenging the legislature's decision to banish her husband because she did so as a wife and mother. Like Sarah Scott, Mary Brown was successful in exploiting her own dependence and need in order to exonerate her husband. The committee decided to grant her petition.[19]

Effectively, women explained that because they had performed their role as dependent wives, their husbands had to protect them, per the social and legal obligations tasked to husbands. In highlighting their husbands' dedication to family, especially as the primary cause for their ostensibly loyalist actions, women essentially took the blame for this treasonous behavior. Susannah Smyth, for instance, claimed her husband, John, had only taken a commission with the British because he did not want to lose "his whole fortune on which his Family altogether depended for Support." If not for her needs and the needs of her children, she held, he never would have made such a decision.[20]

Because of the contested nature of women's political agency, Smyth could openly admit that her dependence fueled her husband's loyalism, and she could do so with little fear of political repercussions for herself. The implication, then, was that John certainly would have joined the American militia (or at least refused to join its British counterpart) had he not been hindered by the need to support and protect his family. By simultaneously positioning herself as a weak, sympathetic figure while insisting that her husband had only forsaken his country to ensure the safety of his family, Susannah played with traditional notions of feminine *and* masculine comportment to successfully bring her husband home to South Carolina.[21] Women's petitions, though often formulaic, display a great adroitness of language and understanding, recognizing the potency of gendered norms while also exploiting upheavals of war to allow for a more malleable interpretation of the expectations of femininity and masculinity.

Women employed this language—their helplessness and vulnerability—as a strategy for convincing the state to return their husband's property or their husbands themselves. In many cases, this method was effective, and in some cases more effective than men's pleas. Sympathetic narratives were often successful in repatriating their husbands from banishment. In their contact with the state, women performed overt political acts (in the form of petitions, a process steeped in humility and subordination), but did so through performing traditional White femininity.

A Challenge?

Historically, military conflict tends to upend, or temporarily suspend, prescribed gender norms. In the examples already discussed, the alteration came in the form of increased petitioning and interaction with the state by a number of women in Charleston. But the evidence presented thus far has not shown women asserting their own political identities—separate and independent from that of their husbands. Women in the aforementioned cases did not position themselves as Whigs or Tories, and did not openly critique their husbands' choices, even when these choices led them into exile and compelled the state to confiscate their property (thus endangering their families). Most women followed the protocols of gendered politics in their petitions; by presenting themselves as both apolitical and dependent—even if this performance belied the very nature of their actions—their sympathetic narratives often elicited mercy from state legislatures. But not all women abided by those unwritten rules. Some criticized their husbands' political choices, others berated the state and its leaders, and still others asserted their own independent political identities. The disruptions of war seemed to give them license, or at least the motivation, to do so.

Women's petitions sometimes used their own political actions, independent of their husbands' decisions, to assert their right to obtain these men's confiscated property.[22] Florence Cooke, for instance, rejected the assembly's denial to her "right of Dower." Cooke's petition highlights the ways in which dower could be perceived or presented as a positive right in itself, but also as a right of dependent wives. In addition to her condemnation of the South Carolina General Assembly for depriving her of her dower, Cooke accused these men of stripping her twelve-year-old daughter of this right, and on "all future claim on the inheritance of her father." Cooke rebuked the assemblymen for their inattention to her daughter's well-being, especially as "her Child received early & strong impressions of real attachment to the liberty of her Native Country; with a Confirmed aversion to our Enemies" given to her not by her father but by her mother. Cooke similarly asserted that if she were "blessed" with sons, she would have raised them "for the Defence and Support of their Country"—the ultimate invocation of female patriotism.[23] Cooke was clear in her contentions that her expressions of patriotism gave her the right to submit her petition, while simultaneously asserting her—and her daughter's—dependence on her husband and, more importantly, his property.

Cooke most fervently asserted her claim to her dower right by sep-arating her politics and her labor from her husband's. She maintained that she earned her dower "by her own Domestic toil." Similarly, Cooke affirmed her right to this property by emphasizing her own "sincere af-fection for the independence and freedom of her Country" despite her husband's (albeit weak) loyalist tendencies. While declaring her own ar-dent patriotism, she simultaneously highlighted her husband's lack of concern or "knowledge of public troubles." James Cooke was, according to his wife, a hard-working man, but she was certain "he had neither in-clination nor influence to execute any mischievous" deed. Her petition included an addendum: an affidavit signed by eleven prisoners of war who testified that she cared for and provided for them in their time of need.[24] James Cooke's political apathy lay in stark contrast to Florence's fervor for the American cause.

Cooke placed much of the blame for her current predicament squarely on the assembly. Painting a bleak picture of the life she and her daughter led in James's absence, Cooke emphasized the "many debts" she had to pay in addition to the care of her child "and a Sickly old Lady, a relation & dependant." Notably, she proclaimed that the assembly's failure to grant her petition would result in her young daughter turning to prostitution: Cooke held that if she was "deprived of the only resource for herself and the maintenance & Education of her Daughter," she "must otherwise be turned into the world, without friend or protector, exposed to that Mis-fortune and affliction which seldom fail to preserve an unhappy female fallen from affluence to poverty."[25] Cooke left no room for these states-men to interpret her situation in any other way. If they did not recognize her right to her husband's property, they were condemning her daughter to a life of sin and destitution.

Cooke segued from her dismal narrative to a depiction of herself as a dutiful wife who, as such, could claim the rights inherent in her de-pendence. Here, Cooke briefly acquiesced to society's vision of a depen-dent, submissive wife, complicating the assertive woman she constructed throughout her plea. Despite critiquing his behavior and politics, for example, she quickly solicited the assembly for the return of her husband (although it was not her primary objective). This demonstrated that she did not only want James's property for herself but also so that the family might be whole again, and she could resume her role as dependent wife. Promising that upon his inevitable acquittal, she "pledge[d] herself that she will exert all the ascendency of a wife & friend to make him a good man and useful citizen."[26] Not only was she a true female patriot in her own right but she extended that sentiment to her husband, who by *her* virtuous reforming efforts could be transformed into an active and ardent patriot.

Florence Cooke manipulated the tenuous notion of women's political roles by couching them in terms of her dependent status as a wife. She distanced herself from her husband's politics (or lack thereof) by identifying herself as an ardent advocate of the "cause of America." She characterized this patriotic behavior, though, as *feminine*. She fit the model of republican motherhood, instilling in her young daughter the ideals of the Revolution while swearing she would have done the same had she bore male children. She emasculated her husband by highlighting his inability to stand firmly against Great Britain, wavering in his political stance and similarly failing to care for his family adequately.

Cooke's petition includes all the hallmarks of a well-behaved woman: emphasizing her performance of White femininity, providing evidence of acquiescence to a wife's dependence on her husband, all the while presenting a wrenching tale of her and her daughter's many distresses. Yet Cooke's plea stands out at the same time. She implicitly critiqued the war, the state, *and* her husband. She maintained that she "earned" the property that the state confiscated by her own "Domestic toil," "not more by the hard industry of her husband." And, notably, her right to dower was hers *not* because of her dependence but because of her *independence*.[27] Cooke's petition was, for a time at least, successful: the General Assembly planned to permit her husband, James, to return to the state. But members of the community, appalled at this mercy, pressured the assembly to rescind their offer. James never returned to the United States.[28]

Cooke asserted her own political identity in an attempt to combat the ill effects of James's actions, but there were instances in which the sins of the husband proved too big a hurdle for some wives to overcome. One such case is that of Mary Fraser. In her petition, Fraser recognized the "unfortunate" decision of her husband to side with the British government. Because of his "becoming obnoxious to the American Government," Dr. James Fraser's name appeared on the list of offenders of the Confiscation Act of 1782. The narrative Mary presented diminished her husband's true influence and activities. In her view, James followed the law, left the country, and as such had been in exile at the time of her petition for thirteen years. Further demonstrating her performance of wifely duty, Mary, "being bound in duty as well as by Affection to follow the fortunes of her Husband, was obliged to quit her Native Country, to abandon her Aged Mother and all her relations and friends, and to take refuge in a foreign land, where she has been made to taste, in Common with her young and unoffending Offspring, of the bitter cup of Sorrow and Affliction." Mary was deeply torn between, on the one hand, her love of country, family, and friends, and on the other, her dedication to her husband and her marital responsibilities.[29]

On the occasion of her mother falling ill, Mary Fraser begged the assembly "to be re-admitted to the bosom of her Country" with her children and husband in tow in order to care for her ailing parent. Mary and her children had already returned to South Carolina; her petition attempted to gain legal sanction for their (and for her husband's) return to the state. Mary was convinced that her husband had already "been severely punished" by the confiscation of his property "to which he submits without reluctance," as well as the family's thirteen-year exile from their home. In her petition, Mary emphasized that she and her children were merely "the Innocent victims of his political errors" and begged for the house to have mercy on her family's situation. The only way, in Mary's view, for these "innocent victims" to receive justice would be for the legislature to forgive her husband's "political errors"; as "the Law . . . banishes her said Husband," it also "virtually banishes your petitioner and her nine helpless Children." Mary clearly demonstrated her dedication to her husband despite his poor political choices and begged the legislature to express their mercy as well.[30]

What made Mary Fraser's petition extraordinary, however, was not her language of devotion to her husband and dedication to her familial duties; this language was strategic and typical. Fraser submitted her petition along with another signed by 191 other women, presumably those "relations and friends" whom she expressed great regret at having to leave upon her husband's exile. These signatures all came from other women who felt compelled to submit a separate plea to the assembly. Convinced of the injustice of the 1782 law, these 191 women explained to the house that "the punishments Imposed . . . reach in their operation far beyond, the person offending." The women were similarly assured that "all who seek should be allowed to enjoy the protection of our mild and excellent Government which above all others knows how to forgive." Here, the petitioners highlighted the patriarchal state's responsibility to provide "protection" to its citizens, particularly dependents and innocents. The female cosigners both emphasized Fraser's dependence on her husband and implicitly recognized her dependence on their support as they petitioned for her husband's offenses to be forgiven so that she might spend time with her ailing mother and return to her home, "which she desires above all earthly blessings."[31] Yet even though she did everything right—providing a sympathetic narrative asserting her own affection for America and gaining the support of the community—James Fraser never returned to South Carolina.[32]

When women were particularly critical of either their husbands or the state (or both!), their pleas fell on deaf ears. Margarett Brisbane acted as the champion of dependent women and children, even highlighting the suffering of her sex more broadly. This was likely a step too far, penetrating the boundaries of gender roles through the opportunities presented in wartime. Brisbane's husband, James, left the country during the war after being accused of harboring loyalist sentiments. Like Fraser, though, Brisbane's petition undervalued the true scale of her husband's actions, and the assembly well knew this. James later absconded from his wife and family, leaving them without any support. Margarett made no attempts to repudiate the case against her husband; instead, she made sure to distance herself from his politics, claiming that "her Sentiments *with regard to the present Contest* never coincided with, but were always contrary to her Husbands."[33]

Here, Margarett stressed her independence of thought while simultaneously reiterating the unfortunate situation of her dependence on her absent husband. This was an implicit critique of women's larger social and marital roles, beyond her own individual situation, and proved problematic. In her case, James left behind an eighteen-month-old infant and a pregnant wife, as well as several children from a previous marriage, in Margarett's care. What he did not leave, however, was a proper method of "support, and Maintenance, or some portion of her Husband's late property."[34] Margarett's petition, then, was similar to others made for the same reasons, but hers included a brave declaration calling on the assembly to recognize her critique of the patriarchal structure that brought her to such an unfortunate position.

Margarett Brisbane not only asked that an exception be made in her case, but in the case of *other* women and children unfortunate enough to find themselves in the same situation. Brisbane boldly made her case to the assembly: "Called on by Humanity toward her Offspring, she finds herself *impell'd* to make this Request, & flatters herself with Hopes, that when the House reflects on the *weak and Defenseless Situation of women & children*, who are not the promoters of the War, nor, from their Sphere in Life, can possibly be disadvantageous to the Contest; and whose Opinions seldom avail, and do not frequently operate on the Judgment of Men."[35]

Brisbane's petition highlights the devastating problem of women's dependence, especially under these circumstances. Her husband, James, was able to leave the country, while she was forced to remain at home not only with her infant son and soon-to-be-born child but also with his children from a previous marriage. The stipulations of the law meant to punish James had the adverse effect of imposing the bulk of the consequences on Margarett and her children. The war, and the state's actions, put her family in this precarious situation, and Margarett refused to remain silent and acquiesce to it.

Margarett Brisbane's petition drew attention to the injustice of the South Carolina Confiscation Act—that dependents, whose political choices the state deemed either considered irrelevant or nonexistent, were made to pay for a husband's, father's, or brother's political affiliations and wartime activity. While Margarett acknowledged these behavioral standards (making a strong case for herself in the process), she was similarly clear in asserting that she and her husband were of contrasting political sentiments. In other words, her family's financial well-being might have been dependent on her husband (despite his absence), but her mind and her political allegiances were not. As a result, Margarett did not believe that she and her children should have to pay for her husband's mistakes; instead, she insisted, it was the *responsibility* of the assembly to return James's property to her family and thus care for them in their dependent legal state. Margarett's language, her accusations, and her overt challenge to the gendered status quo, compounded by her husband's behavior, served to undermine her case; the body rejected her petition.[36] When women did not perform with precision the expectations of helpless femininity, the paternalistic state felt no obligations to those dependents purported to be in their care.

The assembly did not take kindly to women challenging these male officials without acknowledging their authority. Women who criticized male legislators saw their petitions rejected. Ann Williams, for example, petitioned the state to correct what she perceived as a grave injustice on her property rights. Ann's husband, Robert Williams Jr., had signed oaths first to the Whigs and later to the British, addressing General Sir Henry Clinton. Before he absconded from the city, Robert had deeded a substantial amount of property to his wife. Her plea sought to recover portions of her husband's property that he had transferred to her in early 1782, just ahead of the passage of the Confiscation Act. The act, however, nullified maneuvers meant to skirt the statute, explicitly rejecting "colusion or fraud, or . . . an intent of eluding a forfeiture."[37]

Ann, having been made aware of this stipulation, moved forward with her petition, suggesting that Robert had decided to transfer the property to Ann's name before the start of the war but had simply not acted on these wishes. Ann begged that the assembly not follow through with their decree to confiscate the Williams's property, as it was "all she depends on for support, herself and numerous family, consisting of eight helpless Children" who would be "reduced to experience calamities" in such an instance.[38] In that one phrase Ann conformed to the prescriptions of a genteel, White woman. She supplicated herself, she admitted her own dependence on the assembly's mercy, and she offered her children as an example of the destitution that might befall her family if they were not forgiving. In this instance, Ann's petition did, in part, follow the traditional mode of supplicating and deferential language.

The bulk of her petition, however, contains defiant, caustic language that likely cost her the relief she sought. Citing the "weakness and inefficacy upon liberal minds," Ann Williams reprimanded those who, due to "private prejudice and resentment . . . operated considerably to the disadvantage of" both herself and her husband, namely officials in the assembly. Williams claimed to be "uninfluenced by motives of resentment," but the scathing tone of her petition suggests otherwise.[39] Her petition was as much a plea for help as it was a trenchant accusation of wrongdoing (in her view) perpetrated by a vicious legislature hell-bent on punishing innocent men and powerless wives and children. While a number of women transgressed the boundaries of their gender comportment in the language of their petitions, those who saw success despite these offenses were more careful in their performance of unfeminine behavior, couching their challenges to male authority in conceptions of traditional feminine conduct. Williams, however, failed to balance these delicate verbal tensions in her petition. Backed into a corner as a result of the legislature's unforgiving position, she and her children were forced to join her husband in England where they lived the remainder of their lives.[40]

WOMEN'S PETITIONS submitted in the wake of the British evacuation from Charleston reveal the very real personal consequences of constantly shifting, uneven, and unclear political alliances. Women were frequently casualties of political and military decisions and processes in which they had no official part. They thus were compelled to present themselves as hapless victims of circumstance and beg for assistance for themselves and forgiveness for their husbands. The language of their

pleas is replete with conformity to established rules of gender performance. Women were able to exploit and at times manipulate these constraints to work to their advantage. Assumptions that women ought to
be apolitical, financially reliant on men, and, more broadly, incapable of
true independence ultimately aided in supporting their pleas and enabled them to survive and protect their families as well. In certain cases,
women were even able to use their positions of dependence to gain
clemency for their husbands' wrongdoings.

The upheaval of war meant that these normally stark gender boundaries could be fluid under particular circumstances. Women took certain opportunities to challenge their husbands' politics, or the actions
of the legislature itself. They occasionally opined on politics and asserted their own agency, separate and independent of their husbands. But
these boundaries were not completely permeable; despite the upheaval
of war, certain patriarchal structures and values remained impervious to
change. Gender boundaries were thus both rigid and fluid. There were
certain spaces for women to be political (even distinct from their husbands' views), to challenge the status quo, but only *just so*—traditional
femininity might be able to bend, but patriarchal powers would not permit it to break. In fact, women's continued (and at times full-throated)
reinforcement of these tropes may have served to help perpetuate these
prescriptions for generations to come, making resistance to the American
patriarchy all the more difficult.

Notes

1. Scott mentioned her family's "distresses" four times in her petition. Petition of Sarah Scott, 3 February 1783, no. 186, Petitions to the General Assembly, South Carolina Department of Archives and History, Columbia
(hereafter PGA, SCDAH).
2. Theodora J. Thompson and Rosa S. Lumpkin, eds., *Journals of the House of
Representatives, 1783–1784* (Columbia: University of South Carolina Press,
1977), 552.
3. See, for example, Kristin Collins, "'Petitions without Number': Widows'
Petitions and the Early Nineteenth-Century Origins of Public Marriage-
Based Entitlements," *Law and History Review* 31, no. 1 (February 2013):
1–60; Linda K. Kerber, *Women of the Republic: Intellect and Ideology in
Revolutionary America* (Chapel Hill: University of North Carolina Press,
1980); Kerber, "'No Political Relation to the State': Conflicting Obligations
in the Revolutionary Era," in *No Constitutional Right to Be Ladies: Women
and the Obligations of Citizenship* (New York: Hill and Wang, 1998), 3–46;

Cynthia Kierner, *Southern Women in Revolution, 1776–1800: Personal and Political Narratives* (Columbia: University of South Carolina Press, 1998); Mary Beth Norton, "Eighteenth-Century American Women in Peace and War: The Case of the Loyalists," *William and Mary Quarterly*, 3rd series, 33, no. 3 (July 1976), 386–409; and Norton, *Liberty's Daughters: The Revolutionary Experience of American Women, 1750–1800* (Ithaca, NY: Cornell University Press, 1980).

4. Recent studies of women's political roles in the Civil War era have examined the ironies of the Confederate states' values juxtaposed with the activism of dependents like women and the enslaved population. See, for example, Gregory Downs, *Declarations of Dependence: The Long Reconstruction of Popular Politics in the South, 1861–1908* (Chapel Hill: University of North Carolina Press, 2011); Stephanie McCurry, *Confederate Reckoning: Power and Politics in the Civil War South* (Cambridge, MA: Harvard University Press, 2012); and McCurry, *Women's War: Fighting and Surviving the American Civil War* (Cambridge, MA: Harvard University Press, 2019).

5. For examples of recent scholarship on life in British-occupied cities during the American Revolution, see Lauren Duval, "Mastering Charleston: Property and Patriarchy in British-Occupied Charleston, 1780–1782," *William and Mary Quarterly*, 3rd series, 75, no. 4 (October 2018): 589–622, and Donald F. Johnson, "Ambiguous Allegiances: Urban Loyalties during the American Revolution," *Journal of American History* 104, no. 3 (December 2017): 610–31.

6. See Ruma Chopra, *Unnatural Rebellion: Loyalists in New York City during the Revolution* (Charlottesville: University of Virginia Press, 2011); Maya Jasanoff, *Liberty's Exiles: American Loyalists in the Revolutionary World* (New York: Penguin Random House, 2012); and Johnson, "Ambiguous Allegiances."

7. Rebecca Brannon, *From Revolution to Reunion: The Reintegration of the South Carolina Loyalists* (Columbia: University of South Carolina Press, 2016), 5–6.

8. Though her book does a great deal of work to remind scholars of the fluidity of political allegiances during and after the war, even Brannon seems to undervalue the significance that women and tropes of gender played in the petitioning process. Brannon notes the ways in which this process worked but dedicates few pages in a book largely focused on the politics of men; when she does discuss the role of women and the rhetoric they employed in their pleas, she asserts the importance of this language yet neglects to recognize the larger significance of this strategy. See Brannon, *From Revolution to Reunion*.

9. On the significance of sympathy, fellow-feeling, and the culture of sensibility in early America, see, for example, G. J. Barker-Benfield, *The*

Culture of Sensibility: Sex and Society in Eighteenth-Century Britain (Chicago: University of Chicago Press, 1992); Nicole Eustace, "'The Turnings of the Human Heart': Sympathy, Social Signals, and the Self," in *Passion Is the Gale: Emotion, Power, and the Coming of the American Revolution* (Chapel Hill: University of North Carolina Press, 2008), 253–84; and Sarah Knott, *Sensibility and the American Revolution* (Chapel Hill: University of North Carolina Press, 2009).

10. Eustace, *Passion Is the Gale*, 238–39, 241, 247.
11. Petition of Mary Peronneau, 22 February 1783, no. 279, PGA, SCDAH.
12. Ibid.
13. Michael E. Stevens and Christine M. Allen, eds., *Journals of the House of Representatives, 1787–1788* (Columbia: University of South Carolina Press, 1981), 399–400, 424–25.
14. Petition of Mary Peronneau, 22 February 1783, no. 279, PGA, SCDAH.
15. Petition of Mary Brown, 15 February 1783, no. 220, PGA, SCDAH.
16. Ibid.
17. Ibid.
18. Ibid.
19. Thompson and Lumpkin, eds., *Journals of the House of Representatives, 1783–1784*, 552.
20. Petition of Susannah Smyth, 22 February 1783, no. 287, PGA, SCDAH.
21. Kierner, *Southern Women in Revolution*, 94.
22. In her study of petitions for pensions at the federal level after 1812, Kristin Collins similarly argues that "widows' pension petitions pushed Congress to acknowledge common women's particular contributions and vulnerabilities as wives and widows with financial support from the federal coffers." Collins, "'Petitions without Number,'" 48.
23. Petition of Florence Cooke, 27 January 1783, no. 37, PGA, SCDAH. On women's roles as mothers as a political position, see Linda K. Kerber, "The Republican Mother: Women and the Enlightenment—An American Perspective," *American Quarterly* 28, no. 2 (Summer 1976): 187–205.
24. Petition of Florence Cooke, 27 January 1783, no. 37, PGA, SCDAH.
25. Ibid.
26. Ibid. See also Kierner, *Southern Women in Revolution*, 171.
27. My reading of Cooke's petition is more in line with Linda Kerber's analysis than with Rebecca Brannon's. Kerber detects a similar hint of defiance and self-assured patriotism in Cooke's plea, while Brannon sees the Cooke petition as more of a desperate plea for a family who was bereft of any other means of rectifying their difficult situation. In a way, Cooke's petition can, and should, be interpreted with both of these considerations in mind. Cooke could have reasonably seen her own political identity as distinct from her husband's, yet also understood the utility of such a strategy, and the ways in which only her voice could simultaneously elicit the sympathy

of the General Assembly while rebuking them and the constraints put on women's property rights. See Brannon, *From Revolution to Reunion*, 71–72, and Kerber, *Women of the Republic*, 127–29.

28. Brannon, *From Revolution to Reunion*, 72; Kierner, *Southern Women in Revolution*, 171.
29. Petition of Mary Fraser et al., 11 November 1795, no. 7, PGA, SCDAH.
30. Ibid.
31. Ibid.
32. Kierner, *Southern Women in Revolution*, 171.
33. Petition of Margarett Brisbane, 22 February 1783, no. 261, PGA, SCDAH.
34. Ibid.
35. Ibid.; first emphasis in original, second emphasis added.
36. Kierner, *Southern Women in Revolution*, 174.
37. Thomas Cooper and David James McCord, eds., *The Statutes at Large of South Carolina: 1752 to 1786* (Columbia: A. S. Johnson, 1836–41), 556.
38. Petition of Ann Williams, 15 February 1783, no. 241, PGA, SCDAH.
39. Ibid.
40. Kierner, *Southern Women in Revolution*, 118.

The "Widowed State"

WOMEN'S LABOR, SACRIFICE, AND SELF-SUFFICIENCY IN THE AMERICAN REVOLUTION

ALISA WADE

—〰〰〰—

"I MUST BE contented to live a widow for the present," Sarah Hodgkins wrote to her husband, Lieutenant Joseph Hodgkins of the Continental Army, on 16 September 1776, adding, "but I hope I shan't always live so."[1] Sarah Hodgkins, who resided in Ipswich, Massachusetts, corresponded regularly with her distant partner between 1775 and 1779, as Joseph endured the travails first of commanding a unit of Minutemen, then of taking on a company of Continental soldiers.[2] Hodgkins's comparison to living "a widow" was particularly salient, as her husband was himself once a widower. When the couple married in 1772, twenty-one-year-old Sarah inherited the surviving young child from Joseph's previous relationship; by the time of his absence in 1775, she had added two children of her own to the family. With that context in mind, it is no surprise that her letters were full of pleas for his homecoming. "If you should be called to Battle again," she implored, "may he be with you & cover your heads & Strenthen your hands & encorage your hearts and give you all that fortitude and resolution that is left for you and in his own time return you home in Safty."[3]

Despite Hodgkins's reasonable concerns regarding her husband's survival, she was fortunate enough to see him return home in 1779. Many of her peers, however, were not. Yet Hodgkins was not alone in comparing her temporary wartime marital status to that of widowhood.[4] The sentiment was repeatedly echoed by those around her, as women in the revolutionary era grappled with their economic and political functions while their husbands served away from home in military or diplomatic positions. For those women who remained behind, their struggles for survival amid wartime upheaval were complicated by their secondary, *feme covert* legal status in the eighteenth century.[5] The experiences of these women as heads of household during the Revolutionary War—what Laurel Thatcher Ulrich has termed the "deputy husband"—helps reposition their important contribution to the war effort.[6] In fact, the rhetorical decision to conceive of their position as a "widowed state" provides insight, not only into their disrupted lives but into the disrupted economies they, often alone, were required to navigate in the absence of their husbands.

By uniting northern women's intimate life writing with probate records, estate inventories, account books, and other financial ephemera, this essay reconsiders women's managerial position on the home front through the lens of the cultural history of capitalism. It addresses the experiences of northern female patriots who during the revolutionary era were temporarily—or in some cases permanently—widowed, in order to reposition their critical economic contributions to a burgeoning market economy. Some of those represented are familiar, including Abigail Adams and Mercy Otis Warren. Others, however, are less so; for them, their records are more fragmentary, pieced together from collections of family papers and other archival sources. Nonetheless, by relying on printed or written source material, it necessarily draws on a White, literate, primarily urban, and middling or upper-class base. These women's experiences are thus not wholly representative. Instead, many enjoyed access to a level of power through their societal positions and marital connections that lower-class women or women of color did not possess.[7] Their lives tended to be deeply entangled with those of their husbands, and their education and training—often through private tutors but in a mix of ornamental skills and practical knowledge—helped prepare them for and lend confidence to their wartime autonomy.[8] For these women, usage of the designation of widowhood served not just as an expression of self-sacrifice and loss but rather as a tool to mitigate the stress of financial autonomy in the era of coverture.

As provisionally widowed *feme soles*, women like Hodgkins embraced a powerful, albeit daunting, position to secure stability for themselves and their families. This process, of course, did not emerge in a vacuum. There existed in the American colonies a legacy stretching back to the early seventeenth century of women assuming the role of "deputy husband," often informally but in some instances punctuated by the bestowal of power of attorney on the wife in her husband's absence.[9] Yet, as Ulrich and others have argued, this position was limited in its scope and length.[10] In the early colonial period, it tended to serve as a stop-gap measure, used when critically necessary. Thus, Ulrich's study finds that while a limited number of women might have participated in mercantile trade external to New England, most were only active in local, less official methods of exchange.[11]

The Revolution altered these daily patterns of domestic behavior by comprehensively uprooting husbands and lovers from the homes of their families, and though for some this was a temporary loss, others were forced to face the reality of permanent widowhood after a husband's death. While earlier wars for empire and individual business or political obligations might have divided a married couple at some point in their relationship, those separations prior to the imperial crisis were typically short-lived and individual. As Mary Beth Norton points out, they provided no comparison to the protracted interruption of the Revolutionary War, which "affected all Americans, to a greater or lesser degree."[12]

This rupture was complicated by changes in the broader eighteenth-century commercial climate. The transition toward merchant capitalism was accompanied by shifting modes of access to credit and currency that impacted married women in particular.[13] When compounded by scarcity and currency depreciation during the war, the precarious position of those remaining behind becomes clearer. As ad-hoc widows, women thus legitimized their contributions as household managers and harnessed a powerful role through their labor and production within emerging national and international markets of the fledgling nation. They were not participating in an "informal," secondary economy but rather served as critical contributors to capitalist development, both during and after the Revolutionary War.

IN THE wake of the signing of the Treaty of Paris ending the Seven Years' War in 1763, colonists increasingly evaded and protested programs designed to solve problems of postwar finance and debt. The colonies' growing importance to the economy of the British Empire contributed to this crisis; bolstered by a transatlantic consumer revolution, the eighteenth-century colonies evolved from producers of raw materials to a primary market for British goods.[14] As historians have argued, under the Grenville Program, the 1765 Stamp Act—which required revenue stamps on official documents and other records—directly and immediately impacted colonial elites. By the time the Townshend Acts took effect in 1767, however, external taxes on widely utilized commodities like lead, glass, paint, paper, and tea aggrieved increasing numbers of colonial consumers.[15] Colonists along the eastern seaboard pushed for the nonimportation and nonconsumption of British goods as a means by which to resist British mercantilist policies. Women joined in these boycotts, gathering throughout the colonies to manufacture cloth around a common goal: to increase the output of textiles in the colonies and end dependency on materials imported from Britain. In fact, 1,644 women attended spinning meetings—large and typically public gatherings of women to spin cloth and protest dependency on British manufacturing—between 1768 and 1770 alone.[16]

Of course, spinning was not the sole domestic contribution of women in the imperial crisis. Many patriot women altered patterns of purchasing and consumption in accordance with popular resistance.[17] Widespread sentiment in opposition to tea consumption—and emphasis on its boycott—emerged repeatedly in letters and journals in the 1760s and 1770s. Abigail Adams, not one to keep political judgments to herself, voiced a strong opinion against the landing of tea in Boston. She wrote to Mercy Otis Warren, "The Tea that bainfull weed is arrived. Great and I hope Effectual opposition has been made to the landing of it."[18] Esther De Berdt Reed too involved herself in the debate over tea following the passage of the Boston Port Act in 1774, which effectively closed the port of Boston until the cost of the tea destroyed in the Boston Tea Party was repaid.[19] "We are very impatient for the arrival of another ship, to have the particulars of the fate of Boston," she noted. "The news of the removal of their Custom House is just received here, and distresses every thinking person."[20] Even Jemima Condict, who often took a pacifist stance toward war, noted the role played by tea in the conflict between Britain and the colonies, adding, "It seams we have troublesome times a Coming for there is great Disturbance a Broad in the earth & they say it is tea that caused it. So then if they will Quarel about such a trifling thing as that What must we expect But war[?]"[21]

Women's household positions thus took on politicized meaning in the revolutionary era. Women were unquestionably conscious of the impact of their support for the war effort. Mercy Otis Warren, for instance, posited that the consequences of the Revolution were in fact amplified by her position as both a "woman and a mother," writing, "No one has at stake a larger share of Domestic Felicity than myself."[22] Undoubtedly, women's labor within the home helped to bolster the patriot cause, and women's writing reveals many were uniquely aware of their contribution. As an unknown female author under the pseudonym "Sophia

Thrifty" pointed out in the *New York Mercury* in 1765, women were capable of subverting personal desire for public good. "What should induce you to think, gentlemen, that those of us who are daily witnesses to the difficulty of procuring an estate, or even of providing for a large family, should be incapable of feeling for our country, for our husbands, for our offspring?" she wrote, "Let me inform you, we have a good deal of public spirit. We are not unconcerned spectators of the general calamity."[23]

Amid women's increasing activism in the years leading up to and during the American Revolution, however, there were few precedents for female political participation. "What have I to do with politicks?" queried Sarah Livingston Jay, wife of diplomat John Jay, in a letter to her two sisters in 1780, as the war between the United States and Great Britain waged on around her. "Am I not myself a woman, & writing to Ladies?"[24] Yet three years later, Jay's correspondence to Kitty and Susan Livingston belied her disinterest in the subject. She wrote, "My Country & my friends possess so entirely my thoughts that you must not wonder if my pen runs beyond the dictates of prudence when engaged by those subjects."[25] This denigration of civic acumen—significantly, contradicted by Jay's repeated engagement with matters of political importance—served as a common refrain in women's personal writing in the revolutionary era. Mercy Otis Warren proffered similar sentiments in a letter to close friend Abigail Adams, referring to women as the "weak and timid sex[,] only the Echo of the other."[26] Yet, throughout the duration of the American Revolution, Warren—who authored several significant works of patriotic propaganda and in 1805 published her personal interpretation of the Revolution entitled *The Rise, Progress, and Termination of the American Revolution*—proved herself to be far from a passive observer in political matters.[27]

Despite this, women's legal status remained largely static throughout the eighteenth century. Under the British common law doctrine of coverture, a woman's legal identity was subsumed by that of her husband's at marriage. As a married *feme covert*, a woman could not—at least theoretically—sign contracts, write wills, engage in business transactions, or own and administer property without getting prior approval from her husband. Well-known English jurist William Blackstone, in his *Commentaries on the Laws of England*, explained this concept: "By marriage, the husband and wife are one person in law: that is, the very being or legal existence of the woman is suspending during marriage, or at least is incorporated and consolidated into that of the husband." This status, he posited, was actually beneficial to wives. It offered protection, he wrote, for if "judgment be recovered against and husband and wife for the contract, nay even for the personal misbehavior, of the wife during her coverture, the *capias* shall issue against the husband only; which is one of the many great privileges of English wives."[28] Recent works have shown that women could, and often did, find ways to circumvent these legal structures, but nonetheless, coverture could have substantial implications for women's economic stability, particularly when left alone.[29] For those on the home front, this necessitated navigating a potentially precarious situation while simultaneously dealing with fears of personal and familial safety.

These patterns of life were further compounded by shifts in wealth management, forms of payment, and the granting of credit occurring more broadly in the eighteenth-century British Atlantic. Seventeenth-century economies tended to rest on barter systems or "in kind" exchanges. These were not always recorded, but if the head of household chose to track them, it most frequently happened in familial account books. Women thus had access to these while book debt remained the primary ledger system for the settlement of local accounts. Such records were increasingly held in merchant houses or marked by promissory notes as the eighteenth century progressed, however, making married women's ability to regulate debt or gain access to credit more difficult.[30] This, in turn, was accompanied by a transition toward paper money or fiat, in addition to the use of bills of exchange, to settle debts, further distancing women from the market.[31]

Within this context, the impetus behind reframing one's status to that of "widowhood" becomes all the more revelatory. Widows, under British common law, possessed a much greater degree of autonomy than did married women.[32] Under their *feme sole* legal designation, widows could own and administer property, engage in business transactions, and draw on lines of credit in ways that were far more difficult—and in some cases impossible—for married women.[33] Widowhood was a status that many women inhabited; estimates in eighteenth-century New England, for instance, place somewhere around 60 percent of women as experiencing widowhood at some point in their lives, and historians posit that for White women, approximately 10 percent were widowed at any given time.[34]

Autonomy came with its own set of difficulties, and many women in the mid-eighteenth century—particularly when widowed young—might have preferred remarriage to the complicated travails of navigating single life, in some cases with little or no support system. The experiences of West Jersey resident Margaret Hill Morris reflect the sadness and loss that accompanied such a transition. Morris lost her husband, a dry goods merchant, in 1765 and underwent a lengthy period of financial difficulty as a result of the depreciation of currency during the Revolution. She eventually built her own local medical practice in order to keep herself afloat.[35] Significantly, Morris drew a direct connection between her experiences as a widow and those of sister Sarah Dillwynn, whose husband was absent during the war: "I thought of my S. D., the beloved companion of my widowed state—her husband at the distance of some hundred miles from her—I thought of my own lonely situation, no husband to cheer with the voice of love my sinking spirits."[36] As Morris's journal reveals, the connection between self-sufficiency in a husband's absence and the experiences of permanent widows proved to be particularly striking.

Acknowledging one's temporary position as widowhood, then, served as a symbolic acceptance of the mantle of *feme sole* status on the home front. Beyond that, though, it represented a culturally recognized accommodation of women's status and power. Provisional widowhood underscored authority for those nervous about their increased influence.[37] Such behavior legitimized one's role as household manager, repositioning domestic labor as a necessary component to patriot success and American economic independence amid eighteenth-century merchant capitalism. When Joanna Livingston referred to herself as a "commencing woman of business" in 1780, she made explicit the impact of her wartime contribution. "Publick affairs must not be neglected," she added.[38]

Wartime inflation and scarcity made such activities all the more important in the years leading up to 1783. The interruption of trade with England made the acquisition of coffee, sugar, pepper, and other commodities difficult. As Abigail Adams informed her husband, "Every article here in the West India way is very scarce and dear."[39] In this difficult climate, preservation of resources became critical to familial survival. Dry goods merchants frequently hoarded certain staple items, and in some particularly unscrupulous cases raised prices on certain imports to exorbitant levels—especially Bohea tea.[40] To counteract those shortages, women in their managerial positions found clever substitutions to sustain their families: herbs and flowers for tea, walnut ash to preserve food in place of salt, and even new recipes for soap.[41] Amid the paucity of certain necessary provisions, some not only practiced rationing but in certain instances engaged in the regulation of merchants hoarding essential goods.[42]

Analysis of women's contributions to household economies—both physical and emotional—reframes the financial and political meaning of women's labor in the revolutionary era. Under the umbrella of provisional *feme sole* status, women meticulously tracked price fluctuations, frequently keeping absent partners apprised of shifts and waiting to buy until the ideal moment. Adams described the effects of the early years of the Revolution on the family economy in August 1776, noting that "English Goods of every kind are not purchasable, at least by me. They are extravagantly high, West India articles are very high all except Sugars."[43] Sarah Livingston Jay too lamented rising prices, noting to her husband, John Jay, "There is great plenty in the Country yet every thing is immensely high; new hay has been sold all summer at 5/6 & now is 6/. Oats at 3/3."[44] Many women read newspapers and other mercantile circulars, hoping to remain current on the state of economic affairs in the warring nation.[45] Others simply went without, or bartered between each other for necessities. As one woman wrote to two of her friends, "I have heard Coffe is very dear in America and in a few days it will not be permitt'd to export a single pound." Her solution? To send her friends "a Baril of exceeding good Coffe" to accept as "a token of friendship."[46]

Abigail Adams, who strongly advocated manufacturing from within the colonies, wrote to John Adams in 1774, vowing to "seek wool and flax and work willingly with my Hands."[47] Spinning became an action with broader political and economic implications.[48] Supporting American-made products could serve as a source of pride and accomplishment, and women frequently expressed such sentiments in their experiences with the manufacturing of homespun textiles. Esther De Berdt Reed, though residing in England at the time, observed in a letter to her American husband that "all the country people are spinning course linen."[49] Mercy Otis Warren too, writing to Abigail Adams on 1 March 1777, noted, "I suppose when it is done we shall be very proud of Braintree Manufactures." Warren, who, along with Adams, had just finished spinning between "94 and 98 weight" of wool, added that their example—and the example of others in the colonies who chose to spin their own cloth—ought to be remembered with satisfaction. Of Adams, Warren added, "the Females of the united states, must in the Future Look up for the Example of [industry] and economy."[50] Thus, while the tangible impact of women's manufacturing output is difficult to measure, the symbolic effect of homespun is nonetheless apparent.[51] As Kate Haulman argues in *The Politics of Fashion in Eighteenth-Century America*, dress sat at the center of debates over authority and identity in revolutionary-era Philadelphia: "The imperial crisis magnified the already contested cultural politics of fashion, making fashion a critical site of power struggles social, economic, and now political."[52]

Such contributions were nonetheless meaningful amid the disrup-
tion of trade and financial instability of the war. "For tho it was formerly the pride and ambition of American[s] to indulge in the fashions
and Manufactures of Great Brittain," Adams wrote in a letter to Catharine Macaulay, "now she threatens us with her chains we will scorn to
wear her livery, and shall think ourselves more decently attired in the
course and plain vestures of our own Manufactury than in all the gaudy
trappings that adorn the slave."[53] Those handmade items not only clothed
the body but served as a political statement of patriotism, as was the
case for the textiles sent by Maria Livingston Duane to husband James
Duane in 1780. "I thank you for your kind attention in reserving for me
a Share of your Industry," he wrote to her after receiving the packet of
materials; he added, "I shall wear it with great Satisfaction."[54]

Household production, rather than a secondary or informal activity, took on critical significance. Women embraced the mental load of
household management *and* physically worked to sustain their families
through intensive labor. Not only did they continue engaging in domestic
tasks—milking, churning, cooking, baking, sewing, and spinning, among
others—that were common patterns of life prior to the Revolution; they
also inherited additional work left behind by absent husbands, stretching
from farming the fields to balancing finances.

Revolutionary-era women kept records of purchases and meticulously balanced family accounts, serving as agents of financial stabilization. This was true for Susannah French Livingston, who recorded
products purchased for the family's New Jersey household, as it was for
New York widow Cornelia Walton.[55] Others, like Jane Keteltas, invested
in bonds during the war, taking advantage of the opportunity to both
support the Revolution's financing and to hopefully turn a profit after the
war's end.[56] To ensure financial security, Margaret Livingston collected
rents from tenants, in some instances even going after those who failed to
make timely payments.[57] Mary Delaplaine ran her deceased husband Joseph Delaplaine's mercantile storefront in New York City following his
death; this source of income was stipulated to her by his 1771 will, which
gave her £1,000 and the "Dwelling House Lot of Ground and Store
House in the City of New York now in my Possession unto my said
Wife for and during her Widowhood."[58]

Others conducted business affairs for husbands or other absent male
family members during the war. James Duane, for instance, asked wife
Maria Livingston Duane whether "Hughey has been with you and rendered his Accounts and paid you some money."[59] Brockholst Livingston
requested his sister Kitty that she advance a Mr. Vaughan fifty-six dollars

to discharge a debt in his absence, adding that "if you can advance him the money you may depend on being reimbursed in the course of two months at farthest—Should your finances however be too slender to admit of this deduction, I do not advise you to put yourself to any inconvenience on this account."[60] In both of these examples, women took on the position of intermediary in settling accounts for those who, because of distance, were unable to do so.

Of course, embracing temporary widowhood was one thing; being legally widowed was another. Those permanently widowed could—and often did—find themselves in dependent situations following a husband's death, and in many cases were forced to rely on family networks for support. Mary Beekman stepped in to administer her father's estate and enforce the repayment of a sixty-pound wartime bond owed to her mother, a process made ever more complicated by the fact that she herself was recently widowed. Writing to Henry Van Rensselaer at the end of the war, Beekman requested that he "pay off the balance of your Bond which was sign'd over by my Mother to my deceased Husband, as I assure you I am exceedingly in want of money to discharge the Debts that are daily expected to be paid by the Estate of my deceased Husband—Your compliance will very much oblige Sir."[61] Yet even in her own somewhat perilous state, Beekman was left to implore rather than pursue decisive action. Other examples corroborate Beekman's experience, as was the case for widow Jane Byrne, who begged executor William Bayard to provide her with additional financial support. With her husband's estate confiscated during the war, Byrne was desperate for income: "You well know Sir that I have Nothing to subsist upon but a Scanty pittance of Seventy pounds pr Annum left me by my Husband, to whom you are Executor and which you have withheld from me for many years, and whose property to a Considerable amount you Converted to your own life," she charged.[62]

These experiences were frequently undesirable, for both provisional and real widows. Despite the empowering effects of their labor, women also acknowledged the sacrifice and difficulty of such autonomy. Many were directly impacted by inflation and scarcity, both during and after the war. As Abigail Adams complained to John in a letter in 1778, "The miserable state of our currency adds to other difficulties, a hundred Dollors will not purchase what ten formerly would."[63] Widow Cornelia Walton's example highlights the destabilizing consequences of the deficiency of paper money and lack of a stable currency system even further. When Walton tried to collect a staggering £4,000 in unpaid wartime annuity from her nephew William Walton, it created a family crisis. William Walton's inability to collect on bonds taken out during the Revolution made repayment virtually impossible, forcing Cornelia Walton to sue via her executor in 1786.[64]

As Walton's case illustrates, maintaining stability amid the back-drop of the Revolutionary War was often fraught with peril, made even more complicated by women's secondary legal status. Amid few tools of recourse, ad-hoc *feme sole* status offered one alternative. It became an expression of personal loss and self-sacrifice—to both familial stability and the patriot cause—in a period where there was no clear model for women's public behavior. As Abigail Adams informed her husband in 1775, patterns of life were altered by separation. "In the twelve years we have been married," she wrote John, "I believe we have not lived together more than six."[65] Sarah Livingston Jay expressed just such emotions to her husband, confessing, "I find a deficiency, a vacancy, a something want-ing since your absence that even surpasses what I expected."[66] Such state-ments served as a coping mechanism in tumultuous times, and a means by which to process the impact a husband's absence had on daily life. Perhaps, even, it helped to lessen the separation anxiety they were expe-riencing; it would be far less painful to compartmentalize the distance of their husbands than to dwell on the dangers of war.

Unsurprisingly, though women recognized their selflessness in the face of the patriot cause, they also grew weary of distance as time pro-gressed. Reactions varied widely, ranging from sadness and loneliness to frustration, even prompting Jay to write of her "naughty husband who is too lazy to write to his little wife."[67] Perhaps Adams summed the senti-ment up best in a letter to Mercy Otis Warren: "I find I am obliged to summon all my patriotism to feel willing to part with him again," Adams stated. "You will readily believe me when I say that I make no small sac-rifice to the publick."[68]

IN THE spring of 1776, on the eve of the signing of the Declaration of Independence initiating separation from England, Abigail Adams wrote her famous refrain:

> I long to hear that you have declared an independency—and by the way in the new Code of Laws which I suppose it will be necessary for you to make I desire you would Remember the Ladies, and be more generous and favourable to them than your ancestors. Do not put such unlimited power into the hands of the Husbands. Remember all Men

would be tyrants if they could. If perticuliar care and attention is not
paid to the Laidies we are determined to foment a Rebelion, and will
not hold ourselves bound by any Laws in which we have no voice, or
Representation.[69]

Her explicit acknowledgment of women's secondary status under the
"Naturally Tyrannical" male sex was not a plea for political equality but
rather one for the removal of patriarchal structures that made married
women dependent on men. Her push to reconsider women's legal position was, according to some scholars, a potential threat to united patriot
support for the Revolution.[70] But, it was also a critical context for her
own decision to assume the function of provisional widowhood during
the war. Even as she acknowledged the flaws regarding the system of coverture and women's unequal legal status, Adams, at home without her
husband, willingly embraced her position. "To this cause," she wrote to
cousin Isaac Smith Jr., "I have sacrificed much of my own personal happiness by giving up to the counsels of America one of my dearest connexions and living for more than 3 years in a State of widowhood."[71]

Women like Adams and Hodgkins recognized their self-sacrifice and
economic contributions. They were willing to part temporarily with their
husbands and to alter their domestic routines in pursuit of American victory.[72] As Esther De Berdt Reed wrote in a letter to her brother in 1775,
"You see every person willing to sacrifice his private interest in this glorious contest."[73] As provisional—and in some cases permanent—widows,
female patriots participated in nonimportation and nonconsumption,
took the reins of coordinating the family economy and managing domestic finances, and labored to successfully keep their households afloat in
a period of upheaval. This was no accident. As Adams wrote in a letter
to her husband, "I have felt for my country and her sons. I have bled for
them and with them."[74] Referring to their status as widows in a temporary capacity, they reframed their legal position under coverture as a
means by which to underscore the impact of their patriot activism and
labor.[75] At the end of the war, now intimately familiar with the minutiae
of household management and market participation, they were perhaps
less willing to unilaterally concede power back their husbands.[76] More
than just American patriots, they were now capable participants in the
emerging market economy of the early republic.

NOTES

1. Herbert Treadwell Wade and Robert Alexander Lively, *This Glorious Cause: The Adventures of Two Company Officers in Washington's Army* (Princeton, NJ: Princeton University Press, 1958), 208.

2. Emphasizing how much she missed her husband, Hodgkins wrote, "Give regards to Capt Wade and tell him I have wanted his bed fellow pretty much these cold nights that we have had." For a literary analysis of Hodgkins's letters to her husband, see Richard S. Tracey, "'So I Must Be Contented to Live a Widow . . .': The Revolutionary War Service of Sarah Hodgkins of Ipswich," *Historical Journal of Massachusetts* 30, no. 2 (Summer 2002), https://www.westfield.ma.edu/historical-journal/wp-content/uploads/2018/06/Tracey-Summer-2002-complete.pdf.

3. Wade and Lively, *This Glorious Cause*, 178–79.

4. For another example, see Abigail Adams's reference to living "for more than 3 years in a State of Widowhood," in Abigail Adams to Isaac Smith Jr., 30 October 1777, Founders Online, National Archives of the United States, College Park, MD, https://founders.archives.gov/documents/Adams/04-02-02-0291. Other examples include Esther Edwards Burr's assertion that "I am a widdow again. Mr Burr sat out this Morn [early] for [Princeton]," Margaret Hill Morris making note of her friend's "widowed state" in the absence of her husband, and John Beatty's request that his brother visit his wife "whose widowed state requires more attention"; see Esther Edwards Burr, Carol F. Karlsen, and Laurie Crumpacker, *The Journal of Esther Edwards Burr, 1754–1757* (New Haven, CT: Yale University Press, 1984), 87; Margaret Hill Morris, *Private Journal Kept during a Portion of the Revolutionary War, for the Amusement of a Sister* (N.p.: Privately Reprinted, 1836), 5–6; and C. Dallett Hemphill, *Siblings: Brothers and Sisters in American History* (2011; reprint, New York: Oxford University Press, 2014), 80.

5. Under the system of coverture imported from English law and maintained after the American Revolution, a woman's legal status was subsumed by that of her husband's at marriage, as she transitioned from *feme sole* to *feme covert*. For works on women's legal status in early America, see Elaine Forman Crane, *Witches, Wife Beaters, and Whores: Common Law and Common Folk in Early America* (Ithaca, NY: Cornell University Press, 2012); Cornelia Hughes Dayton, *Women before the Bar: Gender, Law, and Society in Connecticut, 1639–1789*, 3rd ed. (1995; Chapel Hill: University of North Carolina Press, 1995); Linda K. Kerber, *Women of the Republic: Intellect and Ideology in Revolutionary America* (Chapel Hill: University of North Carolina Press, 1997); Kerber, *No Constitutional Right to Be Ladies: Women and the Obligations of Citizenship* (New York: Farrar, Straus and

Giroux, 1999); and Marylynn Salmon, *Women and the Law of Property in Early America* (Chapel Hill: University of North Carolina Press, 1986).

6. Laurel Thatcher Ulrich, *Good Wives: Image and Reality in the Lives of Women in Northern New England, 1650–1750* (New York: Knopf, 1982), 44.

7. Many publications on women's roles in the American Revolution have tended to compartmentalize public activism and daily domestic patterns in accordance with the structural framework of "separate spheres" and, in some instances, allowed the experiences of elite White women to stand for all women, regardless of racial, regional, or class background. Nonetheless, these studies demonstrate women's activism through boycotts, spinning, publication of propaganda, crowd activity, and more. See Carol Berkin, *Revolutionary Mothers: Women in the Struggle for America's Independence* (New York: Knopf, 2005); Nancy F. Cott, *The Bonds of Womanhood: "Woman's Sphere" in New England, 1780–1835* (New Haven, CT: Yale University Press, 1997); Joan R. Gundersen, *To Be Useful to the World: Women in Revolutionary America, 1740–1790* (Chapel Hill: University of North Carolina Press, 2006); Kerber, *Women of the Republic*; Kerber, *No Constitutional Right to Be Ladies*; and Mary Beth Norton, *Liberty's Daughters: The Revolutionary Experience of American Women, 1750–1800* (Boston: Little, Brown, 1980).

8. This essay draws on the personal writing—letters, diaries, and memoirs—of fifteen women between the years 1763 and 1783, juxtaposing their personal experiences with financial records drawn from collections of family papers at the New-York Historical Society, New York Public Library, Massachusetts Historical Society, and Library of Congress.

9. For an analysis of married women operating on behalf of absent husbands in New England prior to the Revolution, see Sara T. Damiano, "Agents at Home: Wives, Lawyers, and Financial Competence in Eighteenth-Century New England Port Cities," *Early American Studies: An Interdisciplinary Journal* 13, no. 4 (Fall 2015): 808–35. See also Terri L. Snyder, *Brabbling Women: Disorderly Speech and the Law in Early Virginia* (2003; reprint, Ithaca, NY: Cornell University Press, 2013), 119; Salmon, *Women and the Law of Property in Early America*, 44–53; and Abby Chandler, "'And the Author of Wickedness Surely Is Most to Be Blamed': The Declaration of Debora Proctor," *Legacy: A Journal of American Women Writers* 28, no. 2 (2011): 323.

10. Ulrich, *Good Wives*, 36.

11. Other studies have built on this analysis of women's economic roles, analyzing women's financial contributions and wealth management in the eighteenth century, although in some instances female participation in the market has been treated as a separate, "informal" economy rather than a critical component of capitalist development. Recent work seeks to rectify this. See Sara T. Damiano, *To Her Credit: Women, Finance, and the*

Law in Eighteenth-Century New England Cities (Baltimore: Johns Hopkins University Press, 2021); Ellen Hartigan-O'Connor, *The Ties That Buy: Women and Commerce in Revolutionary America* (Philadelphia: University of Pennsylvania Press, 2011); Woody Holton, *Abigail Adams* (New York: Atria, 2010); Jeanne Boydston, *Home and Work: Housework, Wages, and the Ideology of Labor in the Early Republic* (New York: Oxford University Press, 1990); and Serena Zabin, *Dangerous Economies: Status and Commerce in Imperial New York* (Philadelphia: University of Pennsylvania Press, 2009).

12. Norton, *Liberty's Daughters*, 224.

13. Jeanne Boydston, "The Woman Who Wasn't There: Women's Market Labor and the Transition to Capitalism in the United States," *Journal of the Early Republic* 16, no. 2 (Summer 1996): 183–206; Ellen Hartigan-O'Connor, "Gender's Value in the History of Capitalism," *Journal of the Early Republic* 36, no. 4 (2016): 613–35, https://doi.org/10.1353/jer.2016.0061; and Ann Smart Martin, "Ribbons of Desire: Gendered Stories in the World of Goods," in *Gender, Taste, and Material Culture in Britain and North America, 1700–1830*, ed. John Styles and Amanda Vickery (New Haven, CT: Yale University Press, 2006), 179–200.

14. For more on the consumer revolution, see Zara Anishanslin, *Portrait of a Woman in Silk: Hidden Histories of the British Atlantic World* (New Haven, CT: Yale University Press, 2016); Peter De Bolla, Nigel Leask, and David Simpson, *Land, Nation and Culture, 1740–1840: Thinking the Republic of Taste* (New York: Palgrave Macmillan, 2004); Martha Tomhave Blauvelt, *The Work of the Heart: Young Women and Emotion, 1780–1830* (Charlottesville: University of Virginia Press, 2007); Richard L. Bushman, *The Refinement of America: Persons, Houses, Cities* (New York: Knopf, 1992); Markman Ellis, *The Politics of Sensibility: Race, Gender, and Commerce in the Sentimental Novel* (New York: Cambridge University Press, 1996); Catherine E. Kelly, *Republic of Taste: Art, Politics, and Everyday Life in Early America* (Philadelphia: University of Pennsylvania Press, 2016); Marion Rust, *Prodigal Daughters: Susanna Rowson's Early American Women* (Chapel Hill: University of North Carolina Press, 2008); David S. Shields, *Civil Tongues and Polite Letters in British America* (Chapel Hill: University of North Carolina Press, 1997); and John Styles and Amanda Vickery, *Gender, Taste, and Material Culture in Britain and North America, 1700–1830* (New Haven, CT: Yale University Press, 2006).

15. For additional discussion of mobilization in the American Revolution, see Bernard Bailyn, *The Ideological Origins of the American Revolution*, Fiftieth Anniversary Edition (1967; Cambridge, MA: Harvard University Press, 2017); Benjamin L. Carp, *Rebels Rising: Cities and the American Revolution* (New York: Oxford University Press, 2009); Woody Holton, *Forced Founders: Indians, Debtors, Slaves, and the Making of the American Revolution in*

Virginia (Chapel Hill: University of North Carolina Press, 1999); Brendan McConville, *The King's Three Faces: The Rise and Fall of Royal America, 1688–1776* (Chapel Hill: University of North Carolina Press, 2006); and Gordon S. Wood, *The Radicalism of the American Revolution* (New York: Knopf, 1992).

16. Craig Bruce Smith, *American Honor: The Creation of the Nation's Ideals during the Revolutionary Era* (Chapel Hill: University of North Carolina Press, 2018), 72.

17. Berkin, *Revolutionary Mothers*, 31.

18. Abigail Adams to Mercy Otis Warren, 5 December 1773, in *Adams Family Correspondence*, ed. L. H. Butterfield et al. (Cambridge, MA: Belknap Press of Harvard University Press, 1963), 1:88.

19. See also Benjamin L. Carp, *Defiance of the Patriots: The Boston Tea Party and the Making of America* (New Haven, CT: Yale University Press, 2010).

20. William Bradford Reed, *The Life of Esther De Berdt: Afterwards Esther Reed, of Pennsylvania* (Philadelphia: C. Sherman, 1853), 193.

21. Jemima Condict, *Jemima Condict, Her Book: Being a Transcript of the Diary of an Essex County Maid during the Revolutionary War* (Newark, NJ: Carteret Book Club, 1930), 36–37.

22. Mercy Otis Warren to Abigail Adams, 27 February 1774, in Butterfield et al., eds., *Adams Family Correspondence*, 1:139.

23. Reprinted in T. H. Breen, *The Marketplace of Revolution: How Consumer Politics Shaped American Independence* (New York: Oxford University Press, 2004), 233.

24. Sarah Livingston Jay to Catherine Livingston Ridley and Susan Livingston Symmes, 4 March 1780, in *Selected Letters of John Jay and Sarah Livingston Jay: Correspondence by or to the First Chief Justice of the United States and His Wife*, ed. Landa M. Freeman, Louise V. North, and Janet M. Wedge (Jefferson, NC: McFarland, 2010), 74.

25. Sarah Livingston Jay to Catherine Livingston Ridley and Susan Livingston Symmes, 16 July 1783, in Freeman, North, and Wedge, eds., *Selected Letters of John Jay and Sarah Livingston Jay*, 136–37.

26. Mercy Otis Warren to Abigail Adams, 19 January 1774, in Butterfield et al., eds., *Adams Family Correspondence*, 1:92.

27. "Perhaps," Linda Kerber writes, "the formulaic, ritualized apologies with which they prefaced their political comments were [women's] way of acknowledging that they were doing something unusual." Kerber, *Women of the Republic*, 80.

28. William Blackstone, *Commentaries on the Laws of England: In Four Books* (Chicago: University of Chicago Press, 1979), 1:430; 3:414.

29. For works that assess the ways specific women circumvented laws around separate property, transmission, and inheritance under coverture, see Toby L. Ditz, *Property and Kinship: Inheritance in Early Connecticut,*

1750–1820 (Princeton, NJ: Princeton University Press, 1986); Holton, *Abigail Adams*; Hartigan-O'Connor, *The Ties That Buy*; Kerber, *Women of the Republic*; Suzanne Lebsock, *The Free Women of Petersburg: Status and Culture in a Southern Town, 1784–1860*, rev. ed. (1984; New York: Norton, 1985); Robert K. Miller Jr. and Stephen J. McNamee, *Inheritance and Wealth in America* (New York: Plenum Press, 1998); Salmon, *Women and the Law of Property in Early America*; Karin A. Wulf, *Not All Wives: Women of Colonial Philadelphia* (Ithaca, NY: Cornell University Press, 2000); and Zabin, *Dangerous Economies*.

30. Dayton points out that the increase in the use of promissory notes and bills of exchange toward the latter portion of the century meant that women were increasingly distanced from "their husbands' debt obligations." Dayton, *Women before the Bar*, 79.

31. This process became increasingly complex in the late eighteenth century, as Jeffrey Sklansky points out. A merchant bought from "a farmer or manufacturer, paying for them with a bill of exchange drawn on another merchant to whom the goods would be shipped. The bill was payable in cash—that is, gold or silver specie—when the goods arrived at the other end. Meanwhile, the farmer or manufacturer would sell the bill to a local bank at a discount, meaning that the bank would give in exchange for it a banknote for a lesser value, which could be used to make any other payments." Sklansky, *Sovereign of the Market: The Money Question in Early America* (Chicago: University of Chicago Press, 2017), 127.

32. Recent studies of widowhood include Bettina Bradbury, *Wife to Widow: Lives, Laws, and Politics in Nineteenth-Century Montreal* (Vancouver, BC: UBC Press, 2011); Vivian Bruce Conger, *The Widows' Might: Widowhood and Gender in Early British America* (New York: New York University Press, 2009); and Kirsten E. Wood, *Masterful Women: Slaveholding Widows from the American Revolution through the Civil War* (Chapel Hill: University of North Carolina Press, 2004).

33. Dayton, *Women before the Bar*, 85–86; Kerber, *Women of the Republic*, 146.

34. Cornelia Dayton suggests, "Perhaps 60 percent of all married women in early New England experienced widowhood. They approached it, not as a period of sudden emancipation and autonomy, but rather as an office of trusteeship and stewardship. Kin, neighbors, and probate judges expected a widow to be diligent in preserving the family estate and carrying out the instructions left by her husband." Dayton, *Women before the Bar*, 76. For analysis of White female widows in the second half of the eighteenth century, see Norton, *Liberty's Daughters*, 133.

35. Susan Brandt, "'Getting into a Little Business': Margaret Hill Morris and Women's Medical Entrepreneurship during the American Revolution," *Early American Studies* 13, no. 4 (2015): 775.

36. Morris, *Private Journal*, 5–6.

37. Dayton points out that, in the case of New England, "when long-distance trade was involved, married women were sometimes careful to underscore their 'deputy husband' role." Dayton, *Women before the Bar*, 75.

38. Joanna Livingston to Ann Schaeffe, 19 October 1780, Erving-King Family Papers, box 8, New-York Historical Society (hereafter N-YHS).

39. Abigail Adams to John Adams, 16 July 1775, in Butterfield et al., eds., *Adams Family Correspondence*, 1:249.

40. Arthur M. Schlesinger, *The Colonial Merchants and the American Revolution, 1763–1776* (1917; reprint, New York: F. Ungar, 1968), 211–12.

41. Berkin, *Revolutionary Mothers*, 31.

42. Abigail Adams described an episode in a letter to her husband in which a large group of women persecuted an "eminent, wealthy, stingy merchant" named Thomas Boylston for hoarding coffee. She noted that after asking for his keys, the women "tipd up the cart and dischargd him, then opened the warehouse, hoisted out the coffee themselves, put it into the trucks and drove off." Abigail Adams to John Adams, 31 July 1777, in Butterfield et al., eds., *Adams Family Correspondence*, 2:295.

43. Abigail Adams to John Adams, 25 August 1776, in Butterfield et al., eds., *Adams Family Correspondence*, 2:107.

44. Sarah Livingston Jay to John Jay, 27 September 1794, in Freeman, North, and Wedge, eds., *Selected Letters of John Jay and Sarah Livingston Jay*, 231.

45. For example, in 1774 Abigail noted to John, "All my intelligence is collected from the newspaper." Abigail Adams to John Adams, 14 September 1774, in Butterfield et al., eds., *Adams Family Correspondence*, 1:151.

46. A. Marcorelle to Maria and Nancy Schaeffe, n.d., Erving-King Family Papers, box 1, folder E3, N-YHS.

47. Abigail Adams to John Adams, 16 October 1774, in Butterfield et al., eds., *Adams Family Correspondence*, 1:173.

48. As Laurel Thatcher Ulrich notes, "When the 'Daughters of Liberty' brought down their spinning wheels from their attics, they were responding to a moral imperative as well as to a practical need. Abandoning their 'top knots of pride,' they renounced the luxury of a corrupt England, demonstrating that the descendants of the saints had not forgotten the lesson of Bathsheba." Ulrich, *Good Wives*, 82.

49. Reed, *The Life of Esther De Berdt*, 157.

50. Mercy Otis Warren to Abigail Adams, 1 March 1777, in Butterfield et al., eds., *Adams Family Correspondence*, 2:167.

51. Historian Kathleen Bruce has argued that the 1769 Nonimportation Agreement succeeded based on the prolific activities of women in decades past who produced enough homespun cloth to supply the colonies during the Revolution. Cited in Selma R. Williams, *Demeter's Daughters: The Women Who Founded America, 1587–1787* (New York: Atheneum), 226. Likewise, "As household manufacturers and as major consumers," Carol

Berkin has noted, "white women's cooperation was vital to the success of any proposed boycott." Carol Berkin, *First Generations: Women in Colonial America* (New York: Farrar, Straus, and Giroux, 1996), 173. According to Craig Bruce Smith, women's activities during the imperial crisis were "considered not only to benefit women collectively but also to be representative of united colonial sentiment. Boycotting British goods and making their own clothes became an external sign of their inner qualities and so matched the ethic of honor perfectly." Smith, *American Honor,* 72.

52. Kate Haulman, *The Politics of Fashion in Eighteenth-Century America* (Chapel Hill: University of North Carolina Press, 2011), 153. See also G. S. Wilson, *Jefferson on Display: Attire, Etiquette, and the Art of Presentation* (Charlottesville: University of Virginia Press, 2018).

53. Abigail Adams to Catharine Macaulay, n.d. (1784), in Butterfield et al., eds., *Adams Family Correspondence,* 1:178.

54. James Duane to Maria Livingston Duane, 11 November 1780, Duane-Featherstonhaugh Papers, reel 2 N-YHS.

55. Susanna French Livingston, receipts dated 1781 through 1783, William Livingston Family Collection, reel 2, Massachusetts Historical Society, Boston (hereafter MHS); Cornelia Walton, receipts dated 1772 to 1787, Beekman Family Papers, box 23, folder 4, N-YHS; Account Book of Catherine Alexander Rutherford, Stuyvesant-Rutherford Collection, folder 20, N-YHS. Other examples can be found in Account Book of Maria Erving, 1756, Erving-King Family Papers, box 6, folder E37, N-YHS; Receipt for Jane Byrne, 11 February 1783, Bayard-Campbell-Pearsall Collection, box 6, folder 9, New York Public Library (hereafter NYPL); and Accounts of Mrs. Van Rensselaer, Van Rensselaer-Fort Papers, box 2, NYPL.

56. Estate Settlement, Jane Keteltas, 11 November 1774, Beekman Family Papers, box 15, folder 8, N-YHS.

57. See, for instance, Bill and Settlement for Late Rent for Mr. Lot Trip, May 1786, Robert R. Livingston Papers, reel 29, N-YHS.

58. Will of Joshua Delaplaine, 2 October 1771, Delaplaine Family Papers, box 4, folder 11, N-YHS.

59. James Duane to Maria Livingston Duane, 7 September 1780, Duane-Featherstonhaugh Papers, reel 2, N-YHS.

60. Brockholst Livingston to Kitty Livingston, 11 March 1783, Matthew Ridley II Papers, MHS.

61. Mary Beekman to Henry Van Rensselaer, 7 May 1785, Van Rensselaer-Fort Papers, box 2, NYPL. Mary Beekman's experiences were further addressed by her brother-in-law, who helped settle her deceased husband's estate: "It is the Desire of the Widow of my late Brother that you send her, his Account Currant, and whatever ballance you may have in your hands, that you will be pleased to remit the same to Messrs. Cook and Ralph on Account of her late Husband." He added, "As the above Gentlemen

have a considerable Sum in their hands belonging to the Estate of my late Brother, therefore by the request of his Widow and Executrix, Mary Beekman, I have this day ordered them to remit you the full ballance in their hands, belonging to his Estate, which when you have received you'll please to advise her and [me]." Philip L. White, Gerard G. Beekman, and James Beekman, *The Beekman Mercantile Papers, 1746–1799. Transcribed and Edited by Philip L. White under a Grant from the Beekman Family Association* (New York: New-York Historical Society, 1956), 991, 994.

62. Jane Byrne to William Bayard, 27 September 1785, Bayard-Campbell-Pearsall Collection, box 1, folder 2, NYPL.

63. Abigail Adams to John Adams, 13 December 1778, in Butterfield et al., eds., *Adams Family Correspondence*, 3:135.

64. Walton escalated her attempt to collect the six years of unpaid annuity by reaching out to New York State governor George Clinton in 1782, but it remained unpaid; Walton would eventually rent her home for additional income and move to Newark, New Jersey. Cornelia Walton to George Clinton, n.d. (1782), Beekman Family Papers, box 22, folder 5, N-YHS; Power of Attorney, Catharine Bayard to William Bayard, 26 June 1805, box 7, folder 9, Bayard-Campbell-Pearsall Family Papers, N-YHS.

65. Abigail Adams to John Adams, 21 October 1775, in Butterfield et al., eds., *Adams Family Correspondence*, 1:308.

66. Sarah Livingston Jay to John Jay, 15 October 1783, in Freeman, North, and Wedge, eds., *Selected Letters of John Jay and Sarah Livingston Jay*, 144.

67. Sarah Livingston Jay to John Jay, 3 January 1779, in Freeman, North, and Wedge, eds., *Selected Letters of John Jay and Sarah Livingston Jay*, 56.

68. Abigail Adams to Mercy Otis Warren, 27 August 1775, in Butterfield et al., eds., *Adams Family Correspondence*, 1:276.

69. Abigail Adams to John Adams, 31 March 1776, in Butterfield et al., eds., *Adams Family Correspondence*, 1:370.

70. Robert G. Parkinson argues that John Adams, following this exchange, viewed women as a threat to the "common cause" as he worked on "cataloging, explaining, and dealing with all the Revolution's alleged enemies." Parkinson, *The Common Cause: Creating Race and Nation in the American Revolution* (Chapel Hill: University of North Carolina Press, 2016), 185–86. See also Elaine Forman Crane, "Political Dialogue and the Spring of Abigail's Discontent," *William and Mary Quarterly*, 3rd series, 56, no. 4 (1999): 745–74. For discussion of the relationship between Adams's argument about coverture and larger conversations in the Revolution regarding power and moderation, see Steven C. Bullock, *Tea Sets and Tyranny: The Politics of Politeness in Early America* (Philadelphia: University of Pennsylvania Press, 2017), 221–23.

71. Abigail Adams to Isaac Smith Jr., 30 October 1777, in Butterfield et al., eds., *Adams Family Correspondence*, 2:364.

72. See, for example, Mercy Otis Warren's discussion of her connection to her husband's political contributions: "And though I feel a painful Concern for their safty I acknowledge I feel some kind of pride in being so Closely Connected with persons who dare to act so Noble a part." Mercy Otis Warren to Abigail Adams, 15 May 1775, in Butterfield et al., eds., *Adams Family Correspondence*, 1:199.

73. Reed, *The Life of Esther De Berdt*, 219.

74. Abigail Adams to John Adams, 5 July 1775, in Butterfield et al., eds., *Adams Family Correspondence*, 1:239.

75. Berkin has argued that female citizenship was defined largely through a woman's civic role as "guardians of and instructors in virtue." Berkin, *First Generations*, 200. Kerber adds, however, that the definition of women's citizenship lay more specifically within their obligations to their husbands and the concept of coverture. Kerber, *No Constitutional Right to Be Ladies*, 13.

76. As Joan R. Gundersen wrote of the effect of the American Revolution on marital status, "The process of winning independence helped make married women's dependent status more noticeable and, for some, less desirable." Gundersen, *To Be Useful to the World*, 46.

CONTRIBUTORS

JACQUELINE BEATTY is Assistant Professor of History at York College of Pennsylvania, where she teaches courses in early American history, women's and gender history, and public history. She holds a Ph.D. from George Mason University with the honor of being a finalist for the 2017 SHEAR Dissertation Prize. Her article "Privileged in the Patriarchy: How Charleston Wives Negotiated Financial Freedom in the Early Republic" appears in the July 2018 issue of *South Carolina Historical Magazine*. Her book manuscript, *In Dependence: Women, Power, and the Patriarchal State in Revolutionary America*, is under contract.

CARIN BLOOM is the Manager of Education and Programming at Historic Charleston Foundation in Charleston, South Carolina. She conducted the research for her essay at Middleton Place Foundation where she was previously the Director of Engagement. She earned M.A. degrees in anthropology from the University of Pennsylvania and Temple University, specializing in historic sites of conflict archaeology. She participated in and instructed field schools at St. Mary's City, Maryland, and at Valley Forge National Historical Park, before putting her knowledge of the American War for Independence to use in the South Carolina Lowcountry.

TODD W. BRAISTED specializes in loyalist studies during the American Revolution. He has published numerous books and journal articles on a variety of period subjects, including *Grand Forage 1778: The Battleground around New York City* (2016). His website, royalprovincial.com, has been the leading site for loyalist research since it debuted in 2000. Braisted has lectured extensively on loyalists and other subjects across the United States and Canada and has appeared as a guest historian in such television shows as *History Detectives* and *Who Do You Think You Are?* He is a Fellow in the Company of Military Historians and has served as president of the Bergen County Historical Society, for the Brigade of the American Revolution, and as a history advisor to Crossroads of the American Revolution National Heritage Area. He wrote the 2017 National Park Service Battlefield Studies Preservation Report for Fort Lee, New Jersey.

BENJAMIN L. CARP is the Daniel M. Lyons Associate Professor of American History at Brooklyn College. He is also faculty at the Graduate Center of the City University of New York. He previously taught at Tufts University and the University of Edinburgh. He authored *Defiance of the Patriots: The Boston Tea Party and the Making of America* (2010), which won the Cox Book Prize from the Society of the Cincinnati in 2013, and *Rebels Rising: Cities and the American Revolution* (2007). He is co-editor, with Richard D. Brown, of *Major Problems in the Era of the American Revolution*, 3rd edition (2014). He has written articles in *Early American Studies, Civil War History*, the *William and Mary Quarterly*, and essays for *BBC History, Colonial Williamsburg*, the *Wall Street Journal*, and the *Washington Post*. His most recent essays and articles analyze the Embargo of 1807–9, the destruction of homes during the American Revolution, and Quaker cosmopolitanism in Charleston. He is writing a book about the burning of New York City in 1776.

LAUREN DUVAL is an Assistant Professor of History at the University of Oklahoma. She holds a Ph.D. from American University. She is the author of "Mastering Charleston: Property and Patriarchy in British-Occupied Charleston, 1780–82" in the *William and Mary Quarterly* (2018), which received the journal's Richard L. Morton Award, as well as the Coordinating Council for Women in History's Nupur Chaudhuri Award. She is currently working on a book project that examines revolutionary households, gender, and military occupation during the American Revolution.

STEVEN ELLIOTT earned a Ph.D. in American military history from Temple University and currently works at the U.S. Army Center of Military History in Washington, DC. His research on the social and administrative history of the Continental Army has been recognized by awards and fellowships from the David Library of the American Revolution, the Fred W. Smith Library at Mount Vernon, the Society of the Cincinnati, the North Jersey Heritage Trail, and the New Jersey Historical Commission. He is the author of *Surviving the Winters: Housing George Washington's Army during the American Revolution* (2021). Elliott has worked as a park guide and volunteer for the National Park Service at Morristown National Historical Park and taught national, local, and military history at Rutgers University–Newark. He is currently working on a project exploring the social history of early American military quarters.

LORRI GLOVER is the John Francis Bannon Endowed Chair in the History Department at Saint Louis University. A past president of the Southern Association for Women Historians, she is the author or editor of ten books, including most recently *The Fate of the Revolution: Virginians Debate the Constitution* (2016); *Reinterpreting Southern Histories: Essays in Historiography*, co-edited with Craig Thompson Friend (2020); and *Eliza Lucas Pinckney: An Independent Woman in the Age of Revolution* (2020).

DON N. HAGIST is Managing Editor of the *Journal of the American Revolution* (allthingsliberty.com). His focus on the demographics and material culture of

the British Army in the American Revolution was a response to a paucity of literature on that war's common British soldier and a questioning of conventional
interpretations. This led to his quest for primary sources in Great Britain and
America that provide better understanding of the thousands of professional
British soldiers who served during the 1775–83 war. Hagist's areas of expertise,
besides demographics, include British operations in Rhode Island and wives
of British soldiers. He has published a number of articles in academic journals and books, including *Noble Volunteers: The British Soldiers Who Fought the
American Revolution* (2020), *The Revolution's Last Men: The Soldiers behind
the Photographs* (2015), and *British Soldiers, American War* (2012). Hagist is an
engineer for a major medical device manufacturer and also writes for several
well-known syndicated and freelance cartoonists.

SEAN M. HEUVEL is a faculty member in the Department of Leadership and
American Studies at Christopher Newport University (CNU) in Newport
News, Virginia. An active scholar in the fields of the American Revolution,
American military history, and leadership studies, Heuvel has published essays
in refereed journals, encyclopedias, and magazines. He is also the author or edi-
tor of several books, including *The Revolutionary War Memoirs of Major General
William Heath* (2014) and *From across the Sea: North Americans in Nelson's Navy*
(2020). Through foreign study programs at CNU, Heuvel has also lectured at
Harris Manchester College, Oxford University, in the United Kingdom.

MARTHA J. KING, a historian of early America with a special interest in women's
history, received a doctorate in history from the College of William and Mary
and is Senior Editor with the Papers of Thomas Jefferson at Princeton University. Earlier in her career, she was an editor with the *Papers of General Nathanael
Greene* and became intrigued by the life of Catharine Littlefield Greene. Her
recent published essay on the printer Anne Catharine Green appeared in the
Transactions of the American Philosophical Society (2021) and on the poet Annis
Boudinot Stockton in Barbara B. Oberg, ed., *Women in the American Revolu-
tion: Gender, Politics, and the Domestic World* (University of Virginia Press, 2019).
She is currently completing a book entitled "Making an Impression: Women
Printers in the Southern Colonies in the Revolutionary Era."

BARBARA ALICE MANN is Professor of Humanities, Jesup Scott Honors Col-
lege of the University of Toledo in Ohio. Mann is the author of nine monographs, over four hundred chapters and articles, and co-author of three major
works. Her most recent books include *Spirits of Blood, Spirits of Breath: The
Twinned Cosmos of Indigenous America* (2016) and *President by Massacre: Indian-
Killing for Political Gain* (2019). Other books on settlers and Indians include
The Tainted Gift: The Disease Method of Frontier Expansion (2009), *George
Washington's War on Native America* (2005), and *Iroquoian Women: The Gan-
towisas* (2000). Mann is currently working with a Finnish-Sami scholar on a

book regarding the ancient interface of women and bears across the global north and with an international team of scholars on *The Dark Side of Empire*, a project examining colonial massacres around the world from 1780 to 1820.

HOLLY A. MAYER is Professor Emerita of History at Duquesne University. She has also served as the 2021–22 Charles Boal Ewing Chair in Military History at the United States Military Academy, West Point, and the Harold K. Johnson Chair of Military History at the U.S. Army War College in 2016–17. Her interests in the social, cultural, and military histories of eighteenth-century North America inform her latest book, *Congress's Own: A Canadian Regiment, the Continental Army, and American Union* (2021) and the earlier *Belonging to the Army: Camp Followers and Community during the American Revolution* (1996). Besides authoring various journal and anthology essays, she was co-editor (with David E. Shi) of *For the Record: A Documentary History of America* (multiple editions).

J. PATRICK MULLINS, Associate Professor of History and Public History Director at Marquette University, is a cultural and intellectual historian of the British Atlantic World specializing in the origins of the American Revolution. He received his Ph.D. in history from the University of Kentucky in 2005. Mullins has published articles in the *Massachusetts Historical Review* (2009) and *Age of Revolutions* (2021) and chapters in *Community without Consent: New Perspectives on the Stamp Act* (2016) and *Revolutionary Prophecies: The Founders and America's Future* (University of Virginia Press, 2021). His first monograph was *Father of Liberty: Jonathan Mayhew and the Principles of the American Revolution* (2017). He is now working on a second book called *Killing Kings in America: The Cultural Politics of the Transatlantic American Revolution*.

ALISA WADE is Assistant Professor at California State University at Chico, where she teaches early American and gender history. She earned her Ph.D. from the Graduate Center of the City University of New York in 2016, with a focus on the intersections of gender and capitalism in the early American republic. She was a 2016–17 Bernard and Irene Schwartz Postdoctoral Fellow, jointly held through the New-York Historical Society and the New School, and a 2017–18 Center on Philanthropy and Civil Society Postdoctoral Fellow. Her research has been supported by a Massachusetts Historical Society Ruth R. and Alyson R. Miller Short-Term Research Fellowship, an E. P. Thompson Dissertation Year Fellowship, and an Andrew W. Mellon Pre-Doctoral Fellowship in Women's History. Wade is currently revising her book manuscript, "An Alliance of Ladies: Power, Public Affairs, and Class Consolidation in Early National New York City," which looks at women's investing and the stabilization of the city's leadership class in post-revolutionary New York.

INDEX

Abolitionism (emancipation), 199, 208–9
activism, 10–11, 20n25, 39, 44, 249, 256,
    258n7
Adair, James, 59
Adams, Abigail: on colonial manufactur-
    ing, 252, 253; on economic impact of
    war, 251, 252, 254; as founding mother,
    38; on newspaper reading, 262n45;
    on provisional widowhood, 257n4;
    "remember the ladies" letter by, 255–56;
    on separation from spouse, 150, 255;
    on tea boycott, 248; Warren's cor-
    respondence with, 51, 249; on women
    regulating merchants, 262n42
Adams, John, 264n70
Adams, Samuel, 42
Addison, Joseph, 45, 46, 54n16, 166n41
Adulateur, The (Warren), 38–39, 44–52,
    54n20
African Americans. *See* Black community
agency of women: backlash against,
    31; historical studies of, 6, 9, 150; in
    post-occupied Charleston, 231, 233,
    241; in quartering disputes, 103; rape
    testimonies and, 79, 93–94n23; single
    vs. married women, 8
Alexander, William (Lord Stirling),
    98–99
Allen, Ethan, 119, 213
American Revolution: archetypes of, 10,
    11, 30, 78; bicentennial celebration of,
    6; economic impact of, 175–76, 185,
    247, 251–52, 254; French involvement
    in, 176; incendiaries during, 23–32;
    intellectual origins of, 38, 39; moral
    justification for, 38, 45, 48, 51; political
    equality in rhetoric of, 3; radical
    elements of, 8, 11, 27–28, 32; relational
    experiences during, 9–10; romanticized

notions of, 172, 186n1; as social and
    political movement, 5; strategies and
    tactics in, 2, 16n3, 122; total war cam-
    paigns of, 56, 57, 185; triangularity of
    conflict, 21n32. *See also* British Army;
    Continental Army; loyalists; patriots;
    propaganda; *specific battles*
Anderson, William, 89
Arbuthnot, Marriot, 177
archetypes of women, 11, 24, 30
Armour, John de, 106
army wives, 3. *See also* British Army wives
Arnold, Benedict, 114, 140–41
arsonists. *See* incendiaries
assault, sexual. *See* rape
autonomy, 15, 162, 246, 250, 254

Banbury, John: in *Book of Negroes*, 195,
    200–201, 204; in British Army, 195,
    200–203; debates regarding self-
    emancipation, 198; escape from slavery,
    195–96, 204; in New York City, 201,
    203–5; in Nova Scotia, 200–201,
    204–7
Banbury, Lucy, 195–209; in *Book of
    Negroes*, 201, 204, 208; in British
    Army, 195, 201–3; debates regarding
    self-emancipation, 198; escape from
    slavery, 13, 195–97, 203–4; in New York
    City, 201, 203–5; in Nova Scotia, 14,
    200–201, 204–8; removal to Sierra
    Leone, 14, 208–9
Bancker, Elizabeth, 108
Barnes, John and Mary, 216–17
barter systems, 250, 252
"Battle of the Kegs, The" (Hopkinson),
    121
battles. *See specific battles*
Beard, Mary Ritter, 6

Milton Keynes UK
Ingram Content Group UK Ltd.
UKHW011227280324
440101UK00007B/643